Iconoclastic Departures

Iconoclastic Departures

Mary Shelley after *Frankenstein*

Essays in Honor
of the Bicentenary
of Mary Shelley's Birth

Edited by Syndy M. Conger,
Frederick S. Frank,
and Gregory O'Dea

Assistant Editor: Jennifer Yocum

Madison • Teaneck
Fairleigh Dickinson University Press
London: Associated University Presses

Associated University Presses
440 Forsgate Drive
Cranbury, NJ 08512

Associated University Presses
16 Barter Street
London WC1A 2AH, England

Associated University Presses
P.O. Box 338, Port Credit
Mississauga, Ontario
Canada L5G 4L8

The paper used in this publication meets the requirements
of the American National Standard for Permanence of Paper
for Printed Library Materials Z39.48–1984.

Library of Congress Cataloging-in-Publication Data

Iconoclastic departures : Mary Shelley after Frankenstein : essays in honor of the
    bicentenary of Mary Shelley's birth / edited by Syndy M. Conger, Frederick S. Frank,
    and Gregory O'Dea; assistant editor, Jennifer Yocum.
        p. cm.
    Includes bibliographical references and index.
    ISBN 0–8386–3684–5 (alk. paper)
        1. Shelley, Mary Wollstonecraft, 1797–1851—Criticism and interpretation.
    2. Women and literature—England—History—19th century. I. Conger, Syndy M.
    II. Frank, Frederick S. III. O'Dea, Gregory.
    PR5398.I46 1997
    823'.7—dc21   96–52067
                                                                                                          CIP

336293

To
Jim Conger
Nancy Frank
Alice and Meghan O'Dea

Contents

Part Three: Fictions as Cultural Provocation

Part Four: A Bibliographical Update

Introduction

Reflecting upon her journal entries at the end of the year 1834, Mary Shelley was suddenly "struck" by the contrast between her own sense of self and the virtual self she inferred from the pages before her: "What a very imperfect picture (only *no one* will ever see it) these querulous pages afford of *me*—This arises from their being the record of my feelings, & not of my imagination."[1] If Mary Shelley were now here to perform a retrospective study of the criticism of her imaginative literary endeavors after publication of her monumental first novel, *Frankenstein*, she might well repeat the same theme. Early twentieth-century criticism focused almost exclusively on Mary Shelley's domestic ties, treating her writings as almost the sole context within which to understand her life and—often more important at the time—the lives of her famed parents, William Godwin and Mary Wollstonecraft, and her husband, Percy Bysshe Shelley. In the words of her most recent biographer, Emily Sunstein, "Finding the-persons-in-the-fiction had become a major rationale for reading her work."[2] At the end of the century, on the 200th anniversary of her birth, thanks in large part to the energetic work of the many Mary Shelley scholars listed in Frederick Frank's summary of scholarship at the end of this volume, and also credited repeatedly in the essays in the current volume, she is at last recognized as

> an important Romantic who survived into the Victorian age . . . a major literary figure of the first half of the nineteenth century . . . among the great editors.[3]

In the 1980s and 1990s, there are many milestones on the path of the Mary Shelley renaissance, but several merit immediate notice. For the first time ever, nearly all of Mary Shelley's long and short fiction is accessible to the reading public outside rare-books rooms. In addition to the new edition of Mary Shelley's journals cited above, her letters have been expertly edited by Betty T. Bennett in three volumes, Pickering and

Chatto have published her novels and selected works, and her tales are available in two anthologies.[4] In many cases—*Valperga,* for instance— texts are being reprinted for the first time. Two other groundbreaking books that have made a great deal of difference to the respect and quality of critical attention being accorded to Mary Shelley are Anne K. Mellor's *Mary Shelley: Her Life, Her Fiction, Her Monsters,* with its enlightening revisionist appendix about Percy Shelley's editorial contributions to *Frankenstein,* and the outstanding collection of essays titled *The Other Mary Shelley*, edited by Audrey A. Fisch, Anne K. Mellor, and Esther H. Schor, with its fourteen postmodern essays focusing unswervingly on the originality and subtlety of Mary Shelley's contribution to the literature of Romanticism.[5]

Iconoclastic Departures contributes to this ongoing reevaluation of Mary Shelley as a professional author in her own right with a lifelong commitment to the development of her craft. Many of its contributors acknowledge the importance of Mary Shelley's family to her work, but for them the family has become, in a reversal of the means and ends of scholarship done earlier in the century, an imperative sociopsychological context within which better to understand her contributions to the many literary forms she worked with during her career: journals, letters, travelogues, biographies, editions, poems, dramas, tales, and novels. Its contributors also share the conviction that, even if Mary Shelley, after Percy Shelley's death, gradually retired from public life according to the wishes of his relatives, she retained a resistant, resiliently radical attitude toward many of the established orders of her day that is easily recovered by a careful look beyond her "feelings" to the productions of her literary "imagination."

The essays in part 1, "Authorship Reconsidered," focus on various moments in Mary Shelley's construction of her own sense of authorship. Angela Jones, "Lying Near the Truth: Mary Shelley Performs the Private," cognizant of the ways in which the achievement of Mary Shelley's later literary works remains doubly obscured, once by the brilliance of *Frankenstein* and once by the critical impulse to view her work as autobiographical or collaborative, places Mary Shelley's often quoted 1831 "Introduction to the Third Edition" of *Frankenstein* in the seldom cited context of her 1817 *History of a Six Weeks' Tour* to discover Mary Shelley in the act of producing herself as professional author. In "Author and Editor: Mary Shelley's Private Writings and the Author Function of Percy Bysshe Shelley," Sheila Ahlbrand demonstrates how much Mary Shelley interwove the tasks of editor, biographer, and author in the representations of Percy Shelley that she developed as she assembled his poetry and prose for publication.

Gregory O'Dea, in "'Perhaps a Tale You'll Make It': Mary Shelley's Tales for *The Keepsake*," shows Mary Shelley employing complex models of writing and reading even in the commissioned tale-making she did for the Victorian household annual publication *The Keepsake*.

Essays in part 2, "Myths Revised, Taboos Defied," and part 3, "Fictions as Cultural Provocation," although they foreground other subjects, share with those of part 1 the conviction that Mary Shelley wrote self-consciously, expertly, and innovatively all her life. Syndy Conger's "Mary Shelley's Women in Prison" observes Mary Shelley returning, time and again, to the problem of women's metaphoric and actual confinement (presented dramatically by her mother in *Maria; or, The Wrongs of Woman*), and developing for it in the process a whole series of imaginative fictional solutions. Judith Barbour, in "'The meaning of the tree': The Tale of Mirra in Mary Shelley's *Mathilda*," and Audra Dibert Himes, in "'Knew shame, and knew desire': Ambivalence as Structure in Mary Shelley's *Mathilda*," see Mary Shelley fashioning her risk-taking tale of incest, *Mathilda*, from the works of Dante and Alfieri, as well as of Ovid, Milton, Rousseau and others, in order to broach the delicate subject of a woman's "transgressive desire." Ranita Chatterjee, in "*Mathilda*: Mary Shelley, William Godwin, and the Ideologies of Incest," building on just such an assumption in her own essay, posits as the novel's achievement the successful challenge to social strictures designed to regulate desire. Similarly, Diane Hoeveler's "Mary Shelley and Gothic Feminism: The Case of 'The Mortal Immortal'" demonstrates Mary Shelley confronting and deconstructing an ideology of femininity; and James Carson, "'A Sigh of Many Hearts': History, Humanity, and Popular Culture in *Valperga*," shows her deconstructing and reconstructing the historical novel to allow psychological events to take precedence over external events. Paul Cantor, author of "The Apocalypse of Empire: Mary Shelley's *The Last Man*," believes that Mary Shelley uses the prophetic story of *The Last Man* to launch a "devastating critique" of her culture's ideology; while Lynn Wells, in "The Triumph of Death: Reading and Narrative in *The Last Man*," sees the same novel as a Kristevan imaginary process enabling Mary Shelley to remake that cultural ideology. Like Carson and Wells, Anne M. Frank Wake, author of "Women in the Active Voice: Recovering Female History in Mary Shelley's *Valperga* and *Perkin Warbeck*," and Lisa Hopkins, in "The Self and the Monstrous: *The Fortunes of Perkin Warbeck*," emphasize Mary Shelley's willingness to critique and refashion historical novels in order to challenge prevailing views of genre, gender, and history in her day. Charlene Bunnell, author of "The Illusion of 'Great Expectations':

Manners and Morals in Mary Shelley's *Lodore* and *Falkner*," finally sees
Mary Shelley similarly challenging, and ultimately subverting, the norms
of the sentimental fiction of the eighteenth century.

The Mary Shelley who emerges from this collection of portraits is a
radical, even if a quiet radical. She is a writer who reappropriates
authority for herself (Jones, Ahlbrand, Frank Wake, Hopkins, O'Dea),
then redesigns genres (Bunnell, Carson, Hopkins, O'Dea), redefines
gender (Bunnell, Carson, Dibert Himes, Frank Wake, Hoeveler), rewrites
history and/or biography (Ahlbrand, Carson, Frank Wake, Hopkins),
revises aesthetic expectations (Carson, Jones, O'Dea), and protests
cultural imperialism at home and abroad (Barbour, Cantor, Conger).
More important, this new, radical Mary Shelley was not invented by an
originary "Call for Papers" but emerged on her own in this open selection
of essays written by Mary Shelley scholars from various corners of the
English-speaking world. There seems to be a new, unmistakable, and
crossnational consensus that Mary Shelley is very far indeed from the
passive receptor—the minor figure overshadowed by the major
Romantic—seen by scholarship earlier in our century as one who was
once declared, perfectly seriously, "for all her merits, . . . quite incapable,
both morally and intellectually, of understanding her husband's opinions,
much less of sharing them."[6] The characteristic verbs of these essays tell
quite another story of an immensely talented, fiercely intelligent,
nonconformist Mary Shelley, verbs like "deconstruct," "subvert,"
"critique," "test," "challenge," "refashion," "deny," "protest," "risk,"
"transgress," and "destroy." The Mary Shelley arising from the pages of
this volume remained throughout her literary career, in the spirit of the
misunderstood creature of *Frankenstein*, dedicated to "iconoclastic
departures."

Notes

1. *The Journals of Mary Shelley*, ed. Paula R. Feldman and Diana Scott-Kilvert
(Baltimore, Md.: Johns Hopkins University Press, 1987), 542. The entry quoted in the
introduction is dated 2 December 1834.

2. Emily W. Sunstein, *Mary Shelley: Romance and Reality* (Baltimore, Md.: Johns
Hopkins University Press, 1989), 398.

3. Ibid., 402–3.

4. *The Novels and Selected Works of Mary Wollstonecraft Shelley* are available in
eight volumes from Pickering and Chatto, Brookfield, Vt. (1996). *The Letters of Mary
Wollstonecraft Shelley*, ed. Betty T. Bennett, 3 vols., were published by Johns Hopkins

University Press, Baltimore, Md., in 1983. The two readers that make Mary Shelley's shorter fictions available are *Mary Shelley: Collected Tales and Stories with original engravings*, ed. Charles E. Robinson (Baltimore, Md.: Johns Hopkins University Press, 1976), and *The Mary Shelley Reader, containing "Frankenstein," "Mathilda," Tales and Stories, Essays and Reviews, and Letters*, ed. Betty T. Bennett and Charles E. Robinson (New York: Oxford University Press, 1990). See Frederick Frank's foreword to his "Bibliographical Census" appended to this collection.

5. Mellor's book was published by Routledge in 1989, *The Other Mary Shelley* by Oxford University Press in 1993.

6. Shelley scholar Ellsworth Barnard, writing in 1936, as quoted in Sunstein, *Mary Shelley*, 399.

Iconoclastic Departures

Part 1
Authorship Reconsidered

Lying Near the Truth:
Mary Shelley Performs the Private

Angela D. Jones

Recent years have seen any number of studies attending to Mary Shelley's *Frankenstein* and, even more recently, to the problematic centrality of that text in the author's oeuvre. Feminist critics might well rejoice in a 1989 survey statistic that one of every two undergraduate students of Romanticism has read Shelley's Ur-text.[1] Yet perhaps as many others advocate renewed consideration of the ways in which twentieth-century constructions of this novel have unwittingly obscured Shelley's other generically diverse productions.[2] The editors of the 1993 volume, *The Other Mary Shelley: Beyond Frankenstein*, put the finest point on the matter:

> While *Frankenstein* has become canonized in the classroom, little has changed for Mary Shelley; now it is the pale face of Victor Frankenstein that obscures the pale face of his creator. Ironically, the canonization of *Frankenstein* has institutionalized the marginality of Mary Shelley, throwing her salient and central voice to the edges of Romantic discourse.[3]

If contentions like this one are sound, then they might be adequate to galvanize students of Romanticism and of women's literature to produce more expansive, more historically aware, views of Shelley's canon. But not just of Shelley's canon, as other women writers of the period might be said to have been similarly constructed as one-work wonders, though potentially for different reasons. What follows then is an attempt to examine recent critical constructions of Mary Shelley, making palpable both the need to historicize our post-Romantic notions of authorship and to recontextualize the reception of this particular author.

19

Overwhelming critical impulses to read the novel both as autobiographical and as a collaborative production, though the text bears her name alone, are just two of the vexed if inextricably linked critical trends placing *Frankenstein* in the foreground of literary Romanticism, all the while erasing its author. After giving brief consideration to such readings of *Frankenstein*, I will turn my attention to two separate instances where Shelley may be seen to reconfigure public/private relations, permitting her to produce herself as a professional author as opposed to a gentlewoman with literary gifts: first, Shelley's ostensibly private commentary on her profession, couched in her 1831 "Introduction to the Third Edition" of *Frankenstein,* and, second, and much more obliquely for my purposes here, the author's construction of her half sister, Claire (Jane) Clairmont, and a French tour guide in *History of a Six Weeks' Tour* (1817). Although her 1831 introduction foregrounds authorial identity more conspicuously, Shelley's 1817 travelogue trades in similar issues. In taking the later text as my point of departure, then, I do not mean to imply either that Shelley imagined her authorship in static terms over nearly fifteen years or that these texts are mutually exchangeable such that generic and historical distinctions can be elided. Rather, I am proposing that reconsideration of this author is facilitated by reading these texts against one another, beginning with the one that provides easier access to a discussion of authorial constructions.

Critiques of *Frankenstein* that view the text as a confirmation of Mary Shelley's own harrowing experiences as a mother and/or as a guilt-ridden daughter of a woman who died giving birth to her have become so fashionable that one ought to think twice about producing yet another, lest one reinscribe the text in these clichéd terms. Such autobiographical readings are not limited to narrative turns of the novel but are, unfortunately, extended to the drafting of the text as well. Indeed, Shelley is often imagined as burdened by the daunting task of measuring up to the literary achievements of her parents, William Godwin and Mary Wollstonecraft, and of her husband, Percy Shelley. More specifically, *Frankenstein* has itself been constructed as a joint venture by Shelley and her husband. For instance, in the introduction to his widely circulated edition of Shelley's 1818 text of *Frankenstein*, James Rieger spares no effort in locating and crediting others for their contributions to the novel.[4] To rehearse his commentary briefly, Rieger cites as essential contexts, if not unimpeachable sources, for the text everything from Mary Wollstonecraft Godwin's "intuitions" and William Godwin's novels, to a conversation between Percy Shelley and John Polidori on the natural sciences and Lord Byron's challenge to the foursome (perhaps fivesome) to produce their own ghost stories. The crowning blow comes, however, when Rieger offers to "correct and amplify" (xvi) Mary Shelley's claim, in her "Introduction to the Third [1831] Edition" (appendix A of Rieger's text), that she "did not owe the suggestion of one incident, nor scarcely of one train of feeling, to [her] husband." Insisting that "[Percy] Shelley oversaw his wife's manuscript at every stage," Rieger boldly asserts that Percy might even be considered a "minor collaborator" (xviii).

Anne Mellor attempts to demonstrate that Rieger's introduction "does a disservice to Mary Shelley's unique genius."[5] She accomplishes this not simply by rejecting out-of-hand Rieger's claim that *Frankenstein* owes a great debt to Percy's interventions. Instead, Mellor argues that Rieger has ignored the way that Percy actually does violence to his wife's text. For all her attempts to rescue the novel from the hands of Rieger and others who would dilute Mary Shelley's implicit claim as author, Mellor recontextualizes the novel in a manner that itself must be further recontextualized. Insofar as Mellor confines her arguments to a reactionary either/or proposition—Percy's editorial revisions can be viewed as either improving or damaging the manuscript (most falling into the latter category, according to Mellor)—she persists in the same empirically grounded quest to determine authorship that Rieger undertook. So much so that Mellor languishingly remarks, "Perhaps someday an editor will give us the manuscript that Mary Shelley actually wrote" (62). More importantly, though, Mellor's absorption in accurately cataloguing Percy's interventions—for better or for worse—forecloses the possibility of asking not about where and how often we see Percy Shelley's hand in the text but what we can make of Mary Shelley's comments about her husband's contributions.

Twentieth-century configurations of eighteenth- and nineteenth-century women writers, enabled by, most often, fathers or male partners, have marginalized, if not wholly erased, many authors in addition to Mary Shelley. Maria Edgeworth, celebrated in her day as a prolific and accomplished writer, is currently represented as a one-work author whose "historical/regional" novel, *Castle Rackrent*, is the only work consistently kept in print. Edgeworth hasn't fared much better than Shelley in the collaboration department either, as her work is perennially understood to illustrate the educational theories of her much less prolific father, Richard Lovell Edgeworth.[6] Despite the ways in which Shelley's writing has been read in the context of her mother's literary-political texts, Wollstonecraft, too, might be usefully investigated as a site of erasure. If one reads, say, Catherine Macaulay's *Letters on Education* (1790), a text that Wollstonecraft favorably reviewed in the November 1790 issue of the *Analytical Review*, and that outlines a number of the principles Wollstonecraft will herself articulate two years later in

Vindication of the Rights of Woman, one is forced to consider why Wollstonecraft's text and, indeed, the author herself, is so frequently heralded as a prototype of feminist thinking while Macaulay remains almost completely ignored. One potential response to just such a construction might be to rethink the ways in which Wollstonecraft's associations with canonized literary men like William Godwin and Percy Shelley produce her own canonization. Another strategy would focus on biographical readings accenting the more sensational aspects of Wollstonecraft's life (her affair with Gilbert Imlay, suicide attempts, etc.). Both attempts to reframe Wollstonecraft's canon force the more unfortunate if subterranean effects of biographical readings to the surface, thus particularizing Margaret J. M. Ezell's shrewd observation about the relationship between contemporary biographical readings and nineteenth-century stipulations privileging a female author's conduct over her writing's content:

> We [twentieth-century literary historians] have not heard the voices of earlier commentators such as Dryden or Cibber, who find a way to appreciate and applaud women writers as writers. Instead, we have followed the pattern set out in detail in the nineteenth century of focusing attention on women writers' domestic lives, with their texts being autobiographical revelations, and on the liabilities under which they wrote.[7]

If vitiating women writers' claim to professional authorship and marginalizing their texts are symptoms, then the problem is, perhaps, an ideological bias against "fair authoresses," rooted in a nineteenth-century ethos valorizing women for their ability to be good role models. I offer these readings of Edgeworth and Wollstonecraft here not because it is my intention to attempt a broad characterization of the pitfalls of revisionary literary history but because such readings help situate constructions of Shelley's authorship.

Despite various readings producing *Frankenstein* as at least provisionally autobiographical, very little has been made of some of the more interiorized moments of the "text." While Barbara Johnson explicitly reads the text as "the autobiography of a woman" with all its attending monstrousness because, as she argues, the woman writer must model the "self" on the male subject,[8] she does not interrogate the ways in which Shelley herself misreads the "truth" of stable definitions of authorship or gender. Thus, of Shelley's 1831 "Introduction to the Third Edition"—what Johnson designates as "thin introductory frame . . . an *appendage* to a text" (emphasis added) (58)—she asks, "How does an appendage go about telling the story of her life?" How indeed. It is precisely because this "thin introductory frame" does not elicit the kind of voyeuristic response one might expect of a diary entry or letter that it can far exceed its ostensible ancillary function to the text. If, as Johnson contends, "the problem for the female autobiographer is, on the one hand, to resist the pressure of masculine autobiography as the only literary genre available for her enterprise, and, on the other, to describe a difficulty in conforming to a female ideal which is largely a fantasy of the masculine, not the feminine, imagination" (66), then where better to write the "self" into existence than where nobody is looking for it, where it cannot be as easily recontained in terms of phallogocentric paradigms? Shelley's introduction thus can potentially tell the story of a woman's life, particularly of a literary woman's life in the nineteenth century, *because of*, not in spite of, its apparent marginality.

At the close of her 1831 introduction, Mary Shelley writes: "I certainly did not owe the suggestion of one incident, nor scarcely of one train of feeling, to my husband, and yet but for his incitement, it [*Frankenstein*] would never have taken the form in which it was presented to the world."[9] The subtext of this remark might be understood as: Mary is solely responsible for the novel's content, Percy for its form; Mary is the writer, Percy is the editor. Underpinning this implicit form/content disjunction is a far more subtle distinction: a private/public split where Mary alone writes—and writes alone moreover—but Percy, in readying the novel for the world, transforms her writing into a text. Not unlike Foucault's claim that "a private letter may have a signatory, but it does not have an author,"[10] there is a way in which Shelley's text does not and cannot be properly regarded as a text with an author until it shifts from the private to the public sphere. Insofar as Percy enables this transition from the private to the public—that is, the text is a text because of the way it is presented to the world, and an author, to invoke Foucault again, is an author not simply because she writes but because she produces "the possibility and the rules of formation of other texts" (131)—then Percy might be rightfully considered the novel's author.

Suggesting that Percy Shelley is the author of *Frankenstein* flies in the face of our most basic assumptions regarding the "secondariness" of what seems, according to Mary's comment, to be his editorial role. Although it makes little sense to ask how much credit Mary intended to give her husband in claiming that he was solely responsible for the novel's presentation, it seems potentially instructive to ask how her comment functions in this third edition of the novel. Why, we might want to ask, would Shelley claim that the presentation of the novel fell completely within her husband's purview in the same breath in which she denies her husband's contribution to the composition of the novel? And how does the appearance of such a claim in the third edition of the novel—an edition significantly revised by Mary and offered to the world by her alone—affect how we read that claim?

One plausible response to the question of why she would have credited her husband for presenting the novel to the world relies on the double bind Shelley was confronted with as a woman writer in the nineteenth century. As Mary Poovey observes, Mary Shelley was forced to negotiate her desire to establish herself as an author, thus fulfilling her literary legacy, with the penalty of fracturing the bounds of propriety for doing so.[11] Consequently, if she only accepted responsibility for actually writing the text—which she does unequivocally—then she might have been able to avoid public censure in the same way that a woman writing a private letter would. If, however, Shelley accepts full responsibility for the production and dissemination of her text, then she would simultaneously establish herself as an author and "defy the decorum of the proper lady" (56).

Yet this explanation does not suffice, for, as Poovey notes, "by 1831 Shelley was an established professional author; she was supporting herself and her son almost exclusively by writing" ("HP," 140). In other words, the need to use a trope to conceal her literary efforts would have been sufficiently vitiated between the 1818 and 1831 editions of the novel. Instead, a far more compelling explanation for Mary Shelley's comment is that she offers it in order to *establish* herself as an author. That is, Mary Shelley doesn't simply become an author because she can sustain herself and her son by writing, as Poovey intimates, or because she makes an unescorted foray into the publishing world with a newly revised text, but because the introduction to the 1831 edition foregrounds a public-author/private-writer distinction that can then be used to construct retrospectively Mary Shelley as writer and Percy Shelley as author in earlier editions of the novel. To the extent that Mary Shelley establishes herself as an author in the context of a highly privatized discourse that she ultimately claims for herself—"But this is for myself; my readers have nothing to do with these associations"[12]—she has succeeded in shifting the frame of reference for authorship such that private discourse is an equally valid and valuable ground for writing. It might make sense then to ask not "Who wrote *Frankenstein*?" but rather, "At what point does Mary Shelley become its author?" Is there, for instance, a temporal disjunction between the first and third editions of the novel whereby Mary Shelley only becomes the author of the third edition even though we construct and naturalize her as author of every edition of the text and of every other text she produced? Has she succeeded, as I have begun to suggest, in opening up a place for private discourse as a serious subject of literary study by presenting a performatively privatized discourse in the form of her 1831 introduction to *Frankenstein*?

To apply the label "confessional," or even "interiorized," to the introduction of a novel potentially risks stretching these metaphors to meaninglessness.[13] Though steering wide of the kind of sensationalistic details conventionally embedded in confessional narratives, this text foregrounds, even performatively, the intimate details of its author's life. Shelley personalizes the third edition of *Frankenstein* by suggesting that it is now a placeholder for her dead husband: "Its several pages speak of many a walk, many a drive, and many a conversation" with Percy.[14] Public and private relations get configured quite differently in *History of a Six Weeks' Tour* (1817),[15] though potentially to similar ends: to produce Mary Shelley as a professional author through counterpublic discourse.

Donald Reiman proposes that Shelley's *History of a Six Weeks' Tour* be understood more or less as a public document[16] in that the published text contains Mary's and Percy's revised letters, Percy's poem "Mont Blanc," and Mary's vastly revised journal entries penned during their "elopement tour" of the Continent, with Claire Clairmont in tow. Although Shelley's pseudojournal, constituting the bulk of the text, is largely personal in its observations and intimate in its tone, it anticipates public consumption as part of a trend among tourists who "have sent their journals to the press" (iii). Shelley locates her text in a wider publication tradition but denigrates it, suggesting that she and Percy are less "experienced and exact observers" (iii). She regrets that "since their little History is to be offered to the public, that these materials were not more copious and complete" (iv), a characterization that I think must be read as ironic, given the way she will use this travelogue to revise androcentric imperatives for touring. The possessive "their," used to designate what is overwhelmingly Mary's textual production, once again begs questions of authorial proprietorship and gender, but this *History*, unlike *Frankenstein*, is certainly collaborative in its inclusion of Percy's letters and poetry. While representing Mary Shelley as the sole author of *History of a Six Weeks' Tour* reinscribes ideologies of the author as singular and public, which I have been attempting to critique here, the travelogue should not be understood as simply collaborative. That is, I regard and refer to this text as Mary Shelley's because I am specifically interested in its historical function as a revision of masculinized Romantic tourism. Certainly both writers' gender identities are relevant to this consideration of Romantic touring practices, but I am privileging Mary's represented identity as female traveler over Percy's attempt "to imitate the untamable wildness and inaccessible solemnity" (vi) of the landscape in order to emphasize the way seemingly gender-neutral landscape descriptions are not, in fact, neutral at all.

Ideologies of authorship, gender, and touring converge in Shelley's recurrently sharp segues from personal anecdote to political commentary—commentary that includes descriptions of English and French class distinctions, nationalistic comparisons favoring Protestant Switzerland to Catholic France, and the unfortunate aftermath of the Napoleonic wars on the French countryside. Shelley's text is hardly anomalous in the period for blurring personal and political narrative, often imagined as boundaried and separate. Wollstonecraft's patently ignored *Letters Written during a Short Residence in Sweden, Norway, and Denmark*, to take one example, is almost always discussed in terms of the way the author elides distinctions between strong self-referential meditations and political commentary.[17] Epistolary travelogues such as Wollstonecraft's, as Mary Favret observes, potentially offer competing understandings of the letter form and of epistolary fiction:

> Feminist scholars have read the letters of epistolary fiction as emblems of a social trap, which either locks the woman into marriage (as in *Pamela*) or betrays her into death (as in *Clarissa* or *Julie*). . . . [F]ew scholars have studied letters as tools for political agitation or propaganda in a particular historical moment defined by revolution, reaction and Romanticism.[18]

Favret's claims for the letter as a potential vehicle of social protest, especially for women writers, might be usefully generalized to Shelley's journalizing in *History of a Six Weeks' Tour*. One could, that is, read Shelley's text not simply as functioning to lower whatever imagined barrier exists between personal anecdote and political rhetoric but also as a kind of counterpublic discourse marshaled to revise practices of and assumptions about picturesque touring and aesthetics so prevalent in the early nineteenth century.

William Gilpin's essays theorizing representations of English landscape both produced the fashion for touring and enabled the flourishing cult of the picturesque in the late eighteenth century. His detailed prescriptions for tourists' experiences of landscape through representations of those landscapes—specifically in painting—touched off debates among writers such as Uvedale Price and Richard Payne Knight, to name but a few.[19] Despite his avowed intention to be, as one of his reviewers put it, "engaged in delineating the infinitely varied scenery of his native country,"[20] Gilpin's sketches are anything but varied. Ostensibly representing unique picturesque views, each sketch seems a reincarnation of every other, with the possible exception of more

trees added to a foreground, more rocks to a background. His recipes for
sketching landscape, accenting sensory experience of natural scenery and
formulaic reproduction of that scenery, arguably dulled readers'/tourists'
abilities to relate differently to their surroundings or to make nuanced
distinctions about those environments. The kind of mindlessness
associated with picturesque touring as I have described it in relation to
Gilpin seems precisely the ideology that Shelley is revising in her
History of a Six Weeks' Tour. Specifically, Shelley represents her half
sister, Claire Clairmont, as the quintessentially indiscriminate
picturesque traveler, and, by implicit contrast, herself as the more aware,
more sensitive tourist. At one juncture, Shelley records Claire, nearly
awash in the view: "On looking at this scene, C*** exclaimed, 'Oh! this
is beautiful enough; let us live here.' This was her exclamation on every
new scene, and as each surpassed the one before, she cried, 'I am glad we
did not stay at Charenton, but let us live here'" (15). Although she
represents herself as deeply involved with the sublimity and beauty of
continually changing landscapes, Shelley, by contrast, also often
describes the scenery before her as "perfectly without interest," her tastes
implicitly more refined than Claire's. Shelley's status as a
knowledgeable, sophisticated tourist is further reinforced in descriptions
of desolate French villages whose inhabitants remain unaware that
Napoleon has been deposed, a deliberate contrast to the English traveler
who knows the fate of the French government. Here, then, Shelley's
"descriptive mode" might be understood not simply as counterpublic
discourse on picturesque touring but also as a form of Enlightenment
anthropology. To the degree, that is, that Shelley may be said to figure
herself as a more knowledgeable, disinterested English outsider capable
of rendering impartial judgment on the observed Other—the French,
Swiss, and Germans in this travelogue—she practices a form of social
inquiry that Esther Schor aligns with Enlightenment values.[21]

Shelley's *History* also revises the Burkean construction of the sublime
as threatening or engulfing and, as Anne Mellor has generally argued, as
"an experience of masculine empowerment."[22] Although Shelley only
uses the adjective "sublime" once in her travel book to refer to the Swiss
Alps, she transfers the sublime from the externalized unknowable to the
quantifiable, ludicrous behavior of their male tour guide. I quote at length
from Shelley's description of their journey through the French
countryside:

> Hills had appeared in the distance during the whole day, and we had
> advanced gradually towards them, but were unprepared for the scene that
> broke upon us as we passed the gate of this city. On quitting the walls, the

road wound underneath a high precipice; on the other side the hills rose more
gradually, and the green valley that intervened between them was watered by
a pleasant river; before us arose an amphitheatre of hills covered with vines,
but irregular and rocky. The last gate of the town was cut through the
precipitous rock that arose on one side, and in that place jutted into the road.
This approach to mountain scenery filled us with delight; it was otherwise
with our *voiturier*: he came from the plains of Troyes, and these hills so
utterly scared him, that he in some degree lost his reason. After winding
through the valley, we began to ascend the mountains which were its
boundary: we left our *voiture*, and walked on, delighted with every new view
that broke upon us. (31–32)

Again, Shelley does not characterize this "amphitheatre of hills" as
sublime, but her description of the maddening effect the scenery has on
their *voiturier* is certainly resonant with Burke's sublime as provoking
the illusion of self-annihilation. As Burke observes in his 1757
*Philosophical Enquiry into the Origin of Our Ideas of the Sublime and
the Beautiful*: "Whatever is fitted in any sort to excite the ideas of pain,
and danger, that is to say, whatever is in any sort terrible, or is conversant
about terrible objects, or operates in a manner analogous to terror, is a
source of the sublime."[23] Thus, it is as if Shelley produced this naive tour
guide, rendered vulnerable to the landscape, as a literalized embodiment
of the fear of engulfment by some unobjectifiable Other present in
Burke's account. The threat of self-annihilation, which constitutes the
pain associated with the sublime is, according to Burke, merely illusory,
transitory. In Shelley's account, however, the threat is abiding, and, to
this end, she traces their tour guide's attempts to flee from the hills for
the next several pages of her travelogue. Shelley's coolly distant self-
representation, conspicuously juxtaposed with the *voiturier*'s frenzy,
produces her as the more worldly traveler as it ironically undermines this
construction of the sublime. If, as Mellor contends, Burke fashions the
sublime as "masculine empowerment" and "its contrasting term, the
beautiful, is associated with an experience of feminine nurturance, love,
and sensuous relaxation" (*R & G*, 85), then Shelley's apparently
descriptive mode must be seen as an attempt to regender Burke's
aesthetics. On Shelley's rendering, the sublime is not an experience of
masculine empowerment but quite the opposite: a demasculinization of
the male tour guide. Moreover, while Shelley seems no more self-aligned
with the beautiful than with the sublime here, she comes off as an
unmistakably centered, slightly amused, manifestly female traveler. I
should add that, while any rich consideration of Shelley's gendered
sublime cannot ignore the *voiturier*'s nationality, it is beyond the scope
of this essay to do more than simply note the association.

Reading *History of a Six Weeks' Tour* as a document that was arguably intended to represent personal or private relations yet that also potentially engineers new cultural hierarchies and regulates already existing social relations in early-nineteenth-century England (Shelley's text was published for and consumed by an English readership) dovetails on numerous recent studies relating public and private discourse(s). Such studies compel us to revise not only our temptation to construct the domestic affections and social interests as rigidly separate but also our sense of the relationship such rule-governed discourses share with those who are said to produce them.[24] For instance, my reading loosely tallies with Carole Fabricant's argument for the ways in which domestic travel diaries promote the very public interests of the landed rich by encouraging much less affluent tourists to identify against their own material interests. Fabricant contends that eighteenth-century domestic tourist literature—"the large number of travel journals, guidebooks, recorded tours, estate poems, and the like that appeared throughout the period"[25]—produced the fashion for tourism within England, greatly benefiting the aristocracy:

> Domestic tourism ... was an activity that carefully orchestrated the movement of people through private sectors of the English countryside by defining the terms of their admittance onto the ground of the wealthy, and by seducing them into an identification with the tastes and interests of the landed rich through the manipulation of voyeuristic delights and vicarious pleasures—through the illusion of shared participation in a world not in any meaningful sense their own. In this sense domestic tourism served the interests of the ruling classes, and reinforced their hegemony, by enlisting the complicity of the ruled in the fiction of their *in*clusion in an increasingly *ex*clusionary society. (257)

If one reads Shelley's travelogue against the backdrop of Fabricant's sense of the way domestic touring literature produced a certain false consciousness in its readership, then one might urge that *History of a Six Weeks' Tour* should be located in terms of a somewhat nebulous relationship of private, first-hand narration to social hierarchies. Shelley's description of her travels on the Continent cannot remain exclusively at the level of memoiristic expression, or even at the level of descriptive narrative designed to correct misinformation or to enhance description related in other travel narratives. Rather, Shelley's text seems most usefully read in the context of touring literature of the period that engages the possibility of reshaping notions of the tourist and of producing new discursive possibilities for the practice of tourism. Putting questions about the gender of touring aside, one might profitably reinvestigate Shelley's canon with a more sharply focused sense of the ways in which her literary productions engaged seemingly larger public discourses about authorship itself. For instance, I am suggesting here that Shelley's travelogue not only "indicates a refusal to conform to the dictates of the 'sublime,' which sought absence of the feminine and of detail"[26] but that it also revises aesthetic standards that would relegate it to subliterary standards. That is, lifewriting texts such as *History of a Six Weeks' Tour* remain understudied because the attention to detail, dailiness as a structuring principle, immersed narrative perspective, and the degree of personal revelation run counter to the aesthetics of touring that promote the notion of perspective as distance. Let me put this another way: the kind of journalizing that emphasizes particularity as a way of structuring reality was viewed as inferior as Shelley's travelogue went to press because it was incommensurate with emergent notions of the sublime. Thus, I am suggesting that Shelley was quite self-consciously engaged in a revision of tropes of the sublime, the beautiful, and the picturesque in order to make ideological room for this very text.

The premium placed on the individual author in a post-Romantic era and questions about who can be an author and what constitutes a text are frequent preoccupations of literary critics. If an author, as Foucault and others have suggested, is an author because she alters the possibilities for what can be said or written, then the accent placed on "publicity," as many feminist theorists have noted, effectively and inevitably erases those women authors who have largely written the private. While I make no claims for offering even the beginnings of a typology with which to reevaluate women's Romantic writing, I do mean to highlight the strategies that women authors such as Shelley deployed in order to write themselves into history. Insofar as these authors performatively foreground and then fracture paradigms that would devalue or marginalize writing that represents and is located in the private or the interior, they potentially initiate a kind of discursive practice that, according to Foucault, constitutes the "author-function." Although such a paradigm shift might authorize previously devalued forms of written representation, it, too, necessarily rests on a critique of the presumptions of that very paradigm shift itself. Thus, to the question that Barbara Johnson asks at the end of "My Monster/My Self," "Can [a woman] write anything that would *not* exhibit 'the amiableness of domestic affection'?" (66), I would want to ask, by way of offering a response to that question, "Can a woman write anything that would *only* exhibit 'the amiableness of domestic affection' and still be considered an author?"

Notes

Many thanks to Morris Eaves, Bette London, and Victoria Szabo for their thoughtful criticisms of earlier drafts of this essay.

1. Harriet Kramer Linkin surveyed over three hundred U.S. universities, reporting that more than half of the courses on Romanticism include Mary Shelley ("The Current Canon in British Romantic Studies," *College English* 53 [1991]: 548–70). Audrey A. Fisch, Anne K. Mellor, and Esther H. Schor, the editors of *The Other Mary Shelley: Beyond Frankenstein* (New York: Oxford University Press, 1993), cite Linkin's study, surmising that "one of every two students of Romanticism has read *Frankenstein*" (4).

2. Some of Shelley's more understudied forms include essays, reviews, short stories and tales, and travelogues.

3. *The Other Mary Shelley: Beyond Frankenstein*, 4.

4. Mary Shelley, *Frankenstein, or The Modern Prometheus* [1818], ed. James Rieger (Chicago: University of Chicago Press, 1974). Attempting to document Percy Bysshe Shelley's influence over the 1818 manuscript, James Rieger suggests that "his assistance at every point in the book's manufacture was so extensive that one hardly knows whether to regard him as editor or minor collaborator" (xviii).

5. Anne K. Mellor, "'My Hideous Progeny,'" in *Mary Shelley: Her Life, Her Fiction, Her Monsters* (New York: Routledge Press, 1988), 59. Mellor provides an ambitiously detailed account of the differences between Shelley's and her husband's language in *Frankenstein*. Using the manuscript of *Frankenstein* in the Abinger Collection in the Bodleian Library, she has compiled a chart that compares Shelley's manuscript with her husband's often inferior, inflated revisions.

6. The literary careers of Maria Edgeworth (1767–1849) and Mary Wollstonecraft Shelley (1797–1851), though initially separated by thirty years, span roughly the same historical period and are remarkably similar in terms of the obstacles both confronted as women writers and, more interestingly, in terms of how both have been constructed by twentieth-century critics. Not only do these authors currently share the rather damning reputation of being one-work wonders, their lives converged insofar as Edgeworth was inspired by the writings of Shelley's mother, Mary Wollstonecraft. Indeed, Edgeworth's own *Letters for Literary Ladies* (1795) is commonly read against the backdrop of Mary Wollstonecraft's *Thoughts on the Education of Daughters* (1787) and *A Vindication of the Rights of Woman* (1792)—works that fueled the already hotly debated subject of women's education in the late eighteenth century. See Marilyn Butler's, *Maria Edgeworth: A Literary Biography* (New York: Oxford University Press, 1972) for an extended account of Edgeworth's relationship to her father. See also Janet Dunleavy's essay "Maria Edgeworth and the Novel of Manners," in *Reading and Writing Women's Lives: A Study of the Novel of Manners*, ed. Bege K. Bowers and Barbara Brothers (Ann Arbor, Mich.: UMI Research Press, 1990), 49–65, which attempts to debunk the "myth of modern scholars . . . that following her unassisted writing and publication of *Castle Rackrent* in 1800, Maria Edgeworth . . . was so dominated by her well-meaning, overbearing, moralistic, and single-minded father . . . that thereafter she was never free to produce anything of comparable quality or significance but devoted herself to the production of moral tales that illustrated his theories of education" (50).

7. Margaret J. Ezell, "The Tedious Chase: Writing Women's Literary History in the Eighteenth and Nineteenth Centuries," in *Writing Women's Literary History* (Baltimore, Md.: Johns Hopkins University Press, 1993), 103.

8. Barbara Johnson, "My Monster/My Self," *Diacritics* 12 (1982): 57. Johnson treats *Frankenstein* as one of three texts able to accommodate the preoccupations of many liter-ary critics: "The question of mothering, the question of the woman writer, and the ques-tion of autobiography" (55). Although Johnson does a fine job sketching out some of the pitfalls implicit in women's autobiography, she limits herself to a very literal, one-dimensional understanding of confession as a "resemblance between teller and addressee" in Shelley's text (57). Finally, her failure to interrogate her definition of confession fore-closes the possibility of asking about how such confessional moments in the "text" func-tion in less obvious, less plot dependent ways.

9. Shelley, *Frankenstein, or The Modern Prometheus*, 229 (appendix A of Rieger's text).

10. Michel Foucault, "What Is an Author?" in *Language, Counter-Memory, Practice: Selected Essays and Interviews*, ed. Donald F. Bouchard (Ithaca: Cornell University Press, 1977), 124. Foucault elaborates on specifically modern constructions of authorship.

11. See Mary Poovey's essay "'My Hideous Progeny': The Lady and the Monster," in *The Proper Lady and the Woman Writer: Ideology as Style in the Works of Mary Woll-stonecraft, Mary Shelley, and Jane Austen* (Chicago: University of Chicago Press, 1984), 114–42, hereafter cited parenthetically in the text as "HP," for an extended narrative of professionalized women writers in the nineteenth century.

12. Shelley, *Frankenstein, or The Modern Prometheus*, 229.

13. In her extensive and thoughtful analysis of modes of self-narration and the role that they have played in contemporary women's writing, Rita Felski, *Beyond Feminist Aesthetics: Feminist Literature and Social Change* (Cambridge: Harvard University Press, 1989), defines "confession" as "a type of autobiographical writing that signals its intention to foreground the most personal and intimate details of the author's life" (87). Even the most self-conscious of narratives seeking to reveal the "personal" and the "intimate" encode a kind of truth-telling gesture that, as any good postmodern theorist could tell you, potentially obscures the "truth" of incoherent writing selves. Thus, Felski, drawing on Foucault's discussions of censorship and repression of the self, contends that "the act of confession can potentially exacerbate rather than alleviate problems of self-identity, engendering a dialectic in which the production of ever more writing as a means to defining a center of meaning merely serves to underscore the alienation of the subject even as it seeks to overcome it" (104). The truth telling inherent in confession is not, however, thoroughly mitigated by postmodern incursions on the self, for the readerly expectation that the author is aiming at "honest self-depiction" persists. Perhaps, then, the question is, as Sidonie Smith frames it in "Construing Truths in Lying Mouths: Truthtelling in Women's Autobiography"(*Studies in the Literary Imagination* 23:2 [1990]: 145–63), not whether a clean separation between fact and fiction in confessional narratives is plausible but "'truth' to what? To facticity? To experience? To self? To his-tory? To community? Truth to the said, to the unsaid, to other fictions (of man, of woman, of American, of black, etc.), to the genre? And truth for what and for whom?" (147–48). It is these questions that I circulate throughout my examination of the ways in which Shelley publicizes the private and privatizes the public.

14. Shelley, *Frankenstein, or The Modern Prometheus*, 229.

15. The full title of Shelley's travelogue is *History of a Six Weeks' Tour Through a Part of France, Switzerland, Germany, and Holland; With Letters, Descriptive of a Sail Round the Lake of Geneva, and of the Glaciers of Chamouni* (London: T. Hookam & the Olliers, 1817). hereafter cited parenthetically in the text by page number.

16. Donald Reiman's *The Study of Modern Manuscripts: Public, Confidential, and Private* (Baltimore, Md.: Johns Hopkins University Press, 1993) offers criteria by which all Western textual productions—originating since print culture began to flourish in the fifteenth century—can be designated as "public," "confidential," or "private."

17. Wollstonecraft's *Letters from Norway* are reprinted in *The Works of Mary Wollstonecraft*, 7 vols., ed. Janet Todd and Marilyn Butler (New York: New York University Press, 1989), 6:237–348. Eleanor Ty ("Writing as a Daughter: Autobiography in Wollstonecraft's Travelogue," in *Essays on Life Writing: From Genre to Critical Practice*, ed. Marlene Kadar [Toronto: University of Toronto Press, 1992], 61–77) flatly contends that "in Wollstonecraft's *Letters* there is little or no distinction between the public and the private sphere" (65). Ty, as she herself notes, is thus following on the heels of other Wollstonecraft scholars like Mitzi Myers ("Mary Wollstonecraft's *Letters Written . . . in Sweden*: Toward Romantic Autobiography," *Studies in Eighteenth Century Culture* 8 [1979]: 165–86) who note the "flow" of "personal and social themes" (181). Yet Ty reads this blurred boundary between personal and public commentary not so much as a sign of "sophisticated artistry as a revelation of Wollstonecraft's divided subjectivity" (65).

18. Mary Favret, *Romantic Correspondence: Women, Politics, and the Fiction of Letters* (Cambridge: Cambridge University Press, 1993), 10.

19. Relevant texts to this discussion of the picturesque include William Gilpin's *Observations Relative Chiefly to Picturesque Beauty* (1786), *Three Essays: on Picturesque Beauty; on Picturesque Travel; and on Sketching Landscape* (1792), and *Observations on the Western Parts of England* (1798). Richard Payne Knight's *The Landscape* (1794) and *An Analytical Inquiry into the Principles of Taste* (1805) along with Uvedale Price's *An Essay on the Picturesque* (1794) and *A Dialogue on the Distinct Characters of the Picturesque and the Beautiful* (1801) round out the catalogue. See also J. R. Watson's *Picturesque Landscape and English Romantic Poetry* (London: Hutchinson Educational, 1970).

20. *The Annual Register*, 1789, ed. Edmund Burke (Pall-Mall: J. Dodsley, 1792), 170. The entire review of Gilpin's essay appears on pp. 170–83.

21. See Esther Schor's "Mary Shelley in Transit," in *The Other Mary Shelley: Beyond Frankenstein*, 235–57 for a fuller consideration of Romantic women's writing as Enlightenment anthropology.

22. Anne K. Mellor, *Romanticism and Gender* (New York: Routledge Press, 1992), 85, hereafter cited parenthetically as *R&G*. In this, her most recent contribution to the field, Mellor discusses the female Gothic as a strategy for domesticating the masculine egotistical sublime. She writes:

> How did the women writers of the Romantic period respond to this engendering of the sublime as a masculinized experience of empowerment, of the beautiful as a feminized experience of nurturing and sensuous love? . . . One group of writers, those familiar to us as the authors of Gothic fiction, accepts the identification of the sublime with the experience of masculine empowerment. But they explicitly equate this masculine sublime with patriarchal tyranny. Their novels expose the dark underside of the doctrine of the separate spheres, the sexual division of labor, and the domestic ideology of patriarchal capitalism. The father . . . is unmasked as the author of violence against women. . . . His crimes almost always occur among Alpine landscapes or ruined Gothic towers, the loci of the masculine sublime. By moving the exercise of sublime power into the household, the female Gothic domesticates the

sublime as paternal transgression—represented as father-daughter incest—that is everywhere most monstrous and most ordinary (90–91).

Mellor's domesticated sublime is loosely akin to my claim for Shelley's revision of the sublime in picturesque touring. .

23. Edmund Burke, *A Philosophical Enquiry into the Origin of Our Ideas of the Sublime and the Beautiful*, ed. James Boulton (1958; rprt., Notre Dame, Ind.: Notre Dame University Press, 1968), 39.

24. Nancy Armstrong convincingly argues that "in representing the household as a world with its own form of social relations, . . . [conduct books] revised the semiotic of culture at its most basic level and enabled a coherent idea of the middle class to take shape" (*Desire and Domestic Fiction: A Political History of the Novel* [New York: Oxford University Press, 1987], 63). For further elaboration on the production of public and private spheres in the latter half of the eighteenth century and the beginning of the nineteenth, see her book in its entirety.

25. Carole Fabricant, "The Literature of Domestic Tourism and the Public Consumption of Private Property," in *The New Eighteenth Century: Theory, Politics, English Literature*, ed. Felicity Nussbaum and Laura Brown (New York: Routledge, 1987), 255.

26. Kay K. Cook, "Self-Neglect in the Canon: Why Don't We Talk about Romantic Autobiography?" *Auto/Biography Studies* 5 (1990): 94. I am indebted to Cook for her theorization of neglected Romantic lifewriting, especially private writing by women. However, although she persuasively ties eighteenth-century discourses promoting perspective as distance with the erasure of Dorothy Wordsworth's *Journals*, her argument does not go far enough in suggesting how Romantic women writers intervened to alter these popular aesthetics.

Author and Editor: Mary Shelley's Private Writings and the Author Function of Percy Bysshe Shelley

Sheila Ahlbrand

> It would be just as wrong to equate the author with the real writer as to equate him with the fictitious speaker: the author function is carried out and operates in the scission itself, in this division and this distance.
>
> —Michel Foucault, "What Is an Author?"

> Shelley . . .in the evening goes out to take a little walk and loses—himself.
>
> —Mary Shelley, *Journal*, 26 November 1816

> I have another selfish reason to wish that you would come which I have a great mind not to mention, yet I will not omit it as it might induce you—
>
> —Mary Shelley, Letter to Maria Gisborne, 17 August 1818

When Roland Barthes proclaimed "The Death of the Author" in 1968, Michel Foucault answered him with the question "What Is an Author?" In his essay Foucault challenges the boundaries of the preconceived definitions of author in our time, and substitutes the author function for any particular individual who may previously have been given the label of "author." Jack Stillinger extended Foucault's work in *Multiple Authorship and the Myth of Solitary Genius*, once again challenging the boundaries of the definition of "author."[1] It may at first seem anomalous to view Mary Shelley's letters and journals through the lens of Foucault's author function, especially since I am looking at these documents as performing this function not only for Shelley herself but for Percy

Bysshe Shelley as well. After all, Foucault says that "a private letter may well have a signer—it does not have an author" (*MF*, 107–8). I would contend, however, given the current interest in literary nonfiction, that private letters and journals published for public consumption do indeed have authors, or to use Foucault's phrase, "author functions." For, as Foucault observes, "It does not seem necessary that the author function remain constant in form, complexity and even existence" (*MF*, 119). In the spirit of this statement, this essay challenges the definition of author once more by blurring the lines of authorship with the introduction of the once synonymous term of editor.[2] Furthermore, since I will be discussing the editorial function primarily in its role of editing lives, the definitions of such terms as "biography" and "autobiography" will come under scrutiny as well.

I will begin by examining Mary Shelley's history in regard to both the author and the editor, and how her own experiences, as well as those of the people she cared for, affected the way she was to approach her writing and the way she presented herself and her family to the public. I will then argue that Percy Shelley's search for a female extension of himself gave Mary Shelley both the authority to represent him in her writing, public as well as private, and paradoxically to differentiate herself from him. By using her private writings toward this end she could claim to represent Percy Shelley in as truthful a manner as she could. However, since she probably expected these writings to be read and even published, she carefully set herself up as editor of any representations of her husband. Finally, I plan to examine the specific representations she chose to utilize and propose why these distinct images were important to both Mary and Percy Shelley.

The History of a Name

Mary Shelley's relationship with the functions of authors and editors began before her birth and continues to this day.[3] The daughter of two authors and the lover, and later wife, of a third, the very name Mary Wollstonecraft Godwin Shelley contains a history of both public and private writings that are inextricably woven into a pattern of success, scandal, and failure. When Mary Godwin eloped with Percy Shelley in July of 1814, they began a journal to record their impressions of the journey. This journal became the basis for *A History of a Six Weeks Tour* that was published in 1817.[4] It is not surprising to find that one of the entries in this journal records the reading of Mary Wollstonecraft's similar publication *Letters Written During a Short Residence in Sweden, Norway, and Denmark*.[5] In fact, her *Six Weeks Tour* can be seen as both inspired by, and a reaction to, her mother's *Short Residence*. Mary Shelley was paying homage to her mother in the form of emulation while also attempting to create both her own literary name and her own *History*. The recording of this reading so early in her own journal demonstrates the profound influence that private writing within her familial background, actually the writing of private documents for publication, had on the young Mary Shelley. However, not all of the influences from her parents' writings can be seen as entirely beneficial.

After an initial period of intense grief over the death of his wife, William Godwin decided to undertake the twofold task of writing his wife's memoirs and collecting and editing her posthumous works.[6] However, what he intended as a way of memorializing Wollstonecraft resulted in her posthumous humiliation and the temporary devastation of her work for the rights of women. Marilyn May[7] has suggested that because of this early lesson in the injurious consequences of public exposure, Mary Shelley was hesitant to "bring [herself] forward in print."[8] In his memoir of Wollstonecraft, Godwin represents her in the role of the author reluctant to be brought before the public.

> At the commencement of her literary career, she is said to have conceived a vehement aversion to the being regarded, by her ordinary acquaintance, in the character of an author, and to have employed some precautions to prevent its occurrence. (*WG*, 226)

Shelley obviously idolized her mother; her protestations about public exposure would seem to support May's view of a woman who did not wish to participate in the "conjuring [of] notorious ghosts."[9] I would contend that rather than discouraging his daughter, Godwin's miscalculations in publishing the *Memoirs* served as a lesson in the value of subtlety in disclosure practices, as well as in the power of the editor over an individual's life and works. Through both her public and private writings, Mary Wollstonecraft, despite her earlier misgivings, had established a positive authorial persona for herself, which was later temporarily destroyed through Godwin's well-intentioned, though indiscreet, editing of that persona. With the understanding of how her mother's reputation had been damaged, Mary would have also understood how to save the reputations of both herself and Shelley.

Percy Bysshe Shelley's editing of Mary Shelley's *Frankenstein* is the next strand in this cord of intertwined authors and editors. His influence in the novel is striking, though there is some argument as to whether his hand in the writing is the stroke of genius that put *Frankenstein* on a different plane than any of Shelley's subsequent novels, or whether it was part of the sometimes overblown prose for which the novel has continued to draw criticism.[10] The novel, which was published anonymously in 1818, was originally thought to have been written by Percy Shelley, Sir Walter Scott having attributed the probable authorship of *Frankenstein* to him when the novel was reviewed in *Blackwood's* in March of that same year. Mary Shelley, however, was quick to inform Scott of his misconception and to take the credit of authorship for herself, despite the fact that the tone of the letter seems somewhat purposefully acquiescent. She tells Scott, "I am anxious to prevent your continuing in the mistake of supposing Mr. Shelley guilty of a juvenile attempt of mine."[11] Her use of the word "anxious" along with her adamant desire to be recognized as the true author of *Frankenstein*, evokes Harold Bloom's "anxiety of influence," but with different connotations.[12] Mary Shelley does not feel anxiety about the plagiarism of her forefathers but rather about receiving the credit she deserves for a truly original story that has, in fact, become a cultural icon. Scott's notice of *Frankenstein* was quite favorable, and while Mary Shelley asserts that she is attempting to protect Percy's reputation, she is actually attempting to claim the right to her own.

Through her experience with the reception of *Frankenstein*, Mary Shelley became aware of errors in judgment she had made in understanding both the power of an editor over a work, and the power of an author's name. For, as Foucault asserts, an author's name is not only important for classification purposes but also serves a social function:

> It would seem that the author's name, unlike other proper names, does not pass from the interior of a discourse to the real and exterior individual who produced it; instead, the name seems always to be present, marking off the edges of the text, revealing, or at least characterizing, its mode of being. (*MF*, 107)

Percy Shelley was already established as an author, and his name was performing a perfunctory "author function," marking certain expectations for a text connected with his name and allowing him a modicum of respect in certain literary circles. Even though Mary Shelley had become a published author at the age of eleven[13] and possessed three last names of literary celebrity, she still did not have the power of her own name as an "author function." By choosing to publish *Frankenstein* anonymously, Mary Shelley, because of her lack of authority, made herself vulnerable to the power of the suggestion of Percy's name in connection with a text, a situation that was compounded by the presence of his voice through the editing of the work. Mary Shelley now knew not only the authority of an editor over both an individual's life and works, but she had also learned the editing power of an author's name and how the functioning of that name serves as a commanding influence upon the minds of the reading public. Although she was later to publish the novel under her own name, and published all subsequent novels in that fashion, the difficulty of granting her full authorial credit for the novel continues into present criticism.[14]

William Godwin asserted editorial control not only over Mary Wollstonecraft but over Mary Shelley as well, both in exposing her difficult birth to a voyeuristic public and by his direct dealings with her manuscripts. However, the situations were somewhat different for the daughter than the mother. While Mary Wollstonecraft had no control over her husband's editing of her works, Mary Shelley handed the controls to her father of her own free will. Although, in the case of *Valperga*, this was largely a financial consideration to aid her father in emerging from under the mountain of debt he had accrued, she nonetheless had a very high regard for her father. In a letter to Jane Williams, Mary Shelley wrote, "You have then seen my father. Until I knew Shelley I may justly say that he was my God—& I remember many childish instances of the excess of attachment I bore for him" (*MSL*, 1:296). As with the carte blanche she had earlier given to Percy Shelley in regard to editing *Frankenstein*,[15] *Valperga* was given to Godwin with the "liberty to dispose of it to the best advantage."[16] Unfortunately, the letter that Mary Shelley wrote to Godwin accompanying this manuscript has been lost, so the only version of this presentation of liberty regarding Mary Shelley's text is ironically conveyed to us by Percy Shelley rather than Mary, one god bestowing the fruits of his beloved subject upon another. Godwin is thought to have heavily edited *Valperga*, but his true editorial authority is most clearly expressed with his absolute suppression of *Mathilda*, the semiautobiographical novel that remained unpublished until 1959 despite the fact that Mary Shelley had given him the manuscript for publication.[17]

Mary Shelley, whose name had finally acquired its own authorial context with the acknowledgment of her authorship of *Frankenstein*, later became the editor of Percy Bysshe Shelley's *Posthumous Poems* and *Poetical Works*,[18] thus reversing the author/editor dichotomy that had manifested itself in the composition and publication of *Frankenstein*. Like Godwin, through her extensive notes, Mary Shelley was not only editing the works of her late husband but was assuming the role of his biographer as well. Despite the restrictions concerning publication placed on her by Percy's family, Mary now had not only the authority of her

own name but also the power, at least in a figurative sense, of and over
the name of Percy Bysshe Shelley. A similar reversal takes place in the
dynamic of the editorial relationship between Mary Shelley and William
Godwin. At the end of his life, Godwin expressed the desire, in his will,
that his daughter collect his papers and write his memoirs. Although it is
obvious by the many letters that Mary Shelley wrote to people seeking
information for her father's memoirs[19] that, at least initially, she had the
best intentions of conforming to his wishes, Godwin's memoirs were
never to be completed. She wrote to Edward Trelawney that while "I
certainly could not answer to my conscience to give it up—I shall
therefore do it—but it must wait" (*MLS*, 2:280). She offers excuses for
her procrastination, but the matter seems to come down to a contest of
wills between Godwin's "passion for posthumous fame" and her own
fear of "the misery of . . . scurrility and attacks" (*MSL*, 2:281). While
Mary Shelley may not have planned to suppress her father's voice in the
hope for posthumous fame, she realized that in promoting his name she
ran the risk of diminishing her own, so Godwin's memoirs came to join
Mathilda in a circular pattern of familial trust betrayed.

Recent criticism has focused on Mary Shelley's editing of her
husband's works as a reconstruction of the poet's reputation for
consumption by a previously unsympathetic public.[20] While this concept
operates in tandem with what I am presenting here, there are nonetheless
substantial differences. First, in examining Mary Shelley's private
writings, in view of their performative function of editing the life of
Percy Shelley, I am primarily looking at those letters and journal entries
that were written before his death. A radical change of style is evident in
Mary Shelley's private writings after the death of her husband. In the
writings after 8 July 1822, the once human Percy Shelley is transformed
into the idealized, ethereal, and even divine Shelley. The notes, which
accompany Mary Shelley's posthumous editions of Percy Shelley's
works, would decidedly be categorized as adhering to the adulatory style.
In her note to *Queen Mab,* she explains that "Shelley possessed a quality
of mind which experience has shown me no other human being as
participating, in more than a very slight degree: this was his
unworldliness" (*PW*, 1:99). Secondly, as Judy Simons notes in her work
on literary diarists, a formal autobiography, or as in this case biography,
comes from a position of "historical superiority."[21] Biographers can work
through the benefit of hindsight to shape persons and events to fit into the
representations that they choose to utilize in order to best serve their
ends. Although Mary Shelley had at one time expressed the desire to
write her husband's biography, his father, Sir Timothy Shelley, had
allowed her to reissue his poems only if there was no memoir included.

The notes that she wrote for each of these poems are obviously her way of circumventing Sir Timothy's edict. Therefore, at this juncture, Mary Shelley's role of editor is equally balanced by her role as biographer.

Journals and letters, while perhaps still romanticizing and even fictionalizing their subjects, do not have the benefit of hindsight. The Shelleys read numerous memoirs and other private writings, which were beginning to come into vogue at that time. However, while Mary Shelley continued to edit her representations of Percy Shelley before his death, possibly with the idea of future publication in mind, she could not foresee his sudden, tragic end, which would so pervasively color her later writings. Hindsight may be said to be the linchpin of her later writings that is conspicuously absent in her earlier personal works. Paula Feldman has suggested that Mary Shelley never wrote an official memoir of her husband because of a "secret feeling that she was unworthy to have been his wife,"[22] but I would argue that the memoir never came into being because of her inability to reconcile the truth of her early journals to the idealized Shelley that she created in her later ones. The early personal writings are a suggestion of a biography in progress, a biography that was eventually replaced by the notes to Percy Shelley's poems and that could be seen as a parallel to the truthful and caring memoir written by her father, which ended in the ruin of her mother's reputation. The Mary Shelley who wrote in her journal on 2 October 1822,

> The stars may behold my tears, & the winds drink my sighs—but my thoughts are a sealed treasure which I can confide to none. White paper—wilt thou be my confident? I will trust thee fully, for none shall see what I write. (*MSJ*, 2:429)

is not the same woman who was accused of leaving private documents around where they could be read by servants, and who was aware that her letters were being read by people other than those for whom they were intended.[23] It is this earlier Mary Shelley on whom I focus, in an attempt to understand and explain how she used her writing to reinterpret both Percy and herself for what she saw as their future public.

Unity and Dissolution

Mary Shelley came to find her identity inextricably woven in with that of her husband. Any writer who attempts a work on the Shelleys is immediately aware of how this fact manifests itself, when confronted with the problem of separating and naming these two authors for the simple purpose of differentiation and identification. In a paper on the editing of *Shelley and His Circle*, Donald H. Reiman devoted an entire paragraph to his defense of the standard use of naming practices employed to distinguish Mary Shelley from Percy Shelley, by referring to them as "Mary" and "Shelley." Although many contemporary editors have chosen to refer to Mary as "Shelley" when she is their central subject, Reiman notes that "certainly when dealing with both writers, we cannot call Mary W. Shelley simply by her last name without confusion, as we might refer to 'Austen' or 'Plath.'"[24] A difficulty arises for generations of readers who have come to associate the single name "Shelley" with that of Percy Shelley rather than Mary. However, if referring to each of them by their full name is the only way to overcome these gender biases for future generations, then a little discomfort to readers today would seem to be a small obstacle. Unfortunately for Mary Shelley, gender bias is just one of the problems in the use of her name as an authorial label. The dilemma of classification of names has yet another level of confusion when Reiman's decision to refer to Mary Shelley simply as "Mary" is utilized in a context that includes not only Percy Shelley but Mary Wollstonecraft as well. The history I mentioned earlier in the name Mary Wollstonecraft Godwin Shelley not only made her a living reminder of her rich heritage but simultaneously deprived her of any identity that was purely her own. Thus far I have purposely avoided any standardization of naming practices in an attempt to give Mary Shelley her own identity but also to emphasize the difficulty of expressing separate identities for Mary and Percy Shelley. From this point on, as a compromise between Reiman's historically correct use of "Mary" and "Shelley," and the gender-fair "Shelley" and "PB Shelley," I will refer to Mary Shelley by her first and last name, and Percy Shelley by his last name only.

The struggle between her desire to merge with the identity of Shelley and to find an identity for herself is evident at many places in the private writings of Mary Shelley prior to her husband's death, after which she wanted nothing more than absolute communion with him. It is through this struggle that we begin to see Mary Shelley editing the life of her husband, initially as a way of representing herself in reference to her role as his soul mate and later as she begins to differentiate herself in terms of what Shelley is and what she is not.

Irene Tayler and Gina Luria have pointed out that this merging of the identities of husband and wife was a common practice during the Romantic era and reflected the laws of the time. More importantly, they go on to discuss how the Romantic poets, especially Wordsworth, Byron, and Shelley, employ the repeated motif of women as sisters or, especially in the case of Shelley in such poems as *Alastor* and *The Revolt of Islam*, as an extension of the poet himself.[25] In the young Mary Godwin's intelligence and celebrated family heritage, Shelley saw what he imagined could be the female version of himself, and, in associating himself with her, he found the literary legacy that was missing in his own background. As for Mary Shelley, it is not difficult to understand why she would be willing, and even eager, to merge herself with this illustrious poet. Her lack of an authorial name and the power that comes with it could only be strengthened by a union with the name of Shelley. Her journal entry for 25 August 1814 states, "We arrange our appartment—& write part of Shelley's Romance," and again on 27 August she writes, "Then we write part of the Romance." However, on 10 September of that same year, Shelley records, "S. writes part of *his* Romance" (emphasis added) (*MSJ*, 1:19–20, 24). Apparently, at this point in the relationship Mary Shelley had found the integration of their two identities to be more beneficial than had Shelley, whose literary identity—already having been established—needed the merger of souls for personal, rather than public, gain. Beyond the authorial power that his name offered, he also presented her with the chance for adventure, romance, and independence from her father.

Nevertheless, the autonomy that Mary Shelley gained by removing herself from her father's jurisdiction was initially limited by her love of Shelley, and, although her union with him provided her with the sense of power she lacked, her personal growth was such that she soon realized the need to establish strength on an individual level before their alliance could work. Part of this autonomy was achieved in the context of her journals and letters, where she began to exercise the power that she discovered in the form of subtle self-editing. Moreover, while their identities were joined, any editing of Shelley's life reflected upon her own identity.

The first page of Mary Shelley's *Journal*, which was to record entries encompassing July 1814 through May 1815, offers a fascinating suggestion of her change of attitude in the course of such a relatively short period of time. In Mary Shelley's handwriting we read the words "Shelley and Mary's journal book," however, also in Mary Shelley's hand, above the word "Shelley," the word "not" has at some indeterminate time been inserted (*MSJ*, 1:5). I would interpret this to mean that what began as "Shelley and Mary's journal book" came to be seen by Mary Shelley as no longer belonging to both of them but to her alone, a supposition that is upheld by the dwindling number of entries contributed by Shelley over the years.

On 8 August 1814, fewer than two weeks after the commencement of the journal, something quite interesting happens to the text on a stylistic level: Shelley begins to refer to himself in the third person. At this point, the journal belonged more to Shelley than to Mary Shelley, her only contribution having come on the first entry when, after Shelley records, "Mary was there," she adds, "S.helley was also with me" (*MSJ*, 1:7). By 11 August 1814, when Mary Shelley wrote her first lengthy entry in the journal, she too, refers to herself in the third person. She continued this habit of detachment on a fairly regular basis through 1 October 1814.

This choice of self-representation raises several questions. First, had the two of them already decided to publish an account of their expedition based on the journals? This would certainly explain why they wanted to specify to whom they were referring. The fact that Mary Shelley discontinues writing of herself in the third person shortly after the end of their journey suggests that there might be some truth to this conjecture. If this is accurate, then the journals for this period should be viewed as perhaps even more self-conscious than those to come later.

Second, can we speculate that in eliminating the word *I* in favor of personal pronouns or the generic *we*, these two authors are attempting to emphasize the union of their souls? If this is so, might there be another reason that Mary Shelley decides to stop using the third person? Perhaps this question can be clarified by noting that, although Mary Shelley no longer refers to herself in the third person, neither does she return to a habitual use of *I*. For instance, here is an example of three entries from the week when she first discontinued the use of the third person:

> Monday 3rd—Read Political Justice. Hookham calls—walk with Peacock to the lake of Nangis and set off little fire boats After dinner talk & let off fire works—talk of the west of Ireland plan.
>
> Teusday 4th—Shelley is out all day calling on Finnis Ballachy & Ellis—business all unsettled—read Alexy Haimitoff—study a little greek—read Political Justice, write to Isabel—Shelley writes to Hogg & to Mrs Boinville
>
> Wednesday 5th—Peacock at breakfast. walk to the lake of Nangis & sail fire boats—read Political Justice. Shelley reads the ancient Mariner aloud.—letter from Harriet. very civil—L400 for 2400. (*MSJ*, 1:30–31)

I would suggest that it is at this moment that Mary Shelley first began to differentiate herself from Shelley. Mary Jean Corbett places the dissolution of the unified identity of Mary Shelley and Shelley in the epigraph to the 1816–19 journal, which "cites that loss in the radical diminution of the plural 'our' to the singular 'my.'"[26] Although this may have been the dramatic end of this spiritual alliance, I believe that the genesis of separation began earlier. After all, at this time Mary Shelley was pregnant with their first child, and perhaps the idea of impending motherhood began to give her a sense of maturity along with a certain spiritual growth. This is particularly noticeable in her many entries that mention Shelley and Claire Clairmont. Mary Shelley writes on 30 December 1814: "Shelley & Clary go out *as usual* . . . they do not return till past seven having been locked into Kensington Gardens—both very tired" (emphasis added) (*MSJ*, 1:56). Later, as her pregnancy caused her to be further confined, she began to feel alienated from Shelley both physically and spiritually.

While the subtle unraveling of the fabric of their union finally resulted in a breach after the death of their son William, it is here—in the beginning of October 1814—that we see Mary Shelley take the first tentative steps toward representing herself as an individual inside that union. However, as we know, this separation is far from complete, for while she designates Shelley she does not designate herself, suggesting that she is still immersed in his identity. Furthermore, although there seems to be an implied *I* in these entries, there is also an implied *we*. When she says on 3 October 1814, "Walk with Peacock to the lake of Nangis," it would appear to mean "I walk with Peacock." However, she goes on to say, "And set off little fire boats." It has been recorded that Shelley had a particular fondness for sailing these little boats, so it is fairly safe to assume that he would have accompanied his wife and Peacock on this excursion (*MSJ*, 1:30 n. 3). Conversely, on 5 October 1815, when she notes, "Read Political Justice," we can guess that the implied *I* would be appropriate here because she had indicated on 29 September 1814 that "Mary reads Political Justice" and also because on October 5 she had recorded a different reading for Shelley. But even this argument is not satisfactory, since the reading list for 1814 says that both Mary Shelley and Shelley read *Political Justice* that year, and they often read more than one work a day.

Therefore, although we can see Mary Shelley beginning to assert herself, if only on a reductive level, it is Shelley who is most often identified. However, even though there is still confusion of identity because of the implied *I*'s and *we*'s, a representation of Shelley begins to emerge that is separate from Mary Shelley, or rather a representation where she does not claim to be speaking as if she were both herself and him. It is interesting that, while Mary Shelley discontinues the third person at this time, Shelley continues to use it throughout most of his contributions to the journal. Part of the reason he may have done this was, once again, to alleviate the confusion of the *I*. After all, the journal was "*not* Shelley and Mary's journal book" now but simply Mary Shelley's. Any reference to *I* could now be claimed by her, and, if Shelley failed to make this distinction and to identify himself, it would be likely that he could be mistaken for Mary, especially since during their relationship her handwriting had slowly transformed until it came to resemble his. Biographers of both authors have noted the confusion caused by this similarity.[27] Therefore, by surrendering his right to the use of *I*, Shelley becomes, as Mary Shelley did with *Frankenstein*, the anonymous author in this text. He does, however, manage to distinguish himself by the employment, in the 1814–15 journals, of the distinctive naming practice of often calling Mary by her nickname, "the Maie," simultaneously differentiating the two of them while depriving Mary of her authorial name and substituting for it a term of endearment, which ironically becomes the only name that is distinctly her own.

Despite this practice, the power of his name is now defined by Mary Shelley's representations of him, and although he can, and does, contribute to the forming of his own image, he nonetheless tends to comply with the fairly formulaic style of journal entry that Mary Shelley has adopted. Journal entries written on 20 and 21 December 1814, the first written by Mary Shelley and the second by Shelley, demonstrate the terse pattern of listing events of the day, including readings and business transactions.

> Teusday 20th—S.helley goes to Pikes—take a short walk with him first— unwell—a letter from Harriet who threatens Shelley read Emilia Galotti— Hogg comes—converse of various things—he goes at twelve

> *Wednesday 21st—Mary is better. S. goes to Pikes to the insurance offices & the lawyers. An agreement entered into for 3000 for 10000. A letter from Wales offering Post Obit. S. goes to Humes—M. reads Miss Baileys Plays— In the evening. S. goes to bed at 8. M. at 11. (MSJ, 1:54)*[28]

Shelley is obviously attempting to carry on the journal in Mary Shelley's voice at a time when she was perhaps not well enough to write for herself. This writing, as merely a continuation of Mary's voice, marks the beginning of a disinterest in the journal on Shelley's part. Although the journal had started as an important venture to both of them, Shelley's interest and participation progressively diminished throughout the years. In 1814 he wrote nearly a third of the entries, but by 1815 this had dwindled to less than a fifth, followed by only a tenth of the entries in 1816, and in the six years between 1817 and 1822 he wrote only three full entries, with short appendages to nine others. Although Shelley may have continued to read the journal (Mary Shelley addresses him directly in her journal entry on 28 May 1817), it was no longer a medium he felt inclined to use for self-expression, turning rather to his poetry. Even when Shelley does choose to write a lengthy entry, he abandons all forms of self-identification and relies almost exclusively on the collective *we*. Furthermore, in these entries Shelley devotes most of his efforts to the description of the picturesque in their travels, revealing almost nothing of the self. Mary Shelley was left as the sole interpreter of the life and character of Shelley on a daily basis.[29]

Representations of Shelley

In the first letter that Mary Shelley wrote to her old friend Maria Gisborne after the death of Shelley, she relates that about two weeks before Shelley's death he told her that "he had seen the figure of himself which met him as he walked on the terrace & said to him—'How long do you mean to be content?'" (*MSL*, 1:245). Foucault has stated that within every discourse that performs the author function there is a plurality of self (*MF*, 112). Apparently, for Shelley, this supposedly figurative plurality was literal. Ironically, it is at this point in her private writings that Mary Shelley begins to integrate the many selves she had earlier employed as recurrent motifs to depict Shelley into a single representation of what can only be referred to as the "divine" Shelley, a being who is best capable of pure communion only with himself. In creating this idealization of Shelley, Mary Shelley, in her state of grief, sifted through the various icons of Shelley she had generated throughout her writing and chose those that best suited a poet who was destined to die young. Many of the qualities that she chose to characterize this "divine" Shelley were ones she had utilized earlier, now taken to an extreme. Other attributes from which she draws heavily are ones that Shelley initiated, which she now perpetuates. However, like the memories of many people who are in mourning, there are images of Shelley from before July 1822 that are never to be repeated. Only four and a half months earlier, Mary Shelley wrote in her journal of 25 February 1822:

Let me love the trees—the skies & the ocean & that all encompassing spirit of which I may soon become a part—let me in my fellow creatures love that which is & not fix my affections on a fair form endued with imaginary

attributes—where goodness, kindness & talent are, let me love & admire
them at their just rate neither adding or diminishing & above all let me
fearlessly descend into the remotest caverns of my own mind—carry the
torch of self knowledge into its dimmest recesses—but too happy if I
dislodge any evil spirit or enshrine a new deity in some hitherto uninhabited
nook. (*MSJ*, 1:399–400)

It would appear from this passage that Mary Shelley was aware of her
editorial revision of Shelley in both her writings and her mind, for what
is the primary work of an editor but "adding and diminishing"? It is
disheartening to hear the resolution in Mary Shelley's voice in this
excerpt and to realize that in a few months she would be attaching
more—if not imaginary, then exaggerated—attributes to the "fair form"
of Shelley than she had done at any previous point, and that the new
deity she would enshrine would be the same one as before, only more
godlike than ever. Mary Shelley's representations of her husband can be
divided into five general categories that were eventually reconfigured
into the final image of the Shelley deity. These classifications, while not
all encompassing, are useful, nonetheless, in helping to define such an
intricate text. Shelley's multiple selves include the shocking or
scandalous Shelley, the genius/scholar, the delicate poet, the Gothic
figure, and finally, the lover, husband, and father. These substitutions for
the real Shelley are at the heart of Mary Shelley's editing of him, and
perform in the scission between author and fictional speaker that
Foucault defined as the author function. Mary Shelley the biographer
draws on her work as Mary Shelley the editor to bring the Shelley of
hindsight into accordance with the actual Shelley of the past.

    In their introduction, the editors of *The Journals of Mary Shelley*
discuss the different personalities of each of the journal books. They
maintain that the first book is of a different quality than the others
because it is drawn from "the only period in her life during which Mary's
habitual reserve was temporarily dormant" (*MSJ*, 1:xvi). Therefore it is
not surprising that it is here that we catch the most telling glimpses of the
shocking and scandalous Shelley. In fact, the very first entry that Mary
Shelley composes for the journal, without Shelley as cocomposer,
contains the shocking revelation that her stepsister Claire Clairmont, at
this time called "Jane," slept with them that night for fear of rats. Mary
Shelley records that

    she however rested on our bed which her four footed enemies dared not
    invade perhaps having overheard the threat that Shelley terrified the man who
    said he would sleep with Jane. (*MSJ*, 1:13)

Such an incredible revelation involving both Claire Clairmont and Shelley would appear remarkable not only in its content but in the very fact that it is mentioned at all. Later in the journals, scandalous information involving Claire was often delegated to symbolic notation,[30] and as early as 7 January 1815 there is evidence of possible editing of scandalous information involving Shelley and Claire, where a page is torn out following the words, "Hogg goes away at three—S. & C. do not return till near" (*MSJ*, 1:60). The insertion of the shocking episode in Mary Shelley's first journal entry, taken in conjunction with the evidence of her later reticence involving any mention of scandal involving Claire, suggests that Mary Shelley's attitude toward scandal was quite different at this early stage of her life than it would be later. Mary Shelley was, after all, only sixteen years old at the time, and mature as her experiences make her seem, like many sixteen-year-olds she was ready to rebel. Part of this rebellion, perhaps due to the very history of her name, was bound to manifest itself in scandalous and shocking behavior.

It is conceivable that the very recklessness of the elopement put Mary Shelley in this shocking frame of mind when she first began writing in the journals. The elopement may also explain why, even when her disclosure practices became much more guarded, Mary Shelley continued to hold on to the image of the poet whom society found so shocking, the image of the poet associated with happier times. In a letter to Maria Gisborne on 2 December 1819, Mary Shelley tells her:

> There are some ladies come to this house who know Shelley's family—the younger one was *entousiasmee* to see him—the elder said that he was a very shocking man—but finding that we became the mode she melted and paid us a visit. (*MSL*, 1:118)

Even in this statement the shadows of compromise are easily visible. Mary Shelley readily allows Shelley his reputation for being shocking, but she immediately reconciles that notion with the reality of their conventional "mode" of being. Once again, the presence of the pronoun *we* makes itself felt in this discourse. While it is only Shelley who is accused of being shocking, she represents both of them as the single unit of propriety that allows the old woman to accept him. While Mary Shelley values the acceptance of the public, she nonetheless craves that touch of scandal, which through her family heritage, she has come to associate with the power of authorship. Since her own handle on the ability to shock was quite tenuous, Mary Shelley took full advantage of her relationship to Shelley and his circle. In another letter to Maria Gisborne, written 17 October 1820, Mary Shelley, in trying to mend a

breach between the two women caused by gossip from her stepmother,
can't help adding, "When you said that that filthy woman [Mrs. Godwin]
said she would not visit Hunt how I gloried in our infamy" (*MSL*, 1:161).
However, the lessons she had learned from the observation of her
parents' notoriety taught her to orchestrate the level of scandal very
carefully. In his memoirs of Mary Wollstonecraft, William Godwin
writes about how she dealt with information regarding herself and her
lover, Gilbert Imlay.

> Mary made no secret of the nature of her connection with Mr. Imlay; and in
> one instance, I well know, she put herself to the trouble of explaining it to a
> person totally indifferent to her, because he never failed to publish every
> thing he knew, and she was sure, would repeat her explanation to his
> numerous acquaintance. (*WG*, 260)

Mary Shelley was somewhat subtler. While the suggestion of general
disrepute might add an aura of mystery and even eccentric genius to the
work of an author, specific allegations could prove devastating, as with
Mary Wollstonecraft's love affair with Gilbert Imlay. Therefore, when
Mary Shelley heard the rumors that the Hoppners had been spreading
about an illegitimate child, born of a union between Shelley and Claire
Clairmont, she vehemently denied all the charges in a letter that reveals
one of the rare moments when she was not in control of her emotions.[31]
In contrast, when Byron and Shelley were involved in something of a
scuffle on 24 March 1822, Mary Shelley takes great delight in giving a
very detailed description of all the events in a lengthy letter to Maria
Gisborne, as well as accounts to Thomas Medwin and Leigh Hunt, both
of whom had the power to disseminate information. Although these latter
two were at Byron's bidding, Mary Shelley goes beyond the call of duty
and recounts the events in vivid detail. It was unlikely that this incident
could do any real harm to their reputations, but it added just the right
amount of flair to take their lives out of the ordinary realm. In death,
Shelley would naturally be transported into another realm, and since their
identities were still unified in the eyes of the reading public, Mary
Shelley was, in essence, transported with him. Even though scandal
would continue to follow Mary Shelley throughout her life, she no longer
courted it, and therefore the image of the scandalous Shelley is the only
one that does not become part of the glorification of Shelley in her later
writings.

The journals as a whole can be seen as a monument to the icon of
Shelley the genius and scholar, and while they contain a wealth of information, they have been described as nothing more than a collection of

reading lists. While this description may be making a rash generalization, it nonetheless reveals a certain schematic that was important to Mary Shelley. She once said that she kept the journal more for the sake of dates than anything else,[32] but obviously dates without any reference have no meaning. What fills this calendar with significance is the detailed cataloguing of reading, writing, translating, and transcribing that scholars continue to study for evidence about the inspirations and influences that affected the works of these authors, as well as some insight into the workings of their creative processes. The Shelleys' reading lists included an extensive array of works dealing with people's lives, including memoirs, letters, journals, biographies, and autobiographies, so Mary Shelley was obviously aware of the public interest in such writing. Yet her journals are quite different in style from the works she had been reading. Perhaps she intended the work to be presented in a format that would only interest serious critics and scholars, but more likely she may have been concerned with the importance of dating practices as a way of reminding herself of what she and Shelley had been reading in the midst of the creative process, with the idea of writing a memoir to follow a narrative discourse at a more advanced stage in their careers.

However, Shelley's career ended much sooner than Mary Shelley expected, and although her career certainly did not end with his death, the recording of her scholarly pursuits on a daily basis did. With the beginning of a new journal on 2 October 1822, the next marked change in style in the journals occurs. No longer do the entries recount the minute details of everyday life; instead, they become the receptacle for all of Mary Shelley's grief and emotion. However, as Judy Simons has noted, the emotional release in the journals after Shelley's death is often less illuminating than is the information born of self-restraint in the earlier volumes.[33] Apparently Mary Shelley felt that the recording of readings on a daily basis was more important in association with Shelley than with herself. Unfortunately, in letting go of her reserve, she also managed to neglect the documentation of her intellectual pursuits. Because of this neglect, all of the work to establish the intellectual intensity of both Shelley and herself has resulted in the misconception that Mary Shelley failed to continue any sort of intellectual life after Shelley's death, even though she said in a letter to Thomas Medwin shortly after Shelley's death that her life would now "be one of study only" (*MSL*, 1:243). Despite this declaration and their perceived unity, Mary Shelley's representation of Shelley as the scholar/genius was ineffectual in endowing her with the same qualities in the eyes of the public, even though she continued to write prolifically.

A representation of Shelley that was very important to Mary Shelley, but which she did not attempt to emulate, was the image of Shelley as the delicate poet. In a letter to Marianne Hunt on 27 November 1823, she says in reference to the poet Bryan Waller Procter:

> He is an invalid—& some time ago I told you in a letter that I have always a sneaking (for sneaking, read open) kindness for men of literary & particularly poetic habits who have delicate health; I cannot help revering the mind, delicately attuned, that shatters the material frame, & whose thoughts are strong enough to throw down & dilapidate the walls of sense & dikes of flesh that the unimaginative contrive to keep in such good repair. (*MSL*, 1:404)

Looking back through the letters and journals, the truth of this statement is obvious. Again and again appears the simple notation "S is unwell" or some variation on that theme. Shelley, among other things, has spasms, falls and sprains his knee, is exhausted, and is even attacked by a dog. Conversely, although it is sometimes recorded that Mary Shelley is not well, almost invariably that means she is pregnant. In fact, on 15 February 1815, a week before she was to go into labor, Shelley writes "S & M still unwell," followed by an entry that Shelley begins, but Mary finishes, where she states again, "S very unwell." Finally, after the birth of the child, both authors write on consecutive days that Mary (whom they both refer to as "the Maie" at this juncture) is very well but that Shelley is unwell a total of four times in the two days (*MSJ*, 1:65–66). Apparently giving birth was much harder on Shelley than it was on his wife. The letters are even more explicit about Shelley's health than are the journals. In a letter to him on 24 September 1817, she admits that seeing him was harder than the separation because it was so upsetting to see his increasing illness. Letters written during their stay in Italy are full of discussion about the search for the best location for settling down in a climate that would ensure Shelley's health. It almost seems that Mary Shelley prepared a lifetime for Shelley's death but was shocked when it came, perhaps because it was not the long deathbed scene she had anticipated. She has said that Adonais was "his own elegy" (*MSL*, 1:249), and perhaps if he had died in the manner of Keats, she would have been better prepared. While her version of the divine Shelley no longer has a delicate human frame, his new form is beyond the pain of the human sphere, and yet, at the same time, its ethereal nature reaches a new pinnacle of delicacy. For Mary Shelley, the delicate poet is only able to fulfill his true nature after death.

The figure of the Gothic or supernatural Shelley is the ideal representation for a poet who was to die at a relatively young age. Initially, this image was most often utilized by Shelley himself. In a lengthy entry on 7 October 1814, Shelley recounts the events of an evening in which he and Claire Clairmont became quite frightened through the very nature of their discussion. The figure he presents of himself is especially interesting since it, like many of his other entries, is written in the third person.

> At two they retire awestruck & hardly daring to breathe. S. says to Jane "Goodnight" his hand is leaning on the table. he is conscious of an expression in his countenance which he cannot repress . . .Jane hesitates "Good night" again. She still hesitates . . .Did you ever read the tragedy of Orra? said S. "Yes.—How horribly you look . . .take your eyes off!" "Goodnight" again & J. ran to her room. (*MSJ*, 1:32)[34]

The choice to write in this narrative style, rather than the rigid formula chosen by Mary Shelley, verifies that the evening's events seemed very important to Shelley. But also, it is as if he has cast himself in the role of the Gothic hero, much as he had done in his two early Gothic novels, *Zastrozzi* and *St. Irvyne*.[35] The tone is melodramatic, and Shelley the hero is at once vulnerable and frightening. This passage displays the acute awareness he had of his own being, as well as a sense of awareness about his personal plurality. When he sees his own hand on the table and is conscious of the expression on his face as if he were someone else watching it, Shelley is experiencing the standard Gothic experience of disembodiment. Mary Shelley apparently doesn't find this incident to be as important as does Shelley. Fewer than two weeks later she writes in her journal, "I go to bed soon—but Shelley and Jane sit up and for a wonder do not frighten themselves" (*MSJ*, 1:37). Shelley, however, continues his fascination with the supernatural, most notably in his entry for 18 August 1816. In this passage he relates a discussion with Byron and Monk Lewis, the Gothic novelist, about ghosts, then transcribes five of the tales that Lewis told them that night. Shelley even reveals the supernatural side of Mary Shelley in an entry later that year when he quotes her as saying, "Come & look, here's a cat eating roses—when beasts eat these roses they turn into men & women" (*MSJ*, 1:139). Before this time any connection to be made between Mary Shelley and the supernatural appears to lie solely in the realm of the dreams born of her grief. In Mary's eyes the Gothic and death go hand in hand. The first time we see her relate ghost stories in a fashion similar to that of Shelley's earlier entry comes less than a month after the death of her daughter Clara.[36] However, she does talk about divination using the texts of Virgil and Homer, and she even mentions asking for predictions about Shelley from John Varley, a relative of the Gisbornes who was known for his abilities at divination. Mary Shelley is obviously skeptical, but she nonetheless asks Maria Gisborne if she will ask Varley about her as well.[37] So by the time of Shelley's death, she was becoming more accustomed to the supernatural in her own life.

Because of her inability to completely sever the tie between the Gothic and her own grieving, the transition at the time of Shelley's death is inevitable, and she is finally able to portray Shelley as that Gothic hero he had cast himself as so long before. Not only does she cast Shelley in this role but herself as well. Mary Shelley's letter to Maria Gisborne in which she told the uncanny[38] tale of Shelley meeting his double is full of suggestions of the otherworld, including the fact that Byron and his mistress told her "that on that terrific evening [she] looked more like a ghost than a woman" (*MSL*, 1:247). Even more chilling is her tale of Shelley's night of visions, in which he sees the mangled bodies of the Williamses as the sea is flooding the house, and then the figure of himself strangling Mary. For the first time Mary Shelley is able to project Shelley as the Gothic hero with the mixture of vulnerability and cruelty intact. This is her most powerful representation of the Gothic hero in her private writings. After this, the Gothic figure of Shelley is collapsed into an ethereal spirit that continues to make its presence felt on the earth, but without the terror and dread associated with ghost stories. It is as if Mary Shelley finally acquiesces to her husband's wishes, but only momentarily and as a way of manipulating the hindsight necessary to interpret such earth shattering events.

The final representation of Shelley is that of Shelley the lover, husband, and father. This domestic representation is difficult to put in context with the others discussed earlier, simply because it almost seems to be at odds with them. What kind of a father and husband would Shelley make if he was truly the genius/scholar with a scandalous background and delicate health as Mary Shelley represents him? Mary Shelley's later writings would indicate that there was never a better husband or father than Shelley, and although her earlier writings support this at times, there are other indications that Shelley's very nature was inimical to such a role. In her many letters to Shelley at the beginning of their relationship, she is always very loving to him, but still, occasionally, there are suggestions that Shelley might not have been the ideal father. She writes on 5 December 1816, when William would have been about ten months old,

> The blue eyes of your sweet boy are staring at me while I write this he is a
> dear child and you love him tenderly, although I fancy your affection will

encrease when he has a nursery to himself and only comes to you just dressed
and in good humour. (*MSL*, 1:22–23)

It seems strange that Mary Shelley would find it necessary to inform her
husband that he loved the child, unless she was afraid that perhaps he
didn't. It may not be coincidental that this is the same letter in which
Mary Shelley announces that she has just finished the fourth chapter of
Frankenstein. This is the chapter just prior to the one where Victor
Frankenstein creates the monster and then rejects him. *Frankenstein* has
been interpreted as a criticism of Shelley, and these two bits of
information would seem to support such a theory. However, she does
mention several family excursions, especially on the boat, and in a letter
to Marianne Hunt she explains how, during the last week of their stay at
Rome, Shelley spent "60 miserable—deathlyke hours without closing his
eyes" when William was ill (*MSL*, 1:103). She also notes that this vigil
left him in poor health. As with childbirth, the tolls of fatherhood are
wearing on the frame of the delicate poet.

Domestic life with Shelley was apparently not always easy. When
Shelley was staying with the Hunts in London during the Chancery suit
to gain custody of his children by his first wife, Mary Shelley wrote
Marianne Hunt a letter asking her to take care of Shelley's dirty linen,
giving his thoughtlessness as an excuse. In a letter to Shelley later that
year, she explains the household expenses to him as if he were a child, in
order that he might fully understand the financial difficulties in which
they found themselves.[39] But the letter that places itself in the most
extreme opposition to that of Mary Shelley's idealization of their
relationship comes on 2 October 1817, not quite a week before the last
one mentioned. She tells Shelley:

Your letter received per parcel tonight was very unsatisfactory. You decide
nothing and tell me nothing—. (*MSL*, 1:50)

This is hardly the portrait of two souls in unity with each other, and it is
one of the only times in her private writings that we see her overtly angry
with him. It is at times such as these that Mary Shelley can be seen to
step out of both her editorial and her authorial mode and to actually live
what she is writing. This letter was probably not written with an eye on
an audience and therefore becomes part of the living biography that Mary
Shelley was unwilling to look at when she later wanted to write Shelley's
life. She tends to write less about him as their relationship wears on, and
he is often relegated to a simple "Shelley sends his regards" at the end of
a letter. In the journals, the change is even more marked. There is the

suggestion that Mary Shelley is becoming attracted to other men.[40] She seems to be quite intimate with Edward Williams, taking many walks with him, sitting for a portrait, and even reading *Mathilda* to him. She is rather guarded about this, however, and I would speculate that perhaps she was concerned about Shelley reading her journal. Her admiration for Edward John Trelawney, however, is quite open. In her journal entry for 19 January 1822, Mary Shelley diverges from her usual short form to write an extensive description of Trelawney:

> If his abrupt, but unpolished manners be assumed, they are nevertheless in unison with his Moorish face (for he looks oriental yet not Asiatic) his dark hair his herculean form. And then there is an air of extreme goodnature which pervades his whole countenance, especially when he smiles, which assures me that his heart is good . . . & tired with the everyday sleepiness of human intercourse I am glad to meet with one who among other valuable qualities has the rare merit of interesting my imagination. (*MSJ*, 1:391)

Such a detailed physical description of Shelley appears nowhere in Mary Shelley's private writings. It is not much later than this when she begins to compose entries that reveal the emotional part of her personality and where she begins to assert her use of the word *I*. It still isn't an easy transition for her, as we see in her entry of 8 February 1822, where she substitutes *I* and *my* for *one* and *ones*, allowing the words to refer directly to her rather than to a general emotion. So it is in the portrayal of Shelley as the family man that we see Mary Shelley reveal, although guardedly, his most human side and, through this process, disclose her own humanity as well. The separation between the two united souls is practically complete. However, it never reaches full severance, for on the death of Shelley, Mary Shelley once more immerses herself in him.

Current discussion about representation and images often revolves around the medium of film. The film editor is involved in the process of literally cutting, combining, and splicing film. To compare Mary Shelley to a film editor may seem to exceed the boundaries of this subject at first, but perhaps it is not as unsuitable as it appears, and, indeed, this analogy may help to illustrate my point about Mary Shelley's editing of her husband's life. If we can see Shelley's life as a film, he is the "author" of his own life, or we might even say the director, but when the shooting is finished, the film is out of his hands. Mary Shelley's journals and letters are like the dailies, the film as it is viewed at the end of each day. The final picture, though, is largely the work of the editor, who, when the filming is complete, sifts through these dailies to find the pieces that they want to splice together and combine in order to best represent the whole.

Like a film editor, Mary Shelley has manipulated the original Shelley, through the use of representations that are substitutes for the whole, into a package that is most appealing and accessible to the general public.

The editor, in both literature and film, is a largely anonymous entity but one who wields much power. For Mary Shelley, who once wrote in a letter to Shelley, "I know you will be punctual for you know how I dislike walking up and down in a public place" (*MSL*, 1:4), this powerful anonymity would hold a decided appeal. The difference between the film analogy and Mary Shelley's situation is that she was, to an extent, editing the dailies of Shelley's life as well. This is where the author function exerts itself, for in the dynamic of this function it is impossible to represent the persons who write texts as they truly are. As Betty Bennett has pointed out, "every editor is also a critic" and "any document that is not a photofacsimile represents editorial alteration."[41] To take that statement back a step, every author is an editor, for authors edit what they see before representing it on the page. However, since we are dealing with the author of lives, at what point does the editor and/or the author become the biographer? Furthermore, doesn't Mary Shelley actually perform all of these functions of author, editor, critic, and biographer simultaneously, with only variations of intensity that allow us to view the working of each function independently? By quietly undertaking all of the above-designated roles, Mary Shelley appropriated for herself the power that had been denied to her in her shared name.

Eventually Mary Shelley even comes to have power over her own writing, as we can see illustrated in her two versions of Shelley, where essentially she edits her previous editing. The quantity of private writings she read while she was keeping her journal, her nonchalance about the reading of her letters by those other than for whom they were intended, along with the publication of letters, albeit highly stylized ones, in *History of a Six Weeks' Tour*, suggest that the idea of publishing her letters and journals was, before Shelley's death, always a consideration. However, when her representation of Shelley changed, her letters and journals remained unpublished until after her death, while her new view of him was published as the notes to his poems, presenting an author function for Shelley that has largely remained until this day. Richard Holmes's biography *Shelley: The Pursuit* was acclaimed for its realistic portrait of the poet, claiming that "he has taken the Shelley story out of the realm of myth and made it far more convincing and significant."[42] Mary Shelley had already begun a biography that could make the same claim as that of Holmes, but instead she chose to circulate the image of the ethereal and divine Shelley, an image that has become so ingrained in our cultural consciousness that it is immediately invoked by the very mention of the name Shelley or the words "Romantic poet." This image of Shelley spills over not only to other Romantic poets but to Mary Shelley as well. In the mythologizing of Shelley, she mythologizes herself. Perhaps there is some validity in Paula Feldman's conjecture about Mary Shelley's failure to publish a biography of Shelley because of her feelings of inadequacy. However, if Mary Shelley was reluctant to face the truth about herself, she was even more afraid to bring forward the real Shelley. A biography of Shelley based on her private writings would have been far too painful and would have broken down the walls of illusion she had built around herself upon his death. The double editing of Shelley's life works as a distancing technique similar to those that Mary Shelley often utilized in her novels[43] as a way to keep her audience at arms' length from the real individuals, who were Mary and Percy Shelley, choosing instead to work in that scission where the author function grapples to bridge the gap between the writer and the author.

Notes

Research for this essay was made possible by a grant from the Bush Foundation and the support of Hamline University.

1. Roland Barthes, "The Death of the Author," in *Image—Music—Text*, trans. Stephen Heath, 142–48 (New York: Noonday Press, 1977). Michel Foucault, "What Is an Author?" in *The Foucault Reader*, ed. Paul Rabinow (New York: Pantheon, 1984), 101–20, hereafter cited parenthetically within the text as *MF*. Jack Stillinger, *Multiple Authorship and the Myth of Solitary Genius* (New York: Oxford University Press, 1991), 3–24. The first chapter of Stillinger's book is entitled "What Is an Author?" in direct reaction to Foucault's text.

2. William Harmon and C. Hugh Holman, eds., *A Handbook to Literature*, 6th ed. (New York: MacMillan, 1992), 41.

3. See, for example, Betty T. Bennett, "Feminism and Editing Mary Wollstonecraft Shelley: The Editor And?/Or? the Text," in *Palimpsest: Editorial Theory in the Humanities*, ed. George Bornstein and Ralph G. Williams (Ann Arbor: University of Michigan Press, 1993), 67–96. Bennett discusses the editing practices and interpretations, or rather misinterpretations, of Mary Shelley that she believes have affected current scholarship and public perception.

4. Mary Wollstonecraft Shelley with Percy Bysshe Shelley, *History of a Six Weeks' Tour through a Part of France, Switzerland, Germany, and Holland: with Letters descriptive of a Sail round the Lake of Geneva, and of the Glaciers of Chamouni*, in *The Complete Works of Percy Bysshe Shelley*, vol. 6 (New York: Gordian Press, 1965).

5. Mary Wollstonecraft, *Letters Written During a Short Residence in Sweden, Norway, and Denmark*, ed. Richard Holmes (Harmondsworth, England: Penguin, 1987).

6. William Godwin, *Memoirs of the Author of a Vindication of the Rights of Woman*, ed. Richard Holmes (Harmondsworth, England: Penguin, 1987); hereafter cited parenthetically within the text as *WG*. Mary Wollstonecraft, *The Posthumous Works of the Author of a Vindication of the Rights of Woman*, ed. William Godwin (London: Joseph Johnson, 1798).

7. Marilyn May, "Publish and Perish: William Godwin, Mary Shelley, and the Public Appetite for Scandal," *Papers on Language and Literature* 26.4 (Fall 1990): 489–512.

8. Mary Wollstonecraft Shelley, introduction to the 1831 edition of *Frankenstein*, in *Case Studies in Contemporary Criticism*, ed. Johanna M. Smith (Boston: Bedford Books, 1992), 19.

9. May, "Publish and Perish," 509.

10. Anne K. Mellor devotes extensive space to the discussion of Percy Shelley's contributions to *Frankenstein* in *Mary Shelley: Her Life, Her Fiction, Her Monsters* (New York: Routledge, 1988), 58–69. She contends that Shelley did help the manuscript in many small ways, but that the biggest changes resulted from his changing Mary's simple prose to a more Latinate prose, which he found preferable but which has alienated readers. E. B. Murray ("Shelley's Contribution to *Frankenstein*," *Keats-Shelley Memorial Bulletin* 29 [1978]: 51–68) suggests, despite Mary Shelley's statement to the contrary, that *Frankenstein* does, in fact, owe some of its "train of feeling" to Percy Shelley.

11. Mary Wollstonecraft Shelley, *The Letters of Mary Wollstonecraft Shelley*, 3 vols., ed. Betty T. Bennett (Baltimore, Md.: Johns Hopkins University Press, 1980–88), 1:71, hereafter cited parenthetically within the text as *MSL*.

12. Sandra M. Gilbert and Susan Gubar discuss the Bloomian struggle in a feminist context in *The Madwoman in the Attic* (1979; rprt., New Haven: Yale University Press, 1984), 46–53. Bloom's "anxiety of influence" is also central to the arguments of James P. Carson in "Bringing the Author Forward: Frankenstein through Mary Shelley's Letters," *Criticism* 30.4 (1988): 431–53.

13. Mary Wollstonecraft Shelley's first published work was a verse poem entitled "Mounseer Nongtonpaw," which was published by the Godwin Juvenile Library in 1810.

14. Stillinger lists *Frankenstein* in his appendix to *Multiple Authorship and the Myth of Solitary Genius*. In his introduction to the 1818 text of *Frankenstein* (New York: Bobbs-Merrill, 1974), xliv, editor James Rieger credits Shelley as a minor collaborator on the text.

15. In a letter to Shelley, probably written 24 September 1817, Mary Shelley writes, "I send you my dearest another proof—which arrived tonight in looking it over there appeared to me some abruptness which I have endeavoured to supply—but I am tired and not very clear headed so I give you carte blanche to make what alterations you please" (*MSL*, 1:42).

16. Percy Bysshe Shelley, *The Letters of Percy Bysshe Shelley*, 2 vols., ed. F. L. Jones (Oxford: Clarendon Press, 1964), 2: 372.

17. Paula R. Feldman and Diana Scott-Kilvert, eds., *The Journals of Mary Shelley: 1814–1844*, 2 vols. (Oxford, Clarendon Press, 1987), 2:442 n. 1, hereafter cited parenthetically within the text as *MSJ*.

18. Percy Bysshe Shelley, *Posthumous Poems of Percy Bysshe Shelley*, ed. Mary Wollstonecraft Shelley (London: John and Henry L. Hunt, 1824). *The Poetical Works of Percy Bysshe Shelley*, 4 vols., ed. Mrs. Shelley (London: Edward Moxon, 1839), hereafter cited parenthetically within the text as *PW*.

19. Between 27 May and 16 October 1836, Mary Shelley sent letters to Henry Crabbe Robinson, Henry Colburn, Thomas Abthorpe Cooper, Josiah Wedgewood, and William Hazlitt Jr., soliciting assistance in collecting her father's papers for his biography.

20. See the critical anthology *The Other Mary Shelley: Beyond Frankenstein*, ed. Audrey A. Fisch, Anne K. Mellor, and Esther H. Schor (New York: Oxford University Press, 1993), for two extensive discussions on the subject: Mary Favret, "Mary Shelley's Sympathy and Irony: The Editor and Her Corpus," 17–38, and Susan J. Wolfson, "Editorial Privilege: Mary Shelley and Percy Shelley's Audiences," 39–72.

21. Judy Simons, *Diaries and Journals of Literary Women from Fanny Burney to Virginia Woolf* (Iowa City: University of Iowa Press, 1990), 197. Simons dedicates one chapter of the book to the study of Mary Shelley's journal, but the introductory and concluding chapters are excellent studies of the genre of journal writing in general.

22. Paula Feldman, "Biography and the Literary Executor: The Case of Mary Shelley," *The Papers of the Bibliographical Society of America* 72 (1978): 297.

23. *MSJ*, 1:138 n. 5, says that in a letter to Mary Shelley from Fanny Imlay, Fanny "[chides] Mary for her own carelessness in leaving letters about for the servants to see." In a letter to Leigh and Marianne Hunt, Mary Shelley writes, "I wish you had opened Trelawney's letter—(I am less scrupulous about T's letters because he shew all his & I never write a word to him that I do not expect to be read by those near him)" (*MSL*, 1:368).

24. Donald H. Reiman, "Gender and Documentary Editing: A Diachronic Perspective," *Text: Transactions of the Society for Textual Scholarship* 4 (1988): 358. Reiman's decision to refer to the authors as "Mary" and "Shelley" is based on historical consideration that this is how they were referred to in their own circle.

25. Gina Lauria and Irene Tayler, "Gender and Genre: Women in British Romantic Literature," in *What Manner of Woman*, ed. Marlene Springer (New York: New York University Press, 1977), 98, 115–19.

26. Mary Jean Corbett, "Reading Mary Shelley's Journals: Romantic Subjectivity and Feminist Criticism," in *The Other Mary Shelley*, 78. While Corbett comes to some of the same conclusions that I do in this essay, especially concerning the use of pronouns in tracing the dissolution and unity of the Shelleys, she tends to focus on the perspective of feminist criticism, whereas I am focusing on a textual analysis of the journals.

27. Betty T. Bennett, "Finding Mary Shelley in Her Letters," in *Romantic Revisions*, ed. Robert Brinkley and Keith Hanley, 296 (Cambridge: Cambridge University Press, 1992).

28. I have adopted here the practice used by Paula R. Feldman and Diana Scott-Kilvert, in their editing of *The Journals of Mary Shelley*, of placing words written by Shelley in italics in order to differentiate text written by him from that written by Mary Shelley.

29. For example, see Shelley's entries for 3 September 1816 and 26 March 1818.

30. *MSJ*, appendix 1, 2:579–81, explains Mary Shelley's use of symbols in the journal.

31. This letter, dated 10 August 1821, contains Mary Shelley's most overt attempt to defend their reputations. It also contains an incredible slip of the pen, where Mary Shelley states, "Need I say that the union between my husband and hims myself has ever been undisturbed." This can be seen as further evidence of the dissolution of Mary Shelley and Shelley's union, or as her realization that he was unable to have a true union with anyone other than himself.

32. Simons, *Diaries and Journals*, 62.

33. Ibid., 82.

34. See note 29.

35. I would like to thank Frederick Frank for reminding me of these early Gothic novels by Shelley.

36. Mary Shelley's daughter Clara died on 24 September 1818. On 20 October of that same year, Mary Shelley recorded in her journal three ghost stories she had heard while staying with the Hoppners, using a form similar to that which Shelley used when he recorded the stories told by Monk Lewis.

37. Mary Shelley speaks of these divination practices in letters dated 8 June 1820 and 7 March 1822.

38. Sigmund Freud's essay "The Uncanny," in *The Complete Psychological Works of Sigmund Freud*, trans. James Strachey, in collaboration with Anna Freud, assisted by Alix Strachey and Alan Tyson, 17:219–52 (London: Hogarth Press and the Institute of Psychoanalysis, 1975), offers a fascinating examination of the phenomenon of the "double," which can be directly related to Shelley's meeting of himself.

39. These letters were composed on 18 January 1817 and 7 October 1817, respectively.

40. Although Mary Shelley had written letters earlier to Thomas Jefferson Hogg, these were at the instigation of Shelley. The later attractions are of her own accord. It has also been suggested by Ernest J. Lovell Jr., in "Byron and Mary Shelley," *Keats-Shelley Journal* 2 (1953): 35–49, that Mary Shelley was interested in Byron. Yet, as Lovell remarks, "Mary's letters provide no reference to Byron before 1817, and her journal entries for the summer of 1816 are carefully and significantly non-committal concerning him" (37). However, he also cites Mary Shelley's accounts of the incident of 24 March 1822, mentioned above, as an indication of her attraction to Byron. This would coincide with the other attractions that I discuss here.

41. Bennett, "Feminism and Editing," 89.

42. Stephen Spender, quoted in the 1994 Daedalus Books catalog, p. 27.

43. *Frankenstein* is framed in an epistolary structure, which distances the reader from the author through the many voices that tell the story. *Mathilda* is formed entirely as a letter to a friend, suggesting the authenticity of the text and obliterating the actual writer. Most fascinating of all, though, is Mary Shelley's fictional "Author's Introduction" to *The Last Man*, which not only presents a fictional author but denies that author any authorial power by attributing the story to the Sybilline leaves found in the cave. See Gregory O'Dea, "Prophetic History and Textuality in Mary Shelley's *The Last Man*," *Papers on Language & Literature* 28.3 (1992): 283–304, for an in-depth discussion of this text.

"Perhaps a Tale You'll Make It":
Mary Shelley's Tales for *The Keepsake*

Gregory O'Dea

O Reader! had you in your mind
Such stores as silent thought can bring,
O gentle Reader! you would find
A tale in everything.
What more I have to say is short,
And you must kindly take it:
It is no tale; but should you think,
Perhaps a tale you'll make it.

—William Wordsworth, "Simon Lee"

For much of her later literary career, Mary Shelley was a hack writer. Out of a noble necessity—she found herself a widow neglected by her friends and Percy Shelley's relations, with a young son to feed, clothe, and house—she became a scribbler, making her living in bits and pieces and writing on commission more often than following her own imaginative lights. With *Frankenstein* and Percy behind her, Shelley filled the spaces between her increasingly disregarded novels by turning her pen to essays, reviews, bits of history and travelogue, and, what certainly marks her reduced circumstances, tales for *The Keepsake* (1828–57), a British annual designed especially for seasonal gift giving. *The Keepsake* and its competitors (*The Forget-Me-Not*, *Friendship's Offering*, and *Heath's Book of Beauty*, among others) were enormously popular with the buying public but just as widely reviled in precisely the literary circles to which Shelley by rights belonged. Such works were, after all, little more than pretty baubles, handsomely designed and illustrated but notoriously devoid of serious literary merit.[1] The appeal for Shelley and other writers was an attractive combination of remuneration and expedience: "Writers of reputation," says Wendell V. Harris, "often found their principles melted by the promise of good payment," while the editors were happy to accept shorter contributions so that their tables of contents might appear attractively full.[2]

Shelley wrote fifteen tales for *The Keepsake* between 1828 and 1838. In their continental and historical subject matter and settings, the tales do not depart significantly from the character of her novels of the same period: *Perkin Warbeck* (1830), *Lodore* (1835), and *Falkner* (1837). There are, however, at least two striking differences, the intermingled significance of which I will detail in this essay. First, because the *Keepsake* pieces are "tales" rather than novels, they employ alternative narrative strategies that require a proportioned adjustment of reading strategies. Second, because the *Keepsake* tales had to accommodate accompanying engravings selected and assigned by the annual's editors, they become, in varying ways and degrees, literary elaborations on moments originally proposed in a nonliterary medium. Together, these two points can illuminate Romantic concepts of "tale-making," and particularly the authorial and readerly acts by which fragments— unspeaking objects, disjunctive voices, shattered narrative surfaces—can be (re)fashioned and understood as more fully articulate wholes.

The "tale" is an ancient and amorphous narrative form, but it seems always to have been considered a genre of narrative fragmentation. Unlike the novel and the short story, which are the major narrative genres that came to supplant it, the tale is rendered as a part rather than a whole, insufficient to stand without an external, supporting context. *A Thousand and One Arabian Nights* and Boccaccio's *Decameron* set their tales in larger structures that include not only other tales but also metanarratives, or framing situations in which the tales are told. As it emerged in the eighteenth century, the novel continued to sublimate the tale, but now as digression, a narrative of incidental relation to the main plot. The short story, as it was developed in the mid- and late-nineteenth century, actively sought differentiation from its ancestor on the grounds that it formed a whole by adhering to the dramatic unities of time, place, and action, whereas the tale often depicted more than one significant incident and might cover a period of years by passing over detail in favor of summary narrative devices. The tale is thus fragmented internally, in its sequence of divided incidents, and externally, as it is commonly made a distinct sublevel of larger narrative forms.

Its internal and external fragmentations suggest that the tale itself is an occasional narrative brought into being by an encounter with a disjunctive person, object, or event that requires an elaborative explanation in order to make sense. *Frankenstein*, for example, is largely given over to tale-telling as Walton seeks to justify his Arctic expedition, as Frankenstein attempts to warn against Walton's potentially tragic *hubris*, and as the Creature plays upon Frankenstein's sympathies so that he will create a female companion. Conrad's subtitle for *Lord Jim* is "A Tale" because Marlow's narrative, which takes up the majority of the novel, is occasional and intended to account for Jim's actions and character, a subject under discussion by his companions. These narratives do not exist for their own sakes but in order to bring an external anomaly or uncertainty into consonance with an established pattern of experience. Because tales, so understood, have external but immediate intentional origins, they are neither self-contained nor self-explanatory narratives, nor are they complete in their representations, for they render only what is required by the demands of their external contexts. These circumstances tend to emphasize the teller and the occasion of the tale-telling as much as the tale's content, thus constituting an important aspect of the genre's inherently fragmentary nature: a focus split between the interior and exterior of the narrative, the tale and its telling.

Given such a view of the tale's fundamental form and its place among other narratives, it is not surprising that the Romantics turned again and again to the peculiarities of the tale-as-fragment. As Thomas McFarland has argued, "the diasporactive triad" of "incompleteness, fragmentation, and ruin. . . are at the very center of life," and they "occupy both the theory and the actuality of Romanticism."[3] Romantic poetry, of course, provides the best-known examples of fragmented works in Samuel Taylor Coleridge's "Christabel," John Keats's "Hyperion" and "The Fall of Hyperion," Lord Byron's "The Giaour," and William Wordsworth's monumentally ruined "gothic church," *The Recluse* complex. By extension, fragmentations of all sorts become subjects, too, in poems such as Coleridge's "Kubla Khan" and "The Rime of the Ancient Mariner," Percy Bysshe Shelley's "Ozymandias" and "Julian and Maddalo," and, again, Keats's Hyperion poems. But the prose tale becomes a particularly crucial means of representing such incompleteness in another sphere, in a literary genre that is fundamentally fragmented in itself and yet necessarily more dedicated to overcoming that fragmentation. The tale seeks, by its intentional origins, to involve itself in a larger narrative structure.

Tale-making is thus an effort to achieve organic unity, the attempt to recover and reintroduce the part into a greater (imagined) whole, or what René Wellek long ago posited as the predominating Romantic project: "the great endeavor to overcome the split between subject and object, the self and the world, the conscious and the unconscious."[4] Something of the same artistic endeavor obtains in other Romantic contexts.

Wordsworth's narrative poetry is often doubly intent on achieving organic unity through narrative elaboration. Many of the poems in *Lyrical Ballads* (1798) and certain sections of *The Prelude* (1805) have been read as instances of tale-making, as the poet recollects an image or scene—an old huntsman, a leech-gatherer, a discharged soldier—and then elaborates that image or scene first into narrative and finally into moral meaning. In poems such as "Simon Lee" and "The Thorn" and in the "discharged soldier" episode in book 4 of *The Prelude*, the reader is invited to infer a narrative from sketchy hints, thus doubling the act of tale-making.[5] Wordsworth's method is partly pictorial as he offers up the sense of an isolated image, and partly narrative as he suggests the sequential and causal patterns that lie behind the scene or image described. In these cases, the tale is regarded as a moral medium, and the "meaning" that a tale might embody becomes an essential part of the narrative construct. Tale-making, in this view, is an act of infinite creation; to make a tale is to make meaning.

On the other hand, Romantic tale-making may be a disintegrating enterprise as well. Keats's "Ode on a Grecian Urn" offers the most graphic expression of the tension between narrative and non-narrative, first as it lays bare the process by which potential narratives are imagined, and then as it rejects narrative before the more intense beauty of the unspeaking images on the urn, the "silent form" that "dost tease us out of thought" (ll. 44)—a notable rejection of the "stores" of "silent thought" that Wordsworth requires for tale-making. The voice in Keats's ode has confronted the isolated images and posed narrative questions: "What men or gods are these? What maidens loth? / What mad pursuit? What struggle to escape? / What pipes and timbrels? What wild ecstasy?" (ll. 8–10). The speaker recognizes, however, that any attempt to make tales of the images would necessarily introduce the element of time into the scenes, robbing them of their immortality. Paradoxically, the tale-making effort toward organic unity is an impulse toward reduction, finality, destruction, and death.

This paradoxical effort is especially evident in Mary Shelley's tales for *The Keepsake*, partly because of the publication's material production and partly because Shelley made some striking experiments with the relationships between image and narrative. Composed of tales and accompanying engravings, the *Keepsake* texts pose special considerations for both writer and reader—considerations that are embodied in a violent formal rupture between word and image, between the linear movement of narrative and the stasis of iconography. In practical terms, the *Keepsake* writer's assignment is to produce an interesting, compact narrative that provides some degree of intersection with the subject of the engraving, which was usually chosen by the editors before the tale had been commissioned.[6] This aspect of material production privileges image over narrative from the first, and it clearly engages the writer in tale-making, as the unspeaking image must be narrated toward meaning. Some of the *Keepsake* engravings are static portraits of a single, inactive figure, in which case the author might simply take that figure as a principal character in the tale, or change the name of a principal character in an already-completed tale to match the title of the engraving. This was Mary Shelley's method on a few occasions.[7] But the engravings for her stories more often depict either "scenes," in which figures are disposed in postures indicating that a particular action or event has taken place, or "moods," in which a solitary figure is shown in a particular emotional state. These types of engravings require more than nominal treatment, for the potential degree of intersection between the verbal and visual texts is implicitly more acute; the "scene" or "mood" image suggests *in itself* that it has been severed from a beginning and an end, cut off from a narrative to which it naturally belongs. The tale, then, must elaborate and extenuate the moment depicted in the engraving by narrating events that lead to and away from that moment. The relationship between narrative and image is forged by an imaginative process of tale-making in which a narrative originates in a non-narrative object—one which does not or cannot, in conventional terms, "speak for" or explain itself. Such a static, isolated image may suggest to the imagination a beginning and an end, a narrative that is set in motion and connected to an active, living world of experience and causal association. The result, of course, is potentially ambiguous, as both Wordsworth and Keats imply.

A fairly straightforward example of this affirmative tale-making is "The Trial of Love," which Shelley contributed to *The Keepsake* for 1835. The engraved plate that accompanies the tale, entitled "The Letter," depicts a specific scene of two young women in a sitting room. One woman, dark haired, dressed modestly in black, stands with her hands clasped before her and her head melancholically inclined; the other, light haired, dressed more fashionably in white and sitting at a table, points to a paper (a letter, we presume—a seal is visible) lying on the floor at her companion's feet. The scene is so clearly a fragment from a larger narrative structure that to make a tale from it is not difficult. Almost all of the necessary elements are present. One must simply imagine, first, why the letter is lying on the floor and the rest will follow: the receiver of the letter, its authorship and contents, and the relationship between the women. Two important hints might be taken from the engraving: the man's hat and cloak lying on the table and the fact that the letter rests on the floor between the two women, at the base of the vertical line of the door-frame that divides the engraving nearly in half. The letter seems positioned as a root object, the sign of all that separates the women, even as it connects them by acting as the focal point of the engraving.

Shelley meets these suggestions with a tale of love, faith, and inconstancy that perfectly embodies the plate, accounting for all of its visible elements without introducing anything extravagantly beyond them. The demure, dark-haired woman becomes Angeline, the tale's heroine; she and her lover Ippolito have vowed to remain separate for a year to test their attachment before they are wed. Angeline attempts to keep the vow, but Ippolito, interpreting her distance as inconstancy, makes love instead to her friend Faustina, whom he eventually marries. Shelley fashions her narrative with a characteristically free hand, sliding between a development of the present, shortly before the end of the year of separation, and an exposition of the past. The overall effect is nevertheless successful, for Shelley takes hints from the engraving to

"The Letter"
Drawn by John Massey Wright, engraved by Charles Heath.
Reproduced by permission of Johns Hopkins University Press.

flesh out her characters and shape her plot. Because the dark-haired woman in "The Letter" is dressed and posed modestly, Angeline is made an orphaned boarder at a convent; the light-haired woman is clearly fashionable and at home in the rich surroundings of the engraved scene, so Faustina becomes the daughter of a Venetian nobleman. The letter itself suggests to Shelley a sub-rosa correspondence, as the light-haired woman points vaguely both to it and to the dark-haired woman. The engraved scene is thus made the climax of Shelley's tale: Angeline has written to Ippolito to remind him of their engagement, and in this scene Faustina, ignorant of the relationship between the divided lovers, confronts her friend with the apparent evidence of deception. Here is Shelley's rendering:

> [Angeline] arrived at the villa, and entered the saloon. She heard quick steps, as of someone retreating as she came in. Faustina was seated at a table reading a letter—her cheeks flushed, her bosom heaving with agitation. Ippolito's hat and cloak were near her, and betrayed that he had just left the room in haste. She turned—she saw Angeline—her eyes flashed fire—she threw the letter she had been reading at her friend's feet; Angeline saw that it was her own . . . she was motionless—her hands clasped, her eyes swimming with tears, fixed on her letter. (*CTS*, 241)[8]

Shelley's sense of balance and proportion shows how clearly she understands the theoretical relationship between the engraving and the tale, the frozen moment and the flowing narrative. She does not, like many *Keepsake* authors, overemphasize the engraving in her own tale in an attempt to force the connection between them. To describe the scene in minute physical detail would inflate it out of proportion with the duration of the scene in her tale, or the importance of the setting to that scene. Instead, Shelley allows the momentum of the preceding action to carry the moment, using, for example, the hat and cloak on the table to suggest the third principal character of her tale. The scene is briefly related because it briefly occurred, and the engraving—a frozen moment, a shard of time—is (re)established and given proper proportion in the narrative continuum.

This method is standard for the *Keepsake* texts that include an imaged "scene." A greater difficulty for Shelley is working with a more static "portrait" image, one that naturally contains fewer suggestions of narrative. The typical portrait image, in fact, is purposely devoid of context; the original drawing is intended as a character study, an attempt to capture the essence of personality per se. One might do almost anything with an engraving of this sort, but that very freedom becomes a difficulty when one attempts to make a tale that will have some acute degree of intersection with the assigned image. Shelley's "The Invisible Girl" (*The Keepsake* for 1833), another tale of vows made by separated lovers, offers a clever solution by making the engraved image itself a principal object in the tale.

The engraved plate, titled "Rosina," shows a young woman in a posture common to *Keepsake* portraiture: she is seated, her chin resting prettily against her small hand, while she glances through the pages of a folio book. The stringed instrument reclining at her feet, like the folio, is meant to suggest the girl's polite "accomplishments," in keeping with her genteel surroundings. There is nothing unusually interesting in this portrait, nothing to mark it as a moment extracted from a larger narrative structure. But Shelley's task is to write an interesting tale that makes substantial use of the engraving's rather generic subject. The first sentences of the tale itself speak to these focused and specific requirements: "This slender narrative has no pretensions to the regularity of a story," the narrator writes, "or the development of situations and feelings; it is but a slight sketch ... nor will I spin out a circumstance interesting principally from its singularity and truth, but narrate, as concisely as I can" (*CTS*, 190). "The Invisible Girl" makes use of the frame device with which Shelley was familiar and comfortable. The narrator has taken shelter in what seems to be a ruined tower, though its interior, curiously, "was fitted up somewhat in the guise of a summer-house" (*CTS*, 190). Here he discovers a watercolor painting of a young woman strangely entitled "The Invisible Girl" and becomes the auditor of an old woman who renders "a kind of garbled narrative" that the narrator's "imagination eaked out, and future inquiries rectified," until the tale assumes the textual form available to the reader (*CTS*, 192).

One detects in the narrator's opening remarks a note of Shelley's own resignation to working within the confining limits of the gift-book tale and the defensive posture of the hobbled author offering an admittedly "slender narrative" deficient in "the development of situations and feelings." However, given the narrator's opening *apologia pro modum sua*, the original tale told by the old woman becomes an obscured figure of the "Rosina" engraving itself; selected and assigned to Shelley's tale, the engraving becomes for the author a "kind of garbled narrative" that must be "eaked out" and "rectified" before it assumes a suitable coherence. To narrate an unspeaking or "garbled" object—to make it a tale—is thus Shelley's authorial goal, and that goal itself establishes the tale's narrator as a kind of editor of oral history.

"Rosina"
Drawn by William Boxall, engraved by J. C. Edwards.
Reproduced by permission of Johns Hopkins University Press.

"The Invisible Girl" is unusual among Shelley's *Keepsake* tales in that the painting itself is incorporated as a material object in the tale. "Rosina" does not depict a scene or event in the world of the tale, thus forming an alternative or supplement to Shelley's representation. Instead, it is an object available to Shelley's narrator, and, indeed, the painting becomes for him, as the engraving is for Shelley, a fragment in need of fulfillment, something that will bring forth a tale: "The picture and its singular inscription," the narrator tells us, "naming her invisible, whom the painter had coloured forth into very agreeable visibility, awakened my most lively curiosity" (*CTS*, 192). That "curiosity" not only leads the narrator to hear the old woman's "garbled narrative" but also to seek out additional and corroborative information and, finally, to assemble the tale and present it to an audience himself. Indeed, the point of the tale is not to detail the strains of early affection between Rosina and her lover Henry Vernon, or even their forced separation by Vernon's disapproving father and manipulating aunt; the former, says the narrator, "is a tale often told," while the latter "would require a good-sized volume to relate" (*CTS*, 195). Instead, the tale focuses on the means by which the parted lovers are reunited, an event that explains both the local mystery of "the invisible girl"—a ghostly figure marked by flickering lights in the ruined tower—and the curious tower and painting upon which the narrator first happens.

These two mysteries are the points of incongruity that the tale must resolve in its telling. Vernon himself solves the mystery of the invisible girl, who of course turns out to be Rosina herself, hiding from the imagined curse that Vernon's father has placed upon her. Vernon solves the mystery after discovering a tiny slipper and using this talisman to confront the specter of the tower. The ruined tower itself and the flickering lights that haunt it figure the shattered and incongruous surface of the tale that contains them, while the Cinderella motif of the slipper indicates the degree to which the tale is composed of fragments from other narratives. The narrator's investigations reveal the origin of the incongruous tower, ancient ruin on the outside, modern comfort on the inside: Vernon has "fitted up the tower, and decorated it as I saw" (*CTS*, 202) and fixed the title "The Invisible Girl" to a portrait of Rosina, all to stand as a monument of sorts to their strange but happy love story.

Shelley solves the same problem in a very different way in "The Swiss Peasant," contributed to *The Keepsake* for 1831. Like "The Invisible Girl," "The Swiss Peasant" must attempt to place a common "portrait" image into a larger narrative context. The engraving, "Swiss Peasant," shows a generic female figure of that class gazing up at the child she carries on her shoulders while a lamb follows at her heels. They have just

"The Swiss Peasant"
Drawn by Henry Howard, engraved by Charles Heath.
Reproduced by permission of Johns Hopkins University Press.

come down a mountain path to the stream flowing at the woman's feet. Mountains, groves, and hills make up the landscape background; both a low cottage and a convent are visible near the horizon. The image is certainly more varied and seemingly more active than "Rosina," but for all that, there is no more specific suggestion of preceding events, no more indication of who the woman is or what has led her to this moment. The engraving's title, "Swiss Peasant," tells all.

The question is whether one can make a tale from this generic image—a tale, that is, that bears more than a casual relationship to the engraving. Shelley solves the problem by making the question itself the subject of the tale; rather than shaping a narrative that leads up to and away from the moment depicted in the engraving, Shelley chooses to make the moment part of a narrative frame that will introduce the figure depicted and also raise and address Wordsworthian ideas of infinite tale-making. Shelley's skeptical narrator begins by claiming that he cannot "invent the commonest incident" (*CTS*, 136), then he recounts the recent circumstances of a wager he made with his painter friend, Ashburn. The bet tests Ashburn's Wordsworthian claim that "no living being among us but could tell a tale of soul-subduing joys and heart-consuming woes, worthy, had they their poet, of the imagination of Shakespeare or Goethe" (*CTS*, 137). The two then see Fanny, the Swiss peasant, "descending the mountain-path" (*CTS*, 137). Ashburn, who "insisted that our existence was only too full of variety and change—tragic variety and wondrous, incredible change" (*CTS*, 137), immediately begins composing a painting of Fanny: "'What a figure!' cried Ashburn; 'oh that she would stay thus but one quarter of an hour!—she has come down to bathe her child—her upturned face—her dark hair—her picturesque costume—the little plump fellow bestriding her—the rude scenery around—'" (*CTS*, 137). Fanny then proves Ashburn correct by recounting the events of the revolutionary era that led her to marry her "contrary" husband, Louis Chaumont.

By attaching the engraved image to the introductory frame of her tale, Shelley teaches us to read as Ashburn does, as the Wordsworthian poet does:

"Even," said the painter, "as sky, and earth, and water seem for ever the same to the vulgar eye, yet to the gifted one assume a thousand various guises and hues—now robed in purple—now shrouded in black—now resplendent with living gold—and anon sinking into sober and unobtrusive gray, so do our mortal lives change and vary. ... [T]he meanest peasant will offer all the acts of a drama in the apparently dull routine of his humble life." (*CTS*, 137)

"Constantine and Euphrasia"
Drawn by Edward Corbould, engraved by J. Henry Robinson.
Reproduced by permission of Johns Hopkins University Press.

After hearing Fanny's tale, it is difficult to see the figure in "Swiss Peasant" as generic, or to see the engraving itself as having taken up a generic subject. Shelley manages to imply an origin for the engraving itself (Ashburn, we feel certain, persuaded Fanny to model for that quarter hour) and a distinct purpose for having brought the image before us: to demonstrate that the perceived generic image may be particularized by narrative, by being made to speak.

Shelley experiments with a more complicated tale-making strategy in "Euphrasia: A Tale of Greece" (*The Keepsake* for 1838), and implicit in the fractured, externally motivated structure of her tale is an ironic and confrontational critique of the reader. The accompanying engraving, "Constantine and Euphrasia," depicts a clear "scene," a moment of unquestionable climax, excitement, and danger. Through an atmosphere of smoke and fire, stepping over and perhaps upon the dead, armored bodies at his feet, Constantine carries Euphrasia in his arms (the figures are named in the plate's title). The action portrayed suggests a rescue, and the figures in their dress and names are clearly Greek. There is no doubt that "Constantine and Euphrasia" is a fragment, a scene excised from a larger narrative. Shelley's job, supposedly, is to create the narrative context that will absorb the isolated moment into the larger whole. What could such a scene suggest to Shelley, except a tale of the Greek Revolt of 1821–29? The tale might lead to the engraved scene by recounting the capture of Euphrasia by the Turks, Constantine's attack on the palace where she is held, and her dramatic rescue in his arms. Such a tale could figure, allegorically, the heroism of the Greek freedom fighters as they liberated their beloved land from the invading Turks. The connections seem clear and the meaning manifest.

But Shelley offers something much more complex and obscure in a sequence of narratives that buries the core incident depicted in the engraving deep within a heavily framed structure. Shelley's tale opens on Christmas 1836 in Sussex. A party of snowbound travelers pass the time and attempt to distract a nervous young woman by listening to the tale of one of its members, a young man named Henry Valency who had seen action in a skirmish between the Greeks and the Turks during the uprising. Valency recounts the night he spent with Constantine, a Greek revolutionary, as both lay wounded on the field of battle. As they awaited help, Constantine told Valency the tale of his sister, Euphrasia, and how he had rescued her from the harem of a Turkish prince in occupied Athens. Why might Shelley have chosen to construct such an extensive labyrinth of narrative frames, inevitably blurring the clarity of theme and purpose that the engraving suggests?

First, we should consider Shelley's own connection with the Greek revolt through Byron, who died in its cause at Missolonghi in 1824. Shelley's sense of the revolt was very personal but also very removed; she experienced it as distant news, in scenes reported second and third hand, and that distance becomes figured in the structure of "Euphrasia." Somehow, it seems, the matter of the Greek revolt must be "brought home," an act that Shelley is able to perform only through the successive stages of sequentially framing narratives. Thus, we might see the tale "beginning," as undoubtedly it must have, in Shelley's imagination, with the very scene depicted in the engraving: Constantine's rescue of his sister from the Turkish harem. That action becomes a tale, an externally motivated narrative act, when Constantine and Valency lie wounded after a skirmish with the Turks. Near death, Constantine is naturally reminded of the night Euphrasia died in his arms, and under Valency's questioning he tells the tale. Years later, snowbound at Christmas and awaiting aid in Sussex, Valency is reminded of the night he spent with Constantine, also waiting for help that seemed forever in coming. Like Constantine, Valency is in his turn questioned about his adventure, and he produces the tale.

This sequence obviously reflects the external motivation of Shelley's own tale-telling, which begins with the engraving and seeks to make a tale to explain that isolated image. But with each stage in the succession of narrative acts, from Constantine to Valency to the Sussex party and finally to Shelley's reader, the original senses of danger and romantic heroism are ironically undercut. Valency is not Greek but British, and had been decidedly romantic in his understanding of the revolution: "He longed to have the pages of his young life written over by deeds that would hereafter be memories, to which he could turn with delight. The cause of Greece warmed his soul" (*CTS*, 297). Lying on the field, listening to Constantine's tale, he is one step removed from the center of active, heroic revolutionary struggle that Constantine recounts; his party of soldiers had been hiding from the Turks, lying in ambush when they were attacked and defeated. Even more diminishing are the circumstances under which Valency recounts his tale—a Christmas snowstorm in Sussex. Finally, the tale comes to Shelley's reader, whom we might picture settled comfortably before a Christmas fire, turning the pages of *The Keepsake*. These ironic narrative reductions of the engraving's romantic content suggest that the particular power of a lived moment is often diminished by the context in which it is recounted and received; that the absorption into a larger whole is, as Keats suggests in his "Ode on a Grecian Urn," potentially reductive and destructive. Shelley likely intends her comfortable *Keepsake* reader to feel that reduction most keenly by requiring passage through the distancing sequence of narrative frames, ending in a confrontation near the end of the tale with the engraving itself, an immediate representation of the tale's romantic, heroic origin. "Euphrasia" is thus structured as an implicit critique of the reader, who is made to feel most powerfully the difference between the active life of romantic heroism and the sedate life of home and hearth.

In combining an effort toward organic unity with inevitable fragmentation, the paradox of Romantic tale-making stands as an apt figure for Shelley's own artistic and ideological ambivalence. The format of *The Keepsake* itself seems implicitly to accept Wordsworth's claim that "such stores as silent thought can bring" will reveal "a tale in everything," and Shelley's experiments certainly work harder than most *Keepsake* tales to make good that claim by seeking a meaningful integration of image and narrative. Time and again, however, Shelley's narrators take up the negative Keatsian concept of tale-making as entropic reduction, consistently reminding their readers that the texts before them are not what their originals were. The tales are either reformations of fragments—of "a kind of garbled narrative," as the narrator of "The Invisible Girl" has it—or more often they are admittedly "garbled" themselves. Like Keats's speaker in "Ode on a Grecian Urn," these narrators recognize that they strip the original renderings of their "soft, silvery accents" and "greatest charm" ("The Swiss Peasant," *CTS*, 137), their "lively earnest interest" ("Euphrasia," *CTS*, 296). They set them in motion, reduce and degenerate them, and, because they must ultimately end and fall silent, lead them to a kind of death. Of course, in this Keatsian sense, complete wholeness is impossible; either the part remains separate, or it joins a larger continuum and flows forward to an end, proving merely a part once more.

In studying Shelley's *Keepsake* tales, then, one feels the author taking up something of Coleridge's epistemological complaint:

> I can contemplate nothing but parts, and parts are all *little*—!—My mind feels as if it ached to behold and have something great—something *one and indivisible*—and it is only in the faith of this that rocks or waterfalls, mountains or caverns give me the sense of sublimity or majesty!—But in this faith *all things* counterfeit infinity![9]

As her journals so often attest, Mary Shelley longed to be integrated with the larger body of life, to be given back a literary and intellectual context she had seemingly lost. Instead, like the image and the tale, she most often felt divided and isolated from "something great." In their attempts to hold both the unifying and entropic views of Romantic tale-making in tense proximity, Shelley's tales for *The Keepsake* find her once again testing the soundness of Romantic idealism.

Notes

1. For a fuller view of what the annual gift books offered, see Bradford Booth, *A Cabinet of Gems: Short Stories from the English Annuals* (Berkeley: University of California Press, 1938), 1–19, and Andrew Boyle, *An Index to the Annuals (1820–1850)* (Worcester, Mass.: Boyle, 1967). Anne Renier's *Friendship's Offering: An Essay on the Annuals and Gift Books of the Nineteenth Century* (London: Private Libraries Association, 1964) provides a substantial discussion of the general gift book phenomenon.

2. Wendell V. Harris, "English Short Fiction in the Nineteenth Century," *Studies in Short Fiction* 6 (1968): 8.

3. Thomas McFarland, *Romanticism and the Forms of Ruin: Wordsworth, Coleridge, and Modalities of Fragmentation* (Princeton, N.J.: Princeton University Press, 1981), 5, 13.

4. René Wellek, "Romanticism Re-examined," in *Concepts of Criticism*, ed. Stephen G. Nichols Jr. (New Haven: Yale University Press, 1963), 220.

5. Don H. Bialostosky offers a complex, careful reading of *Lyrical Ballads* as a set of experimental narratives, some of which he terms "tales," or narratives that "establish a framework of expectations which may be met or modified by other interests and constraints that affect the speaker's sense of himself and the others" (*Making Tales: The Poetics of Wordsworth's Narrative Experiments* [Chicago: University of Chicago Press, 1984], 68). Bialostosky also subscribes to Barbara Herrnstein Smith's definition of tales as "distinctly framed and conventionally marked tellings" that depend upon "the specific conditions that elicit and constrain them" (Smith, "Narrative Versions, Narrative Theories," *Critical Inquiry* 7 [1980]: 232, 234).

6. Charles E. Robinson, introduction to *Mary Shelley: Collected Tales and Stories, with Original Engravings*, ed. Charles E. Robinson (Baltimore Md.: Johns Hopkins University Press, 1976), xvi.

7. For the textual details of each of Shelley's tales (manuscript and printing histories, editorial emendations, and so forth), the reader is referred to Charles E. Robinson's excellent notes in *Mary Shelley: Collected Tales and Stories*.

8. Citations of Mary Shelley's tales refer to *Mary Shelley: Collected Tales and Stories* and are hereafter noted parenthetically in the text with the abbreviated title *CTS*.

9. Coleridge to John Thelwall, 14 October, in *Collected Letters*, ed. E. L. Griggs, 6 vols. (Oxford: Clarendon Press, 1956–71), 1:349.

Part 2
Myths Revised, Taboos Defied

Mary Shelley's Women in Prison

Syndy McMillen Conger

This essay investigates the early fictional solutions that Mary Shelley offers to her mother, Mary Wollstonecraft's, most frequently restated problem: women's metaphoric imprisonment arising "out of the partial laws and customs of society."[1] Its aim is to demonstrate that the daughter—as sole surviving heir and chief executor of her mother's intellectual estate[2]—cautiously acknowledges and advances protofeminist gains passionately fought for by the mother. Inspired by the revolutionary fervor of her day, Wollstonecraft's works turned an increasingly critical eye on English institutions and attitudes that she believed promoted or perpetuated the physical confinement, emotional or intellectual restraint, or criminalization of women.[3] Her style was polemical; her thinking, radical; her ultimate aim the transformation of both the public and private spheres in English society to allow women better education, more physical, emotional, and intellectual freedom, more public responsibility and respect.

In contrast, her daughter—having grown up in an increasingly conservative England in which the press had savagely denounced the French Revolution and its advocates (among them both her parents, both of whom she adored)—focuses circumspectly in her fictions on individual women protagonists rather than society at large. These characters are often political prisoners unjustly shut in or out; yet the metaphoric "chains," "shackles," "fetters," "whips," "cages," and "prisons" liberally sprinkled throughout Wollstonecraft's polemical treatises are literalized, narratized, and, to some extent, ideologically diffused in the fictions of the daughter.[4] Doubting revolution's efficacy, Shelley highlights her heroines' subversive but less disruptive strategies for extricating themselves from constraints or—a probable response to the posthumous slander of her mother—vindicating themselves from slander.[5] Her style, usually either detached or sentimental, is nonconfrontational; her thinking skeptical to guardedly optimistic; her ultimate aim the moral conversion of all citizens from an ethic of individual rights to an ethic of social—and especially familial—responsibility.

The mother, it should be said at the outset, might not have wholeheartedly endorsed her daughter's devices and intellectual positions, had she lived. Mary Shelley's remythologization of the virtues of sensibility her mother worked so hard to demythologize in *A Vindication of the Rights of Woman*,[6] for example, might have met emphatic maternal disapproval. Mary Shelley's heroines display many of the passive attributes of the woman of sensibility admired by Wollstonecraft as a young woman, then later rejected by her as an enervating and self-defeating feminine role model: amiability, sensitivity, genius, compassion, and a tendency to melancholy. The best-known example among these heroines is undoubtedly Elizabeth in *Frankenstein*, a wraith of a character with a docile, "affectionate" disposition, a "luxuriant imagination," and a "light, airy figure" and soft eyes[7] that all seem to repudiate Wollstonecraft's later feminine ideal. Just as Wollstonecraft ridiculed submissive wives as "house slave[s]" in *Rights of Woman*, she might well have winced to read her daughter's apparent praise of Elizabeth: "No one could submit with more grace than she did to constraint and caprice."[8] "Such a woman ought to be an angel—or she is an ass," her mother might have lamented, "for I discern not a trace of the human character, neither reason nor passion in this domestic drudge, whose being is absorbed in that of a tyrant's."[9] Nevertheless, Wollstonecraft was too acutely conscious of both the linguistic and sociopolitical pressures to which women were subject not to have understood the cultural constraints under which her daughter worked. Certainly it is possible to see today that Mary Shelley's stories, despite some divergence from Wollstonecraft's feminine ideal, pay covert homage to her mother's political vision in multiple, if subtle, ways:[10] by excavating the concealed socioeconomic or political forces motivating the oppression—whether psychological or physical—of innocent women; by presenting many of Wollstonecraft's lifelong wishes for her sex— better education, more independence of mind, greater freedom of movement in the public sphere—as faits accomplis; and by representing the resistant woman as heroine.

* * *

One of Shelley's favorites among her mother's works was a novel-in-progress at her own birth, *Maria; or The Wrongs of Woman*. It was among the books by Wollstonecraft that Godwin allowed his motherless daughters to read quite early in their education; and daughter Mary, according to her biographer Emily Sunstein, "devoured" it, reading its interpolated heroine's memoir to her infant daughter as her mother's last "testament to herself."[11] The sensational story of a husband's unjust consignment of his wife to a mental institution, *Maria* is a daring exposé of the customs and laws in England that put women in constant jeopardy of dispossession and mistreatment. Maria's debauched husband first depletes her material resources, then attempts to peddle her sexual wares, and finally has her confined as insane when she refuses to cooperate. As outlandish as Maria's "history" may seem, it "ought," Wollstonecraft's preface insists, "to be considered as of woman, than of an individual."[12] Similarly, *Maria* invites its readers to take the heroine's double confinement, in the mental institution and in the institution of marriage, figuratively: "Was not the world a vast prison, and women born slaves?" (27) asks the narrator at the tale's outset. Later, Maria answers, "Marriage had bastilled me for life" (103).

The novel fragment chronicles Maria's painful exile from respectable society, an exile, however, that only increases her sense of being confined and scrutinized. First her husband stigmatizes her as "hysterical" after she insists that he has, by his actions, broken the wedding contract, declares herself free, and runs away. He has her followed, drugged, and abducted, separating her in the process from her child. Thereafter she is incarcerated, closely monitored, and finally criminalized in the asylum, when she breaks rules in order to maintain her sanity. Summoned to court by her husband's continuing legal proceedings, Maria at last has the chance to defend her right to a legal separation from her husband. Unfortunately, the presiding judge sides with her husband, not only disregarding her request but impugning her character for even contemplating such a request:

> What virtuous woman thought of her feelings? It was her duty to love and obey the man chosen by her parents. ... [I]ndeed ... the lady did not appear sane. (149–50)[13]

After this scene the story breaks off into various brief sketches of possible endings, probably cut short both by its author's indecision and untimely death shortly after the birth of a daughter. In all the sketched endings of the story, Maria manages to escape from the asylum, her literal prison, but she remains—as she was before she ever met her husband—a metaphorical prisoner of a patriarchal institution: confined by society's interdicts, myths, seductions, and fictions about women. Two of the several sketched endings include suicide attempts, good signs that Maria sees herself trapped in a classic no-exit situation (a double bind): she can return to a loathsome husband or she can live in disgrace with a lover. The tale's many endings leave her ultimate fate unresolved. Just how does she negotiate the continuing limitations of her existence? Does she have a "miscarriage" or does she live happily ever after for her child? Does her lover stay or disappear? Does she live or die?

Mary Shelley may have had a special urge to complete the incomplete *Maria*, to make at least a textual restitution to a mother—and a story— she had unwittingly arrested at her own birth. She never says so, but then, she rarely speaks about her mother, whose posthumous reputation was so ruined by her political enemies as to render her name taboo. In the literary works of Shelley's first decade of authorship, images of incarcerated women appear in two novels (*Frankenstein* and *Valperga*), four tales ("A Bride of Modern Italy," "The Heir of Mondolfo," "The False Rhyme," and "A Tale of the Passions"), and one mythological drama (*Proserpine*). In each of these, Mary Shelley tests a new way to set imprisoned women free—or rather, to have them set themselves free: by extricating themselves from bondage, by transforming their persecutors, or by clearing their names of unjust slander. The range of independence and ingenuity in these heroines attests at once to Mary Shelley's close understanding of the "Maria problem" of being "bastilled for life"[14] and to her determination to seek solutions to it, to commute society's life sentences for all the "Marias" of her world.

The most haunting of these heroines is the religious enthusiast Beatrice of Mary Shelley's second novel, *Valperga* (1823), who has been recently identified as one of several Wollstonecraftian figures in her fiction.[15] A gifted young woman, whom many believe to have prophetic powers, Beatrice falls in love with the local warlord Castruccio, only to have that love consume her talents, divert them from religious to political activities, and then drive her to delirium when Castruccio abandons her. She is eventually abducted as a political pawn, tortured, and twice imprisoned when she refuses to cooperate with captors. During these trials, Beatrice declines physically and psychologically, first succumbing to fever and hysteria, then to despair and death. On a literal level, Beatrice's brief, tragic story recapitulates the dark fears for women that are central to *Maria*—miseducation and oppression; madness, misogyny, and persecution; love and betrayal—and it represents Mary Shelley's greatest moment of doubt about women's capacities—however gifted they may be—to liberate themselves from the "iron cages" in which they "starve." Much in her mother's recorded life and fictions may have impelled her to wrestle with these fears. Wollstonecraft's lifelong, ultimately futile struggles against rage, ennui, and suicidal despair within, and injustice and oppression without, all drive home the degree to which she herself was trapped by the antiquated systems she deplored. Yet Beatrice never loses either her sense of integrity or her Cassandran clairvoyance: "Listen to me," Beatrice prophesies near the end of her life, "while I announce to you the eternal and victorious influence of evil, which circulates like air about us, clinging to our flesh like a poisonous garment, eating into us, and destroying us."[16]

On the metaphoric level, Shelley's novel forges covert links to her mother's ideas, paying homage to, then modifying, them. The cages and the Medean poisonous garment that Beatrice imagines clinging to her and eating her flesh are hyperbolic versions of the prevailing sentiment in *Rights of Woman* that women taught to be preoccupied with self-adornment are, in a sense, prisoners for life in their own bodies: "Confined then in cages like the feathered race, they [women] have nothing to do but to plume themselves, and stalk with mock majesty from perch to perch."[17] But Shelley has erased her heroine's culpability in her figures of speech—she has, in other words, at least extricated her from the twin burdens of debilitating guilt and self-doubt—something her mother was never entirely able to do. Enveloping evils, not Beatrice herself, are responsible for her destruction.

Two other early-imprisoned heroines, Justine Moritz, a well-loved servant of the Frankenstein family (1818), and Clorinda Saviani, a "Bride of Modern Italy" (c. 1824), might seem at first glance to have very little in common either with each other or with Wollstonecraft's concerns. Justine is a model servant: devoted, pious, and obedient. Bred to such utter dependency that she can be persuaded of nearly anything, she is unjustly accused of the murder of Victor's young brother William, imprisoned, and interrogated. She offers neither resistance nor denial: "I did confess," she tells her beloved mistress Elizabeth, "but I confessed a lie. . . . [M]y confessor . . . threatened and menaced, until I almost began to think that I was the monster that he said I was."[18] Clorinda, in stark contrast to Justine, is a rebellious Italian daughter confined by her parents to a convent until a suitable marriage can be arranged for her. Flitting from one suitor to the next, always in the hope of finding one bold enough to storm her convent-prison to elope with her, she is at last caught in her own subterfuge. Confronted with her guilt, she nevertheless insists on her innocence, refusing to take responsibility for a heart she claims has "escaped from [her] control."[19]

Wollstonecraft would have had little trouble seeing a likeness between her daughter's fictional constructs despite their contrasting personalities. Both Justine's vulnerability to persuasion and Clorinda's inconstancy in and obsession with love are, she would have said, natural consequences of the inadequate and partial education of women described pointedly in *Rights of Woman*, then fictionalized in *Maria*:

> Their senses are inflamed, and their understandings neglected, consequently they become the prey of their senses. . . . All their thoughts turn on things calculated to excite emotion; and feeling, when they should reason, their conduct is unstable, and their opinions wavering. . . .
>
> When the sensibility is thus increased at the expense of reason, and even the imagination, why do philosophical men complain of their fickleness?[20]

Maria is Wollstonecraft's case in point. Once she is branded as irrational and criminal, and forced to subsist on solitude and fleeting prison conversations, borrowed books and painful memories, even though she had considerable "strength of mind" to begin with, she becomes the thrall of her senses, her sensibility, and her passions: "What chance then had Maria of escaping [love]," the narrator asks, "when pity, sorrow, and solitude all conspired to soften her mind, and nourish romantic wishes, and, from a natural progress, romantic expectations?"[21] Maria's lifelong restriction to nonintellectual spheres at last renders her—about this she is crystal clear as she records her own memoirs—monstrous: "By allowing women but one way of rising in the world, the fostering the libertinism of men, society makes monsters of them, and then their ignoble vices are brought forward as a proof of inferiority of intellect" (88).

Although Mary Shelley never speaks so directly or pointedly, she implicitly concurs with her mother, both here and elsewhere, about the importance of educating women to think as well as to feel. She takes care to demonstrate in these two cases that socioeconomic conditioning makes the heroines what they are: Justine, pliable;[22] Clorinda, sly and rebellious.[23] Two of Wollstonecraft's other persistent concerns also surface in these two stories: women's vulnerability to slander and social ostracism and their all-too-frequent reduction, in the eyes of others, to material worth: beauty, physical chastity, dowry. Justine's story illustrates that even the most virtuous woman is not safe from quick and irrevocable condemnation in a society designed by men for men. Clorinda's story shows that women often serve as mere pretexts for commodity exchange; that they are—and this is Shelley's hyperbolic magnification of her mother's vision—little more than the refuse of their societies.

Women's inescapable vulnerability to male slander is articulated as a fear by Elizabeth in *Frankenstein* in predatory, cannibalistic figures soon after Justine's execution. She is haunted by visions of men as "monsters thirsting for each other's blood" and sees herself exiled to society's life-threatening margins:

> Alas Victor, when falsehood can look so like the truth, who can assure themselves of certain happiness? I feel as if I were walking on the edge of a precipice, towards which thousands are crowding, and endeavouring to plunge me into the abyss.[24]

Clorinda, the presumably representative "bride of modern Italy," lives literally on life's margins, and the actions of her various caretakers—foregrounded in her story—underline her society's strictly mercenary motives in dealing with young women. While she pleads with suitors and prays to a series of saints to deliver her from her bondage, her parents put out a bid for the suitor willing to accept the lowest dowry; and the convent's Mother Superior barters with Clorinda's admirers, who are allowed to visit only when the bribes flow freely.[25] Meanwhile, Shelley's description of the convent and its garden transforms the setting into a material emblem of "modern Italy's" neglect of unsalable women, who are at last literally devalued to an equivalency with garbage:

> Clorinda and Teresa walked up and down the garden of the convent of St. S.———, at Rome . . . bounded by a long, low straggling, whitewashed, weather-stained building, with grated windows, the lower ones glassless. It is a kitchen garden, but the refuse of the summer stock alone remained, except a few cabbages, which perfumed the air with their rank exhalations. The walks were neglected, yet not overgrown, but strewed with broken earthen-ware, ashes, cabbage-stalks, orange-peel, bones, and all that marks the vicinity of a much frequented, but disorderly mansion. . . . You saw the decayed and straggling boughs of the passion-flower against the walls of the convent; here and there a geranium, its luxuriant foliage starred by scarlet flowers, grew unharmed by frost among the cabbages; the lemon plants had been removed to shelter, but orange trees were nailed against the wall, the golden fruit peeping out from amidst the dark leaves; the wall itself was variegated by a thousand rich hues; and thick and pointed aloes grew beneath it. Under the highest wall, opposite the back door of the convent, a corner of ground was enclosed; this was the burial place of the nuns. (32)

"Luxuriant foliage" and "rank exhalations," nuns' graves and cabbages, the convent of St. S— at Rome is quite clearly a place where dreams—

and initially healthy young novices—languish and then die. It never quite occurred to Wollstonecraft, caught up as she was in the eighteenth-century rhetoric of the value of the individual, that women could literally become—either by circumstances or social ostracism—disposable objects, [26] even though it follows from her own often reiterated premise that their worth is too dependent on things ephemeral. But it does occur to Mary Shelley, who doggedly pursues this premise of her mother's to its logical extreme yet who dodges critics' detection, in this case, by veiling her potentially volatile point in metaphoric description. Her discontent does not drive her to an invective made of chiseled satiric epigrams, as it did her mother, but instead to fantastically and evasively labyrinthine tropes that manage a literal exposé of metaphors her society lives by (in Justine's case, the "monstrosity" of an accused woman) or a metaphoric parody of her society's material values (in Clorinda's case, the "dispensable," "disposable" spinster).

Neither Justine nor Clorinda—the most conventional of Shelley's imprisoned women—openly defies restrictions imposed upon her; at the same time, neither is quite reduced—despite incarceration—to a Maria-like attitude of passivity, guilt, or suicidal despair. Each, in her own way, attains peace of mind. Justine does so by anticipating her reunion with William in heaven and by rejoicing over the loyal friendship of Elizabeth and Victor. "I feel," she says to Elizabeth during their last interview, "as if I could die in peace, now that my innocence is acknowledged by you, dear lady, and your cousin." [27] Clorinda, who devises several clever escape plots to Maria's one, also proves herself much more clever than Maria in avoiding loss of reputation. At the last possible moment, she lowers her expectations ("My sole aim is to escape from this prison" [28]), agrees to marry the low-budget suitor her parents have found for her, and gains her freedom; only a slow reader would not know by the story's end what she intends to *do* with that freedom.

Both Viola, the heroine of "The Heir of Mondolfo" (early 1820s), [29] and Emilie de Lagny, heroine of "The False Rhyme" (1829), embody Wollstonecraft's stated feminine ideal in the *Rights of Woman*: women who are "more observant daughters, more affectionate sisters, more faithful wives, more reasonable mothers—in a word, better citizens." [30] Although not the Wollstonecraft ideal now most often emphasized, it was one her daughter absorbed early and championed often. [31] Viola and Emilie are two clever, loyal, and intrepid wives who risk all to be reunited with their husbands. They endure slander, hardship, and imprisonment; yet, in stark contrast to the unhappily married Maria, they ultimately gain the restitution of both character and partner.

Viola, a poor orphan, agrees in secret to marry Ludovico, the heir-apparent of Mondolfo, unaware that his tyrannical father, Fernando, has arranged a more profitable marriage for his son. Once Fernando discovers the truth, he sends Ludovico on a fabricated errand and then confronts Viola, first trying to transform her by words and actions into a kept woman—"You call yourself, I believe, the wife of Ludovico Mondolfo? . . . The dream has passed. ... You will receive a yearly stipend"—and then forcibly removing her and her infant son to a remote coastal area.[32] There, locked in a lonely beach house tower with her son, as Viola stands near the window hoping to catch the attention of some passerby who might carry a message to Ludovico, "that her fate might not be veiled in the fearful mystery that threatened it," it suddenly strikes her "that her person would pass between the iron grates" (325). She waits until the darkest hour of night, then, during a violent thunderstorm, slips through the bars to the ground with her child bound to her waist and trudges resolutely into the gloom. Her trek eventually reunites her with Ludovico, and her love, loyalty, courage, and faithfulness at last effect a positive transformation in those around her, even her indomitable father-in-law:

> Time softened painful recollections; they paid him the duty of children; and cherished and honoured in his old age, while he caressed his lovely grandchild, he did not repine that the violet girl should be the mother of the Heir of Mondolfo. (331)

Unlike Maria, who needs help to escape from her prison and who remains permanently alienated from her husband and society, Viola singlehandedly extricates herself from a patriarch's prison, vindicates her slandered character, and builds a loving family circle. The "violet girl," her epithet in the tale, heralds the end of a tyrannical father's winter of discontent.

Emilie de Lagny, the favorite maid of honor of Margaret of Navarre in "The False Rhyme," not only does the same, she manages as well, with Margaret's help, to vindicate symbolically all womankind in the eyes of Margaret's capricious royal brother Francis. Shortly after her husband of one year is unjustly accused of treason and imprisoned for life in the "miserable dungeon" of King Francis, Emilie disappears with her jewels and her page. Slanderous rumors abound, and, at Margaret's command, Emilie's name is banned at court while all further attempts to find her are curtailed. Spurred by a wager with her brother to find "one true tale of woman's fidelity,"[33] Margaret renews her search for Emilie, only to discover that she exchanged places with her husband in the dungeon, "assumed his chains"—and his identity—so that he could be free to regain the king's favor in battle. The narrator does not describe the dungeon but does describe its effects on Emilie, still in disguise as she comes before the king to ask his pardon for her husband—by now a much decorated but unidentified knight in the king's service:

> Attended by guards, the prisoner was brought in: his frame was atenuated by privation, and he walked with tottering steps. He knelt at the feet of Francis, and uncovered his head; a quantity of rich golden hair then escaping, fell over the sunken cheeks and pallid brow of the suppliant. (120)

Francis, his faith in the possibility of loving, faithful wives rekindled, admits that Margaret and Emilie have won the wager and acknowledges the fact by giving a tournament to celebrate the "Triumph of the Ladies" (hence the title) and by restoring the faithful couple to his favor. Yet, at the moment she kneels before him, Emilie embodies much more than the good wife; she also exemplifies Wollstonecraft's notion of virtue as gender-neutral, articulated in *Rights of Woman*, as a matter of fact, in a chivalric figure of speech: "I here throw down my gauntlet, and deny the existence of sexual virtues, not excepting modesty."[34] Wollstonecraft long resisted the Burkean notion that there existed masculine and feminine virtues. She wanted chaste men and courageous women; in short, she wanted both sexes to have access to the widest possible range of virtues. Mary Shelley embraces this notion of gender-neutral virtue, but—as is often her practice—under ironical cover. Her women characters often look beautiful in Burke's sense of that term—small, soft, symmetrical, smooth to the touch, and pleasing. But they also have access to Burke's stern, "manly" virtues as well: keen intelligence, courage, physical stoicism.

By far the most daring of these Shelley characters are two whose stories both see print in 1823: Despina in "A Tale of the Passions" and Euthanasia in *Valperga*. Like Wollstonecraft's Maria and Shelley's Viola and Emilie de Lagny, both Despina and Euthanasia make choices that they fully realize may result in arrest, imprisonment, even death; and both do, in the end, die. Unlike those previous heroines, however, these two operate as independent agents with gender-neutral virtues in male-dominated worlds. They choose the public sphere as their theatre of operations, and they take their risks for political—indeed for republican—causes. Considering women's limited economic and nonexistent political rights at the time, the creation of such heroines is an act of authorial fortitude and one of the best proofs of Mary Shelley's continuing, if cautious, loyalty to her mother's revolutionary ideas. Wollstonecraft envisioned women as daring as Despina and Euthanasia only in the brief "Utopian dreams" of *Rights of Woman*:[35] liberally educated, in command of themselves, and deeply engrossed by the political well-being of their homelands. She even hoped for a future time when women would be able to pursue a wider variety of careers in the public sphere, such as medicine and politics. [36] Shelley's heroic women characters give her mother's utopian dreams literary substance.

Despina enters strife-torn Florence disguised as a mysterious young nobleman, partisan to the Ghibellines. Her character is gentle but firm; none around her guess her to be a woman. Perhaps her informed discussion of "various cities of Italy . . . their modes of government and . . . their inhabitants"[37] deflects suspicion. Her plan is to go secretly to the palace of "the enemy," the local Neapolitan commander, Lostendardo, to win him back to the Ghibelline cause. Her hope is to reveal her identity to Lostendardo and to try to revive the love she knows he once had for her in order to persuade him of the justice of her cause.

Hers is not a task for the faint-hearted. Lostendardo's "unnatural hatred" of the Ghibellines has become legendary. Despina knows that, should she fail in this mission, she faces imprisonment, death, or worse; but she has achieved a level of resolution and courage beyond concern for personal security: "I do not fear thee," she tells Lostendardo during their interview, "for I do not fear death" (10–11). In immediate political terms, her interview fails. Lostendardo feigns interest and promises to consider her proposition, but he is actually too intent upon revenge to accept it. After leaving her confined for hours in the apartment where they first meet, he spirits her away to prison under cover of darkness. The reader never sees her again alive. Still, in psychological terms, Despina triumphs both over herself and Lostendardo. During her lonely all-night vigil in his apartments, she intuits that she has become a political prisoner yet maintains a calm, stoical resolution in the face of imminent danger. She sits quietly and reviews the large, empty chamber, where Lostendardo has left her, the moon and stars visible through its grated windows, with the same clarity and detached view that they seem to take of her:

> One by one these torches went out, and the shadows of the high windows of the hall, before invisible, were thrown upon its marble pavement. Despina looked upon the shade, at first unconsciously, until she found herself counting, one, two, three, the shapes of the iron bars that lay so placidly on the stone. "Those grates are thick," she said: "this room would be a large but secure dungeon." As by inspiration, she now felt that she was a prisoner. No change, no word, had intervened since she had walked fearlessly in the room, believing herself free. But now no doubt of her situation occurred to her mind; heavy chains seemed to fall around her; the air to feel thick and heavy

as that of a prison; and the star-beams that had before cheered her, became the dreary messengers of fearful danger. (16)

Before the interview begins, Despina hopes that her courage will "not desert [her] at the moment of trial" (11). By dawn she has proved her courage, while Lostendardo—offered the choice of abandoning his pursuit of revenge and changing his political affiliation—has failed her test of his character. After this first "moment of trial," as if in periodic, revisionary return to the humiliating mock trial of Wollstonecraft's *Maria*, "A Tale of the Passions" dramatizes one trial after another, each one a more resounding success than the last for Despina and her political cause. Lostendardo tries the leader of her party, Prince Corradino, and the mockery of justice it represents reveals his villainy to all observers. He seeks to try her once more by bringing her to her prince's execution, but she eludes his grasp, slipping away in death before he can mock her:

She must have endured much; for when, as Corradino advanced to the front, of the scaffold, the litter being placed opposite to it, Lostendardo ordered the curtains to be withdrawn, the white hand that hung inanimate from the side was thin as a winter leaf, and her fair face, pillowed by the thick knots of her dark hair, was sunken and ashy pale, while you could see the deep blue of her eyes struggle through the closed eyelids. . . . [S]he was dead! (23)

At the last, overcome by remorse, Lostendardo turns his remaining life into a trial, a monastic existence of "self-inflicted torture," and dies "murmuring" her name (23).

It might be tempting to deny the notion that Shelley's model of pyrrhic heroism could have anything to do with Wollstonecraft; yet Wollstonecraft was hardly a stranger to the notion of death as triumphant exit. She attempted suicide on two occasions, and she also considered it for her heroine in one of the optional endings to *Maria*. In *Letters from Norway*, another book of her mother's that Mary Shelley read often and admired, Wollstonecraft confided her view of death to the reader as she contemplated the barren Scandinavian countryside with its "aged pines" and its "sapling[s] struggling for existence": "I cannot tell why—but death, under every form, appears to me like something getting free—to expand in I know not what element."[38] Mary Shelley offers her heroine Despina such a liberating death, but one much less loaded with potential social opprobrium than Maria's: a heroic death for a public, political cause.

Euthanasia, the other heroine as political martyr in the novel *Valperga*, makes two choices that she knows could have fatal political consequences. First, she declines an offer of marriage from the local warlord Castruccio. "A lady of great prudence, beauty, and learning," Euthanasia, the sole surviving heir of her father, is the much-loved countess of Valperga: "her assistance was perpetually claimed and afforded in every little misfortune or difficulty of her friends."[39] She falls in love with Castruccio, but when he invades and subdues her own castle and beloved city of Florence, "callous to blood" (2:171), she vehemently refuses his offer of a reconciliation-marriage:

> We are divided; there is an eternal barrier between us now, sealed by the blood of those miserable people who fell for me. . . . If these have been your actions of courtship, pardon me if I say, that I had rather woo the lion in his den to be my husband, than become the bride of a conqueror. (2:284–84)

When Castruccio's ambitious depredations become more and more lawless, Euthanasia makes a second, fateful decision: to join the conspiracy against him. It is discovered, and all the conspirators are rounded up and imprisoned, including Euthanasia. Her prison apartment recalls Maria's, but her calm, resigned piety in prison is quietly revisionary of Maria's romantic fantasies and melodramatic, suicidal melancholy:

> Morning succeeded to a winter's night . . . clear, and sunshiny, but cold. The cheering beams poured into her room; she looked upon the azure sky, and the flock of giant mountains which lay crouching around, with a strange pleasure. She felt as if she saw them for the last time, but as if she were capable of enjoying until the latest moment those pleasures which nature had ever conferred upon her. She repeated some of Dante's verses where he describes in such divine strains the solemn calm and celestial beauty of paradise. "When will it be my lot to wander there also," she said, "when shall I enjoy the windless air, the flower-starred meadows of that land?" (3:242–43)

Castruccio, still in love with Euthanasia, frees her from prison to send her into an exile-sanctuary, but she dies in transit. Nevertheless, hers is a "merciful death," as her name suggests. She does not die in shame as a political traitor with her fellow conspirators (although she actually wishes for it). Indeed, she is not murdered by anyone. She drowns in a shipwreck, and her heroic example lives on in the minds of her faithful subjects.

Mary Shelley's mythological heroine Proserpine, the last of her early imprisoned heroines, makes few choices and takes no risks, with her fate firmly in the hands of the male gods Jupiter and Pluto and, to a lesser extent, her mother-goddess Ceres. Her chief virtues are her adaptability and filial devotion to Ceres. Abducted to the ultimate prison, Tartarus, by Pluto to reign there as queen, she becomes a model hostage, accepting her fate without a murmur: "If fate decrees, can we resist?"[40] It is through Ceres's defiance of the gods—her refusal to accept their decree—that Proserpine wins an annual reprieve: "Six months to light and Earth,—six months to Hell" (42). For her part, the daughter promises to spend her months in Tartarus, dreaming of her flowers and summers with Ceres; her imagination, then, wins her additional solace and subverts Pluto's absolute claim over her.

As the mention of defiance, imprisonment, eloquence, and imagination might suggest to those acquainted with both Wollstonecraft and her daughter, *Proserpine* also revisits and revises *Maria*. Maria's response to separation from her daughter is impassive despair, to incarceration, self-defeating fantasies; her plaintive eloquence in the courtroom has no effect on her husband, her family, her society, or the judge who might have granted her a separation from her husband. Ceres and Proserpine together fare better: the impassioned words of one and the imagination of the other undermine the laws of a dual patriarchy and win significant concessions. Mothers and daughters working together—Mary Shelley seems to say in her own mythological allegory of justice—can create a force strong enough to change the world just as certainly as a Ceres in mourning changes the surface of hers, or Proserpine's fertile imagination transforms the subterranean sterility of Tartarus:

> [Ceres] Sweet Prophetess of Summer, coming forth
> From the slant shadow of the wintry earth,
> In thy car drawn by snowy-breasted swallows!
> Another kiss, & then again farewel!
> Winter in losing thee has lost its all,
> And will be doubly bare, & hoar, & drear,
> Its bleak winds whistling o'er the cold pinched ground
> Which neither flower or grass will decorate.
> And as my tears fall first, so shall the trees
> Shed their changed leaves upon your six months tomb:
> The clouded air will hide from Phoebus' eye
> The dreadful change your absence operates.
>
> (43–44)

This tribute is in response to her daughter's vow to dream her incarceration away:

> Dear Mother, let me kiss that tear which steals
> Down your pale cheek altered by care and grief.
> This is not misery; 'tis but a slight change

From our late happy lot. Six months with thee,
Each moment freighted with an age of love:
And the six short months in saddest Tartarus
Shall pass in dreams of swift returning joy.
Six months together we shall dwell on earth,
Six months in dreams we shall companions be,
Jove's doom is void; we are forever joined.

(42)

If Ceres represents Mary Shelley's wish-fulfillment fantasy of a living, loving, and supportive, yet courageously defiant, mother, Proserpine is most certainly her as a daughter. Notice, moreover, what kind of daughter she is: utterly devoted—indeed, in league with her mother—and demonstrating that loyalty by ignoring, even denying, tyrannical paternal authority and creating her mother imaginatively in her absence. If you want to find the daughter of Wollstonecraft, she seems to whisper to us from the last scenes of *Proserpine;* look for her in her quiet acts of defiance and in her fictional imaginings.

It might be easy enough to think that these confined women in early Mary Shelley stories are mere fictional shadows, simply medieval fantasies. Certainly all the prison images are antiquated, prepanopticon dungeons.[41] Yet each presentation of punishment is a manifestation of princely power, and the imprisonment of each of these women characters—Beatrice, Justine, Clorinda, Viola, Emilie, Despina, Euthanasia, and Proserpine—is largely political. They are not incarcerated because they have committed heinous crimes but because they have resisted or upset the plans or decrees of men who rule their worlds, because they require discipline, punishment, and subordination. Mary Shelley's conservative milieu makes her subdued, yet no less determined than her mother, to continue to address the problem of both the literal and the metaphoric confinement of women. Taking *Maria*'s lesson to heart, she creates a series of fictional worlds in which women can achieve some small measure of respect and autonomy.

Notes

1. Mary Wollstonecraft, author's preface to *Maria; or The Wrongs of Woman*, ed. Moira Ferguson (New York: Norton, 1975), 21.

2. This essay concurs with Emily W. Sunstein's conviction in her biography *Mary Shelley: Romance and Reality* (Baltimore, Md.: Johns Hopkins University Press, 1989) that Mary Shelley is "indeed her mother's daughter" (403).

3. Some of what Michel Foucault says about techniques of power utilized in Western societies to punish perceived crimes in *Discipline and Punish: The Birth of the Prison*, trans. Alan Sheridan (1975; rprt., New York: Pantheon, 1977), is relevant to this discussion, especially his discussion of the Panopticon effect in chap. 3.

4. A fine exposition of Mary Shelley's predilection for the literal can be found in Margaret Homans's "Bearing Demons: Frankenstein's Circumvention of the Maternal," chap. 5 of *Bearing the Word: Language and Female Experience in Nineteenth-Century Women's Writing* (Chicago: University of Chicago Press, 1986), 100–19.

5. Sunstein speculates convincingly on the lasting effect Wollstonecraft's slander had on her daughter. See, for example, *Mary Shelley* 54, 268, 273, 303–4, and 315–16.

6. Mary Wollstonecraft, *A Vindication of the Rights of Woman*, in vol. 5 of *The Works of Mary Wollstonecrft*, ed. Janet Todd and Marilyn Butler (Washington Square: New York University Press, 1989), chap. 5, hereafter cited as *Rights of Woman*. I agree with Virginia Sapiro, *A Vindication of Political Virtue: The Political Theory of Mary Wollstonecraft* (Chicago: University of Chicago Press, 1992), 64, that Wollstonecraft's attitude toward sensibility was far from "unambiguous."

7. Mary Wollstonecraft Shelley, *Frankenstein, or The Modern Prometheus*, ed. James Rieger (New York: Bobbs-Merrill, 1974), 30.

8. Shelley, *Frankenstein*, 30.

9. Wollstonecraft, *Rights of Woman*, 165.

10. As three remarkable mother-daughter pairs in Shelley's earliest fictions confirm— Ceres and Proserpine in *Proserpine*, Safie and her mother in *Frankenstein*, and Wilhelmina and Beatrice in *Valperga*—Shelley tended to see herself as a second-generation feminist whose mother's "lessons were indelibly impressed on the mind" (Shelley, *Frankenstein*, 119). More and more recent Shelley scholarship speaks of her in relationship to her mother. In addition to Sunstein's biography, see Betty T. Bennett's introduction to *The Letters of Mary Wollstonecraft Shelley*, 3 vols. (Baltimore, Md.: Johns Hopkins University Press, 1980); Anne K. Mellor's *Mary Shelley: Her Life, Her Fiction, Her Monsters* (New York: Routledge, 1989); and *The Other Mary Shelley: Beyond Frankenstein*, ed. Audrey A. Fisch, Anne K. Mellor, and Esther H. Schor (New York: Oxford University Press, 1993).

11. Sunstein, *Mary Shelley*, 37, 53. Godwin had begun the girls' education with a primer designed by Wollstonecraft, but he did not allow them at first to read his *Memoirs* of her life, the book that had—unwittingly—contributed to the destruction of Wollstonecraft's posthumous reputation by telling the story of her unconventional life and loves rather too completely.

12. Wollstonecraft, *Maria*, 21.

13. See Michel Foucault's story of the hysterization and criminalization of certain members of the social community—children, women, and homosexuals—during the eighteenth century in vol. 1 of his *The History of Sexuality*, trans. Robert Hurley (New York: Vintage Book Random House, 1978).

14. Sapiro also identifies Maria's problem as one of Wollstonecraft's problems in *Vindication of Political Virtue*, 40–41.

15. Barbara Jane O'Sullivan's "Beatrice in *Valperga*: A New Cassandra," in *The Other Mary Shelley*, 140–58, develops this hypothesis.

16. Mary Shelley, *Valperga; or, The Life and Adventures of Castruccio, Prince of Lucca* (London: G. & W. B. Whittaker, 1823), 3:44.

17. Wollstonecraft, *Rights of Woman*, 125.

18. Shelley, *Frankenstein*, 81–82.

19. Mary Shelley, "The Bride of Modern Italy," 39, in *Collected Tales and Stories*, ed. Charles E. Robinson (Baltimore, Md.: Johns Hopkins University Press, 1976), 32–42.

20. Wollstonecraft, *Rights of Woman*, 129–30, 133–34.

21. Wollstonecraft, *Maria*, 48, 88.

22. Shelley, *Frankenstein*, 60–61.

23. Shelley, "Bride," 34.

24. Shelley, *Frankenstein*, 88.

25. Shelley, "Bride," 34–35.

26. One could argue that Jemima's story in *Maria* comes closest to articulating this idea. Competing with another impoverished woman for a local tradesman's sexual favor, she recommends that he evict her from his house; the young woman subsequently commits suicide and Jemima is guilt-struck.

27. The guilt-ridden cousin Victor envies Justine her achievement: "She indeed gained the resignation she desired. But I, the true murderer, felt the never-dying worm alive in my bosom" (Shelley, *Frankenstein*, 83–84).

28. Shelley, "Bride," 41.

29. "The Heir of Mondolfo," in *Collected Tales*, 308–31, was not published until 1877, long after Mary Shelley's death.

30. Wollstonecraft, *Rights of Woman*, 220.

31. Mellor's *Mary Shelley* identifies domestic affection (and the bourgeois family ideal that sustains it) as a key idea in Shelley's works.

32. Shelley, "Heir," 323.

33. Shelley, "The False Rhyme," in *Collected Tales*, 119.

34. Wollstonecraft, *Rights of Woman*, 120.

35. Ibid., 105.

36. "Is not that government then very defective, and very unmindful of the happiness of one half of its members, that does not provide for honest, independent women, by encouraging them to fill respectable stations?" (Wollstonecraft, *Rights of Woman*, 219).

37. Shelley, "A Tale of the Passions," in *Collected Tales*, 7.

38. Mary Wollstonecraft, *Letters Written during a Short Residence in Sweden, Norway, and Denmark*, ed. Carol H. Poston (Lincoln: University of Nebraska Press, 1976), 132.

39. Shelley, *Valperga*, 1:169.

40. Mary Shelley, *Proserpine and Midas* (London: Humphrey Milford, 1922), 37–38.

41. The distinction between medieval and early modern forms of punishment is made by Foucault in the early chapters of his *Discipline and Punish*.

"The meaning of the tree": The Tale of Mirra in Mary Shelley's *Mathilda*

Judith Barbour

The Meaning of the Tree

The meaning of the tree is proclaimed to the pilgrim-poet in Dante Alighieri's *Purgatorio* 32 by the lady Beatrice from her station in the car of paternal deity (the imperial Roman church). It is one meaning of men folded within another meaning of women: the one is the patriarchal plot of succession by male primogeniture on the genealogical dynastic tree; the other is the pagan romance of maternal self-immolation and sacrifice of the virgin daughter to the seminal male divinity. In the tenth book of Ovid's *Metamorphoses*,[1] King Cinyras's daughter Mirra seduces her father, flees his curse, and is metamorphosed to a myrtle tree that cracks when she births Adonis, beloved of Venus. Immobilized, mute, a grand hysteric, Ovid's Mirra resorts to narrative only in extremity, "between fear of death and loathing of life." Her plea to the gods, "Change me!" purloins her literal doom into the magical evasions of *couvade* (the brooding sleep of the placenta) and *charivaria* (the barrage of noise that signals the cutting of the umbilical cord between mother and son).

In Dante's *Inferno* 30, Mirra is the lowest of all women damned to eternal torment. In contrast to Mirra, another young girl, the fair Matelda, in *Purgatorio* 28, is lyrically compared to Proserpine before she was raped by Dis, and to Venus when she fell in love with Adonis. In Dante's plot, Adonis is not Mirra's son but the pagan type of the beautiful youth and dying god, of which Jesus Christ is the *figura*, fulfillment of providential meaning in a human physiognomy. In Mary Shelley's *Mathilda* (1819–20), lyric inversions of Dante's Mirra and Matelda, no

98

longer fixed apart by judgments of guilt and innocence, are invoked in the temporal asymmetries of quotation and pastiche. In 1821, when Percy Bysshe Shelley's work-in-progress, *The Triumph of Life*, makes a skeptical reentry into the garden of Dante's Matelda, it is stirring with the presentiments that Jean-Jacques Rousseau, master tutor of the female heart, has left behind him there.[2]

Folded within the meaning of the tree is a second level of mystery, also gendered masculine and feminine. The pilgrim-poet beholds the tree at one moment stripped bare (*spogliata*), and at the next flowering with rose and violet light. In Dante's mythological plot, Christ's redemptive action from Crucifixion (on the despoiled tree) to Resurrection (as the tree of life) is underwritten by Mary his pregnant mother's hidden passage from Annunciation to Nativity. Deeper than deep runs the parallel passage of pregnant Mirra from incestuous rape to birthing Adonis, and from birthing the infant Adonis to separating from Adonis the man. Thus, Western theology curses the female birth-giving body and reassigns the redemptive meaning of the tree to the son-sacrificer in action on his father's world.

Fields of Fancy

In August 1819, Mary Shelley, childless after the death in Rome of her three-year-old son, William Godwin Shelley, and pregnant with her fourth, wrote *Mathilda*, a novella based on the story of Mirra[3] in Ovid, Dante, and Vittorio Alfieri; in 1820, in collaboration with Percy Bysshe Shelley, she wrote two plays on Ovidian fables, *Proserpine* and *Midas*.[4] Mary and Bysshe together were reading the *Divina Commedia* in the original Tuscan, as Bysshe composed his father-daughter incest drama, *The Cenci,* and experimented with Dante's Tuscan metre (*terze rime*) for a poem in progress, *The Triumph of Life*. Tuscan was once again the language of Italian political and cultural resurgence but not yet the language of Italian public life. Alfieri's patriotic verse tragedy, *Mirra,* was in the repertoire in the theater season of 1818. Written in 1786 for the theater in Pisa founded by Alfieri, and with famous stage actresses proud to take the leading role of the incestuous Mirra, the play revolutionized the English tourists' expectations of public theater and encouraged Percy Bysshe Shelley to believe that his work-in-progress, *The Cenci*, might feasibly find a backer for a London stage production. It is also on record that the topic of father-daughter incest, acted live on stage, disturbed while it excited Lord Byron. The text of *Mirra* in Charles

Lloyd's 1815 English translation was probably already known to Mary Shelley, and in 1818 Bysshe had been urging her to attempt her own translation from Alfieri's stately Tuscan. This was to be a private language exercise, and Bysshe was tutoring Mary in Greek at the same time. He had translated the *Symposium* of Plato as a study text for Mary, with the title *Plato's Banquet* and with the homoerotic and pedophilic character of Greek love considerably excised. In 1818 or 1819, he also translated Euripides' fragmentary "The Cyclops," a bloodstained pastoral satire based on an episode in the Homeric tales of Odysseus.[5]

A timetable of composition has been pieced together[6] from manuscript and published evidence. In August 1819, in Leghorn, Mary Shelley was reading and translating *Purgatorio* with Bysshe, was five months pregnant, and wrote a draft of a novella modeled on Wollstonecraft's "Cave of Fancy," entitled *Fields of Fancy*.[7] She finished it in early September, around the date of her mother's death and her own twenty-second birthday. She began to write again under the title *Mathilda* when she decided to offer the book to William Godwin so that he could pay off his debts. Godwin's icy cold letters from London dunning Bysshe Shelley for a promised £500 had not relented even when little William died, and the £100 that Bysshe raised from money lenders for the old man did not mollify him.[8]

In the first week of November, Mary learned that the Scottish obstetrician Bell, who was to have confined her, was gravely ill, and she faced the prospect of delivering the child alone among foreigners and strangers. She resumed writing after Percy Florence was born on 12 November and took the manuscript to Maria Gisborne in April 1820 to take to England and deliver to Godwin.[9] Godwin's adverse reaction was recorded verbatim in Maria Gisborne's London journal for August 1820 and, later, diplomatically conveyed to Mary.[10] She had already begun work on a historical novel on the Renaissance Italian prince Castruccio; this too she planned to sell to raise the desired £400 for Godwin. She read and researched with earnest minuteness and earned a criticism of her writing from Bysshe: writing to Thomas Love Peacock in 1820 to urge him to contact London theater managers with the manuscript of *The Cenci*, Bysshe complained that Mary had racked *Castruccio* (later retitled *Valperga* by Godwin), "out of fifty old books."[11] The rift between Mary's writing and Bysshe's tutoring had begun with *Fields of Fancy*, and it helps to measure the difference between Bysshe's ease with canonical European literature and Mary's efforts to master it. With *Valperga*, Godwin after Bysshe's death assumed the mantle of editor and judge of Mary Shelley's writing.

Mary Wollstonecraft's posthumous fragment "Cave of Fancy" is a fable of the birth and fostering of a woman genius, philosopher, and female educator. It allegorizes her own intellectual and erotic expectations of Richard Price, Joseph Johnson, and Henry Fuseli, muddying the waters by adding and subtracting traits from different milieus. Unlike Mary Shelley, who was an avid reader as a child, Wollstonecraft as a writer did not intuitively identify with young girls, and her protagonist is the teacher in training, earning her commission and her constituency of young, faceless pupils. Sagesta is an adult woman of sensibility before she enters into any of the learning experiences offered by crossgender, face-to-face pedagogy. Her education is fostered, monitored, and patronized by men and, in particular, by the aged satyr figure of Sagestus. But since the fable is a showcase for Wollstonecraft's theories and policies for female education, it is bound by the decorums of pedagogy in Wollstonecraft's London of the 1790s. Sagestus is neither sexual nor knowledgeable about sex, especially not about female sex or women's erotic lives. The fable is embarrassed by the presumed competence of Sagesta in all that pertains to the female body and mind and the corresponding blankness of the masculine personae. Heterosexual pedagogic exchanges are to yield instrumental information as to how Sagesta is to fare forward and found her second-generation academy. Wollstonecraft's utopian academy consists of a sole woman, surrounded by male bachelors and masters of the arts.

Mary Shelley's *Fields of Fancy* inherits and compounds the embarrassed tacit limits of the Wollstonecraft piece. She offers a fable that centers itself in a world where women are posed picturesquely together, but where all the news of past, present, and future comes from and goes out to men and the world of men. The sexual and birthing experiences of women cannot be a topic for literature or pedagogy, and the sexually experienced woman cannot teach girls out of that experience. The experienced face of the matron Diotima blurs as the young girl (Mathilda) enters the rapt mood of confessional mourning to tell of her sexual initiation into *her father's* incestuous passion. The manuscript breaks off and the narrative peters out without catharsis: "tomorrow" will be the same, it will be rehearsed again. The name Diotima, of course, is borrowed from Bysshe's translation of *Symposium*, where Diotima is the female satyr. But Mary Shelley's Diotima is debarred from enlightening the girl by the very fact of knowing what she is talking about, and the narrative declines into tableau, the statuesque poses and portrait faces of a broken circle of women.

If Mary Shelley could not find any woman to teach her about the love of women in Wollstonecraft's text, where could she find it? The pathos of *Fields of Fancy* is drawn from the children's tale "Elizabeth Villiers"

by Charles and Mary Lamb.[12] Little Elizabeth learns her letters from
Papa, a clergyman, and practices writing her own name sitting on her
mother's grave and copying the letters engraved on the headstone, for
baby girls were named for their dead mothers in England at this period.
Only the bar of death releases women and girls from the taboo on
empathetic communication of the facts of female life.

The Mathilda of *Fields of Fancy* had poured her faltering tale into the
uncircumcised ears of Diotima, but the heroine of *Mathilda* addresses her
narrative to a young man with a future in the world, the English poet
Woodville. In the retitled manuscript begun in November 1819, the tale
relapses from the woman-centered didacticism of the *Fields* to the
agonistic lyricism of *Mathilda*. The feminine portrait figures,[13] the
tableau vivant with its genteel costumed stances, and the utopian vision
of a scene of female instruction are cast off (leaving several loose threads
behind) before the incoming force of a Gothic romance of the solitary
bride alone of all her sex and alone among the male sex. Pivotal changes
are the shuffling off of other women and the internalizing by Mathilda of
the male poet's imperative of withholding his self-identifying
knowledge. She hovers on the brink of confessional abjection but does
not fall.[14] She evades extrinsic determinations by the production of florid
symptoms and narcissistic self-identifications, through echoes and
mirror-image quotations from uncountable poets, all male. She writes for
a posterity she has the power to nominate and call into being, and she
triumphs (a pyrrhic, suicidal triumph) over the lesser sort, all women
whatsoever, and Woodville in particular. In the closing autumnal vision
of the after-death, she flies in writing (the repression of presence) to the
father, now metamorphosed into her coming son.

Mirra

Ovid's Mirra (*Metamorphoses* 10) impersonates a young girl, a
stranger to the father-king Cinyras, smuggled into his bed by her
accomplice, the nurse. Ovid borrows the nurse from the plot of
Euripides' *Hippolytus*, where Phaedra is the foreign woman left
neglected in her husband's palace during his frequent absences on
hunting and trading expeditions. Caught in the claws of Venus, Phaedra
first hints at her shameful passion for her stepson Hippolytus to the
woman who has tended her since girlhood, her old nurse. The only other
woman who speaks her language and knew her as a girl, the nurse is an
ignoble figure simply because she is a slave. Slaves by definition have no

patria and cannot be dignified by terms like "exile." Phaedra's incestuous and adulterous passion is a symptom of modernity. She destroys the patriarchal simplicity of the Homeric family triad of Odysseus, Penelope, and Telemachus. In the ancient tale, Odysseus wanders twenty years and takes back kingdom, wife, and son when he returns, virility unimpaired. Phaedra is no faithful Penelope, but Theseus is no navigator of the broad ocean. He is a bisexual island-hopper and subtle master of the city of Thebes. He has learnt the lost language of cranes and taught it to foreign boys. He has subdued one wife by violence, Hippolyta the Amazon, and abducted the Cretan magician's daughters, Phaedra and Ariadne. Ovid's borrowings from Euripides draw out these traits of modernity: the cosmopolitan city, the straying husband, the mixed marriage, the stepmother. However, female sexual knowledge and childbirthing remain the province of women and slaves: the nurse is a bawd, a breast-feeder. Men do not study this lost language or field of fancy, where satyrs and Amazonians roam.

"Nurse" in Roman city satire doubles with "bawd," and Ovid's nurse goes offstage to solicit the king to have a hot and lively girl come to him at night. There is no suggestion in Ovid that Mirra is impersonating her own mother in order to deceive her father into marital sex in the darkness of the curtained bed. That detail is a medieval interpolation of Christian doctrine on adultery, a modern misprision of a wife's "rights" in the domestic sexual order. Cinyras knowingly beds a young whore and is destroyed by the discovery that it is not the peccadillo he thought and that he has committed incest with his daughter. Ovid plays down private relationships and emphasizes the public stake in a crime of sexual generation, the aging man made a prey to the young woman and her backers, the gens of Cinyras (we would add, the genes) cut off short by this unnatural pairing. The folk customs of *charivaria* (less formal than a rite of passage) signal, often with uproarious noise, the culturally critical joinings and partings of male and female, old and young, clan and individual, which took place typically at weddings, births, and the outbreak of war. Ovid's Mirra is a Gothic tale of "omitted anxiety,"[15] the stonifying spectacle of a "too late" drawing back from perdition, the violent flinging apart of ill-met lovers.

Ovid's Mirra dies twice, smothered inside breathless wood, then torn apart in giving birth to Adonis. The sadistic conflation in her one person of womb and fetus is irresistible, and Mirra is saluted in her metamorphosed shape as "murra," or myrrh for embalming corpses. The teller of Mirra's tale, Orpheus, also dies twice, drowned and dismembered by the Hyperborean hags. Ovid's plotting is antithetical; a shape before and after the metamorphic change is at a diametric angle or half-turn from itself. This *volte face* in Mirra's tale is conveyed in the perfect parallelism of Ovid's verse lines: Cinyras snatches (*deripit*) his sword from its hanging sheath (*vagina*) to kill his daughter; he snatches his penis from her vagina to abort his fate. Too late, Mirra is already impregnated and escapes with his seed as he goes for his sword. Cinyras is obliterated, but Mirra later is prized as a fetish—her "tears" of gum sweeten and preserve dead male flesh.

In Ovid, patriarchal simplicity is preserved only as a reminder, by the sword hanging in its sheath on the wall of Cinyras's bedchamber. [16] All else is modern: the private, secretive, curtained household; the father's jaded sexuality; the precocious, oversexed daughter; the nurse a very ready bawd; and last but not least, the mother's unwifely absence. She is attending the rites of Ceres (Kör), an aggregation of women, which leaves her daughter unmonitored and her husband unserviced and which in itself, as an assembly of women, signifies the heterogeneity of the city and breaks the romance plot that puts into circulation the single cathected and capitally invested "bride." The distance between Euripides' Phaedra and Ovid's Mirra is measured in this urbanized family household and the traffic in gendered commodities that links it to its world. Mirra impersonates the multiple orders of the city itself.

James Frazer's *The Golden Bough* (1898) is an anthology of Victorian male sexual myths and highlights the anxiety of aging men in financial and sexual competition with younger men. Freud's trope of the unconscious mind opened the space of asylum for aging men in the nuclear family household with its superannuated wife's generation of women understudied by their replacements from the daughter's generation. Ovid's Mirra goes straight into Frazer's nightmare of the sacred wood of Diana at Nemi, without the palliative of the Freudian unconscious. Metamorphosed into a myrtle tree, Diana incorporates phallus and loaded womb and parodies the genealogical fictions that perpetuate the father in the son and lead the son back to the father.

Linked in a female genealogy with Semele of Thebes and Hecuba of Troy, but paired in eternity with a vicious man (*The Divine Comedy* 1:30.22–27, 37–45), Dante's "cursed Mirra" is one of two grub-white, naked shades running among the impersonators in hell. She is the most damned of all women in Dante's book. Those damned with her are not the father, who sinned with her, or Adonis, the son she bore him, but a man entirely unconnected with her in life, Gianni Schicchi. Schicchi was hired to impersonate an already dead man (Buoso Donati). He climbs into the death bed and forges a will in favor of a greedy nephew, who pays him off with a sexual bribe. Schicchi accepts a woman from the stews, "la donna della torma,"[17] as his price, and this vileness skewers him to a vile woman, Mirra. The nephew is not displayed among the damned: cheating the church and legal heirs out of his uncle's money is not interesting, not gender-compromised.

Dante charges his Mirra with metamorphosis itself—"falsificando sè in altrui forma," shape-changing rhetoric, the falsifying turns and bends of metaphor and prosopopoeia. Schicchi's imposture tampers with powerful taboos on trafficking between the dead and the living, and Mirra reneges on sacred obligations between parent and child. However, Dante's whole enterprise traffics with the dead, calling up dead poets to be relieved of their mastery over his new text and circulating phantasms of beautiful women to pave his access to masculine supreme fictions.

Mirra's crime, like Phaedra's, traduces the authority of the male and the virile virtue of the masculine authority figure. That is the worst of her offense, in Dante's polemic against Firenze, playing on Mirra's alternate name, the Greek city Smyrna. Her masquerade serves the order of the just city only by sinking underneath it with the death-cheating, shit-eating toady, Schicchi. The law of scarcity that rules systems of value and hierarchy is mocked by the two delinquents, Mirra by turning the father's seed back into the tight nuclear unit (doubly invested in her own body) and Schicchi by wasting the deference of the living to the dead, on which depends the fragile social compact between dying man and heirs. Schicchi himself is a carnivalesque figure of mockery who plays a perennial joke at the expense of the mercantile order. Ben Jonson's *Volpone* (1607) frames the Schicchi figure in the decaying opulence of a Venetian magnifico, exposing the farcical underside of all cultural dealings with dead bodies.

Alfieri's neoclassical drama *Mirra*[18] propounds a fascist mystique of female sacrifice to the father who embodies the state. The work of the late Dame Frances Yates has shown that ancient magics and cults revived in Renaissance Italy, and the myth of founding the city-nation in the sacrifice of the nubile girl revived again in Italian and German nationalist movements after Napoleon. Goethe's *Iphigenia in Tauris*, for example, was known to both the Shelleys, and Robert Browning later turned from mythological settings to the historical Roman girl murder of *The Ring and the Book*. The Tuscan-language *Tragedie* of Alfieri form a belated founding myth of the Italian risorgimento. Invoking Aristotelian unity of effect, Alfieri strikes an augmented balance between the high value of the sacrifice (a noble princess) and the trauma of her loss to the city. Mirra is the exemplary victim whose prophetic prescience of imperial future greatness is seized and bound into the fasces, the ever rigid bundle of rods that guarantees the continuity of the Roman imperial line. She has interpellated the name of the father's power and is big with it. After protracted mental torture, she delivers it and dies. The female obstetric deities and demiurges are defunct: two women, Mirra's mother and nurse, stand by and shake their heads at her in collusion with the inquisitor father.[19]

Alfieri adapts the technique of stichomythia, a question-and-answer exchange where the two speakers complete each other's half-line, feinting with each other as in a weightless duel. Stichomythic duels and interrogations between Alfieri's Mirra and her father turn on the tight circle of rhetorical irony, punning, and double entendre. This suggests that the two speakers are collusive with each other, or apprehensive of each other, anticipating each other's next or half-formed words. Stichomythic dramaturgy carries erotic and aggressive tensions between the couple. Shakespeare provides the classical examples: Macbeth and Lady Macbeth on the night of Duncan's murder and the wooing of Lady Anne over her husband's corpse in *Richard III*.

In the end, Alfieri's Mirra's secret is forced from her but triumphantly vindicates her because it is too monstrous for the others to contain, to put a face to. She reburies her shame and her father's honor in her body with his sword, snatched from the sheath at his side. The tendency I have traced from Euripides to Dante, to blame the woman's desire for the decadence of patriarchal masculinity, is arrested and rebuffed here by the rigid decor of the incorporated state. A supplementary detail carries the archaic patriarchal mark. Although the scene is set in Cyprus, following Ovid, the nurse is named for Odysseus's nurse, Euriclea. It is Euriclea who recognizes Odysseus on his return to Ithaca by reading the scar of the boar's tusk that had initiated the virile youth into social manhood. Alfieri's Euriclea reverses the nurse character's slide into sexual chicanery that had begun with Euripides, and, significantly, she is paired with the Queen, Mirra's virtuous mother, as a solid supporter of the King's absolute rule.

Mirra and Phaedra are mythical sisters to Cassandra, women rendered prophetic and unclean by the *até* of a destiny that they have not psychologically conceived. In the works of Mary Shelley's European contemporaries—Alfieri's Mirra, Hebbel's Antigone, and Goethe's Iphigenia and Marguerite of *Faust*—heroines are statuesque models of the Romantic woman as poet-prophetess and sacrificial holocaust. Bysshe had steadily ventured into the open in his portrayals of sexual women, and in 1820 Beatrice Cenci[20] was not only his boldest dramatic portrait but written expressly to try the public stage with a woman's role as strong as Alfieri's Mirra. These are the works of contemporary mythmakers and nation-founding propagators: Alfieri and Goethe in their countries of birth, Shelley in 1819–20 "unacknowledged" in exile.

Goethe deplored the fact that his Germany was not a united nation, and he envied the English Shakespeare for his mastery of a language common to both highest and lowest. However, there was an advantage in writing of exceptional figures in an exceptional, even artificial, language, especially if these were figures of women. British publishers, the busy censors of the Society for the Suppression of Vice and the Tory reviewers attacked any work of fiction that could conceivably be held to represent actual, contemporary English women and girls, and the major mode of English novel was realistic, domestic, and drawn from contemporary middle-class life. Mary Shelley ventured in *Mathilda* to place her portrait of a young girl in the lightly veiled circumstances of her own girlhood in Scotland and London (Yorkshire too, where the middle class and gentry discreetly boarded their illegitimates and discarded dependents). She did not take warning from the scandal that had greeted Godwin's attempt in *Memoirs* (1798) to blend into his portrait of the late, well-known Mary Wollstonecraft some heightened colors of the Ovidian grand lover, Dido, or Sappho, or Laodamia. During the months in which Godwin was writing *Memoirs* (September to December 1797), his journal entries record that he was reading Ovid's *Heroides* and *Metamorphoses*. Godwin always kept several books going at once, and he taught Mary Shelley to do the same, for he wanted the stimulus and variety of reading experiences to energize his own writing. With Byron, Percy Bysshe Shelley, and Godwin as the living writers against whom she measured herself, Mary Shelley aimed in *Mathilda* at high poetic effects and fashioned a promiscuous and serendipitous text. This mixing of styles and genres, sure to be attacked as gender transgression, was risky writing.[21]

Mathilda

> *I chanced to say that I thought Myrrha the best of Alfieri's tragedies; as I said this I chanced to cast my eyes on my father and met his: for the first time the expression of those beloved eyes displeased me, and I saw with affright that his frame shook with some concealed emotion that in spite of his efforts half conquered him.*
>
> —"Mathilda," *The Mary Shelley Reader*

On delivery of the manuscript by the Gisbornes to Godwin in London in about August 1820, Godwin commented that he thought it "disgusting and detestable" and in need of a preface "at least if it is ever published" to prevent readers "from being tormented by the apprehension . . . of the fall of the heroine." Maria Gisborne strongly dissented from Godwin's opinion: "I have read 'Mathilda.' This most singularly interesting novel evinces the highest powers of mind in the author united to extreme delicacy of sentiment."[22]

In the tale, the revelation of the father's incestuous passion occurs as an angry censoring and self-censoring response to Mathilda's "chance" approving mention of Alfieri's incestuous Mirra, a response that prefigures Godwin's violent reception of the manuscript of *Mathilda*. Mathilda's inklings of a violent "change," a "fatal period" to the daughter-father bond guaranteed by the sacrificial mother, haunt her childhood past and future, repeating the family and artistic crises of 1817 as Godwin published his tale of a demonic puritan, *Mandeville*, and reluctantly received *Frankenstein* into the niche vacated by Bysshe in 1814. In August 1820, *Mathilda* similarly passed from Mary Shelley back to her father as tribute.

Fields of Fancy has a naturalizing preamble. An unnamed woman poet has a dream of fair women who appear in an after-death scene like the Elysian fields of Plato, or like the island of grand amorous women of Ovid's *Heroides*, only bowdlerized of sexual reference. *Fields* is the broken-off portico of a women's academy or secular nunnery where well-tempered instruction, autobiographical récit, and talking cure are spoken and listened to in stately concert. After *Fields* was abandoned, Mary Shelley started over with the title *Mathilda*. This time, there is only one female figure, the fair penitent who brought her burdensome tale to Diotima in the first draft and is now surrounded exclusively by men who are alone real to her and in the real time of action. Confession has shifted from childlike and apolitical *chora* to the contested ground of blame and vindication. Mathilda becomes the righteous confessor, urging confession from her father and banishing him when he has confessed. In her second relationship, she is strong enough to withhold confession from Woodville and send him about his business in a world she has put aside. Mathilda's half-turn between the two men is symmetrically arranged in two sets of six chapters each. The twelve chapters form a little epic, or epyllion.

The trading and sequestering of secrets and occult knowledge are thematized in *Mathilda* as the reciprocal feints, disclosures, and retractions of the romantic reading experience. Eddies of premonition move about the intertwining subjectivities of father and daughter. They have become addicted to sounding out each other. Adhesiveness to the face-to-face relation, which was the intense core of *Frankenstein*, is stigmatized. Stammered disclosures, stumbling confessions, and half-apologetic accusations increase suspicion rather than purge and dispel it. Tension snaps when the father, under Mathilda's interrogation, blurts out the very words, "My daughter—I love you," that Mathilda had previously spoken to herself as her father's pledge of "innocent," that is, voluntarily withheld, desire. The sexually labile woman pores over the imago, or mental picture, of an impassive man. Mathilda pictures her father's frequent absences and withdrawals as a promissory note. She desires to attract male desire that by tacit agreement is never to be posited.

The shocking thing about father-daughter incest in *Mathilda* is not that it happens but that it does not work. As the mingled thrill and taboo of writing and reading fantasy, it disappoints because it is not cathartic but rather addictive. Mathilda and her father fail to generate a convincing third party to mediate their attractions and repulsions. Woodville is mechanically separated from the father by Mathilda's two years of solitary manless life, which leaves the briefly appearing and nameless "young man of rank" of chapter 4 as the trigger to the father's incestuous jealousy, ominously supplemented by the altercation over "Alfieri's Myrrha." However, holding father and suitor apart makes Woodville not less but more like a tame son-in-law, an epigone. This makes the second half of the story, Woodville's half, an appendage and sequel to the first half.

There is, however, a ritual climax to the second part of Mathilda's epyllion. The chapter 11 scene between Mathilda and Woodville is deliberately framed as a citation for the *Faerie Queene*, where Guyon, Spenser's most protestant hero, is tempted by the Giant Despair, and Una, the feminine persona of the Church of England, preaches the gospel of self-reliance to him and turns him back from suicide. Spenser's Una remains bracketed within the ambit of European Catholicism and *amour courtois*. In Milton's revision of the Spenserian scene for *Paradise Lost,* Eve is a wife and pregnable. Suicide temptation comes from her, and it is Adam who rises above temptation and subjects Eve to a homily on parenthood.

Mary Shelley replays the Milton scene, and it is Mathilda who sets out the glasses of poison. This is also Ovid's Mirra, staging a scene of false instruction and seduction. However, when Mathilda retrieves the option of true instruction and sends Woodville off to be a liberal humanist poet in England (the home thoughts from abroad of Byron's *Don Juan*), the feeble hope of a Mathilda-Woodville marriage is collapsed back into crossgender, crossgenerational pedagogy. Mathilda quietly dismisses Woodville, evading the moment of maternal supersession.

Matelda

The name, in Italian spelling, is Matelda in Dante's *Purgatorio*, and she appears first in "the Earthly Paradise, the fair lady and the stream, the seeds dispersed on the earth" (2:28.364–75). The fair singer Matelda is linked back to Mirra (*Inferno* 30) by an epic simile comparing the gaze from her eyes with Cupid's dart that pierced Venus in play and caused her to fall in love with Adonis, Mirra's "tree-born" son (2:28.64).[23] Beatrice retrospectively names "Matelda . . . la bella donna" (2:33.129–30) when Matelda and Beatrice repeat to Dante the names of the twin streams in Matelda's garden: Lethe, forgetfulness of sin, and Eunoë, remembrance of every good deed.[24] This ripple of likeness along the female line blends Venus, Matelda, and Mirra together in the "mistura" of all earthly streams (2:28.29)[25] and furthers the chiastic play between the serial appearances of a "fair lady" and the revelations of and by Beatrice from the car of paternal deity in cantos 29–33.[26] Beatrice is the culminating point of the feminine series, but only insofar as she is turning back under the aegis of the male deity.

The dark glassy stream (2:28.30–33) in Matelda's garden evades the series of structural dichotomies clear/opaque, oblivion/memory, girl/matron, and the overriding dichotomy unmixed/mixed. The preteritive symbolism of the divided stream strategically divides Matelda from the polluting stain that is female nature in life, and it places her at a diametric angle of opposition to infernal Mirra. However, Matelda is poised before the final step that is Beatrice herself, and she must retain some tincture of female nature to offset Beatrice. When they are seen together in *Purgatorio* 33, the difference lies between young girl Matelda and grave matron Beatrice. The literal thresholds between Mirra and Matelda, Matelda and Beatrice, articulate natural female sexual knowledge of rape and supernatural female sexual knowledge of the father. *Purgatorio* 33 is a chiasmatic interchange between the "mistura" of all other streams and the transparent darkness of this one. The mystery of the dark glassy stream, like the meaning of the tree, is that knowledge of the father in the woman is not knowledge, let alone the woman's knowledge, but the very father himself in his seed before all seeds. "Mistura," sexual mingling, in the figure of Mirra is a romance of male gestation and delivery, in the figure of Matelda is a romance of the ever-renewing virginity of the son's identity with the father.

The description of the stream in Matelda's garden is quoted by Mary Shelley's Mathilda in chapter 12, but it omits the phrase that I have translated as "glassy." Dante's phrase is "che nulla nasconde," literally "which hides nothing." Mary Shelley's fictional heroine may hold back from the sign of "transparency," a key term in Rousseau's *Confessions*. Or, she may hold back to herself what she has to hide from Woodville at this late point in her story. She writes to Woodville: "I pictured to myself a lovely river such as that on whose banks Dante describes Mathilda gathering flowers, which ever flows . . . bruna, bruna/ Sotto l'ombra perpetua." Woodville is an English poet, so presumably the echo of Milton's "Proserpine gathering flowers" is also meant for his ears.

With this self-naming, Mathilda in her final chapter, 12, brings her artistry of quotation and chrestomathy to a crescendo. She improvises a finale that brings both mother and father back to her and replays the drama of the gaze and the reading of each other's faces that had proved fatal to her and her father when they were in their bodies. This concluding vision is recursive, and it recaps the starting moment of chapter 1, "Oedipus has come to die," with its missing speaker, Antigone, who has come to bury him. Mary Shelley takes considerable license with Dante's effects, mixing the colors of *Purgatorio*, with its magisterial Beatrice in the car, and *Paradiso*, where Beatrice "like a mother with her delirious child," and the pilgrim-poet with his eyes "lost" for wonder, both quoted in earlier chapters of Mathilda's tale, now revive their presences as Mathilda raises her eyes to her restored father and *neither he nor she looks away*. The adhesiveness of the Romantic poet to imaginary origins and originary imaginings repeats, as if for a final time, the obliteration of the sexual mother and the elevation of the nubile daughter to her father's knowledge.

Unlike Percy Bysshe Shelley, who by 1819 had launched himself as a European poet in expatriate exile,[27] Mary Shelley's poetic prose art could not abide foreigners, and her techniques of bricolage and macaronic pastiche in *Mathilda* are apotropaic fencings around her Godwin patronymic heritage, in which the maternal icon of Mary Wollstonecraft was niched. The name "Woodville" for the Shelleyan figure was a late choice, replacing "Lovel," a stage-aristocratic name. Woodville, like Florence, is a locality name, of the kind favored by Ann Radcliffe for her English protestant protagonists, moving in masquerade for their European excursions. The second half of *Mathilda* is notionally set in the north of England, but it is hard to avoid the impression that Mathilda sends Woodville back to England to take up his work.

Mathilda did not make its way into print because Godwin's reading of it was not of capable imagination to discover in it either the domestic realist or the protestant mythopoetic, English traditions. As it turned out, Godwin's rejection confirmed *Mathilda*'s diagnosis of the protagonist Mathilda's woe. Her father has never picked her up and named her, and she moves in an ellipse with no center, Proserpine at risk from Dis, at bay to Kör.

I have not sought to contain Mary Shelley's *Mathilda* within the frame of Dantesque pastiche or as an English prose paraphrase of Alfieri's *Mirra*. These are only vehicles of the text's eclectic fashioning. It is characteristic of the English protestant mythopoeic tradition, which Mary Shelley engages as a newcomer and latecomer, that it borrows freely from European and Catholic sources and adapts them to English cultivation. Bunyan's *Pilgrim's Progress* and the lifelong protestant dramaturgy of spiritual election are stronger presences than Dante's Catholic paradise or Alfieri's monarchist Duce. The Romantic dilemma of Mathilda's inward-turning gaze is that the gaze *cannot* turn away.

Notes

All parenthetical references to *The Divine Comedy of Dante Alighieri* in this essay, unless otherwise identified, are to the Italian text with translation and commentary edited by John D. Sinclair in 3 volumes (Oxford: Oxford University Press, 1971). Volume 1 contains *Inferno*, volume 2 *Purgatorio*, and volume 3 *Paradiso*.

1. *Metamorphoses of Ovid*, trans. Frank Justus Miller, 2nd ed., rev. G. P. Goold, 2 vols. (Cambridge, Mass.: Harvard University Press; London: Heinemann, 1984).

2. Peggy Kamuf's *Fictions of Feminine Desire: Disclosures of Heloïse* (Lincoln: University of Nebraska Press, 1982) maps the characters of Rousseau's novel *Julie; ou la Nouvelle Heloïse* onto the triad of God-Beatrice-Dante in *La Divina Commèdia*. Beatrice's final "turn" toward the "eternal fount" (*The Divine Comedy* 3:31.92–93) is reconfigured in Rousseau's novel as Julie-Heloïse's renunciation of her claims on Abelard-St Preux. Claire Tomalin, *The Life and Death of Mary Wollstonecraft* (New York, 1974; rprt., New York: Meridian/New American Library, 1983), 289, lists a London edition of *La Nouvelle Héloïse* in English translation in 1784, a Dublin edition in 1761.

3. I have used the Latin "Mirra" in preference to the Greek transliterated "Myrrha" throughout.

4. Alan Richardson, "*Proserpine* and *Midas*: Gender, Genre, and Mythic Revisionism in Mary Shelley's Dramas," in *The Other Mary Shelley: Beyond Frankenstein*, ed. Audrey A. Fisch, Anne K. Mellor, and Esther H. Schor (New York: Oxford University Press, 1993), 138. Richardson describes the Ovidian plays of 1820 as "revisionist responses to Ovid and the tradition he represents, as generic experiments related in a complex, critical manner to the 'visionary' lyrics [by P. B. Shelley] framed within them, and as early, if oblique, attempts to explore the cultic roots of Greek tragedy and myth."

5. *The Plays of Euripides in English*, introduction by V. R. Reynolds, 2 vols. (London: J. M. Dent; New York: E. P. Dutton, 1906–8), 1:121.

6. See especially *The Journals of Mary Shelley 1814–1844*, ed. Paula R. Feldman and Diana Scott-Kilvert (Baltimore, Md.: Johns Hopkins University Press, 1987); *The Letters of Mary Wollstonecraft Shelley*, ed. Betty T. Bennett, 3 vols. (Baltimore, Md.: Johns

Hopkins University Press, 1980–88); Emily W. Sunstein, *Mary Shelley: Romance and Reality* (Baltimore, Md.: Johns Hopkins University Press, 1989).

7. Elizabeth Nitchie, ed., "Mathilda; Fields of Fancy" (Chapel Hill: University of North Carolina Press, 1959), 81, notes two lengthy drafts, and a number of fragments, in the Bodleian, Oxford, Godwin-Shelley Collection of Abinger manuscripts of *Fields of Fancy*.

8. Cf. Sunstein, *Mary Shelley*, 174 and n. 22, quoting passages of Godwin's letter to Mary Shelley on 19 September 1819.

9. Ibid., 179.

10. Godwin denounced the manuscript as a "detestable" work by one of the "authors of the modern school" (cited in Sunstein, *Mary Shelley*, 436 n. 41, citing *Maria Gisborne and Edward E. Williams, Shelley's Friends: Their Journals and Letters*, ed. Frederick L. Jones [Norman: University of Oklahoma Press, 1951], 44). He refused repeated requests to return this sole copy to Mary Shelley, which prevented her from reworking or publishing it. The manuscript finally published by Elizabeth Nitchie in 1959 bore few revisions or corrections, according to Terence Harpold, "'Did You Get Mathilda from Papa?': Seduction Fantasy and the Circulation of Mary Shelley's *Mathilda*," *Studies in Romanticism* 28.1 [1989]: 51 n. 22.

11. Sunstein, *Mary Shelley*, 190.

12. "Elizabeth Villiers" is the first story, illustrated by the frontispiece, in *Mrs Leicester's School: or, The History of several Young Ladies, Related by Themselves*, 2nd ed. (London: M. J. Godwin, 1809). Printed for the family firm of M. J. Godwin and Co., at the Juvenile Library, no. 41 Skinner Street, this is one of the books likely to have been read by the child Mary Godwin before her departure to Scotland in 1812. Seven of the ten stories in the collection were written by Mary Lamb.

13. Mary Shelley may have known the celebrated group portrait, painted by Richard Samuel c.1779, of the *Nine Living Muses of Great Britain*, showing the women of the "Bluestockings" generation immediately before Wollstonecraft's as the statuesque muses—of history (Catharine Macaulay), music (Elizabeth Linley Sheridan), and so on.

14. Godwin's hostile reaction in 1820 is perceptive in making the Gothic reader's suspense about Mathilda's "fall" central to the drama (of Mathilda's poetic election, I have argued).

15. Michelle Massé, *In the Name of Love: Women, Masochism, and the Gothic* (Ithaca: Cornell University Press, 1992), revises Freud's description of the repeated circlings of the site of archaic trauma, so symptomatic of anxiety. The return of an original "forgetfulness" opens a second chance, an exergue on which the subject fantasmatically inscribes an altered signature.

16. This is a classic locus for (the absence of) the father, as in Homer's description of the sword on the wall of Telemachus's bedroom in Ithaca during Odysseus's absence.

17. Dante's "la donna della torma" may possibly throw light on William Blake's name "Theotormon" for the punitive keeper of the seduced and abandoned Oothoon in *Visions of the Daughters of Albion* (1793).

18. Notes to the performances of Alfieri's *Mirra* attended by the Shelley party, including Byron, are in *The Journals of Claire Clairmont,* ed. Marion Kingston Stocking, with the assistance of David Mackenzie Stocking (Cambridge, Mass.: Harvard University Press, 1968), 52, 502. Other references to Alfieri are to be found in *Letters of Percy Bysshe Shelley*, ed. Frederick L. Jones, 2 vols. (Oxford: Clarendon Press, 1964), 2:39.

19. A significant departure from Dante appears in P. B. Shelley's *Prometheus Unbound*, act 4, written in autumn 1819, at the same time as Mary Shelley's *Fields of Fancy/Mathilda*. The car of the moon (of maternal rather than paternal deity) appears with a sleeping baby (an "it" not a "he" or a "she") in the vision of Asia's two sisters, Ione and Panthea. These angelic helpers at the birth of the new Promethean world are impeccably sisterly.

20. Sunstein, *Mary Shelley*, 178, argues from the evidence of *Mathilda* and the letters of Mary and Bysshe Shelley that he was using Mary as a "sitter" for the portrait of Beatrice Cenci. But it was the Irish actress Eliza O'Neill that he wanted for the stage debut, as Mary Shelley states in her notes to *The Cenci* in *The Poetical Works of Percy Bysshe Shelley*, 4 vols. (London: Edward Moxon, 1839).

21. Gary Kelly, *The English Jacobin Novel 1780–1805* (Oxford: Clarendon Press, 1976), 209–10, points to the play on royal Jacobite names in Wollstonecraft's *Wrongs of Woman*, e.g. Maria=Maria Stuarda, Darnford=Darnley, giving it a spin toward "commonlife" morganatic romance and royal scandals memoir.

22. Journal entry of 8 May 1820, in *Maria Gisborne and Edward E. Williams, Shelley's Friends: Their Journals and Letters*, 27. Gisborne's description of Godwin in Skinner Street in August 1820 is distinctly unflattering to him (44).

23. See the notes to canto 28, in *Dante's Purgatory,* translated with notes and commentary by Mark Musa (Bloomington.: Indiana University Press, 1981), 306–7. Musa glosses "the meaning of the tree" in canto 32 as "Beatrice as guardian of the recessed seed of all righteousness" (430).

24. Matelda had earlier instructed Dante: "Da questa parte con virtù discende/ che toglie altrui memoria del peccato;/ dall'altra d'ogni ben fatto la rende" (*The Divine Comedy* 2: 28.127–29).

25. The word "mistura" is glossed in English translations as: "defilement" (Sinclair), "some mixture" (Longfellow, Norton edition), and "cloudy tinge" (Musa).

26. William Blake's engraved series of illustrations of Dante, showing Beatrice and the car, are near contemporary with the composing of Mary Shelley's *Mathilda*.

27. Sunstein, *Mary Shelley*, 177, dates the Shelley couple's acceptance of expatriation to their move to Florence in October 1819 for Percy Florence's birth.

"Knew shame, and knew desire": Ambivalence as Structure in Mary Shelley's *Mathilda*

Audra Dibert Himes

"Such is my name, and such my tale,
Confessor—to thy secret ear,
I breathe the sorrows I bewail,
And thank thee for the generous tear
This glazing eye could never shed."

—Lord Byron, "The Giaour" (1813)

Mathilda is an arresting, riveting work, strange in its representation of incestuous love yet believable in its evocation of forbidden desire. The tightly confined internal and external spaces of and around the title character, who is the scriptor of this confessional work, force the reader to participate with Mathilda in the text. The reader cannot objectively receive the novel but must engage with Mathilda in her psychological landscape, and that is an area fraught with ambivalence created by vacillation between two equally powerful poles: Mathilda's position as both the subject and the object of the verb "to desire." This ambivalence provides the structural and intellectual underpinning for the story as a whole, both within the text and, by extension, within the consciousness of the responding reader.

Mathilda's father and his desire for her are the figure and force that determine her internal world and her responses to the external one. Of course, incest is one conventional theme in eighteenth- and nineteenth-

115

century British literature; therefore, we should not be titillated to find that Mary Shelley, an informed reader and writer, used it in her own writing as well. Yet in her novel, Mary Shelley considers the theme of incest in a way that is quite different from the portrayals of incestuous pairs that are found in her sources' works, including Ovid and Vittorio Alfieri,[1] and her contemporaries' writings. The difference is the way in which the novel treats the issue of Mathilda's desire, an especially transgressive one, and how she attempts at once to confess and cloister herself and her desire, both by choice and imposition.

Before beginning an exploration of the novel's sources, we must demarcate the ground between Mary Shelley and Mathilda. I treat Mary Shelley as an author function in this study; her proper name is that which assures a "classificatory function."[2] Treating Mary Shelley in this way prevents a biographical reading of *Mathilda*, a reading that has been ventured already by other students of Shelley's work.[3] As Roland Barthes asserts about biographical criticism, "*Explanation* of the work is still sought in the person of its producer, as if, through the more or less transparent allegory of fiction, it was always, ultimately, the voice of one and the same person, the *author*, which was transmitting [her] 'confidences.'"[4] Treating Mary Shelley as an author function allows us to focus more clearly on Mathilda as the *scriptor* of *Mathilda* who "is born *at the same time* as [her] text." Mary Shelley "is not the subject of which [her] book would be the predicate"; rather, Mathilda is the book, and the book is Mathilda (52).

Yet examining two works that contain plots based upon father-daughter incest that Mary Shelley, the biographical author, read leads us toward a better understanding of how differently the same subject is treated in *Mathilda*.[5] Shelley's principal sources for her unsettling story are Ovid's *Metamorphoses* and Vittorio Alfieri's tragedy *Myrrha*.[6] *Myrrha* is a story of incestuous desire and passion felt by the title character/protagonist of the play for her father, Cinyras. Throughout the play, Myrrha suffers from guilt that is provoked by something that remains unnamed until the terminal moments of the action. Every character in the play (which includes only Myrrha, Myrrha's beloved father, and her mother, nurse, and fiancé) and the audience/reader guess at the cause of Myrrha's misery, evidenced by her physical and verbal expressions of despondency and affliction. However, the dramatic structure itself functions as a nondisclosing narrator.

The master stroke of Alfieri's work is the remarkable, forced nondisclosure of Myrrha's desire. The nondisclosure unfolds the narrative slowly and thereby compels the audience/reader to stay with the play in order to partake of the pleasure of discovering what impels the text. Franco Betti notes that we, the audience to Myrrha's suffering, "become so engrossed with [her] behavior that we forget what causes it. . . . [A]lmost paradoxically, [Alfieri] can create an eventful action where apparently there would be none."[7]

Ambivalence underpins the structure of Alfieri's play as it does in *Mathilda*. Alfieri promotes ambivalence in the reader's response to *Myrrha* by pairing the implication that the young woman's passion is as unnatural as it is misdirected with the verbal underscoring of Cinyras's paternal love for his child. Over and over again, Myrrha's father asserts his sensitivity and his wish for her happiness. The most pointed of these exclamations of his love occurs in the first act:

> Nature made me a father; chance a king.
> Those which are deem'd by others of my rank,
> Reasons of state, to which they are accustom'd
> To make all natural affections yield,
> In my paternal bosom would not weigh
> Against a solitary sigh of Myrrha's.
> I, by her happiness alone, can be
> Myself made happy. [8]

In this passage, Cinyras's words stress his concern and love for his daughter. Against that filial responsibility, we compare what we might suspect already to be Myrrha's misplaced and transgressive passion and sexual desire for him.

Alfieri treats Myrrha's ardor more subtly than Ovid treats the same theme in *Metamorphoses*, Alfieri's acknowledged source.[9] In Alfieri's play, Myrrha's yearning drives her mad because she believes that it is immoral and unnatural to feel such an emotion. She commits suicide because she thinks that her desire has contaminated her completely, making her a wholly unnatural creature. She is a human degraded to a beast—an Ovidian transformation that happens because Myrrha fails to recognize and regulate her appetites. Her filial affection transposes into a discordant key, that of physical passion for her father. In *Metamorphoses*, Ovid's Myrrha is tormented by her desire, but not for the same reason as in Alfieri's *Myrrha*; in fact, Ovid's Myrrha consents to a sexual quenching of her fires, while Alfieri moralizes the myth.

Alfieri's Myrrha can neither name her desire nor its object for most of the play, and when she finally does, it costs her her life to voice her craving. Myrrha's naming the object of her desire is her final confession. Her confessor is her father/beloved, who forces the confession from her by threatening to withhold from Myrrha his adoration of her. After

Myrrha tells Cinyras finally that he is the one she wants and then stabs herself with his dagger, she gasps, "—Thou thy-self, . . . / By dint of violence, . . . from my heart . . . didst wrest . . . / The horrid secret . . . But since . . . with my life . . . / It parted . . . from my lips, . . . I die . . . less guilty. . . ."[10] Confession equals expiation from her sin of transgressive desire for Myrrha. She has called herself "an impious wretch" before this confession, so Myrrha is very much concerned with the idea that her desire is a sin (Act 4, Scene 7). In Ovid's "The Story of Cinyras and Myrrha," Myrrha is able to murmur, "O mother, mother, happy in your husband!" which is enough to galvanize her nurse to the action of tricking Cinyras into accepting his daughter into his bed.[11] Thus, the main point of Ovid's story is not the struggle within Myrrha, the struggle that silences her and leads to her climactic confession, as it is in the tragedy. Instead, Ovid focuses our attention on Myrrha's emotional state after her sexual union with her father and the consequent conception of her sibling/offspring Adonis.

The narrative voice of *Metamorphoses* states explicitly that the passion the reader is to witness is morally unnatural, something left implicit in Alfieri's play. The *Metamorphoses* narrator exclaims:

> The story
> Is terrible, I warn you. Fathers, daughters,
> Had better skip this part, or, if you like my songs,
> Distrust me here, and say it never happened,
> Or, if you do believe it, take my word
> That it was paid for. Nature, it may be,
> Permits such things to happen. I would offer
> Our land congratulations, that it lies
> So far away from such abominations.
>
> (10.5.299–306)

The dichotomy here between what might be considered strictly "natural" and what is actually socially permissible, and even legal, admits that a culture's demands can override the desires of Nature, an idea to which we will return.

Whether or not the Ovidian narrator recognizes that something such as incestuous love might be strictly "natural," both Myrrhas are devastated and driven to annihilation after they realize their desire to the outer world either by word, as with Alfieri's character, or by deed, as with Ovid's. Nevertheless, neither of these characters is able to express precisely what she feels; indeed, Ovid's Myrrha is unable to name what she has done in having sex with her father. Even after she has conceived her father's child, she is able to pray for her own eradication with only these words:

> O gods,
> If any gods will listen, I deserve
> Punishment surely. I do not refuse it,
> But lest, in living, I offend the living,
> Offend the dead in death, drive me away
> From either realm, change me somehow, refuse me
> Both life and death!
>
> (10.5.483–89)

Forbidden desire, alluded to in this prayer, silences both Ovid's and Alfieri's Myrrhas, but the insularity and narcissism of their desires also make each of them mute. However, Mary Shelley's Mathilda does not voice or show her transgressive desire to her father during his life or in his presence, and that is not the only difference between Shelley's conception of incestuous desire and that of her sources.

The first difference between *Mathilda* and the two Myrrha stories lies in the novel's narrative scheme. Instead of an outside narrator recounting an age-old tale, as in Ovid, or a gradually unfolding structure governed by the main character's actions, as in Alfieri, *Mathilda* is narrated by the young woman who is at first the object of her father's desire but who then realizes that her desire for him has surrounded his for her, for her desire has preceded his and endures and follows it. No other characters intervene in this transgressive relationship. In fact, there are few characters who act in Mathilda's story; Woodville, her father, and she are the only three who directly affect the unfolding plot (her mother, aunt, childhood nurse, and would-be lover are mentioned). Mary Shelley's limited cast is like that of Alfieri's tragedy, in which five characters make up the dramatis personae. The few actors and the limited time-frame in which the work is written by the dying Mathilda make the book necessarily condensed. Mathilda certainly could not write many volumes in her weak condition during the "three months" left to her before she succumbs, yet the novel has been criticized for following this logic.[12] Jane Blumberg states that the book "does not rank as one of Shelley's important novels; it is remarkably slim compared to her customary three-volume works of fiction. . . . [I]t is undisciplined and uncomfortably personal,"[13] and Tilottama Rajan asserts that "*Mathilda* is a short, bare narrative of trauma."[14] The book is not short or slim because it is "uncomfortably personal" or traumatic; rather, it is uncomfortable for the reader because it is so devoid of any perspective except Mathilda's.[15] Consequently, the reader must share Mathilda's vision of the world because it is the only moral, emotional, and intellectual universe offered to her or him. This exceptionally tight focus on Mathilda's inner realm does not mar the work. It is part of the overall design of the novel, a design like the one that Mary Shelley recognized to be at work in Alfieri's tragedies.

In her biocritical essay on Alfieri, Shelley delineates his narrative strategy:

> Energy and conciseness are the distinguishing marks of Alfieri's dramas. Wishing to bring the whole action of the piece into one focus, he rejected altogether the *confidantes* of the French theatre [explained later as "the action being carried on by a perpetual talk about it"], so that his dramatis personae are limited to the principals themselves. The preservation of the unities of time and place also contributed to curtail all excrescences; so that his tragedies are short, and all bear upon one point only, which he considered the essence of unity of action.[16]

Mathilda and *Myrrha* are similar in their limited numbers of principals, and even as, according to Mary Shelley, Alfieri's "tragedies are short, and . . . bear upon one point only," so is and does her novel. The unities of time and place are established otherwise in *Mathilda*, however. In Mary Shelley's work, they are congruent within Mathilda's mind. In her consciousness and memory, everything that has happened to her over the preceding four years and all the locations where she has been are fused, and every event is happening at every place at this moment, the moment of her writing her final confession.

As Michel Foucault writes, "For us, it is in the confession that truth and sex are joined through the obligatory and exhaustive expression of an individual secret."[17] *Mathilda* and its creator/creation, Mathilda, is such an expression. The novel is what Foucault calls a "discourse of truth":

> The confession is a ritual of discourse in which the speaking subject is also the subject of the statement; it is also a ritual that unfolds within a power relationship, for one does not confess without the presence (or virtual presence) of a partner who is not simply the interlocutor but the authority who requires the confession, prescribes and appreciates it, and intervenes in order to judge, punish, forgive, console, and reconcile. (62)

The naturalness versus unnaturalness of incestuous desire is what creates ambivalence in *Mathilda*. Our own ethical system—the guidelines for social behavior in which we live—defines Mathilda's passion as unnatural. Thus, because she has violated our ethics, Mathilda's culture—again, our own—demands a confession from her about her father's and her transgressive desire so that she may expiate her guilt, just as Alfieri's Myrrha confessed her desire and believed that she died less guilty of it. As Mathilda begins her tale, she writes, "Perhaps a history such as mine had better die with me, but a feeling that I cannot define leads me on."[18] This feeling is the pressure on her of the reader's desire—and the reader is the law's representative as she or he participates in the text—to know about Mathilda's position as the creation and creator of this text of incestuous desire. This relationship based on desire—the reader/advocate of the law's desire to know Mathilda's relation to her and her father's desire—makes the text seem "uncomfortably personal." The reader gains pleasure initially through the power of being Mathilda's confessor, but the pleasure is mitigated first by the reader's realization that the pleasure can come only through an intimate knowledge of a transgressive, unlawful desire, and second by the reader's realization that Mathilda wants only a listener, not a confessor who might offer her absolution.

Mathilda's work is a testament that constitutes a voicing of her desire and a confession of what she has felt and continues to feel until the conclusion of the tale as she waits to die in her self-made cloister. Mathilda is actively cloistering her emotional and physical desire by turning life into art—into discourse. Foucault explains that during confession "a twofold evolution tend[s] to make the flesh into the root of all evil, shifting the most important moment of transgression from the act itself to the stirrings—so difficult to perceive and formulate—of desire."[19] Within her story, Mathilda divulges to the reader the culmination of her father's confession of his stirred desire for her in the form of the revealing epistle that he addresses to her, a letter that mirrors in a reduced size her own confessional document that inhabits the space around that smaller text. Also, the narrative frame formed by confessional document surrounding confessional document echoes the way in which Mathilda's longing for her father precedes, surrounds, and endures his desire for her. Mathilda replicates her father's confession for her reader; she then reveals how his confession affects her feelings. Although the act of physical incest never takes place between father and daughter—the incest is psychic, and her remorse arises from thought, not deed—Mathilda traces and retraces "the stirrings" of desire that move in both of them.

Her father's letter traces the stirrings of only his desire, but after she has read it, Mathilda's tumultuous phrasing reveals a deep ambivalence as she brushes against the subject of her feelings for her father:

> He must know that if I believed that his intention was merely to absent himself from me that instead of opposing him it would be that which I should myself require—or if he thought that any lurking feeling, yet he could not

think that, should lead me to him would he endeavor to overthrow the only hope he could have of ever seeing me again.[20]

Mathilda's father has already made a demand on her by communicating to her, however ambivalently, his desire when he stated, "'Yes, yes, I hate you! You are my bane, my poison, my disgust! Oh! No! . . . [Y]ou are none of all these; you are my light, my only one, my life.—My daughter, I love you!'" (201). Jacques Lacan writes, "As an unconditional demand of presence and absence, demand evokes the want-to-be under the three figures of the nothing that constitutes the basis of the demand for love, of the hate that even denies the other's being, and of the unspeakable element in that which is ignored in its request."[21] These three figures conflict in *Mathilda* to create the ambivalence in the desire of the protagonist (Mathilda) and the antagonist (her father) for each other.

Undoubtedly, Mathilda feels a keen desire for her father. She has practically willed and prayed her father back to life, and in her intense desire to know him, she has developed a deep desire for his presence in her life and for him as a person—his body. He was dead to her; she had never met him. Her father had lived only as a letter, another text within the text of *Mathilda*, and Mathilda underscores that letter's significance when she confesses, "I bestowed on him all my affections; there was a miniature of him that I gazed on continually; I copied his last letter and read it again and again."[22] She relates that he was "the idol of my imagination," and her actions toward the relics of him that he has left behind are very much like those of a lover who has lost her beloved. Mathilda desires her father, and his absence allowed her longing for his presence to develop into idealizing him and, finally, idolizing him.

After Mathilda reads her father's confession to her, she realizes that he reciprocates her desire, indeed, her sexual passion. She states that her father is "a lover, there was madness in the thought, yet he was my lover" (211). Malcolm Bowie asserts that any person to whom another person makes an appeal cannot answer it unconditionally, and "he too is divided and haunted, and his *yes*, however loudly it is proclaimed, can only ever be a *maybe*, or a *to some extent* in disguise."[23]

When Mathilda states unequivocally that her father is her lover, she accepts her father's demand, although she never proclaims a loud *yes*. In spite of the fact that her desire has preceded his, Mathilda is especially "divided and haunted"; her feelings about her father's confessed desire for her are conflicting, and her answer to her father is particularly equivocal. All of her ambivalence is caused by the socially defined unnaturalness of the desire that she perceives, a definition with which she agrees, despite her yearning for her father. When Mathilda recognizes her own passion as she reads his letter, a recognition signaled by her understanding that her father is her lover, the novel begins to travel on one path of development—others are closed for the story, Mathilda, and the reader. Thus, the act of reading performs a cardinal function in the narrative. Mathilda's declaration of awareness, instigated by reading—"a lover, there was madness in the thought, yet he was my lover"—is the core of this novel.

When the plot of her life and her text takes this turn, Mathilda turns with it. Instead of willing her now dead father back to life, she wills herself to death. Mathilda states that she looks forward to death because "alone it will unite me to my father when in an eternal mental union we shall never part."[24] Her death is a *liebestod*, an extension of her sexual desire. Her phrase "an eternal mental union" is her carnal desire disguised and an excellent demonstration of her use of ambivalence as a technique of self-cloistering.

The first step that Mathilda takes to make herself dead to the world, and hence closer to her father, is to cloister herself. This is a state to which she is accustomed. As a child, Mathilda was cloistered in solitude in the cathedral of nature. She had loved with a deep attachment the inanimate nature she had found on her aunt's Loch Lomond estate. When her father came to her finally, Mathilda stayed in the woods the night before his arrival, sequestered by nature for the last time. When she tried to return home the next day, the woods attempted to encompass her and to keep her in their embrace. Shelley's trees might be related to Ovid's Myrrha, who has turned into the myrrh tree after her prayer to the gods to obliterate her as a human. It is tempting in this context to see the Scottish woodlands as attempting to keep Mathilda from experiencing the maddening physical desire that Myrrha felt, as if Ovid's metamorphosed Myrrha were attempting to protect Mathilda from herself.

However, after her father confesses verbally to Mathilda, she turns away from the natural world. Rather than retreating into nature to find solace for her pain, which is what we might expect, Mathilda puts a barrier between herself and it. Indeed, "perfect solitude" from everything well describes the state of existence that Mathilda strives to find. Mathilda emphasizes her solitude when she writes:

> Even after this, I thought, I would live in the most dreary seclusion. I would retire to the Continent and become a nun; not for religion's sake, for I was not a Catholic, but that I might be for ever shut out from the world. (204)

Here we find the first explicit evidence that Mathilda wishes to cloister her body, her desire, and her entire self. The only way that she can think of to cope with what she feels is to remove herself in every possible way, but not from desire.

Mathilda considers removing herself from the social world by assuming a facade. She concludes that she "must heap an impenetrable heap of false smiles and words: cunning frauds, treacherous laughter, and a mixture of all light deceits" (216). Her mind continues to wander, creating many different types of mental and emotional cloisters where she might shelter herself. She writes, "I dared not die, but I might feign death" (216).

One of the most effective ways to "feign death" from the world, to annihilate herself from the world of the living while yet retaining life, would seem to be to silence her writer self about her experiences with her father and her desire for him. Mathilda, though, attempts to subdue herself by removing herself from all human company. She leaves London for the wild heath of the north country and describes herself as she appeared on her journey:

> A youthful Hermitess dedicated to seclusion and whose bosom she must strive to keep free from all tumult and unholy despair—The fanciful nun-like dress that I had adopted; the knowledge that my very existence was a secret known only to myself; the solitude to which I was for ever hereafter destined nursed gentle thoughts in my wounded heart. (219)

Mathilda's story has broached the classic element of the recognition of desire. That recognition leads to a cloistering of the self from the world, which leads to confession in order to explain her reasons for cloistering herself. It is this confessional and seclusive aspect of self that Mathilda creates through her writing and that, in turn, creates her.

Seclusion was supposed to lead a woman into the contemplative life, a life in which she could empty herself of concern for the world.[25] The cloister, or anchor hold, was to function as a tomb, making its inhabitant "dead to the world" (3). From there, the anchorite was to live a life of quiet thought, prayer, and meditation, preparing herself for her union with God, a union that was often consummated in a spiritual marriage between the woman and the Holy Spirit or Christ.

Mathilda enters her own self-made cloister on the heath in northern England, and there she arrives through her writing at an intellectually active life rather than a contemplative one. Her verbal self will not be silenced. It feels the demand of the law to know her desire, so it gives a voice through writing to Mathilda's sins of thought. Her writing functions in several ways: it acts as an exercise in remembering and keeping alive her love, and it serves as a confession, ostensibly for Woodville's eyes but in reality for any other reader's.

Another unconventional aspect of Mathilda's self-cloistering is her method of prayer: "And morning and evening my tearful eyes raised to heaven, my hands clasped tight in the energy of prayer, I have repeated with the poet—

> Before I see another day
> Oh, let this body die away!"[26]

Nowhere does Mathilda mention a complete turning away from the world, toward God. Indeed, in this passage, she bases her appeal on contemporary Romantic poetry, not around traditional invocations, as we would expect from a woman who had cloistered herself in the conventional sense of the term. Myrrha's prayer in Ovid, quoted above, is unconventional, as is her inability to give her act a name and thus confess to the gods what she has done. Throughout most of her confession, Mathilda never states explicitly her desire to satisfy her father's desire. She is part of a culture that deems such desire nefarious; therefore, she is ambivalent about her own feelings. Neither Ovid's Myrrha nor Shelley's Mathilda can articulate why she wants to be removed from humanity or the world. Their transgressive desires, which put them so far outside the standards of their communities, preclude their full confessions because they have no language with which to portray what they feel.

In the very act of confession, however, Mathilda forms another cloister for herself. We can see that she attempts to explain her desire to her reader by confessing it, "by the mere fact of transforming it—fully and deliberately—into discourse."[27] The conversion of desire into discourse, an act that gives the unnamed passion formal bounds, invests in the reader a great deal of power over judgment. The reader becomes Mathilda's confessor through the process of participating in the text, but in the end, Mathilda does not wish for expiation from the reader/confessor for her sin of desire because that would amount to an emptying of desire from herself. Instead, she wishes for an even closer union with her father, the "eternal mental union" from which "we shall never part."

This is not a comfortable ending for the reader. Because Mathilda's incestuous desire crosses the taboo line, the reader instinctively wishes for a closing that will rectify the character of Mathilda.[28] However, the reader's desire for an ending in which Mathilda would renounce her "unnatural" desire clashes with Mathilda's desire to experience the desire of her father more fully. The reader, who presumably believes and obeys the Electra taboo surrounding father-daughter incestuous love, cannot accept Mathilda's desire and absolve her of its societally defined sinfulness. The subject of the story, then, the reader's inability to resolve the tensions between her or his desire for an ending that is empty of desire, and Mathilda's desire to fulfill her desire, prevent any neat closure.

The reader is left, too, with the tension created between the concepts of "natural" and "unnatural." Another dichotomy of naturalness versus unnaturalness involves the description of the fresh, blooming season of the year and Mathilda's imminent death in that month: "It was May, four years ago, that I first saw my beloved father; it was in May, three years ago that my folly destroyed the only being I was doomed to love. May is returned, and I die."[29] In this, the penultimate paragraph of her confession, Mathilda breaks her silence about her passion for her father and names it "love." Perhaps this naming of her desire is really the purpose of this confession. She does not seek absolution; she seeks realization for herself of what she feels.

Peter L. Thorslev Jr. states, "Parent-child incest is universally condemned in Romantic literature" and goes on to assert that "when it does appear—notably in England in Walpole's *The Mysterious Mother* and in [Percy Bysshe] Shelley's *The Cenci*—it is always the object of horror."[30] Mathilda reveals, though, that she feels the same desire as her father and yearns to join him at some other level of consciousness, a less than horrified reaction to his initially expressed want for her. The Romantic norm might be to seek transcendence from the physical world through a metaphysical affair with nature or art; however, Mary Shelley's revised Romanticism has her Mathilda seeking the metaphysical in the physical, or more exactly, carnal union with the forbidden figure.

In approaching Mary Shelley's work as it resides within the context of persistent Romantic themes, it is not interesting in and of itself that she chose the theme of incest as a subject early in her writing life. Many writers of the eighteenth and nineteenth centuries chose it, chief among them her contemporaries, who surrounded her in Leghorn as she wrote the tale that would become *Mathilda*. But the structure of her story, the sources that she drew on in creating it, and her inversion of certain ethical and traditional aspects of incest, such as the movement toward spiritual unification of the emotionally incestuous pair, make her work intriguing. The highly individualistic creativity apparent in Mary Shelley's *Mathilda* shows this novel to be a vital work of art worthy of serious and sustained consideration.

Notes

I thank Professor Stephen C. Behrendt for his generosity in giving me the opportunity to begin this work. I thank Professor Frederick S. Frank for his astute, critical eye. And, as always, thank you, Glenn T. Dibert-Himes, for the innumerables.

1. Jean de Palacio minimizes Alfieri's influence on most of Mary Shelley's work but admits its effect on *Mathilda* when he writes, "Quant à Alfieri, son influence se limite pratiquement au seul motif littéraire de l'inceste; aussi trouvera-t-on ce point traité dans le cadre des éléments gothiques" (*Mary Shelley dans son oeuvre: Contributions aux études Shelleyennes* [Paris: Éditions Klincksieck, 1969], 23). He also hints at a biographical reading of the novel: "Sans nier ici l'influence de la *Myrrha* d'Alfieri, on retrouve dans ce livre des résonances profonde qu'une simple rencontre littéraire ne suffirait pas à expliquer. *Mathilda* n'est pas une oeuvre de circonstance, mais le développement d'un thème qui lui tenait à coeur et dont son propre cas peut fourmir le point de départ" (133).

2. Michel Foucault, "What Is an Author?" trans. Josué V. Harari, in *Textual Strategies: Perspectives in Post-Structuralist Criticism*, ed. Josué V. Harari (Ithaca: Cornell University Press, 1979), 141–60. Reprinted in Robert Con Davis and Ronald Schliefer, eds., *Contemporary Literary Criticism: Literary and Cultural Studies*, 3rd ed. (New York: Longman, 1994), 342–53. Foucault suggests that such a name used as an author function "permits one to group together a certain number of texts, define them, differentiate them from and contrast them to others" (346).

3. For biographical and psychobiographical readings of *Mathilda*, see the following writers: Jane Blumberg, *Mary Shelley's Early Novels: "This Child of Imagination and Misery"* (Iowa City: University of Iowa Press, 1993); Paula R. Feldman and Diana Scott-Kilvert, eds., *The Journals of Mary Shelley, 1814–1844*, 3 vols. (Oxford: Clarendon Press, 1987); Terence Harpold, "'Did You Get Mathilda from Papa?': Seduction Fantasy and the Circulation of Mary Shelley's *Mathilda*," *Studies in Romanticism* 28.1 (1989): 49–67; Anne K. Mellor, *Mary Shelley: Her Life, Her Fiction, Her Monsters* (New York: Methuen, 1988); Bonnie Rayford Neumann, *The Lonely Muse—A Critical Biography of Mary Wollstonecraft Shelley*, Salzburg Studies in English Literature 85 (Salzburg, Austria: Institut für Anglistik und Amerikanistik, 1979); Elizabeth Nitchie, "Mary Shelley's *Mathilda*: An Unpublished Story and Its Biographical Significance," *Studies in Philology* 40 (1943): 447–62; Audrey A. Fisch, Anne K. Mellor, and Esther H. Schor, eds., *The Other Mary Shelley: Beyond Frankenstein* (New York: Oxford University Press, 1993); Tilottama Rajan, "Mary Shelley's *Mathilda*: Melancholy and the Political Economy of Romanticism," *Studies in the Novel* 26.2 (1994): 43–68; Janet Todd, *Mary, Maria and Matilda* (New York: New York University Press, 1992); William Walling, *Mary Shelley* (New York: Twayne, 1972).

4. Roland Barthes, "From Work to Text," in *The Rustle of Language*, trans. Richard Howard (Berkeley: University of California Press, 1986), 50.

5. From Feldman and Scott-Kilvert, *The Journals of Mary Shelley,* we find that in October 1814 she read *Vita di Vittorio Alfieri . . . scritta da esso* (1804), translated as *Memoirs of the Life and Writings of Victor Alfieri . . . written by himself* (1810) (632); in April and May 1815, she read Ovid's *Metamorphoses* (665); a few months later, between 4 August and 12 September 1815, she wrote "The Fields of Fancy," the first version of *Mathilda* (294, 296); in September and October 1818, she read Alfieri's *Work* (632); on Monday, 14 September 1818, she had begun to translate Alfieri's *Myrrha* (226); and on 15 March 1819, she might have been continuing her translation of Alfieri (253). The

beginning of Mary Shelley's drafting *Mathilda* and Percy Bysshe Shelley's ending *The Cenci* overlap—he ended his work on 8 August 1819, she began *Mathilda* on 4 August; she ended her work on *Mathilda* on 12 September 1819 (Mary Shelley, *The Letters of Mary Wollstonecraft Shelley*. ed. Betty T. Bennett, 3 vols. [Baltimore, Md.: Johns Hopkins University Press, 1980], 104, 105). (Palacio examines the period of Percy's writing of *The Cenci* and Mary's writing of *Mathilda* [*Mary Shelley dans son oeuvre,* 134–35]). Feldman and Scott-Kilvert note that when Mary Shelley recorded "write & correct—" in her journal entry for Friday, 11 February 1820, she meant "probably *Mathilda*," and they add that "The fair-copy version . . . is dated 'Florence Nov. 9th 1819'" (308).

6. Mathilda names Vittorio Alfieri in chapter 4 of *Mathilda*: "I chanced to say that I thought *Myrrha* the best of Alfieri's tragedies" (Mary Shelley, "Mathilda," in *The Mary Shelley Reader*, ed. Betty T. Bennett and Charles E. Robinson [New York: Oxford University Press, 1990], 192).

7. Franco Betti, *Vittorio Alfieri*, ed. Anthony Oldcorn (Boston: Twayne, 1984), 83.

8. Vittorio Alfieri, "Myrrha," in *The Tragedies of Vittorio Alfieri; Translated from the Italian*, 3 vols., trans. Charles Lloyd (London: Longman, Hurst, Rees, Orme, and Brown, 1815), Act 1, Scene 3. This is the edition that Feldman and Scott-Kilvert believe Mary Shelley read (226 n. 7).

9. In Mary Shelley's biographical sketch of Alfieri, she quotes his discussion about Ovid's Myrrha from his autobiography: "'I had never thought,' he says, 'either of Myrrha or Biblis as subjects for the drama. But, in reading Ovid's 'Metamorphoses,' I hit upon the affecting and divinely eloquent speech of Myrrha to her nurse, which caused me to burst into tears, and, like a flash of lightning, awoke in me the idea of a tragedy. . . . My idea was, that she should do in my tragedy what Ovid describes her as relating, but do it in silence'" (Mary Shelley, "Alfieri: 1749–1803," in *Lives of the Most Eminent Literary and Scientific Men of Italy, Spain and Portugal*, 2 vols. [London: Longman, Rees, Orme, Brown, Green and Longman, 1835], 2:291–92).

10. Alfieri, "Myrrha," Act 5, Scene 2.

11. Ovid, "The Story of Cinyras and Myrrha," in *Metamorphoses*, trans. Rolfe Humphries (Bloomington: Indiana University Press, 1955), 10.5.423.

12. Shelley, "Mathilda," 245.

13. Blumberg, *Mary Shelley's Early Novels*, 225.

14. Rajan, "Mary Shelley's *Mathilda*," 43.

15. In contrast, Jean-Jacques Rousseau's *Confessions,* or even St. Augustine's, are structured to appeal to the reader's power to see, to sympathize, and to forgive. This structure, which includes the reader's perspective and appeals rhetorically to him or her, is more typical of confessional literature than of *Mathilda*.

16. Shelley, "Alfieri: 1749–1803," 282.

17. Michel Foucault, *An Introduction*, vol. 1 of *The History of Sexuality*, 3 vols., trans. Robert Hurley (New York: Vintage/Random House, 1990), 61.

18. Shelley, "Mathilda," 175.

19. Foucault, *Sexuality*, 1:19–20.

20. Shelley, "Mathilda," 211.

21. Jacques Lacan, "The Direction of the Treatment and the Principles of Its Power," in *Écrits: A Selection*, trans. Alan Sheridan (New York: W. W. Norton, 1977), 265.

22. Shelley, "Mathilda," 185.

23. Malcolm Bowie, *Lacan* (Cambridge, Mass.: Harvard University Press, 1991), 136.

24. Shelley, "Mathilda," 244.

25. Linda Georgianna, *The Solitary Self: Individuality in the Ancrene Wisse* (Cambridge, Mass.: Harvard University Press, 1981), 3.

26. Shelley, "Mathilda," 221.

27. Foucault, *Sexuality*, 1:23.

28. Certainly, William Godwin wished for a "proper" conclusion. He called the subject of *Mathilda* "disgusting and detestable" and urged Mary Shelley to amend the story by putting a disclaimer at the beginning of the tale, assuring the reader that Mathilda never committed physical incest (Maria Gisborne and Edward E. Williams, *Maria Gisborne and Edward E. Williams, Shelley's Friends: Their Journals and Letters*, ed. Frederick L. Jones [Norman: University of Oklahoma Press, 1951], 44).

29. Shelley, "Mathilda," 246.

30. Peter L. Thorslev Jr., "Incest as a Romantic Symbol," *Comparative Literature Studies* 2.1 (1965): 41–58.

Mathilda: Mary Shelley, William Godwin, and the Ideologies of Incest

Ranita Chatterjee

Although Mary Shelley sent her fictional autobiographical novel *Mathilda* (1819)[1] to her father and literary agent William Godwin, he curiously refused either to return or to publish her manuscript. Only a letter to the daughter from a mutual friend, Maria Gisborne, indicates that Godwin's feelings toward Shelley's second work were strong but strangely mixed. While Godwin is reputed to have said that the pursuit and catastrophe that end the narrative are "the finest part of the whole novel," the same letter reports him finding the theme of father-daughter incestuous desire "disgusting and detestable."[2] Significantly, Godwin's reaction to Percy Shelley's lyrical tragedy *The Cenci* (1820), written the same year as *Mathilda*, is not as vitriolic, although it too portrays parent-child incest.[3] Unlike *Mathilda*'s sensitive depiction of potential father-daughter love, in *The Cenci* incest is committed, albeit offstage. In addition, William St Clair's biography describes Godwin liking *The Cenci* because it involved "individuals not abstractions."[4] Thus, while Percy's *The Cenci* was published in 1820 with Godwin's approval, *Mathilda* was not published until Elizabeth Nitchie's edition in 1959. Godwin's strong censure of Mary's suggestive reference to incestuous desires in *Mathilda,* when juxtaposed with his tolerance for a more concrete inscription of this theme in the action of Percy's *The Cenci,* suggests that personal matters, pertaining to the private libidinal dynamic between father and daughter, played a role in his suppression of her text. Clearly, for both William Godwin and Mary Shelley, the potential publication of *Mathilda* had broader implications beyond the simple matter of whether it was commercially and aesthetically viable for the Romantic literary market of 1819.

Overshadowed by *Frankenstein* (1818), *Mathilda* has until recently attracted little scholarly attention despite its crucial role as a critique of the Romantic incest trope and in the circulation of desire among the Godwins and the Shelleys. Recent readings have renewed critical interest in the daughter of Wollstonecraft and Godwin, opening up discussions of the significance of *Mathilda*'s fictional autobiographical form and incest theme.[5] Some of the critical works on *Mathilda*, however, still tend to indulge in an analysis of only those segments of the narrative that parallel certain biographical details of Shelley's life.[6]

Written as the narrator is dying, *Mathilda* is a tragic narrative that both resembles Shelley's experiences and suggestively comments on the fate of Romantic women writers who express their own desires. As Mathilda recounts the death of her mother (Diana) in childbirth, the departure of her father (whom she does not name), and her subsequent childhood spent rereading her father's last letter and worshipping his image, she sets the stage for the inevitable and yet innocent emotions of complete affection she will feel for her father upon his return sixteen years later. Mathilda's autobiography dwells on this long-awaited reunion and the period of shared happiness, which is rudely shattered by the father's confession of his incestuous desire and the daughter's recognition of and revulsion toward her desires. Her father's suicide and her own melancholia cause Mathilda not only to flee society in shame but also in her grief to write her "tragic history" (Shelley, 175). This "history" is addressed to the sympathetic Shelleyan poet Woodville, who encourages Mathilda to find happiness in her solitude. Because of the overwhelming resemblance of the plot of *Mathilda* to the life of Shelley, the novel has suffered from a history of ideological readings embedded in the biographical space of the Godwin/Shelley family circle.

Domna C. Stanton in "Autogynography: Is the Subject Different?" states that the "autobiographical [is] wielded as a weapon to denigrate female texts and exclude them from the canon."[7] It is often the case that women's writing, regardless of genre, is read autobiographically, especially when the theme is one of possible sexual violence. Indeed, *Mathilda*'s reception has been predetermined by Godwin's autobiographical reading of the text. Though *Mathilda* is an intensely personal work, if read fictionally it is also a severe critique of the period's idealization of incest as the ultimate literary expression of creative fulfillment for male Romantic poets. *Mathilda* portrays this Romantic preoccupation with the pursuit of subjectivity, often depicted as an incestuous relationship, from the perspective of the female writer. While the fictional character

Mathilda writes about her experience of incestuous love, the author Mary Shelley writes the novel *Mathilda* using incest as a trope, as Percy Shelley had done in his lyrical tragedy *The Cenci*. By depersonalizing Godwin's reaction to the novel, namely the scandal of private disclosure, we can consider the novel's theme of incest as a trope that plays a significant role in the Romantic literary tradition.[8]

Anne Mellor claims that in a patriarchal, heterosexist society in which women are forever cast into the role of daughter, even in their marriages, "procreation thus gives life, not to the future, but only to the past. When the child-bride's daughter is also her sister and peer, significant generational and psychological development becomes impossible."[9] In this structure, women are never allowed to grow up; they are permanently infantilized in the service of the Father's Law both literally, in their exclusion from structures of power, and symbolically, in their relations with men. In *The Reproduction of Mothering*, Nancy Chodorow argues that a woman never really separates from her mother and as a result can only resolve her relationship to her through one with her own daughter.[10] The young girl receives her mother's sense of feeling inadequate as a woman in a patriarchal culture, and is, therefore, not encouraged, as is her brother, to be an autonomous self. Mellor's concept, then, may be regarded as a reproduction of daughtering in which the adult woman, even through her relationship with her own daughter, is incapable of solving her conflictual relation with her mother. Both models have negative connotations for women: in the reproduction of mothering, the woman solves her psychic conflict with her own mother but reproduces this tension for her daughter; in the reproduction of daughtering, neither tension is solved—it is a static system.

For the essentially motherless Mary Shelley, the way to restore her subjectivity and separate herself from the memory of an absent/dead mother was not to identify with the mother, for this would mean her own death, but to write her "self" in fiction. I argue that to create an identity through the act of writing was for Shelley her act of mothering herself. Moreover, Shelley's *Mathilda* portrays a fictional, motherless daughter who also needs to write her own story. Mathilda writes her "tragic history" for Woodville in the hopes that he will not "toss these pages lightly over," as she expects others will (Shelley, 176). By constructing a fiction of her "self" in autobiography, both the fictional autobiographer Mathilda and the writer of fictional autobiography Shelley manage to ward off Woodville's and the reader's desire to penetrate even further into their tragic lives. The genre of autobiography reveals enough tantalizing details both to satisfy the reader/voyeur and to protect the secrets of the author. This double gesture of disclosure and protection keeps the power not with the reader/voyeur but with the producer of the show, as it were. It is at this level of the textualization of the "self" that Shelley and her fictional creation share a common role. The narrator Mathilda states, "I shall relate my tale therefore as if I wrote for strangers" (176). While Mathilda, then, writes her tragedy for an implied public sphere, so too does Shelley write *Mathilda* for her contemporary readership.[11] In this sense, despite its foundation in personal, private experiences, *Mathilda* addresses a literary reading public through its enactment as narrative. In textualizing the act of writing about desire—both Mathilda's desire to record her sufferings and Shelley's to narrate those of a motherless female writer—the novel thus destroys the gendered social boundary instituted to regulate desire, masking it as the family structure in the private realm and juridical authority in the public one.[12]

I am using the word *desire* quite simply to refer to the libidinal drives and energies that contribute to our erotic, sexual, and subjective perceptions of ourselves and that direct our interactions with other people and objects. The regulation, organization, and expression of desire is enacted through culture and its institutional practices created for this very purpose. Hence, operating within a social system, desire is affected by power. Literary texts, private journals, the social construction of the family: all of these are cultural institutions that are produced by specific ideologies designed both to control desire and to naturalize this control. It is useful to recall Mary Poovey's addition to Althusser's definition of ideology:

> Ideologies exist not only as ideas, however. Instead, they are given concrete form in the practices and social institutions that govern people's social relations and that, in so doing constitute both the experience *of* social relations and the nature of subjectivity.[13]

Desire circulates through ideological practices which, in themselves, as Poovey indicates, constitute both the subject and its social interaction. Therefore, the division between private/feminine and public/masculine space in the nineteenth century, most rigorously instituted in the Victorian period, collapses in the face of desire that is all pervasive. I refer then to the circulation of desire, since desire is never a static process that can be attributed to subjects in their relations to objects. Rather, desire is an energy: an effect both of the unconscious and of language and always based on lack or absence because it is, in Lacanian psychoanalytic terms, the other's desire.[14] My notion of circulation maintains the dynamic nature of desire, that is, the channeling or

movement of libidinal/erotic energies within the social. The writing of
Mathilda; the reciting of the text to Percy Shelley, the Williams, and the
Gisbornes; the circulation of the manuscript from Mary Shelley via
Maria Gisborne to Godwin; the novel's explicit content of desire: all
occupy significant positions within the circulation of libidinal energy.
However, it is the socially constructed symbolic position of Mary Shelley
as daughter within this circulating system that needs to be investigated.

In discussing the relevance of Shelley's incest trope in *Mathilda*, it is
necessary to reconsider both the function and desires of the daughter
within a familial, libidinal economy. Two of the more powerful discourses attempting to explain the circuitous path of desire are Freudian
psychoanalysis (with its linguistic variation theorized by Jacques Lacan)
and the structural anthropology of Lévi-Strauss. My specific focus is on
Freud's Oedipus complex and Lévi-Strauss's kinship structures.[15] These
two models overlap in their discussion of the incest taboo, which is
always the prohibition of the son's desire for the mother. Like Gayle
Rubin's sophisticated analysis of the use and exchange of women, my
intention is not to recover these two models for a feminist project but to
uncover the complex, oppressive subservience of women that these models require.[16] In both Freud's and Lévi-Strauss's traditional theories of
desire, I am particularly interested in the position of the daughter: her
perspective on her desire and the possibility of her agency through resistance. How does the daughter's articulation of her desire, the restriction
of which is the cornerstone of these two models, effectively deconstruct
the patriarchal, hierarchical, heterosexist structure of both the bourgeois
family and the capitalist society? With respect to my discussion of
Mathilda, I want to consider how the daughter's textualization of her
desire disrupts the libidinal economy to the point that Godwin refuses to
publish or return Shelley's manuscript.

Beginning with Lévi-Strauss's theory of kinship structures, it is significant that the prohibition of the incestuous desires of the son for his
mother is instituted to regulate an exogamous exchange of women in the
form of daughters. This is done so as to extend social alliances between
families. The father is the possessor of the goods—the daughter—whom
he exchanges as a gift with another man for the purchase of a son, who in
turn possesses this daughter as a wife. Women have no subjectivity in
this system except as they occupy the most economically viable role of
daughter. As mothers, they are merely vessels of procreation, devoid of
desire. As daughters, their desire is explicitly guided by the hand of the
father toward profitable exchanges. Rubin also points out that if "it is
women who are being transacted, then it is the men who give and take
them who are linked, the woman being a conduit of a relationship rather

than a partner to it."[17] Women then are the glue that cements the homo-erotic relations under patriarchy. Furthermore, Foucault's description of the family as the site for "the interchange of sexuality and alliance: it conveys the law and the juridical dimension in the deployment of sexuality," reveals that the repression of desire and its "proper" channeling are in the hands of the authoritative father figure.[18] He delineates the private and public expression of desire. Indeed, Judith Butler is correct in assuming that "desire and its repression are an occasion for the consolidation of juridical structures; desire is manufactured and forbidden as a ritual symbolic gesture whereby the juridical model exercises and consolidates its own power."[19] In other words, the Father's Law can only be instituted by creating and then suppressing desire. The incest taboo both acknowledges desire and redirects it through the power of the Father/the Law toward heterosexual exogamous relations in which women as daughters become the signifier/figure of exchange. The implications of this for a reading aimed at discovering the role of the woman in society strongly suggest that the father's desire toward his daughter is tacitly encouraged, since his desire for her becomes the index of her exchange value in the libidinal economy.

Within the family, endogamous desire is regulated through the Oedipus complex. The prohibition against incest is once again the repression of the son's desire for the mother. Both the little boy and the little girl have to separate from their mother through a connection with the father in order to enter the symbolic order. The little boy can do this through an identification with his father, which is therefore similar to the homoerotic structure of his later relations with men. The little girl can only achieve this separation through a desire for her father, which must be subsequently transferred onto other men. Hence, the little girl is encouraged and expected to express toward the parent of the opposite sex (her father) the very same incestuous desire that her brother is prohibited from expressing toward *his* parent of the opposite sex (his mother). Clearly, "for the boy, the taboo on incest is a taboo on certain women. For the girl, it is a taboo on all women."[20] Far from being a complementary system, the Oedipus complex is a "screen for the exchange of women and for father-daughter incest."[21] The complex does not empower the mother to prevent father-daughter incest, nor does it provide a valid justification for the daughter's need to change her love object from the mother to the father to a future lover or husband. Furthermore, there is no guarantee that because the daughter leaves the familial unit in a system of exchange, she has not already become damaged goods, or a victim of her father's incestuous desires. The Father's Law is erected precisely so that the father will not desire his own daughter, whom he must exchange in exogamous relations, and so that he may maintain relations with other men through the use of his daughter as a conduit for this homoerotic connection. To this end, the incest taboo regulates female desire. The taboo "imposes the social aim of exogamy and alliance upon the biological events of sex and procreation," and, I would add, desire. The incest taboo clearly demarcates the path of desire by distinguishing, in Rubin's terms, between "permitted and prohibited sexual partners."[22]

Prior to the incest taboo in these theoretical articulations, there is the more ancient taboo against homosexuality. Another purpose of the earlier taboo is to ensure the exchange of women by redirecting the son's desire away from the father and toward the mother. Although this latter desire for the mother is also prohibited, it must be tacitly encouraged in order to channel the son's desires for a heterosexual economy of female exchange. Because the son cannot desire the father within a heterosexist society, the son must transfer his desire to what the father possesses, namely the mother. To have what the father has is to *be* the Father. From a feminist perspective, however, the taboo against homosexuality plays its dominant role in protecting its most valuable merchandise: the daughter. For the daughter to desire the mother is a threat to the father. Not only does this desire for the mother, transferred to other women in the adult woman's life, threaten the father's position as the subject of the exchange of women, it competes with the father's singular possession of the mother. Thus, the daughter's lesbianism threatens the heterosexual economy upon which the Father's power is based.

In light of these two models, *Mathilda* can be read as a novel of subversion in which the daughter disrupts the traditional flow of desire offered by Lévi-Strauss and Freud. The novel's structure of death, desire, and abandonment operates around gender lines because the men (Mathilda's father and Woodville) exit the narrative in the middle—within the symbolic order—whereas the novel opens and closes with the death of women (Mathilda's mother and Mathilda). In a curious twist of the exchange and the departure of women within the libidinal economy, men are to a certain degree exchanged—after rejecting the desires of her father, Mathilda yearns "for one friend to love" her (Shelley, 222)—while the daughter manages to maintain a symbolic connection with her mother, albeit through death. It is significant that in Mathilda's tale the pattern of the daughter's desire from father to lover is directed by the daughter, not by the Father's Law. Although the father, in desiring his daughter and warding off a potential lover, delays her entrance into the economy of exchange, his incestuous attentions are rejected by the daughter. This rejection insures the father's death and the end of his control over the daughter's desires, which allows Mathilda to meet Woodville on her terms, not her father's.

A more detailed reading shows similar patterns of subversion stemming from the daughter's desire. To begin with, although Mathilda's mother is named, her father is not. He remains the abstract concept of a father: he is the Father, the Law that attempts to hold up the patriarchal order. Mathilda's mother is given the name Diana. We may recall that Diana, or Artemis in Greek mythology, is the virgin goddess of the hunt, the protector of the young, and the patron of childbirth, nursing, and healing.[23] The choice of this name implies that the mother in *Mathilda*, though a minor figure, is far from a passive vessel. Although Terence Harpold rightly characterizes the portrayal of Diana "as the object of the father's passion, with no independent initiative or interest," there are tensions in the narrative with respect to the mother.[24] She is described by the daughter as the one who had "torn the veil which had before kept . . . [Mathilda's father] in his boyhood: he was become a man" (Shelley, 179). The symbol of losing virginity through rupturing of the veil or hymen is explicitly applied to the father in this case. Furthermore, the narrator makes it quite clear that her mother was older than her father. In a society that condones the marriages of young women to older men, thus implying that the older, experienced man will sexually initiate his young wife, the reversal of this model recalls the true power of the mother within the libidinal economy, for she is the "Other" whose desire the father wishes to satisfy. It is the "(M)other" who incites the father's desire to satisfy her desire. However, the narrative cannot restrain such maternal power; thus, she too is absented from the economy of desire, as is the father's mother and eventually his sister, who acts as guardian to Mathilda. In a world with no female role models, no generational connection among women, the scene is set for Mathilda's seduction by her father.

Without the presence of the mother, the daughter's need to locate her subjectivity in relation to the father is accomplished not by separating from her mother and becoming his possession as a daughter but by occupying the place of the mother and becoming his possession as a lover. The mother's absence converts Mathilda's primal scene, her site of origin, into a seduction scene at the hands of her father. Harpold points out that "the abstraction of the seduction fantasy over the entire novel signals its function as a primal fantasy: every character in the novel is an accomplice to the seduction, because every position in the fantasy is cathected by the daughter who records it."[25] Thus, the timely deaths of Mathilda's grandmother, mother, and guardian all prepare for the seduction. Additionally, earlier in her description of the father, Mathilda notes that, while her father "earnestly occupied himself about the wants of others his own desires were gratified to their fullest extent" (Shelley, 177). She makes the caveat that her father was not a selfish man but that his desires had not "been put in competition with those of others" (177). Through these details the narrative prepares the reader for the seduction fantasy.

Chapter 2 contains the primal fantasy that is recast as a paternal seduction fantasy. Although Mathilda acknowledges the memory of her mother, her desire is to remember her father. Because of the literal death of the mother, Mathilda's libidinal energies are transferred onto a living father with whom she may be able to reunite:

> I clung to the memory of my parents; my mother I should never see, she was dead: but the idea of [my] [sic] unhappy, wandering father was the idol of my imagination. I bestowed on him all my affections; there was a miniature of him that I gazed on continually; I copied his last letter and read it again and again. Sometimes it made me weep; and at others I repeated with transport those words,—"One day I may claim her at your hands." I was to be his consoler, his companion in after years. (185)

Mathilda's pronouncement that her mother "was dead" forecloses not only the possibility of actual reunion but, more importantly, the possibility of symbolic reunion. If we concede that a female subject can desire instead of be desired within the symbolic order, then her desire within the psychoanalytic framework would be to replace the mother so as to become the object men desire, implicitly the object of the father's desire. However, for Mathilda to identify with her mother is symbolically to assume her own death. To be in the place of the mother is to be dead: absent from the circulation of desire. Therefore, Mathilda transfers her desire onto her only surviving parent. However, there is a paradoxical desire to be still associated with the mother because the implications of Mathilda's desire for the father are that he will return home from his wanderings to her: she will be "his consoler, his companion." The woman in psychoanalytic terms can never truly return to her origins because she *is* symbolically the origin: men can return to her, but if she desires an origin it must be elsewhere. In this sense, Mathilda does identify with the figurative position of the mother: she desires to be the comforter of the father "in after years"; it never occurs to her that her father might return with a companion, or that he might later desire one other than herself. Hence, the fantasy of a return to the origin is precisely that: a fantasy *of* one's desired site of origin. For Mathilda, although a return to the mother would constitute the primal fantasy, because her mother dies so soon after her birth, Mathilda recasts her primal fantasy into a reunion in the future with a father she has never known except textually, through his last letter. What Mathilda is actively searching for—desiring—is an existing originary connection from which she can later individuate. Her gazing at her father's miniature further implies her active participation in the libidinal economy as she returns, in one sense, the Father's prerogative to gaze, and therefore, elicits desire.[26]

There are two more points to make about Mathilda's fantasy. Most likely unconscious of the implications, Mathilda dreams of the "extatic" moment of her father's return and his first words: "My daughter, I love thee!" (Shelley, 185). Ironically, these are the very words that destroy Mathilda's idyllic reunion with her father. In other words, the seeds of the seduction are already planted in the daughter's unconscious desires, encouraged by a patriarchal system in which the mother is insignificant or, in Mathilda's case, always absent. Of more interest to my reading of the novel's subversive plot is Mathilda's statement that, "disguised like a boy . . . [she] would seek . . . [her] father through the world" (185). Earlier in the paragraph, Mathilda refers to Miranda, Rosalind, and the lady of Comus as her companions, "imagining . . . [herself] to be in their situations" (185). Mathilda's identification with these three literary characters in addition to her desire for transvestism (only to facilitate her search for her father) suggests that Mathilda, like Rosalind, desires to be the active subject in her fantasized erotic encounter with her beloved father. While she anticipates an idyllic relationship alone with her father, like the one Miranda shares with Prospero, Mathilda is also aware of the dangers of seduction by one who is assumed to be her protector, like Comus. In other words, Mathilda may see herself as an innocent daughter with only a father to love, like Miranda. However, because this unknown father may be an evil seducer like Comus, she must be an active participant in the circulation of desire, like Rosalind, for which she must assume the socially constructed symbolic position of the boy, or son, as I will argue later on. Mathilda's seduction fantasy then may be interpreted as a displaced primal fantasy for the mother with Mathilda in the position of the son. In this sense, Mathilda's desire to return to a pre-oedipal stage of complete loving harmony with a parent, although she projects this desire into the future, is akin to the male Romantic poet's desired union with the mother. The Narrator's desire to penetrate/unveil the Mother's "innermost sanctuary" in Percy Shelley's *Alastor* (1816) is one such example.[27]

While chapter 3 describes Mathilda's "Paradisaical bliss" with her father, it is apparent that she also views this reunion with her father as somehow similar to a pre-oedipal stage, since she refers to herself as living "in an enchanted palace, amidst odours, and music, and every luxurious delight" (Shelley, 189, 190). Moreover, Mathilda mentions that "it was a subject of regret to . . . [her] whenever . . . [her father and she] were joined by a third person" (190). It is striking that Mathilda views her father as a maternal figure with whom she shares the first early pleasures of smells, sounds, and sensual delights, jealous of any intrusion by a third person into this imaginary union. However, Mathilda also views this reunion as an Edenic paradise of lover with beloved. She explicitly states that she "disobeyed no command . . . ate no apple, and yet . . . was ruthlessly driven from it" (189). The lack of early maternal affection creates a palimpsest of mixed emotions in Mathilda: while she is always already oedipalized because of the absent mother and can therefore only consider the father as a lover, she also looks to the father as a mother and thus recreates the pre-oedipal stage to compensate for the loss of the mother. Consequently, when the chapter closes with her despair over the father's emotional distance from her, this separation is not her first entrance into the symbolic order but her conscious reentrance or fall into a post-lapsarian world.

Although the father and daughter share an early period of Edenic bliss, as in Milton's paradise the evil is already present. In a curious bit of orientalism, the father's later incestuous desires are justified by his travels in India:

> Lonely wanderings in a wild country among people of simple or savage manners may inure the body but will not tame the soul, or extinguish the ardour and freshness of feeling incident to youth. The burning sun of India, and the freedom from all restraint had rather encreased the energy of his character: before he bowed under, now he was impatient of any censure except that of his own mind. (188)

Since being in India—away from "civilized society" (188)—has not sufficiently restrained the father's desires (as an internalization of the Eurocentric Father's Law would), his passion for his daughter is possible. While the daughter justifies her father's desires through an orientalized description of his travels abroad, the father justifies his by all too clearly articulating what the patriarchal system of exchanging women encourages. In his confessional letter to Mathilda, the father explains that

> the sight of this house, these fields and woods which my first love inhabited seems to have encreased . . . [my love for you]: in my madness I dared say to myself—Diana died to give her birth; her mother's spirit was transferred into her frame, and *she ought to be as Diana to me*. (emphasis added) (210)

In explaining his motives for desiring the daughter, the father rationalizes his actions through a connection between Mathilda and her mother, Diana. Specifically, his sense of the interchangeability of the two women implies that each woman is only a receptacle for his desires, signifiers of erotic pleasure in a libidinal economy based on the traffic of women. In giving birth to a daughter, Diana gives birth to an erotic replacement of herself to service the desires of the father. This reproduction of daughters insures that the father's desires for an innocent younger woman will always be satisfied. It is significant that Diana's last request to her husband before she dies is to make "her child happy" (210). Harpold's analysis is apt: "The mother who commands the father to make their daughter 'happy' provides in fantasy the maternal approval of oedipal succession."[28] Thus, the father in the narrative can view himself as the rival of the "young man of rank" (Shelley, 191) who begins to visit Mathilda. This competition discloses both the father's inadequacy to "properly" circulate desire within the libidinal economy and the flaws of a system that demands that men simultaneously distinguish their own daughters from other women and yet consider all women as sexual objects. As I have argued, the Law of the Father is instituted precisely to protect the father from acting on the desires he has encouraged in his daughter. The father's inability to protect himself from his desires exposes the gap between the Law that he represents and his own self in actual relations. The father is not all-powerful but has erected the Law to suggest otherwise.

This is apparent in the actual scene of confession, in which Mathilda controls the situation, not the father. It is Mathilda who is determined to gain her father's confidence and thus know the reasons for his sudden coldness toward her. She directs the scene of desire, which reveals the devastating emotional toll of a social system in which mothers are absent, fathers must depend on daughter figures to satisfy their desires (since wives as such do not exist), and daughters regard their fathers as their only "friend, . . . hope, . . . [and] shelter" (199). In such a patriarchal system, Mathilda has no choice but to actively seek her own desires if she wishes to recover her subjectivity, as evidenced by her need to reenact another primal fantasy with her father. Mathilda again occupies the position of a son with respect to her father as she tries to master the father.[29] It is Mathilda who prompts the father to say, "Why do you bring me out, and torture me, and tempt me, and kill me" (Shelley, 200), implying that he is threatened by the possibility not only of being seduced by a daughter but also of being replaced by her. Symbolically, Mathilda comes to occupy the position of the son who wishes to replace the father in the new generation. In addition, the father's description of himself as being "struck by the storm, rooted up, laid waste," in contrast to Mathilda, who "can stand against it [for she is] . . . young" (Shelley, 200), points to the father's inability to redirect his desires outside of his family and, thus, symbolically represents his social impotence, since he cannot uphold the Law. In other words, this imagery depicts the destruction of the father's "family tree" as it is "laid waste" by his incestuous desires. The father's confession of his incestuous desire ultimately exposes what his Law was meant to hide, namely that his power rests on encouraging his daughter's desire for him, not on being replaced by the daughter through her own desire.

Without the presence of a strong female role model or mother, the gap left from the father's collapse takes its toll on the daughter as well. Far from a simple recognition of her own erotic desires for her father, Mathilda's despair and revulsion in hearing her father's confession manifests itself as a fear of the mother:

> For the first time that phantom seized me; the first and only time for it has never since left me—After the first moments of speechless agony I felt her fangs on my heart: I tore my hair; I raved aloud; at one moment in pity for his sufferings I would have clasped my father in my arms; and then starting back with horror I spurned him with my foot; I felt as if stung by a serpent, as if scourged by a whip of scorpions which drove me—Ah! Whither—Whither? (Shelley, 202)

A simple reading of this scene may imply that, for Mathilda, the phantom is the absent mother. It is the mother's "fangs," the mother as "serpent," that returns to punish Mathilda for attempting to replace the mother in the father's embrace. Harpold has suggested that "the absent mother may still punish her rival; indeed, the rival will share her mother's fate if she takes her mother's place—she, too, will be subject to the fatal effect of the father's desire."[30] However, recalling that Mathilda transfers her desire for a return to the mother onto the father, I propose that in this instance Mathilda is once again transferring her libidinal energies. In this case, the horror of the father's incestuous desires is transferred to the mother. While the description is phallic, with the mother as serpent sinking her fangs into Mathilda, it is not necessarily that of a phallic mother. Mathilda's early sensual pleasures with her father resurface here as a fear of rejection by the loving parent (the father, in Mathilda's case). This anxiety of separation is manifested as a horror of the mother who, from the daughter's perspective, has abandoned her. Thus, the mother is imagined as devouring, ravishing, and hungry, greedily sinking her "fangs" into the child instead of nourishing her. This projection of unwanted/horrifying emotions onto the figure of the absent vampire-like mother is a defense mechanism geared to prevent the sexualization of what Mathilda has experienced as an innocent, affectionate, pre-oedipal-like relationship with her father. Far from desiring her father sexually, she desires to be loved as a child, as is evidenced by her curse: "This is my curse, a daughter's curse: go, and return pure to thy child, who will never love aught but thee" (Shelley, 204). Her transference is a preventive tactic that maintains the illusion of the innocent primal fantasy that can only be for Mathilda a seduction fantasy. It is also a way to redirect the flow of libidinal energies by reversing the power dynamics: Mathilda is neither the victim of her father's desires, for she ultimately rejects them, nor is she the victim of her mother's perceived desires, for she has merely transformed her mother's anger into jealousy. Mathilda's own resentment toward her father can only surface in her unconscious, in a dream in which she pursues her father to his death, a dream that Anne Mellor takes to be indicative of Mathilda gratifying her "repressed desire to punish her father."[31] In this sense alone, *Mathilda* is not so much about father-daughter incest, as Godwin imagined, but about the active resistance to it in a social polity geared toward controlling the daughter's desire through the F/father.

Anne Mellor claims that "from the moment of his death, Mathilda wishes only to reunite with her father, to embrace him passionately in the grave."[32] Mellor supports this point by interpreting Mathilda's sinking "lifeless to the ground" upon discovering her father's corpse as "something stiff and straight" (Shelley, 214) as "an ecsta[tic] . . . incestuous necrophiliac desire that leaves her exhausted, consummated, 'lifeless,' yet yearning for a repetition of this experience."[33] Far from feeling ecstasy, Mathilda feels nothing: "I did not feel shocked or overcome" (Shelley, 214). In fact, there is no evidence to suggest that the sight of her dead father's body "covered by a sheet" (214) is something from which Mathilda derives erotic pleasure. Neither is there any indication that Mathilda desires to repeat this experience. Indeed, the last sentence of the chapter, "all had been at an end" (214), suggestively frees Mathilda from the grip of her father's desires.

To argue that Mathilda desires to repeat the experience of seeing her father's corpse, one would have to interpret Mathilda's longing for death in the subsequent chapters as her desire to reunite with her father once more. But the narrative does not support this argument, for what Mathilda desires is affection: "I wished for one friend to love me" (222). Although she recognizes her inability to love again, she still clings to life, hoping that someone may desire her. Woodville, who, after the death of his new bride, befriends Mathilda, turns out to be less than ideal. When asked to join Mathilda in a suicide pact, he reveals his selfish desire to seek Mathilda to fill his own loneliness, not to appease hers. It is this second rejection, this second time of being used to satisfy someone else's desires that persuades Mathilda that death is all that remains for her. Mathilda is not so much enamored of death as she is of being loved. Thus, when Mathilda does contemplate death as a maiden wrapped in her "bridal attire" (244), preparing to meet her father, far from enacting a desire to be erotically united with him, as Mellor argues, I suggest that Mathilda is merely reenacting her primal scene. As an always already oedipalized daughter, Mathilda's primal scene, and hence return to origin through death, can only be figured as a seduction scene. She is once again refiguring her need for compassion in the only way she knows: an erotic way. Her desire to occupy the place of the mother, something she has not articulated before this point, is an acknowledgment that she no longer fears the mother, who has always been associated with death. To occupy the place of the mother, then, is not so much *to be her for the father but to simply be with her as one oblivious to the father.* The possibility of loving the mother, of identifying with the mother without the intervention of the father, is restored through Mathilda's death in a fulfillment of her desire for "sinless emotion" (204).

While Diana dies to give birth to Mathilda, the daughter dies to give birth to her new self, that is, to liberate herself from the clutches of the father's desires. In this sense, Mathilda mothers, or rather gives birth to, herself through the act of writing. For Mathilda, the narration of her primal scene, which in her case is a seduction scene, enables her to pass through the mirror stage again, this time emerging from out of the grasp of the F/father. It is as if the narrator has to go through the mirror stage and separate from her primary love—a father—because she never had a chance to do this with the mother, as the narrator is always already oedipalized. However, since the narrator's identity is linked to the father, she too must die in killing the father. For Shelley, the manuscript of *Mathilda* itself becomes the vicarious path to a new self, the old self allegorically represented by the character of Mathilda.

For the woman writer, the escape or destruction/critique of the Father's Law and, hence, patriarchy is, to a certain degree, the death of self. Because her identity is so intricately bound up with that of the father, of patriarchy, and of the weight of a historically masculine literary tradition, to criticize these in order to find a place for herself is also to embrace death (as Mathilda does). So, *Mathilda* becomes a critique of the impossible situation of the woman writer who must simultaneously individuate/separate herself from the father but also, because of her gender, occupy the place of the absent/dead mother. The woman writer who articulates her own specific desire has to write/speak herself out of silence. But, in so doing, she also enters into a crumbling symbolic order that she disrupts through the very act of breaking *her* silence, upon which the order is built. To use Luce Irigaray's term, she becomes the "disruptive excess" of the order.[34]

Diane Hoeveler argues that the male Romantic poets were self-consciously employing "the feminine as 'Other'" in their pursuit of a "new and redeemed/expanded self in an androgynous ideology that stressed union with one's complementary opposite."[35] Hoeveler is referring to the trope of the male Romantic poet's desire to merge psychically with one's sister. Recalling that Freud considered the illicit sexual attraction to one's sister as a displacement of the desire for the Mother, the role of resistance for the woman writer who occupies the position of the feminine "Other" of this male Romantic trope of literary creativity is to position a male family member as "Other." In Shelley's case, she recast Godwin in this role. Unable to escape from the shackles of her gender, being symbolically represented as the Other in her husband's poetry, Shelley attempted to otherize her father by sending him *Mathilda*, effectively disrupting Godwin's sense of who occupies the place of alterity. Through the writing and transmission of this text of patricide—*Mathilda*—Shelley returns Godwin's/the Father's gaze by providing an alternative narrative, one that does not obey the Father's Law. By doing so, she dephallicizes Godwin and exposes the weakness of his law. Similarly, her fictional narrator's rejection of her nameless father's incestuous desires leads to his death and her creativity, for she writes her autobiography.

Although Shelley's *Mathilda* is rather autobiographical, it contains many significant details that cannot be readily accounted for by a reading that assumes Mathilda is Mary Shelley. Indeed, *Mathilda* portrays a life, making the narrator Mathilda a fictional autobiographer. Whether that life is Mary Shelley's or not is irrelevant to our understanding of the novel as a scene of writing or of hermeneutic understanding. In Janet Varner Gunn's words, "As the reader of his or her life, the autobiographer inhabits the hermeneutic universe where all understanding takes place. The autobiographer serves by this habitation, as the paradigmatic reader."[36] *Mathilda* enacts this hermeneutic function. Further, "the real question of the autobiographical self then becomes *where do I belong?* not, who am I?" (23). Far from being simply about Shelley's desire for Godwin, through *Mathilda* Shelley questions her ability to create a subjectivity for herself in a patriarchal family unit overshadowed by an absent mother. She also questions her situation as a widowed writer and failed mother in a culture that identifies women with their relational roles to men. Thus, Mary Shelley is not so much inscribing herself in the figure of Mathilda but questioning a set of propositions through the world and circumstances she creates for her fictional character. We might productively recall Daphne Marlatt's term "fictionalysis" as applicable to what Mary Shelley accomplishes with *Mathilda*:

> It is exactly in the confluence of fiction (the self or selves we might be) and analysis (of the roles we have found ourselves in, defined in a complex socio-familial weave)—it is in the confluence of these two that autobiography occurs, the self writing its way to life, whole life.[37]

Shelley attains a subjectivity through her fictional creation. Furthermore, as Sidonie Smith suggests, "the autobiographer confronts personally her culture's stories of male and female desire, insinuating the lines of her story through the lines of the patriarchal story that has been autobiography."[38] Through her fictional autobiography on female desire, Mary Shelley thus creates her own place in the patriarchal fiction of desire.

As the daughter of William Godwin, Shelley's representation of a father-daughter incestuous passion becomes a trope for the apprenticeship of the literary daughter to her father's patriarchal, hierarchical profession. In Elizabeth Kowaleski-Wallace's discussion of literary daughters, this is a willing "forsaking [of] . . . [the] literal mother," but for Shelley, I suggest, it meant an identification with the position of her literary mother, Mary Wollstonecraft.[39] As Mathilda's longing to merge with the mother is accomplished only through death, Shelley's desire is gratified through complicity with the patriarchal literary structures that her mother occupied and challenged. Indeed, Shelley may be writing over the literal body of her dead mother, but she is also identifying with the literary body of her mother's corpus. Godwin's reaction to the novel's private disclosures implies a social ideology that considers the imaginative use of the incest trope in fiction and poetry as a male writer's preserve. Therefore, Shelley's novel and its theme of incest may be regarded as a counterdiscourse to this type of Romantic masculine ideology. Shelley's transmission of her novel to Godwin enacts her desire to communicate openly her critical perspective of the familial libidinal economy to a parent who had been known for his political views of justice. Hence, *Mathilda* is a political novel in its sharp critique of a Romantic social structure that requires obedience from women, subsequently transforming all sexual relations between men and women to a symbolic form of father-daughter incest. *Mathilda*, then, also functions to force Godwin's political writings and their fictional manifestations into a dialectical encounter on the subject of female libidinal energies while offering a severe criticism of the male Romantic's investment in the ex- cision and appropriation of female desire. Although Shelley's *Mathilda* subverts this Romantic aesthetic use of the incest trope, the novel also implicitly comments on the disastrous consequences of the incest motif for the female writer. Through the textualization of a female writer's (Mathilda's) tragic history of her refusal to participate in a literal inces- tuous relationship, Shelley points to the violence that underlies the liter- ary representation of incest. The struggles of the female Romantic writer are also conspicuously mirrored in the novel's publication history, which replicates the threat of incestuous family violence found in the novel. Whereas the fictional character Mathilda is able to deny her father and write her text, the author Shelley cannot escape from her father's judg- ment, which prevents her from publishing her text. Godwin essentially violates Shelley's right to publish her text by refusing to acknowledge her work. Ultimately, Godwin robs his daughter of her voice in a sym- bolic form of father-daughter incestuous violence.

Notes

Acknowledgements: Preparation for this essay was assisted by funds from the Social Science and Humanities Research Council of Canada.

1. Mary Shelley, *Mathilda*, in *The Mary Shelley Reader*, ed. Betty T. Bennett and Charles E. Robinson (New York and Oxford: Oxford University Press, 1990), 173–246. Reprinted from "Mathilda," by Mary Wollstonecraft Godwin Shelley, edited by Elizabeth Nitchie, from *Studies in Philology: Extra Series #3*, 1959. Copyright © 1959 by the University of North Carolina Press. Used by permission of the publisher. References to *Mathilda* will be hereafter cited in the text as "Shelley."

2. Elizabeth Nitchie, "Mary Shelley's *Mathilda*: An Unpublished Story and its Bio- graphical Significance," *Studies in Philology* 40 (1943): 447–62.

3. Percy Bysshe Shelley, *The Cenci: A Tragedy, in Five Acts*, in *Shelley's Poetry and Prose*, ed. D. H. Reiman and S. B. Powers (New York: Norton, 1977), 236–301.

4. William St Clair, *The Godwins and the Shelleys: The Biography of A Family* (London and Boston: Faber and Faber, 1989), 453.

5. See Tilottama Rajan's "Mary Shelley's *Mathilda*: Melancholy and the Political Economy of Romanticism," *Studies in the Novel* 26.2 (1994): 43–68, for an excellent dis- cussion of the novel's form.

6. William Veeder, "The Negative Oedipus: Father, *Frankenstein*, and the Shelleys," *Critical Inquiry* 12 (Winter 1986): 365–90; Anne K. Mellor, *Mary Shelley: Her Life, Her Fiction, Her Monsters* (New York: Routledge, 1988); and Terrence Harpold, "'Did you get Mathilda from Papa?': Seduction Fantasy and the Circulation of Mary Shelley's *Mathilda*," *Studies in Romanticism* 28 (Spring 1989): 49–67.

7. Domna C. Stanton, "Autogynography: Is the Subject Different?" in *The Female Autograph: Theory and Practice of Autobiography from the Tenth to the Twentieth Century*, ed. Domna C. Stanton (Chicago: University of Chicago Press, 1984), 4.

8. I do not deny the possibility of real occurrences of incest influencing the form and content of *Mathilda*; at the same time, we must not limit our reading of the text to autobiography.

9. Mellor, *Mary Shelley*, 200.

10. Nancy J. Chodorow, *The Reproduction of Mothering: Psychoanalysis and the Sociology of Gender* (Berkeley: University of California Press, 1978).

11. While Shelley's initial audience (her father, husband, and friends) was located in a more private domain, her intention to publish *Mathilda* expressed her desire to address a wider readership.

12. By juridical authority, I am referring to the social imperatives that control the expression of sexuality and desire, such as the various legal institutions, as well as the Lacanian notion of the Father's Law.

13. Mary Poovey, *Uneven Developments: The Ideological Work of Gender in Mid-Victorian England* (Chicago: University of Chicago Press, 1988), 3.

14. Elizabeth Grosz, *Jacques Lacan: A Feminist Introduction* (London: Routledge, 1990), 67.

15. Sigmund Freud [1905], *Three Essays on the Theory of Sexuality*, in *The Standard Edition of the Complete Psychological Works*, ed. and trans. J. Strachey et al., 24 vols. (London: Hogarth Press, 1953–74), 7:125–245; and Claude Lévi-Strauss [1949], *The Elementary Structures of Kinship*, trans. J. Bell et al. (London: Eyre and Spottiswoode, 1969).

16. Gayle Rubin, "The Traffic in Women: Notes Toward a Political Economy of Sex," in *Toward an Anthropology of Women*, ed. Rayna R. Reiter (New York: Monthly Review Press, 1975), 157–210.

17. Rubin, "Traffic in Women," 174.

18. Michel Foucault [1976], *The History of Sexuality. Volume I: An Introduction*, trans. R. Hurley (New York: Vintage, 1980), 108.

19. Judith Butler, *Gender Trouble: Feminism and the Subversion of Identity* (New York: Routledge, 1990), 75–76.

20. Rubin, "Traffic in Women," 193.

21. Madelon Sprengnether, "*Undoing Incest: A Meditation on* Daughters and Fathers," *Modern Philology* 89 (May 1992): 521.

22. Rubin, "Traffic in Women," 173.

23. Barbara G. Walker, *The Woman's Encyclopedia of Myths and Secrets* (San Francisco: Harper and Row, 1983), 233.

24. Harpold, "Seduction Fantasy," 53.

25. Ibid., 56.

26. While a woman's gaze does not serve the same function as the patriarch's, which both constructs and controls the other, the woman's returning gaze significantly restricts the power of the male gaze.

27. Percy Bysshe Shelley, *Alastor; or, The Spirit of Solitude*, in *Shelley's Poetry and Prose*, 69–87.

28. Harpold, "Seduction Fantasy," 55.

29. I should clarify that by daughter, son, mother, or father, I am not referring to Freud's biological descriptions but rather to the socially constructed positions within a familial libidinal economy. What solidifies these positions with respect to gender are social and cultural practices and institutions.

30. Harpold, "Seduction Fantasy," 57.

31. Mellor, *Mary Shelley*, 201.

32. Ibid., 195.

33. Ibid.

34. Luce Irigaray, 1977, *This Sex Which Is Not One*, trans. Catherine Porter and Carolyn Burke (Ithaca: Cornell University Press, 1985), 78.

35. Diane Long Hoeveler, *Romantic Androgyny: The Women Within* (University Park: Pennsylvania State University Press, 1990), 79.

36. Janet Varner Gunn, *Autobiography: Toward a Poetics of Experience* (Philadelphia: University of Philadelphia Press, 1982), 22.

37. Daphne Marlatt, "Self-Representation and Fictionalysis," in *The Anatomy of Gender: Women's Struggle for the Body*, ed. D. H. Currie and V. Raoul (Ottawa: Carleton University Press, 1992), 245.

38 Sidonie Smith, *A Poetics of Women's Autobiography: Marginality and the Fictions of Self-Representation* (Indianapolis: Indiana University Press, 1987), 19.

39. Elizabeth Kowaleski-Wallace, *Their Fathers' Daughters: Hannah More, Maria Edgeworth, and Patriarchal Complicity* (Oxford: Oxford University Press, 1991), 11.

Mary Shelley and Gothic Feminism: The Case of "The Mortal Immortal"

Diane Long Hoeveler

During the month of May 1794, the most popular drama in London, playing nightly to packed houses at Covent Garden, was Henry Siddons's *The Sicilian Romance; or The Apparition of the Cliff*, loosely based on Ann Radcliffe's second novel, published in 1790. One of the more interesting changes in the play concerns the villain of the Siddons piece, who keeps his inconvenient wife chained to solid stone in a rocky cave in the forest, a place he visits only to feed her and blame her for inflicting wounds of guilt on his heart. Although the Gothic villain would later metamorphose into the Byronic hero consumed by unspeakable guilt over illicit sins, the villain of the Siddons drama is a bit more prosaic. He simply desires to marry a younger and more beautiful woman, one who will further improve his social and political status, because his first wife, the mother of his children, has become redundant. The young woman he desires, whom we would recognize as a future trophy wife, is pursued from castle to convent to cavern, aided by the hero, the villain's son-turned-outlaw. As the above synopsis makes obvious, female Gothic novels like Radcliffe's *Sicilian Romance* provided the subject matter, techniques, and melodramatic formulae that, first on the stage in England, later on the French stage, and much later in the Hollywood "women in jeopardy" films such as *The Silence of the Lambs*, have continued to promulgate the primal Gothic tradition of "good" or femininity triumphing over "evil" or masculinity.

The typical female Gothic novel presents a blameless female victim triumphing through a variety of passive-aggressive strategies over a male-created system of oppression and corruption. The melodrama that suffuses these works is explicable only if we understand that, as Paula Backscheider has recently demonstrated, a generally hyperbolic sentimentalism was saturating the British literary scene at the time, informing the Gothic melodramas that were such standard fare during the popular theater season.[1] But melodrama, as Peter Brooks has demonstrated, is also characterized by a series of moves or postures that made it particularly attractive to middle-class women. Specifically, Brooks lists as crucial to melodrama the tendency toward depicting intense, excessive representations of life that tend to strip away the facade of manners to reveal the primal conflicts at work, leading to moments of intense confrontation. These symbolic dramatizations rely on what Brooks lists as the standard features of melodrama: hyperbolic figures, lurid and grandiose events, masked relationships and disguised identities, abductions, slow-acting poisons, secret societies, and mysterious parentage. In short, melodrama is a version of the female Gothic, while the female Gothic provides the undergirding for feminism as an ideology bent on depicting women as the innocent victims of a corrupt and evil patriarchal system.

If husbands can routinely chain their wives to stone walls and feed them the way one feeds a forsaken pet that will not die, then what sort of action is required from women to protect and defend themselves against such abuse? Demure, docile behavior is hardly adequate protection against a lustful, raving patriarch gone berserk. According to Brooks, the Gothic novel can be understood as standing most clearly in reaction to desacralization and the pretensions of rationalism.[2] Like melodrama, the female Gothic text represents both the urge toward resacralization and the impossibility of conceiving sacralization other than in personal terms. For the Enlightenment mentality, there was no longer a clear transcendent value to which one could be reconciled. There was, rather, a social order to be purged, a set of ethical imperatives to be made clear. And who was in a better position to purge the new bourgeois world of all traces of aristocratic corruption than the female Gothic heroine? Such a woman—professionally virginal, innocent, and good—assumed virtual religious significance because, within the discourse system, so much was at stake. Making the world safe for the middle class was not without its perils. Gothic feminism was born when women realized that they had a formidable external enemy—the lustful, greedy patriarch—in addition to their own worst internal enemy—their consciousness of their own sexual difference, perceived as a weakness.

A dangerous species of thought for women developed at this time and in concert with the sentimentality of Samuel Richardson and the hyperbolic Gothic and melodramatic stage productions of the era. This ideology graphically educated its audience in the lessons of victimization.[3] According to this powerful and socially coded formula, victims earned their special status and rights through no action of their own but through their sufferings and persecutions at the hands of a patriarchal oppressor and tyrant. One would be rewarded not for anything one did but for what one passively suffered. According to this paradigm, women developed a type of behavior now recognized as passive aggression; they were almost willing victims not because they were masochists but because they expected a substantial return on their investment in suffering. Whereas Richardson's Clarissa found herself earning a crown in heaven for suffering rape by Lovelace, the women in female Gothic texts were interested in more earthly rewards. The lesson that Gothic feminism teaches is that the meek shall inherit the Gothic earth; the female Gothic heroine always triumphs in the end because melodramas are constructed to suit this version of poetic justice. The God we call Justice always intervenes and justice always rectifies, validates, and rewards suffering. Terrible events can occur, but the day of reckoning invariably arrives for Gothic villains. This ideology fostered a form of passivity in women, a fatalism that the mainstream feminist would be loathe to recognize today. Yet Gothic feminism undergirds the special pleading of contemporary women who see themselves even today as victims of an amorphous and transhistorical patriarchy. When the contemporary feminist theorist Naomi Wolf identifies what she calls "victim feminism"—characterized by a loathing of the female body and a reification of victimization as the only route to power—we can hardly be faulted for hearing the echo of Mary Shelley's literary visions.[4]

As the daughter of Mary Wollstonecraft and William Godwin, Mary Wollstonecraft Godwin Shelley was destined to be an overdetermined personality. A heavy intellectual burden rested on her slight shoulders, and for the most part she fulfilled that expectation not only by marrying extravagantly but by writing well. In fact, her union with Percy Shelley may have been her greatest literary performance—her real and imagined victimization on his account, first as wife, then as widow, being only slightly less painful than the sufferings experienced by her fictional heroines. And although her husband's presence haunts all of her works, the real heroes or hero-villains of Mary's life were always her parents, who also recur obsessively in various mutated forms in everything she wrote. Mary Wollstonecraft may have left us only two inadequately real-ized fictions and two vindications, but she also left us Mary Shelley, in many ways destined to complete and fulfill her mother's aborted philo-sophical and literary visions.[5] If Wollstonecraft failed to understand the full implications of her suggestions for women—that they effectively "masculinize" themselves and shun "feminine" values as weak and debilitating—her daughter understood all too well the consequences of such behavior for both men and women. Mary's major work, *Frankenstein* (1818), stands paradoxically as the Gothic embodiment of the critique of Gothic feminism. If Wollstonecraft could barely imagine a brave new world for women inhabited by sensitive Henrys, Mary Shelley puts her fictional women into that world and reveals that the sensitive male hero is a mad egotist intent on usurping feminine values and destroying all forms of life in his despotic quest for phallic mastery. Her other two works most clearly in the Gothic mode, *Mathilda* (1819) and the short story "The Mortal Immortal" (1833), also critique the female Gothic formulae as they had evolved by the time she was writing. For instance, *Mathilda* rewrites *Frankenstein*, turning the prior text inside out, revealing the incestuous core of the Gothic feminist fantasy as she experienced it. Everyone in Mary Shelley's corpus is a victim, but her female characters are the victims of victims and thus doubly pathetic and weak.

We do not think of Mary Shelley as a feminist by contemporary standards, nor did she think of herself as one. She once stated: "If I have never written to vindicate the rights of women, I have ever befriended women when oppressed—at every risk I have defended and supported victims to the social system. But I do not make a boast." But she understood all too well what her mother failed to grasp—that woman's protection was in her studied pose of difference and weakness. In fact, she went so far as to observe that "the sex of our [woman's] material mechanism makes us quite different creatures [from men]—better though weaker."[6] But Mary's notion of the social system—the legal, financial, class, religious, and educational superstructure that undergirded nineteenth-century British culture—was finally codified and symbolized by her in the patriarchal bourgeois family. Her fathers are not simply demigods of the family hearth, they are representatives of a larger, oppressive, patriarchal system. They inherit and bequeath wealth because they represent and embody that lucre themselves, in their very persons.[7] The body of the male in Mary Shelley's fiction is always a commodity of worth, an object to be valued, reconstructed, reassembled, and salvaged, while the bodies of the women in her texts are always devalued, compromised, flawed, and inherently worthless.

At the core of all of Mary Shelley's works, however, is the residue of what Freud has labeled in "A Child Is Being Beaten" (1919) as variations on the beating fantasy that children generally experience between the ages of five and fifteen. In these repeated scenarios of desire and repression a girl will typically move through three psychological positions. In the first and third positions, her stance is sadistic and voyeuristic—"another child is being beaten and I am observing the act"—but in the second psychic position her posture is masochistic, erotic, and deeply repressed: "I am the child being beaten by my father." For the boy, the psychic transformation is less complex due to the elimination of one stage. For him, the first position, "I am loved (or beaten) by my father," is transformed into the conscious fantasy "I am being beaten by my mother." According to Freud, the roots of the phallic mother (the all-powerful mother in possession of the father's phallus) can be located precisely in this early fantasy,[8] but for Mary Shelley, the psychic terrain is complicated by the fact that she, as a woman writer, typically seeks to elide gender by assuming the position of a male protagonist. The basic beating fantasies we see throughout her works— the attacks the "creature" makes on various members of Victor Frankenstein's family, the incestuous attack on Mathilda by her father, the attack on the body of the idealized female icon in "The Mortal Immortal"—all represent variations on the beating fantasy, expressing the child's ambivalence and impotence when confronted with the power and mystery of the parental figures.

Why does incest hover so blatantly over Mary (not to mention Percy) Shelley's Gothic works in ways that do not occur quite so self-consciously in the works of other female Gothic writers? Why are her heroines always defined and self-identified as daughters first, wives second, mothers only briefly? Why would she send the text of *Mathilda*, a shockingly graphic (for its time) portrayal of a father's incestuous love for his daughter, to her own father? And why would she then be surprised when he failed to arrange for its publication?[9] Writing on the very margins of her unconscious obsessions, Mary Shelley played the role of dutiful daughter to the end, leaving the ashes of Percy in Rome and having herself buried with her parents and son in England. In many ways, Percy was as ephemeral a presence in her life as she was in his. It would appear from a reading of their letters and journals that both of them were playacting at love with ideal objects of their own imaginary creation. Unfortunately, as Mary learned too late, the real loves in both their lives were their parents, both real and imagined.

"The Mortal Immortal: A Tale" (1833),[10] one of the many short stories Mary wrote for money in her later life, plays in its oxymoronic title with ambiguity and impossibility, suggesting that there may be a way to make mortals immortal, just as Mary desperately wanted to believe that there may be a way to equalize women with men. Note, however, that the fear and loathing of the female body that activated *Frankenstein* and *Mathilda* recur as dominant motifs in a majority of Mary's short stories, not simply in this one. *Frankenstein* punished every female body in that text, scarring and disfiguring all female attempts to rewrite the generative body as sacred and whole. It replaced the maternal womb with chemical and alchemical artifice, only to blast masculine attempts at procreation as futile and destructive. In *Mathilda,* the male principle once again would appear to be the only effectual parent; but, as in the earlier work, the father produces his progeny only to consume it, feeding on his daughter as a vampire feeds on victims in order to sustain a perverse form of death-in-life.

"The Mortal Immortal" situates the reader within the same psychic terrain, and, like the other works, it plays with variations of beating fantasies, with sometimes the male protagonist as victim, sometimes the female. But we begin this narrative initially within the frame of legendary discourse, this time of the Wandering Jew. We learn early in the text that the narrator defines himself in negative terms, in terms of what he is not. He tells us that he is not the Jew because he is infinitely younger, being only 323 years old (TMI, 314). "The Mortal Immortal" actually reads as if it were inspired not by that particular old legend but by E. T. A. Hoffmann's "The Sandman" or "The Devil's Elixirs," the latter reviewed in *Blackwood's* in 1824 (16:55–67). Mary Shelley does not record in her journal having read "The Sandman" in either a French or Italian translation, and her knowledge of German was certainly not strong enough for her to have read it in the original, but the tale was well-known in England by 1833, the year she wrote and published "The Mortal Immortal."[11]

Like the Hoffmann tale, "The Mortal Immortal" is told by a naive narrator attempting to decode the scientific experiments of a quasi crank and supposed quack, Cornelius Agrippa, the famous German alchemist whose assistant supposedly "raised the foul fiend during his master's absence, and was destroyed by him" (TMI, 314). A deep fear of death and its association with the father's phallic power motivate Hoffmann's "Sandman," while they occur in more muted form in the Shelley tale. The invocation of the name of Cornelius Agrippa, the association of Agrippa and Satan, both of whom figured so prominently in *Frankenstein* as the inspiration of Victor's dabbling in reanimating the base metal of the human body, suggest that masculine, scientific, and phallic powers are as dangerous as they are crucial to the development of human civilization. Once again, the human body is the obsessive focus of this tale, as it was in the two earlier Gothic works by Mary Shelley. Now, however, the issues are not only clear but very clearly delineated: the female body is decayed and fraudulent; it is a pale and inadequate copy of the prior and superior male body. The tale is predicated on the decline of the body of the beauteous Bertha, whose fading is contrasted to the continuing phallic power of the immortal Winzy, her body rotting while his flourishes over the course of their marriage.

Mary Shelley constructs her tale over the body of Bertha, but before she gets to Bertha, the narrator, Winzy, introduces the reader to his own desperate state of mind. He is a man who has lived for 323 years and fears that he may indeed be immortal. He is a man who feels "the weight of never-ending time—the tedious passage of the still-succeeding hours" (TMI, 314). Traditionally read as a slightly veiled autobiographical statement expressing Mary Shelley's own repugnance at having survived her husband, parents, and three of her children, the fear of time in this text actually expresses a fear of death, a terror about the nonexistence of an afterlife.[12] Life at least prolongs the uncertainty that there may indeed be an afterlife where one will be reunited with the souls of one's beloveds. Death will bring the final and unequivocal answer, and that is something that Mary Shelley was as unprepared to face in 1833 as she was in 1818.

Like a fairy tale, this short fiction begins with the poor, young assistant—"very much in love"—working for the notorious "alchymist" Cornelius Agrippa, who keeps killing all of his assistants because of the inhuman demands he makes on them. One need not search far to see Winzy as the victim of a beating fantasy at the hands of this father substitute. Thwarted in his efforts to persuade his recently orphaned childhood sweetheart Bertha to live "beneath [his] paternal roof," Winzy suffers greatly when Bertha goes off to live with "the old lady of the near castle, rich, childless, and solitary" (TMI, 315). Rather than have a child herself, this wealthy woman "buys" (or, as we might more euphemistically say, "adopts") a beautiful adult woman and then tries to barter her off to the highest bidder. Bertha is dramatic and self-dramatizing. She begins to dress in "silk," pose in her "marble palace" (TMI, 315), and generally amuse herself by taunting and tormenting the frustrated Winzy. Bertha wants Winzy to prove his love by accepting the risky job of working for Agrippa: "'You pretend to love, and you fear to face the Devil for my sake!'" (TMI, 315). Accepting a "purse of gold" from Agrippa makes Winzy feel "as if Satan himself tempted me" (TMI, 315). Bertha wants to put her would-be lover through a test, and she can think of no better one than to subject him to the ultimate evil father, the ultimate beater. No simple coquette, Bertha specializes rather in psychic and emotional abuse of her lover, continually subjecting him to anxiety and jealousy: "Bertha fancied that love and security were enemies, and her pleasure was to divide them in my bosom" (TMI, 316). Notice, however, that everything

Bertha metes out to Winzy is later delivered to her. She plays the role of Gothic villainess and later Gothic victim in this work.

If Cornelius Agrippa as the masculine and phallic aspect of the narrator is identified with the fires of Satan, Bertha as the feminine principle is associated with water and the fountain, "a gently bubbling spring of pure living waters" (TMI, 315). While ordered to work overtime stoking the furnaces of Agrippa, Winzy loses the favor of Bertha, who rejects him in favor of the rich suitor Albert Hoffer. Consumed with frustrated jealousy, Winzy decides to drink the magical elixir that Agrippa is preparing because he has been told that the brew is "'a philter to cure love; [if] you would not cease to love your Bertha— beware to drink!'" (TMI, 317). But that is precisely what Winzy wants— he wants to be free of his attachment to the feminine, or to put it another way, Mary Shelley wants to be free of her tie to the female body. Once again, her male narrator expresses Mary Shelley's own ambivalence and repugnance toward not only the female body but female sexuality and the chains of love. Listen to these revealing words from Winzy about his state of mind and motivations:

> False girl!—false and cruel! . . . Worthless, detested woman! I would not remain unrevenged—she should see Albert expire at her feet—she should die beneath my vengeance. She had smiled in disdain and triumph—she knew my wretchedness and her power. Yet what power had she?—the power of exciting my hate—my utter scorn—my—oh, all but indifference! Could I attain that—could I regard her with careless eyes, transferring my rejected love to one fairer and more true, that were indeed a victory! (TMI, 317)

What power had she indeed? Questioning the source and the power of the female body stands as the central query of Mary Shelley's corpus. The answer she discovers suggests that the female body has only as much power as the male chooses to allot to it. But the focus in this passage is on the male response to the female body, running the gamut from hate to scorn to indifference. Notice the progression of emotions. Only when one reaches indifference is one free of the obsessive hold of the other on one's consciousness. Mary Shelley throughout her works strives to escape just exactly this—the corrosive effect of the passions on her heart and body, seeking the cool indifference, the frigidity, the stark embrace of reason that she represented in the climactic presentation of the Arctic Circle in *Frankenstein*.

Grabbing the elixir and drinking, Winzy declares his intention to be cured "of love—of torture!" He finds himself sinking instead into a "sleep of glory and bliss which bathed [his] soul in paradise during the remaining hours of that memorable night," only to awake and find his appearance "wonderfully improved" (TMI, 317, 319). When he ventures out to Bertha's neighborhood, he finds himself the amorous object not only of Bertha but also of her rich old protectress, the "old high-born hag," "the old crone." The ugly old woman represents a standard feminine archetype, the double-faced goddess motif that Mary and Percy would have been familiar with through their readings in classical mythology. Blake (in "The Mental Traveller"), Keats (in "Lamia" and "La Belle Dame Sans Merci"), and Percy himself (in "Prince Athanase") had used the duplicitous female figure. The old hag in this text represents not simply what Bertha will become, a sort of humanized foreshadowing element, but also a version of the phallic mother as class avenger. Now conceiving a lecherous attraction to Winzy, the old hag aggressively pursues him, sending Bertha back to the castle with the peremptory command, "Back to your cage—hawks are abroad!" (TMI, 319). Ironically, the only hawk is the old hag, seeking to feast on her prey, the masculine flesh of Winzy.

But Winzy is now free of the earlier "respect" he had for the old hag's "rank." Now he boldly runs after Bertha, only to discover that he is as much in love with her as ever: "I no longer loved—Oh! no, I adored—worshipped—idolized her!" (TMI, 319). The two triangles operating here—Winzy/Bertha/old hag and Winzy/Bertha/false suitor—place the young lovers in the two varieties of oedipal rivalry that recur throughout Mary Shelley's fiction. The prior and more powerful association for her heroes and heroines is always the paternal and maternal home. The old hag represents the child-consciousness's (re)construction of the father and mother as one potent figure, all-powerful and all-consuming. This father/mother monad has been traditionally understood within psychoanalytical discourse as the phallic mother, the mother with the father's phallus, the fearful composite of maternity with power.[13] If Ann Radcliffe was finally able by the conclusion of her novels to kill the phallic mother, Mary Shelley is able to flee only temporarily from her. Rather, Bertha decides to reject the old hag's wealth and power and to run away to an alternate maternal abode: "'O Winzy!' she exclaimed, 'take me to your mother's cot.'" But not only does Bertha gain a new mother-figure, Winzy's father also "loved her" and "welcomed her heartily" (TMI, 320). Winzy is not so much gaining a wife as Bertha is gaining new parents. Or, to put it another way, Winzy is not so much gaining a wife as a new sibling.

Five years of bliss pass quickly, and one day Winzy is called to the bed of the dying Cornelius, who finally explains that his elixir had been not simply "a cure for love" but a cure "for all things—the Elixir of

Immortality" (TMI, 321). Love is here presented as another form of disease, a weakening and debilitating condition that leaves one prey to the ravages of mortality. To be "cured of love" is to be made immortal, impregnable, godlike, because to be human is to embody all the opposite qualities (TMI, 321). Love here is also presented as something that feminizes or weakens the masculine self, but the narrator is hardly a realistic presentation of a male character. His consciousness, his sensibility is feminine. He loves; therefore, he is as vulnerable as Mary Shelley found herself. He seeks to escape the ravages to which the flesh is prone, the never-ending pregnancies that Mary endured for six years, the repeated processions to the cemetery to bury babies. Winzy is the idealized masculine component of Mary Shelley—her reason and her intellect—that she desperately wants to believe will provide a means of escape for her. If she can be like a man—free from the biological curse—she would be like a god, immortal, inhabiting a world of the mind.

But the feminine aspect of Mary Shelley lives in the figure of Bertha, the female body that rots and decays before the saddened eyes of Winzy. Years pass and Bertha is now fifty, while Winzy appears to be her son. The two are "universally shunned" (TMI, 322) by their neighbors, largely because they embody the most pernicious incestuous dream of all—the tabooed love of a mother and son. Winzy has finally married the old crone, much to his dismay. Fleeing to a new country, the two decide to "wear masks," although Bertha's mask is infinitely less successful than Winzy's. Resorting to "rouge, youthful dress, and assumed juvenility of manner," Bertha is a parody of her former self. A desperate caricature of femininity, she has become a "mincing, simpering, jealous old woman." In other words, she has become another phallic mother, guarding her son Winzy with a "jealousy [that] never slept" (TMI, 323). The female body—once so beautiful and perfect—has become a flawed and diseased artifice, a shell fitted over a mass of stinking corruption. The male body, in stark contrast, continues to exist as statuesque and youthful, a perfect emblem of the triumph of masculinity and masculine values over the feminine. The female body has become the target and object of the beating given to it by the ultimate Nobodaddy—life, time, and mortality.

The years pass until Bertha is finally bedridden and paralytic and Winzy functions as her nurse: "I nursed her as a mother might a child" (TMI, 324). The wheel has come full circle. The mother is the child, while the husband/son has become a "mother." All gradations in the family romance have been tried in much the same way that Blake depicted them in "The Mental Traveller." Confined within the bourgeois domicile, the sexes feed on each other parasitically until they have consumed themselves in the process of playing all their gendered and ungendering roles to a limited audience. When Bertha finally dies, Winzy decides to escape the family romance. He lives alone in melancholy depression, contemplating suicide, until he decides to "put [his] immortality" to the test by journeying to the Arctic Circle. Like Victor Frankenstein, he decides to seek his destruction in the embrace of the "elements of air and water" (TMI, 325). This desire to reconcile opposites, to bathe and immerse himself in mutually exclusive physical elements, represents Mary Shelley's attempt to depict the catastrophic merging of masculine and feminine elements in the human psyche. If men are associated with the realm of air, the intellect, reason, and the mind, then women are identified with water, the physical, and the body and its fluids. Winzy's seeking oblivion in the extremely gender-coded landscape of the Arctic Circle suggests that the apocalypse Mary Shelley imagined for herself and her characters involved an escape from all polarities, or rather a freezing and holding of the two elements in a static situation. We do not know what becomes of Winzy, just as we never know what becomes of the creature at the conclusion of *Frankenstein*.

But the dream of desire is the same at the end of all of Mary Shelley's texts: to escape the body and live in the realm of pure mind. Like her mother, Mary Shelley was a reluctant sensualist. She needed, philosophically, to embrace free love and open marriage, but her disappointments in her philandering husband could not be concealed. Claiming to support free love is easy as long as one does not have a husband who has a history of collecting pretty young things and bringing them home. Finally a deep revulsion toward the female body emerges as clearly in Mary Shelley's works as it does in Wollstonecraft's.

Gothic feminism for Mary Shelley entailed the realization that women would always be life's victims, not simply because social, political, economic, and religious conventions placed them in inferior and infanticizing postures, but because their own bodies cursed them to forever serve the wheel of physical corruption. Being a mother, bringing to life a child who would die, and perhaps would die soon, condemned women to serve a merciless god—the cycle of generation, birth, and death—in a way that men did not. The nightmare haunting Mary Shelley's life was not simply that she caused the death of her mother but that she recapitulated a reversed version of the same tragedy with three of her own children. She experienced her life as a sort of curse to herself and the ones she loved, and why? She understood that her life, her very physical being, fed on her mother's body parasitically, cannibalistically consuming it. Later she watched her children wither, unable to be sustained by her. These recurring nightmares fed her fictions, but they also spoke to a deeper fear that has continually plagued women.

Gothic feminism seeks to escape the female body through a dream of turning weakness into strength. By pretending that one is weak or a passive victim, one camouflages oneself in a hostile terrain, diverting attention from one's real identity. Mary Shelley knew that on some level she was no victim; she knew her strength and intelligence were more than a match for anyone's. But she also sensed danger in that strength, or at least experienced it ambivalently, fearing that it caused the deaths of others. The grotesque freakishness of the creature in *Frankenstein,* made material in the description of "his" oddly assembled body and his continual rejection by everyone he seeks to love, trope Mary Shelley's own sense of herself and all women as diseased, aberrant, and freakish composites of the hopes and dreams of other people. Gothic feminism for Mary Shelley is embodied in the sense of herself and the female body as a void, an empty signifier, a lure into the cycle of painful birth and disappointing death. Railing against the female body—sometimes disguised as male and sometimes blatantly presented as female—is finally the only position that Mary Shelley can take. She can laud the bourgeois family, she can valorize community and what we now label "family values," but she ultimately cannot escape the mortality that gives the lie to everything she seeks to praise. She inhabits a female body, she bleeds and causes bleeding in others, and those unfortunate facts define for her and her fiction the Gothic feminist nightmare in its starkest terms.

Notes

1. See the suggestive discussion of "Gothic Drama and National Crisis" in Paula R. Backscheider, *Spectacular Politics: Theatrical Power and Mass Culture in Early Modern England* (Baltimore, Md.: Johns Hopkins University Press, 1993), 149–234.

2. For the best discussion of the stock tropes of melodrama, see Peter Brooks, *The Melodramatic Imagination* (New Haven: Yale University Press, 1976), 3, 16–17. Brooks acknowledges the importance on his thinking of Eric Bentley's "Melodrama" in *The Life of the Drama* (New York: Athenaeum, 1964), 195–218.

3. The best discussion of the development of sentimentality (also known as "sensibility") as a change in consciousness can be found in Jean Hagstrum's *Sex and Sensibility: Ideal and Erotic Love from Milton to Mozart* (Chicago: University of Chicago Press, 1980). On the same subject, also see the valuable collection of essays titled *Sensibility in Transformation: Creative Resistance to Sentiment from the Augustans to the Romantics*, ed. Syndy McMillen Conger (Totowa, N.J.: Fairleigh Dickinson University Press, 1990). On weakness as a central component of sentimentality, see R. W. Brissenden, *Virtue in Distress: Studies in the Novel of Sentiment from Richardson to Sade* (New York: Barnes and Noble, 1974) and Janet Todd, *Sensibility: An Introduction* (London: Methuen, 1986).

4. Naomi Wolf, *Fire With Fire: The New Female Power and How It Will Change the 21st Century* (New York: Random House, 1993), 136–37.

5. The relationship, real and imagined, between Mary Shelley and her dead mother and flawed father is explored most revealingly in William St. Clair's *The Godwins and the Shelleys: The Biography of a Family* (New York: Norton, 1989). Sandra M. Gilbert and Susan Gubar's *Madwoman in the Attic: The Woman Writer and the Nineteenth-Century Literary Imagination* (New Haven: Yale University Press, 1979) discusses Mary Shelley's relationship with her mother and its influence on her works (213–47), as does Janet M. Todd's "Frankenstein's Daughter: Mary Shelley and Mary Wollstonecraft," *Women and Literature* 4 (1976): 18–27. On the influence of Godwin on her works, see Katherine Powers, *The Influence of William Godwin on the Novels of Mary Shelley* (New York: Arno, 1980), and on Mary's relationship with her father, see U. C. Knoepflmacher, "Thoughts on the Aggression of Daughters," in *The Endurance of Frankenstein*, ed. George Levine and U. C. Knoepflmacher (Berkeley and Los Angeles: University of California Press, 1979), 88–119. Several recent biographies of Mary Shelley explore the parental influence on her writings. In particular, see Anne K. Mellor, *Mary Shelley: Her Life, Her Fiction, Her Monsters* (London: Routledge, 1988); Emily Sunstein, *Mary Shelley: Romance and Reality* (Boston: Little, Brown, 1989); and Muriel Spark, *Mary Shelley* (1951; rprt., London: Constable, 1987).

6. The full text of Mary's well-known journal confession reads:

With regard to "the good Cause"—the cause of the advancement of freedom & knowledge—of the Rights of Woman, &c.—I am not a person of opinions. . . . Some [people] have a passion for reforming the world:—others do not cling to particular opinions. That my parents and Shelley were of the former class, makes me respect it. . . . I was nursed and fed with a love of glory. To be something great and good was the precept given me by my Father: Shelley reiterated it. Alone & poor, I could only be something by joining a party— & there was much in me—the woman's love of looking up & being guided, & being willing to do anything if any one supported & brought me forward, which would have made me a good partizan—but Shelley died & I was alone. . . . If I have never written to vindicate the Rights of women, I have ever befriended women when oppressed. (21 October 1838) (*The Journals of Mary Shelley*, ed. Paula R. Feldman and Diana Scott-Kilvert [Oxford: Clarendon, 1987] 2:553–54)

The second Shelley quotation is taken from her letter of 11 June 1835 (*Selected Letters of Mary W. Shelley*, ed. Betty T. Bennett [Baltimore: Johns Hopkins University Press, 1995], 257).

7. Analyzing fathers and mothers in Mary Shelley's fiction has been a persistent focus in the literary criticism of her work. A useful overview of the critical history on this topic can be found in Jane Blumberg, *Mary Shelley's Early Novels: 'This Child of Imagination and Misery'* (Iowa City: University of Iowa Press, 1993). See also Marc A. Rubinstein, "'My Accursed Origin': The Search for the Mother in *Frankenstein*," *Studies in Romanticism* 15 (1976): 165–94; James B. Carson, "Bringing the Author Forward: *Frankenstein* through Mary Shelley's Letters," *Criticism* 30 (1988): 431–53; and Kate Ellis, "Mary Shelley's Embattled Garden," in *The Contested Castle: Gothic Novels and the Subversion of Domestic Ideology* (Urbana: University of Illinois Press, 1989), 181–206.

8. See Sigmund Freud, "'A Child is Being Beaten': A Contribution to the Study of the Origin of Sexual Perversions," in *The Standard Edition of the Complete Psychological Works of Sigmund Freud*, trans. and ed. James Strachey et al., 24 vols. (London: Hogarth Press, 1953–74), 17:175–204. The fullest attempt to apply the beating fantasy motif to

female Gothic fiction can be found in Michelle Massé, *In the Name of Love: Women, Masochism, and the Gothic* (Ithaca: Cornell University Press, 1992). In particular, see her chapter "'A Woman Is Being Beaten' and Its Vicissitudes," 40–106.

9. Mary Shelley sent the manuscript of *Mathilda* to Godwin via their mutual friend Maria Gisborne in May 1820. After almost two years of fruitless inquiry, she finally concluded that Godwin would not help see the manuscript into publication, so she began trying to recover it. She never succeeded, and the novella was not published until Elizabeth Nitchie prepared an edition for press in 1959 (*Mathilda* [Chapel Hill: University of North Carolina Press, 1959). Terence Harpold explores the incestuous core and motivation of *Mathilda* in his article "'Did you get Mathilda from Papa?': Seduction Fantasy and the Circulation of Mary Shelley's *Mathilda*," *Studies in Romanticism* 28 (1989): 49–67. Harpold concludes that the novel "represents a fantasy of seduction," and that the submission of the novel to Godwin "signals Mary's effort to engage him in the seduction fantasy, but to acknowledge the authority of his desire in the primal scene which determines her understanding of herself and her relations with each of her parents" (64).

10. All quotations from "The Mortal Immortal" are taken from text reprinted in *The Mary Shelley Reader*, ed. Betty Bennett and Charles E. Robinson (New York: Oxford University Press, 1990), 314–26, hereafter cited in the text as TMI. The first printing of "The Mortal Immortal" was in *The Keepsake* (1834), 71–87.

11. Although I have been unable to document Mary Shelley's reading of the Hoffmann tale through her own record of her readings in the journal, I believe she may at least have been familiar with the story's rough plotlines through the text's circulation in British literary circles by 1833. E. T. A. Hoffmann's "The Sandman" is itself a seminal literary source in psychoanalytic discourse systems. Freud developed his theory of the uncanny while reading the story, and it has inspired a number of French feminist meditations on "the phallic gaze," most notably Hélène Cixous's fruitful "Fiction and Its Phantoms: A Reading of Freud's 'The Uncanny,'" *New Literary History* 7 (1976): 525–48. An overview of the psychoanalytic history of the Hoffmann story can be found in Sarah Kofman, *Freud and Fiction*, trans. Sarah Wykes (Cambridge: Polity Press, 1991), while its status within the Romantic tradition is examined by Marianne Thalmann, *The Literary Sign Language of German Romanticism*, trans. Harold Basilius (Detroit: Wayne State University Press, 1972).

12. Like *Mathilda* and the other novels besides *Frankenstein*, the short stories of Mary Shelley are now the focus of critical interest. For a very different reading of the female body in this text, see Sonia Hofkosh, "Disfiguring Economies: Mary Shelley's Short Stories" in *The Other Mary Shelley: Beyond Frankenstein*, ed. Audrey A. Fisch, Anne K. Mellor, and Esther H. Schor (New York: Oxford University Press, 1993), 204–19.

13. For useful overviews and summaries of the theoretical and psychoanalytical background on the phallic mother, see Marcia Ian, *Remembering the Phallic Mother: Psychoanalysis, Modernism, and the Fetish* (Ithaca: Cornell University Press, 1993); and Dana Birksted-Breen, ed., *The Gender Conundrum: Contemporary Psychoanalytic Perspectives on Femininity and Masculinity* (New York: Routledge, 1993).

Part 3
Fictions as Cultural Provocation

"A Sigh of Many Hearts": History, Humanity, and Popular Culture in *Valperga*

James P. Carson

To the degree that Mary Shelley's first two novels are didactic works, they promote the same moral about the superiority of domestic affections "in blameless obscurity"[1] to the ambition for glory and fame. However, there is a generic difference between these two works. In the philosophi‐cal novel *Frankenstein* (1818), Shelley seeks to define humanity in a deliberately theoretical way, by examining the nature and education of a fantastic monster and his claims on our sympathies. In her second novel, *Valperga* (1823), Shelley seeks to define humanity historically, in a study of the influence of passion, imagination, and conscience on fourteenth-century Italians. While we cannot rigorously maintain an opposition between theoretical and historical modes of definition, the greater length of and the more detailed social fabric presented in *Valperga* permit Shelley to analyze more explicitly popular culture, crowd psychology, and feminist ideology. While Shelley discusses government in her first novel, especially in the episode in which the monster overhears Felix de Lacey's lectures from Volney's *Ruins of Empires*, the opposition between tyranny and republicanism forms the central conflict of her second novel. Shelley's commitment to Italian unification, liberty, and independence from Austria motivates both a series of historical analogies in *Valperga* and certain changes for the 1831 edition of *Frankenstein*. Thus, in the revised text of Shelley's first novel, Elizabeth Lavenza's father is transformed from "an Italian gentleman," about whom we have no further information, into "one of those Italians nursed in the memory of the antique glory of Italy,—one among the *schiavi ognor frementi*, who exerted himself to obtain the liberty of his country."[2] In *Valperga*,

Shelley writes a historical novel of sensibility—that is to say, a novel in which a temporal succession of feelings takes priority over a chronology of public events—in order to explore political ideals for the self-government and policing of socially and culturally conditioned human agents. Her ideals derive from classical republican thought, from the historical and economic views of J. C. L. de Sismondi and from the rationalism and sentimentalism of Mary Wollstonecraft and William Godwin.

After *The Last Man* (1826) and, of course, *Frankenstein*, *Valperga* has received the most critical attention of any of Mary Shelley's works. Indeed, Frederick Jones, praising both the "creative force" and "thoroughness of scholarship" it exhibits, called *Valperga* Shelley's "best novel."[3] Among the most notable essays on the political ideology of *Valperga* are those by Betty Bennett and Joseph Lew. Bennett has persuasively argued that *Valperga* reveals Mary Shelley's commitment to liberal social reforms and, specifically, to the view formulated by Percy Shelley that the opposition between the forces of liberty and despotism (represented in *Valperga* by the Guelphs and Ghibellines respectively) motivates and structures historical progress.[4] Joseph Lew, on the contrary, finds an opposition between Mary Shelley and male Romantic authors, including her husband. He seeks to confirm that she, like Jane Austen, is an exponent of what Anne Mellor terms "female Romantic ideology," which stresses Enlightenment values, rationality, domesticity, and selfless sympathy for others.[5] For Lew, female Romanticism proves to be a conservative ideology. Characterizing the government of Florence, which Shelley idealizes, as "moderate aristocratic," Lew asserts that *Valperga* is marked by a Humean "disdain for and fear of the lower classes."[6] In contrast to Lew, and in general agreement with Betty Bennett, I shall argue that *Valperga* is a liberal work, that Mary Shelley would have associated early-fourteenth-century Florence with republicanism rather than aristocracy (and rightly so), and that at times she shows substantial sympathy for both the people and popular culture.

I shall first define Shelley's mode of historical fiction in *Valperga*, showing how she values history for its potential to expand the narrow perspective of individuals caught in the present moment and how she places sentiments above political events in her representation of the past. Secondly, I shall show that Shelley, recognizing the threat of dehumanization posed by early-nineteenth-century industrial and state institutions, seeks to represent and analyze the fourteenth-century forces that similarly threatened autonomy and humane sentiments, even while she suggests that love and compassion might create superior specimens of humanity. Thirdly, I shall provide evidence that Shelley regarded Florence as a republic, characterized in Godwinian terms, and I shall detail her ambivalent attitudes toward the common people and their culture.

History and Sensibility

In 1823 Shelley embodied her liberal and feminist rationalism in what I am calling a historical novel of sensibility. Her understanding of history derives in part from the classical republican model of masculine virtue, preeminently found in the figure of the autonomous farmer/soldier who possesses a disinterested and extensive view of the public good. In this view, landed property provides the best guarantee of independence. Usury and the dubious maneuvers of financial capitalism are condemned, whereas commerce, though perhaps narrowing the views of its practitioners, benefits the state.[7] In classical republican ideology, historical change is partly a process of decline, as luxury threatens autonomy and self-interest displaces public spirit. For the English, the gap between ancient Romans and modern Italians provided clear evidence for this process of historical decline. But if self-interest and narrow views could be overcome, such decline might be forestalled. Shelley celebrates classical learning and the knowledge of history, including that obtained from a historical novel like *Valperga*, because both enable the transcendence of partisan, provincial, and present-centered views and thus stave off corruption.

Shelley embodies such learning in a female character—Euthanasia dei Adimari, a Guelph republican aristocrat and the heroine of the novel. Euthanasia's father, Antonio dei Adimari—after retiring from public life to devote himself to study, at the beginning of a great period in the revival of learning—is struck with blindness. Euthanasia turns her father's misfortune to her own advantage, learning Latin in order to assist him in his studies and thus to share in them. Her education preserves her from "that narrow idea of the present times, as if they and the world were the same, which characterizes the unlearned" (*Valperga*, 1:28).[8] There is an autobiographical dimension here, as Shelley imagines her own father, William Godwin, now much less of a public figure than he was in the 1790s, to be disabled, giving her the oppportunity to affirm her filial virtue in caring for him.[9] However, more than a mere autobiographical positioning of Godwin in the role of Adimari and herself in Euthanasia's roles of teacher and nurse, the passage also reveals Shelley's politics and a justification for historical fiction.

History, the classics, and foreign travel extend one's views both temporally and geographically, thus inhibiting the historical movement toward decline. So, when Euthanasia visits the Pantheon in Rome, she becomes an ideal figure of the historical novelist, in her attempt to bring her classical reading to life: "I called on the shadows of the departed to converse with me" (*Valperga,* 1:203). Euthanasia's future fiancé, Castruccio Castracani, begins his education under the tutelage of his father's friend Francesco de Guinigi, who, living in exile in Este, has given up his military role and, obeying the messianic injunction (Isaiah 2:4), has "turned his sword to a ploughshare" (*Valperga,* 1:46).[10] An enlightened figure, Guinigi is characterized by "a freedom from prejudice" (1:65). While Castruccio reveals his narrow views by expressing elitist contempt for the "grovelling" minds of peasants, Guinigi conceives of a utopian state, which will refute the mistaken notion

> that a peasant's life is incompatible with intellectual improvement. . . .
> [W]hen I would picture happiness upon earth, my imagination conjures up
> the family of a dweller among the fields, whose property is secure, and whose
> time is passed between labour and intellectual pleasures. (1:53)

Shelley derives Guinigi's sentiments from the arguments in favor of equality of property in book 8 of Godwin's *Enquiry Concerning Political Justice* (1793). There, Godwin argues that, were everyone to contribute to the labor necessary for subsistence, the labor of any individual would be light. In that case, "none would be made torpid with fatigue, but all would have leisure to cultivate the kindly and philanthropical affections, and to let loose his faculties in the search of intellectual improvement."[11] Thus, while Shelley expresses her admiration for republican Rome through the character of Euthanasia, she endorses the Godwinian revision of classical republican ideology through that of Guinigi. In Godwin's view, neither substantial landed property nor freedom from manual labor is a prerequisite for acquiring extensive views, liberal learning, impartial judgment, and public spirit.[12] Godwin, Wollstonecraft, Sismondi, and Mary Shelley are proponents of radical agrarianism: all celebrate independent peasants, who labor on small farms that they either own outright or hold on long and secure leases.[13]

Both classical republican ideology and Godwinian political philosophy prior to the mid-1790s posited an autonomous, stoical model of personality. From the time of *St. Leon* (1799), however, Godwin paid much greater attention to sensibility and the domestic affections. Both Godwin and Mary Shelley advocate a sentimental hierarchy of communicative modes, in which the languages of the heart, of tears, of the eyes, and of the countenance take priority over speech, which in turn has higher value than writing. This antirhetorical and antitheatrical hierarchy embodies the values of spontaneous expression and unmediated truth. So, in *Frankenstein*, Robert Walton remarks that even letter writing, which approaches the condition of speech, "is a poor medium for the communication of feeling"; he seeks instead a friend "whose eyes would reply to mine."[14] While the cruel and ambitious Ghibelline tyrant of Lucca hardly counts as a man of feeling, he too has his occasional sentimental moments. At the end of *Valperga*, Castruccio Castracani visits Euthanasia in prison, where she has been confined for her reluctant participation in a conspiracy against him. The glistening eyes of Castruccio and the single tear visible on his cheek prompt a narrative commentary that formalizes sentimental communicative theory:

> They talk of tears of women; but, when they flow most plenteously, they soften not the heart of man, as one tear from his eyes has power on a woman. Words and looks have been feigned; they say, though I believe them not, that women have feigned tears: but those of a man, which are ever as the last demonstration of a too full heart, force belief, and communicate to her who causes them that excess of tenderness, that intense depth of passion of which they are themselves the sure indication. (*Valperga*, 3:250)

Sentimentalism entails a new conception of masculinity, for which Castruccio is ill-suited, given his seduction of Beatrice (a young religious enthusiast from Ferrara)[15] and his refusal to abandon military and political ambition in favor of the domestic pleasures he might have enjoyed with Euthanasia. Here, however, he experiences a moment of regret for having rejected sentimental values.[16]

But sentimentalism, as Shelley's discussion of male tears shows, is also crucially concerned with the epistemological question of the relationship between language and truth—a question that preoccupied eighteenth-century novelists in general[17] and historical novelists in particular. So, the prime attraction of male tears resides not in the evidence they supply for the appearance of a new sympathetic and humane masculine character. Rather, male tears are a natural, entirely reliable, and not at all arbitrary sign: they are beyond feigning, they provide demonstration in the last analysis of an overflow of feeling, they enforce belief, and they are a "sure indication" of deep passion. A historical novel of sensibility like *Valperga* turns from public events, which are the objects of interested and partisan misrepresentation, to the supposedly less contested representations of the subjective and emotional responses of historical personages. As such, *Valperga* seems consistent with Godwin's theory of fiction, as formulated in a 1797 manuscript essay entitled "Of History and Romance." This essay begins by indicating a preference for individual history (i.e., biography) over general history, since the latter, as David McCracken notes, "is usually the pursuit of those who abhor feelings."[18] Godwin then proceeds to claim that fictional biography is superior to documentary biography.

Shelley begins her historical novel with a preface in which she disparages as a "romance" Machiavelli's *Life of Castruccio Castracani*, which she claims is the English reader's major source for knowledge about this tyrant (*Valperga*, 1:iii). Shelley's disparagement is warranted, since Machiavelli's *Life*, written in 1520, has been characterized by Allan Gilbert as "essentially a work of fiction."[19] However, more important than any opposition between the genres of romance and historical fiction is that between two radically different conceptions of human beings: either as passive objects of fortune or as subjective interpreters of events. Machiavelli seeks to demonstrate how fortune brings about human greatness. As the dying Castruccio in Machiavelli's biography says, "Fortune . . . is admitted to be arbiter of all human things."[20] For Shelley, on the contrary, fortune operates in the realm of *accident*, whereas feelings constitute *essences* or *realities*. As Euthanasia learns from her father, "content of mind, love, and benevolent feeling ought to be the elements of our existence; while those accidents of fortune or fame . . . were as the dust of the balance" (*Valperga*, 1:198–99). Earlier in the same chapter, Euthanasia recounts for Castruccio the past few years of her life:

> I have had few hopes, and few fears; but every passing sentiment has been an event; and I have marked the birth of an new idea with the joy that others derive from what they call change and fortune. What is the world, except that which we feel? Love, and hope, and delight, or sorrow and tears; these are our lives, our realities. (1:192–93)

In her role as narrator of her own individual history, Euthanasia provides a model for the author of the historical novel of sensibility, which should simultaneously limit the power of fortune by reducing external events to accidents and extend the power of sentiment by transforming subjective feelings aroused by actions in the world into internal events. Shelley stages a narration within the novel in order to delineate a subgenre of historical fiction in which feelings, because they are essential and substantial, count as events.

However, Euthanasia's observation that "every passing sentiment has been an event" provides evidence not only about genre but also for Shelley's identification with her heroine. After the death of Percy Shelley and just prior to the publication of *Valperga*, Mary Shelley wrote to Jane Williams about her loneliness in Italy: "Solitary as I am, I feed & live on imagination only—feelings are my events—." [21] The twenty-five-year-old Shelley, having lost her husband, identifies with her solitary Italian heroine, who, by the age of twenty-two, has suffered the loss of not only her beloved father but also her mother and two brothers. Shelley's works are not only autobiographical but also highly allusive, drawing particularly on the works of the authors in her own family and circle. Euthanasia's statement that "every passing sentiment has been an event" would have been encountered by Shelley in her mother's most famous and least sentimental work, *A Vindication of the Rights of Woman* (1792). In Wollstonecraft, the statement appears within a description of how women's sentimentalism results from their having been denied political rights, an exclusion that distracts women from "the interest of the whole community" and "the general good":

> The mighty business of female life is to please, and restrained from entering into more important concerns by political and civil oppression, sentiments become events, and reflection deepens what it should, and would have effaced, if the understanding had been allowed to take a wider range. [22]

A certain intertextuality—the problem of where Shelley's language has already been and the textual locations to which it will subsequently migrate—might introduce a critique of sentimentalism into the very heart of the historical novel of sensibility. In *Valperga*, the idea that feelings are events initially serves to mark the refusal passively to accept the power of fortune in human life. It delineates a type of history that, while less public, may be more useful and more true than "general" history. However, when the idea is taken into Shelley's letters, we might be enabled retrospectively to discern a note of self-pity in Euthanasia's admirable attempt to reconcile sentimentalism and the fostering of civic virtue. Moreover, that Shelley, in her letter to Jane Williams, conceives of the situation in which feelings are events as one in which one feeds oneself on imagination instead of on reality would seem to overturn the philosophical opposition between accident and essence, shadow and substance. If, for Euthanasia, sentiments and thoughts are real and substantial, in Shelley's letter to Jane Williams, by contrast, sentimental events reside merely in the imagination. Then, once a probable source for the idea that feelings are events is discovered in Wollstonecraft, a critique of sentimentalism as an ideology imposed on women by their having been denied more extensive views could be imported into Shelley's novel. Thus, the idea that feelings are events simultaneously defines the historical novel of sensibility and calls into question the value of sentimentalism. Even while *Valperga* provides the knowledge that might preserve the reader from "that narrow idea of the present times, as if they and the world were the same" (*Valperga*, 1:28), the sentimental aspects of the novel may well be the product of the political oppression that has denied "a wider range" to female understanding.

Defining Humanity

The central problem of *Valperga*—that of providing a historical definition of humanity—leads to innumerable questions and comments about "man," women, gods, rulers, monsters, machines, and tools in the course of the three volumes of the novel. Castruccio introduces the topic early in the work, when he asks his pastoral tutor, Guinigi, the Promethean question: "Is it not fame that makes men gods?" (*Valperga*, 1:54). As one might expect from the author of *Frankenstein*, Shelley's ultimate answer is "no." However, in *Valperga*, as opposed to *Frankenstein*, Shelley clearly distinguishes between Castruccio's ambition for worldly power and renown and a laudable desire for posthumous fame (1:161–62). The initial question of what "makes men gods" reverberates through a novel that explores the forces that raise people above or sink them below humanity.

For Shelley, four things may transform a person into a superior being: education, broad cultural forces, compassion, and love. Euthanasia—by means of her father's lessons in history, the classics, and the poetry of Dante—comes to think that human nature has declined from ancient Roman times and "that no man lived now, who bore affinity to these far shining beacons of the earth" (1:195). Human nature changes with historical and cultural conditions. Looking back from nineteenth-century Florence to Castruccio's time, Shelley posits a similar decline to that which Euthanasia believed had occurred since the days of ancient Rome. The architectural monuments of Florence surviving from the fourteenth century, writes Shelley, were "better suited to those warlike and manly times, than to the taste of the present age, when the Italian heaven shines on few who would defend their own home" (2:124). Shelley's historical perspective here derives from the classical republican discourse in which luxury corrupts and effeminizes a heroic and warlike people. Shelley shares Euthanasia's view that a transcendent heroic virtue is the product not of nature but rather of historical and cultural conditions. While the "Italian heaven" has not changed, human beings have.

When Euthanasia heroically and disinterestedly sacrifices her personal love for Castruccio to her devotion to the principle of liberty, Shelley sketches the character of the tyrant of Lucca in order to show what the ruling passion of ambition has made of him: "Neither compassion which makes angels of men, nor love which softens the hearts of the gods themselves, had over him the slightest power" (2:172). That is to say, the idol of fame leads Castruccio to reject two emotions—compassion and love—that have the power to raise human beings above themselves.

Military glory (and Castruccio is too ambitious to be admirably self-denying) is countered by sympathetic nursing of the sick and wounded. During the siege of Valperga by Castruccio's troops, Euthanasia is observed "flitting like an angel" as she "mingled with the women who ministered to the wounded" (2:265). The force of the word *angel* here is revealed when, in Castruccio's subsequent siege of Florence, Euthanasia is "lifted . . . above humanity" in her heroic endeavors to alleviate the suffering caused by her former professed lover (3:179). While classical republican thought leads to admiration for public spirit in civic duties and to self-sacrifice in military service, sentimentalism privileges self-sacrifice in domestic, compassionate, and charitable acts, such as nursing. Shelley explicitly contrasts Euthanasia and Castruccio in order to show that the sentimental woman succeeds, whereas the ambitious man fails, in the endeavor to become godlike. The rationalist, sentimentalist, and feminist ethic of compassion wins out over the desire for fame through conquest—if not in the fates of the characters (the realm of narrative *event*), then surely in the feelings of both author and reader (sentiments as *events*).

If education, favorable political and cultural conditions, compassion, and love can raise human beings to the status of angels or gods, Shelley likewise finds many sources of human degradation and atavism. Party (as opposed to *public*) spirit, military discipline, and the desire for power (gained through political machinations, finance, or sex) are the negative forces Shelley discovers in fourteenth-century Italy that are analogous to the commercial, industrial, and utilitarian institutions and theories of the early nineteenth century. Shelley shares with civic humanists the view that a liberal education acquired through classical and historical literature and through foreign travel enables one to gain extensive views of the public good. Trade, finance, and partisanship, on the contrary, may result in narrow and self-interested views. Galeazzo Visconti, friend to Castruccio and tyrant of Milan, is led by Ghibelline partisanship to dehumanize others—specifically, to reduce the Guelphs to the status of "vermin" (2:7). Employing a gambling metaphor in advising Castruccio to attempt the conquest of Florence, Galeazzo claims that "men are both our die and our stake" (2:11)—mere instruments and counters for tyrants' play. Castruccio has already become "accustomed . . . to count men as the numerals of a military arithmetic" (1:245–46). He subordinates human beings to his designs of conquest and control, so that people become body parts to be organized and administered: "He began to count heads to be removed, and hands to be used" (2:145). Given Castruccio's skillful disposition and insistent enumeration of human bodies, his peacetime administrative interests should not surprise us: he establishes "a vigorous system of police" in Lucca (2:174).[23] Even while Shelley is especially appalled by Castruccio's frequent recourse to capital punishment and his increasing use of torture, Castruccio's government also represents something new—namely, the disciplinary institutions of punishment, education, and industry that were being developed at the beginning of the nineteenth century in order to exert power over the masses by individualizing them.

Like sadists and Machiavellian tyrants of earlier times, the new institutions that deploy demographic data and bureaucratic techniques conceptualize humanity in terms of instrumentality and utility. Thus, the various forms of imprisonment and tyranny to which the major female characters in Shelley's novel are subjected reflect on modern as well as medieval institutions and attitudes. Beatrice is arrested by Dominican inquisitors at various times. When she is abandoned by Castruccio, she embarks on a pilgrimage for Rome, only to be abducted and confined for three years in a "ruinous house" on the Campagna di Roma (*Valperga*, 3:82). There, she is starved, tortured, and sexually assaulted by a diabolical and sublime figure and his "carnival of devils" (3:86), including the infidel priest Battista Tripalda. In an inverted echo of Castruccio's earlier question, "Is it not fame that makes men gods?" (1:54), Beatrice asks if "the author and mechanist of these crimes" even belongs to the human race: "He bore a human name; they say his lineage was human; yet could he be a man?" (3:85).

If the word *author* refers to the intellectual activity of original conception and relates the sublime sadist of *Valperga* to Victor Frankenstein, the "author" of the creature, the word *mechanist* refers to the lower activity of perpetrating crimes with one's own hands and body.[24] In the context of Shelley's critique of disciplinary and industrial administration, the word *mechanist* implies that a utilitarian and instrumental view of human beings may lead to manipulating them as if they were machines. The fourteenth-century mechanists of crime or tyranny use their penetration into human character to obtain the requisite biographical and psychological insights, which disciplinary institutions will later compile through bureaucratic means. When Galeazzo Visconti, for his own political ends, seeks to disrupt the proposed marriage between Castruccio and Euthanasia, he at first avoids conversation with the countess, "until, finding out the secret chords of her mind, he might play upon them with a master's hand" (2:126). The power-hungry witch of the Apennines, Fior di Mandragola, who herself "seemed hardly human" and "unlike humanity" (*Valperga*, 3:129), operates in the same way on Beatrice: "The witch had now tuned her instrument, and she proceeded to play on it with a master's hand" (3:133). When, a few pages later, she is taken out to meet the witch, Beatrice moves "her arms like inanimate machines" (3:148). No doubt, in employing a musical metaphor for treating people as instruments, Shelley has literary precedents in mind— specifically, Hamlet's attack on Guildenstern: "You would play upon me, you would seem to know my stops, you would pluck out the heart of my mystery, you would sound me from my lowest note to [the top of] my compass."[25] But, as a historical novelist, Shelley also knows that playing on people as if they were instruments, or operating them as if they were machines, signifies different though sometimes analogous things in different circumstances—in medieval Italy, Shakespearean England, and the Industrial Revolution.

Even though there are no specific references to industrial mechanization or the division of labor in *Valperga*, Shelley does critique classical political economy and the idea that rational self-interest provides a key to human behavior. When Euthanasia consents to join a conspiracy to overthrow Castruccio, she objects to the personal immorality of one of her fellow conspirators, Battista Tripalda. Bondelmonti, a Florentine aristocrat, responds that a conspiracy, like other political associations and governmental organizations, requires instruments and not full human beings: "Edged tools are what we want; it matters little the evil name with which they may be branded" (*Valperga*, 3:199). Another conspirator, Ugo Quartezzani, attempts to answer Euthanasia's objection in a more philosophical way: "A man may be one day wicked, and good the next; for self-interest sways all, and we are virtuous or vicious as we hope for advantage to ourselves. The downfall of Antelminelli [i.e., Castruccio] will raise [Tripalda]; and therefore he is to be trusted" (3:213– 14). But the proponents of self-interest and those who subordinate evil means to good ends prove to be wrong, as Tripalda betrays the conspiracy.

The question of means versus ends in the Godwinian context opens out into speculation about whether social change should be achieved through revolutionary violence or through discussion, education, and the gradual diffusion of knowledge. The belief in the necessity of violent means derives from the idea that material forces determine human consciousness: that is to say, since class allegiance and political ideology are the products of rational calculations of material self-interest,[26] people cannot be *persuaded* but must be *forced* to give up wealth and power. Given Godwin's and Shelley's advocacy of self-denial and disinterestedness, it is not surprising that they should prefer that social change be achieved through gradual reform promoted by education and enlightened discussion. For Godwin, lasting political improvements, as well as changes in the distribution of wealth and property, must follow a change in consciousness—a change, as it were, in the ideological superstructure rather than the material base. Rational agency for Godwin and Mary Shelley cannot be reduced to the material calculations of *homo economicus* but rather should be expanded to include extensive views of the good of the whole society, characteristic of the republican citizen.

The Godwinian novel, in which we should include *Valperga*,[27] reinscribes the question of means versus ends as the opposition between daggers and tales, edged tools and narratives. Euthanasia disputes with her coconspirator, the "edged tool" Tripalda, over whether Castruccio must merely be overthrown or whether it is necessary that he be put to death. Tripalda's mode of argumentation is *ad feminam* derision:

> "Women! women!" said Tripalda, contemptuously. "By the body of Bacchus! I wonder what Bondelmonti meant by introducing a woman into the plot. One way or another they have spoiled, or ever will spoil, every design that the wisdom of man has contrived. I say he must die." (*Valperga*, 3:209–10)

Believing that she can reform Castruccio through love, that she can raise the tyrant's consciousness, Euthanasia responds by attempting to control the bacchanalian Tripalda by narration. She threatens to tell a tale about him that will "fill mankind with detestation" (3:212)—the tale that Beatrice has recounted about Tripalda's participation in the sadistic "carnival of devils" on the Campagna di Roma. Shelley traces a parallel between contempt for women and sadistic sexual practices. Her opposition between edged tools and tales recalls *Hamlet* once more, this time through the mediation of Godwin. Anticipating the closet scene with Gertrude, Hamlet seeks self-control: "I will speak [daggers] to her, but use none."[28] Anticipating his judicial confrontation with Falkland, Caleb Williams exclaims, "Tyrants have trembled surrounded with whole armies of their Janissaries! What should make thee inaccessible to my fury?—No, I will use no daggers! I will unfold a tale—!"[29] In the

Godwinian novel, then, the dagger or edged tool is a metaphor for revolutionary violence, whereas narrative represents the reformist mode of extensive discussion and uncensored communication. Once more, Euthanasia becomes a figure for the historical novelist, given her plans both to reform Castruccio and to overawe Tripalda *through narrative*.

Tripalda is a monster who must be controlled, whereas Castruccio can be reformed. Castruccio has illegitimately divorced the feeling human being from the rational, Machiavellian ruler. Euthanasia's sentimental project is to remake the man by healing this split. In response to an earlier plot against him, Castruccio banishes three hundred families from Lucca, the innocent along with the guilty. This act of injustice results from the remorselessness of the "ruler; for he loses even within himself the idea of his own individuality" (*Valperga*, 2:154). For Castruccio, "the head of a state is no longer a private man, and he would act with shameful imbecility, if he submitted to his enemies because he dared not punish them" (2:158). The government of Castruccio, then, along with that of his fellow Ghibellene tyrant Galeazzo Visconti, operates through a double dehumanization, which nonetheless entails a dissymmetrical application of the strategy of individuation. First, the ruler must act with cruel and inhumane policy while losing the very "idea of his own individuality." Those subjected to power, on the other hand, are reduced to enumerated parts of human beings and to utilitarian machines, but this second form of dehumanization appears simultaneously with the individuating strategies of efficient administration, discipline, and police.[30] In place of politicians who have stripped themselves of their humanity along with their individuality, Shelley would install humane legislators, whose vision is more extensive and whose feelings are more intense (since their sentiments are themselves events). In opposition to the mechanized but individuated subjects of bureaucratic power, Shelley betrays at least a guarded sympathy for the, admittedly superstitious, crowd and its traditional popular culture.

Republicanism and Popular Culture

Mary Shelley would have regarded early fourteenth-century Florence as a republican, not an aristocratic, government. Her conception of late medieval Italian politics derived largely from her major source for contextualizing the life of Castruccio: J. C. L. de Sismondi's sixteen-volume *Histoire des républiques italiennes au moyen age* (1809–18). Better known today for his writings on political economy than for his histories, Sismondi (1773–1842) began his career as "a fervent disciple of [Adam] Smith."[31] However, by the time he completed his Italian history, he had begun to express indignation at laissez-faire economics: "He boldly declared himself the adversary of the English school, of the Ricardos, of the Maccullochs, of the Says, of all those who see in the mass of men only a machine to create the wealth which will afterwards crush them."[32] Sismondi describes Florence as "the Athens of Italy" for, among other qualities, "the generosity which seemed the national character, whenever it was necessary to protect the oppressed or defend the cause of liberty."[33] In virtually every context, he distinguishes Florence from other Italian states: "Florence was the city where the love of liberty was the most general and the most constant in every class; where the cultivation of the understanding was carried farthest; and where enlightenment of mind soonest appeared in the improvement of the laws" (75–76). Sismondi holds the conventional Enlightenment view that the arts and sciences arise soonest and flourish best where liberty is fostered and preserved, and he observes that by the thirteenth century "the Florentines became still more attached to the most democratic forms of liberty" (103).

Sismondi notes that when Guelph cities (those loyal to the pope) fell to the armies of the German (Holy Roman) emperor, "the triumph of the aristocracy generally accompanied that of the Ghibeline party" (64). His account of the two parties at the time of Castruccio's ascendancy to power is essentially the same as that in *Valperga*:

> In the fourteenth century, the faction of the Ghibelines had become that of tyranny,—of the Guelphs that of liberty. The former displayed those great military and political talents which personal ambition usually develops. In the second were to be found, almost exclusively, patriotism, and the heroism which sacrifices to it every personal interest. (120)

Not only does Shelley derive information on Italian politics from Sismondi, but she largely shares his ideological perspective. Like Shelley, Sismondi prefers republican Guelphs to despotic Ghibellines, but also views party conflict itself as potentially "fatal to the cause of liberty" (85). Thus, even while history is structured on the opposition between parties, both Sismondi and Shelley value disinterested, nonpartisan, and extensive views. In drawing heavily on Sismondi, Shelley uses the best history of Italy available to her, which was, moreover, one written by a liberal Enlightenment figure. Sismondi's influence led Shelley to situate early Renaissance Florence among other notable, if imperfect, sites of freedom, such as democratic Athens, republican Rome, seventeenth- and eighteenth-century Holland, Rousseau's Geneva, and Franklin's Philadelphia.[34]

In *Valperga,* republican and popular politics are largely characterized in the words of those opposed to them. At the beginning of his military career in France, Castruccio serves under an Italian commander named Alberto Scoto—Shelley's name for the historical figure Alberto Scotti of Piacenza.[35] From Scoto, Castruccio imbibes not only military skill but the devious politics of Renaissance Italians. In Scoto's "evil school" (*Valperga,* 1:94), Castruccio learns that a prince should rely on the sword, on gold, and on ideological control, whereas "woe and defeat are to that chief, who reigns only by the choice of the people; a choice more fickle and deceitful than the famed faithlessness of woman" (1:96). The antifeminist excess in this comparison between the fickleness of the people and "the faithlessness of woman" is a strong indication of Shelley's criticism of Scoto's views on democracy and thus, by implication, of her own approval of republican politics.

Immediately upon his return to Italy, Castruccio encounters Benedetto Pepi, who detests the republicans of Florence for "asserting the superiority of the vulgar, till every petty artizan of its meanest lane fancies himself as great a prince as the emperor Henry himself" (1:119).[36] In the course of the novel, Shelley discredits Pepi even more thoroughly than Scoto. Far from idealizing a "moderate aristocratic" state, Shelley appears to believe in a leveling "commonwealth," such as that which Pepi and Galeazzo Visconti (*Valperga,* 2:12) abhor, in which commerce produces security if not liberty.

The ideal of freedom in *Valperga* resides neither in peaceful retirement nor in a stable pastoral state. Instead, liberty is a condition of instability, change, conflict, and energy. Such progressive energies will sometimes require restraint, yet the ideal republic permits neither despotic force nor ideological control. Thus, Shelley adopts the Godwinian solution of self-censorship and mutual surveillance among equals. Godwin proposes a "natural" rather than administrative form of restraint in communities of limited size. No penal system would be necessary, he argues, since "every individual would then live under the public eye; and the disapprobation of his neighbours, a species of coercion not derived from the caprice of men, but from the system of the universe, would inevitably oblige him either to reform or to emigrate."[37] So, Castruccio, prior to his descent into tyranny, is led by his love for Euthanasia to "talk of republics, and the energy and virtue that every citizen acquires, when each acting under the censure of each, yet possesses power" (*Valperga,* 1:188). The republic for Godwin and Shelley, then, maintains order by fostering self-discipline and by creating conditions of transparency and visibility in which public opinion can operate "naturally," with maximum effectiveness.

The character who best realizes the ideal of the republican citizen is Euthanasia, and Shelley once again contrasts her with Castruccio. Following the deaths of her parents and brothers, Euthansia finds herself in a state of independence, moderated only by "the rigid censorship of her own reason, and the opinion of her fellow-citizens" (1:170). Conscience and duty are the other names for this faculty of self-censorship. Throughout the novel, Euthanasia engages in self-regulation enforced by a nightly procedure of self-examination (3:66). While there is little evidence of Roman Catholicism in this novel about medieval Italy, apart from the persecution and torture of heretics by Dominican inquisitors, a fundamentally Calvinist internalization of the practice of confession guides the behavior and, indeed, the very thoughts of the ideal republican citizen.

To be sure, there is a certain feminist elitism in presenting the liberally educated and nobly born Euthanasia as the ideal republican citizen. The common people in *Valperga* lack both Euthanasia's classical cultivation and her capacity for self-regulation, but it would be incorrect to follow Anne Mellor and Joseph Lew in characterizing Shelley's attitude toward the lower social orders as disdainful or fearful. Early in the novel, Shelley raises the question of the control of the common people through the ideological means their own popular culture makes available and through disciplinary mechanisms of surveillance (as opposed to Godwinian public opinion). Again, Alberto Scoto presents the young Castruccio with political lessons—in this case, explaining the usefulness of minstrels, actors, and other *Uomini di Corte*: "These latter . . . can penetrate every where, see every thing, hear every thing, and if you acquire but the art of getting their knowledge from them, they become of infinite utility" (1:98).[38] We have already seen how Shelley discredits Scoto by emphasizing his antifeminism. Here, he is discredited by his devious politics, since Machiavelli himself argued that a wise prince "engages the people's attention with festivals and shows."[39] Machiavelli's advice, less modern than Scoto's administrative utilitarianism, derives from the Juvenalian *panem et circenses*, though Machiavelli here emphasizes circuses rather than bread. In Shelley's view, if the people lack enlightenment, social order should be fostered through education and not maintained through ideological manipulation and the use of surveillance to obtain bureaucratic information.

Even though her novel is subtitled *The Life and Adventures of Castruccio, Prince of Lucca*, Shelley's conception of history and historical fiction includes popular culture and mass movements as well as accounts of elites and great men. Failing to understand Shelley's ideal of socially comprehensive representation and her broad social view of historical causality, the reviewer for *Blackwood's Edinburgh Magazine* dismisses the descriptions of popular culture and the accounts of religious heresies as extraneous historical details possessing no aesthetic significance: "We cannot spare four days of the life of Castruccio Castracani to singers and tale-tellers, and so forth, with whom he and his story have nothing to do."[40] However, Shelley intentionally devotes the last three chapters of the novel's first volume to the May festival at the castle of Valperga—not merely because she wishes to display her historical research or authenticate her late medieval setting but rather because the early-nineteenth-century rediscovery of popular culture and the problem and power of the masses impressed themselves on her consciousness.

While Mary Shelley does not simply ignore or disdain popular culture, neither does she offer unqualified praise for it. She views popular culture as backward and superstitious; it sometimes involves cruel and unjustified shame punishments; it is not a pure and authentic expression of the folk but may derive from sources in the elite tradition; it sometimes reveals national character, but it may also seem timeless and geographically universal. The second chapter of *Valperga* describes a theatrical representation of Dante's Hell, on the bridge of Carraia in Florence.[41] This spectacle, deriving from a work of high culture, has terrific power because it appeals to the superstitions of the people: it is an external embodiment of "what then existed in the imagination of the spectators, endued with the vivid colours of a faith inconceivable in these lethargic days" (*Valperga*, 1:20).

If this initial manifestation of popular culture reveals a historical disjunction in the construction of consciousness or imagination, a later incident betrays the cruelty of the people, both random and ritualized. Common soldiers in the Ghibelline army outside the walls of Florence rape the women of the city who fall into their hands, whereas Florentine men are subjected to a skimmington (a procession exposing traditional targets of popular ridicule) through a gauntlet of soldiers: "To lead a prisoner naked through the camp, seated on an ass, with his face turned towards the tail, was a common mockery" (3:176). Shelley's reference to the charivari does not simply evince an interest in popular culture for its own sake but is integrated into a novel in which popular justice is almost as prominent as despotic and inquisitorial imprisonments and tortures. Shelley believes that certain popular entertainments, particularly nonverbal ones such as juggling and fire-eating, are universal— performed "from the shores of the Ganges to those of the Thames, from the most distant periods, even down to our own times" (1:269). On the other hand, one may also find evidence for national character in popular culture—for example, the Italian predilection and talent for mime and improvisation (1:288). Popular culture presents a contradictory terrain for the historical novelist: now an index to temporal and geographical specificity, now evidence for universal qualities of the common people (from the perspective of the elite observer); now authentically "popular," now something that has trickled down from the culture of the elite; now spontaneous celebration, now violence and humiliation.

The first volume of Shelley's novel ends with the lengthy account of the four-day celebration at Valperga; the second volume begins with Castruccio and Euthanasia's arrival in Florence, an arrival that coincides with a spontaneous festival. The festival, prompted by the birth of "five whelps" to one of the lionesses that serve to symbolize and magically protect Florence's prosperity and strength (2:2), occasions a debate between the two lovers. To the Ghibelline lord's mockery of the "childish omens" in which republicans put their faith, the Guelph countess replies with a justification of popular superstition. Euthanasia rejoices to discover such evidence of active imagination: "It is this same imagination more usefully and capaciously employed that makes them decree the building of the most extensive and beautiful building of modern times" (2:3–4). Euthanasia celebrates the human faculty of imagination, even while she recognizes that it may be misdirected; but better misdirected than inactive or extinct. Public benefits and the fine arts may have the same source as chauvinistic and superstitious faith in omens.

Even when what is at stake is not popular festivity but rather potentially frightening crowd violence, Shelley seems to accord at least qualified approval to popular sentiments and actions. The inhuman and sublime sadist who imprisons Beatrice in his ruinous house is eventually destroyed by crowd action: "The moment that a leader appeared, the whole peasantry flocked as to a crusade to destroy their oppressor" (*Valperga*, 3:88). Shelley's qualifications in this case are twofold: first, the peasantry behaves not rationally but rather in a kind of knee-jerk response to the direct experience of oppression; secondly, a leader, not himself a peasant, proves to be necessary for the crowd to be incited to act at all. On the other hand, Shelley and her readers almost certainly believe that, in this instance of popular violence, justice has been done.

The major crowd scene in the novel takes place in Ferrara, where Beatrice is first arrested by the Dominican inquisitors and then subjected to a highly theatrical trial by fire, which itself has been staged so that she will escape uninjured. While ostensibly charged with uttering heretical false prophecies, Beatrice has come to the authorities' notice, or so the crowd believes, for the political crime of favoring restoration of the marquess Obizzo to the lordship of Ferrara. In response to the initial arrest, the crowd seems inclined to attempt a rescue: "The people armed themselves with stones, sticks, knives, and axes" (2:46). Beatrice's trial consists of walking blindfolded over white-hot ploughshares placed in furrows in a Ferrara square. Shelley's description initially reveals disgust with the huge crowd, which she compares to a "timid herd" and which resembles that in attendance at hangings in London: "Their bodies and muscles were in perpetual motion; some foamed at the mouth, and others gazed with outstretched necks, and eyes starting from their sockets" (2:58). But when Beatrice is brought out, Shelley employs a nature metaphor that suggests a certain respect both for the power of the crowd and for their sympathy with the sufferer, which they restrain only with difficulty: "A sound, as of the hollow north-wind among the mighty trees of a sea-like forest, rose from among them; an awful, deep and nameless breath, a sigh of many hearts" (2:59). When Beatrice survives her trial unscathed, Shelley approves—though not without the condescension of the elite commentator—the wild, superstitious joy of the multitude and their threat of violence that causes the inquisitors to slink away and their Gascon troops to retreat (2:61–62). Shelley's attitude toward the people and their culture is that of an elite, enlightened, and liberal observer. The escalating list of the arms of the crowd, from stones and sticks to knives and axes, perhaps suggests fear, but then their violence is directed against the despotic inquisitors. Shelley cannot approve of superstition, but in a gesture of radical populism she honors the shared human faculty of imagination, which may feed superstition.[42] Similarly, she is disgusted by the bloodthirsty crowds who flock to public executions, but then, as if after further reflection, she recognizes that the crowd may have been led to such scenes of suffering by curiosity about the liminal space between life and death, by a love of the marvelous, or by an admirable sympathy.

What is most striking is that "sigh of many hearts," the people speaking in one voice—hardly a voice. In accord with the sentimental hierarchy of communicative modes, which values the nonverbal above the verbal, the people express themselves immediately, spontaneously, and unanimously. Today, we are aware of the dangers of Enlightenment and Romantic fantasies of the unanimity of the people speaking in one voice, of how such fantasies may coincide with the eradication—often violent—of difference. But, for a member of the intellectual elite born two hundred years ago, the problem was to extend sympathy and shared humanity into the lowest ranks of society. The problem is that of extending one's vision, not by the leisure that property confers, though assuredly by knowledge of history and the classics. However, our feelings and vision, which are potentially so narrow, can also be extended by love of a kindred spirit or by joining our breaths in the "sigh of many hearts":

> The human soul disdains all restraint, and ever seeks to mingle with nature itself, or with kindred minds; to hope and fear for oneself alone often narrows the heart and understanding; but if we are animated by these feelings in unison with a multitude, bound by the same desires and the same perils, such participation of triumph or sorrow exalts and beautifies every emotion. (1:237)

Conclusion

In her historical novel of sensibility, Shelley justifies the reading of history and historical fiction for the criticism it enables of narrow, present-centered views. *Valperga* represents a new kind of historical novel, one in which sentiments are events. Here, as in *Frankenstein*, Shelley maintains a sentimental linguistic theory, or sentimental suspicion of rhetorical modes of communication and even of verbal language itself. She exhibits a preference for the immediacy and spontaneity found in the language of the heart, of the countenance, and of tears—especially of the entirely reliable tears that mark the emergence of a man of feeling. While Shelley may be guilty of anachronism in situating the sentimental hero and heroine in late medieval Italy, she does seek to delineate the fourteenth-century forces that might transform people into superior beings or, on the contrary, brutalize them or their victims. However, in examining fourteenth-century dehumanizing forces, Shelley very much has in mind a critique of the early-nineteenth-century industrial and state institutions that employed surveillance and bureaucratic techniques in order to make human beings into knowable and useful machines. As a student of the French Revolution, Mary Shelley shows a particular interest in the workings of popular justice and the psychology of the crowd. While she defines humanity historically, she is also attracted to universality, to a union in solidarity with a multitude of human beings to whom she feels herself superior but whom she cannot condemn, not even for their superstitions, not even for their attendance at public displays of despotic force directed against suffering human bodies.

Notes

1. Mary W. Shelley, *Valperga; or, the Life and Adventures of Castruccio, Prince of Lucca*, 3 vols. (London: G. and W. B. Whittaker, 1823), 1:43. ; subsequent references to this novel will be noted parenthetically in the body of the text as *Valperga*.

2. Mary Shelley, *Frankenstein; or, The Modern Prometheus: The 1818 Text*, ed. Marilyn Butler (Oxford: Oxford University Press, 1994), 20, 206. Shelley uses the same Italian phrase, which means "slaves always trembling with restlessness," in an 1826 book review ("The English in Italy," *Westminster Review* 6 [October 1826]: 325–41; reprinted in *The Mary Shelley Reader*, ed. Betty T. Bennett and Charles E. Robinson [New York: Oxford University Press, 1990], 345 n. 10). Arguing against the view that Mary Shelley grew more conservative and conventional after the death of Percy Shelley, Emily W. Sunstein provides substantial evidence that Mary Shelley "was an ardent partisan of Italian national liberation" (*Mary Shelley: Romance and Reality* [1989; rprt., Baltimore, Md.: Johns Hopkins University Press, 1991], 6). See also Sunstein, *Romance and Reality*, 296, 328, 378.

3. Frederick L. Jones, introduction to *The Letters of Mary W. Shelley*, 2 vols. (Norman: University of Oklahoma Press, 1944), 1:xxx.

4. Betty T. Bennett, "The Political Philosophy of Mary Shelley's Historical Novels: *Valperga* and *Perkin Warbeck*," in *The Evidence of the Imagination: Studies of Interactions Between Life and Art in English Romantic Literature*, ed. Donald H. Reiman et al. (New York: New York University Press, 1978), 354–71. In contrast to Bennett and others who trace continuities between *Valperga* and the works and thought of Godwin and Percy Shelley, Jane Blumberg believes that Mary Shelley had greater intellectual if not emotional independence, composing her novels out of "a fundamental intellectual conflict with the men in her life" (*Mary Shelley's Early Novels: 'This Child of Imagination and Misery'* [Iowa City: University of Iowa Press, 1993], 6).

5. Joseph W. Lew, "God's Sister: History and Ideology in *Valperga*," in *The Other Mary Shelley: Beyond Frankenstein*, ed. Audrey A. Fisch, Anne K. Mellor, and Esther H. Schor (New York: Oxford University Press, 1993), 163.

6. Ibid., 162. In *Mary Shelley: Her Life, Her Fiction, Her Monsters* (New York: Routledge, 1988), Anne K. Mellor similarly finds a "deep aversion to the lower classes," "racist chauvinism," and a "commitment to the preservation of a class-system" in Mary Shelley's journal entries for August 1814 (25). Mellor argues that Shelley posits an ideal of the bourgeois family, an ideal whose limitations lead her to endorse "a conservative vision of gradual evolutionary reform, a position articulated most forcefully during her times by Edmund Burke" (86). It will be apparent from my argument that I am not persuaded that Shelley is a Burkean conservative.

7. I am indebted here and throughout my account of classical republican ideology to the work of J. G. A. Pocock. For the opposition between speculative finance and productive trade, see, especially, Pocock, *The Machiavellian Moment: Florentine Political Thought and the Atlantic Republican Tradition* (Princeton, N.J.: Princeton University Press, 1975), 436–37, 445–49, and 456.

8. A preference for the classics over current events, partisan conflict, and utilitarian and vocational relevance characterizes humanism whether it appears in Romantics or Marxists. In his reflections on the ideal college in *The Prelude, or Growth of a Poet's Mind: Text of 1805*, ed. Ernest de Selincourt and Stephen Gill (Oxford: Oxford Univer-

sity Press, 1970), William Wordsworth recommends that the unchanging body of ancient truth be denuded of superficial and ephemeral fashions:

> The passing Day should learn to put aside
>> Her Trappings here, should strip them off, abash'd
>> Before antiquity, and stedfast truth,
>> And strong book-mindedness; and over all
>> Should be a healthy, sound simplicity,
>> A seemly plainness, name it as you will,
>> Republican or pious.
>>
>> (3:401–7)

In a striking passage on the value of studying a dead language like Latin, Antonio Gramsci revives the reanimation metaphor, so important to Shelley:

> It has been studied in order to accustom children to studying in a specific manner, and to analysing an historical body which can be treated as a corpse which returns continually to life; in order to accustom them to reason, to think abstractly and schematically while remaining able to plunge back from abstraction into real and immediate life, to see in each fact or datum what is general and what is particular, to distinguish the concept from the specific instance. (*Selections from the Prison Notebooks*, ed. and trans. Quintin Hoare and Geoffrey Nowell Smith [New York: International Publishers, 1971], 38)

While it would be naive to deny the element of elitism in Shelley's liberalism, there are significant similarities between her project and that of Gramsci, who likewise compared the history of nineteenth-century Italy to the medieval communes of Tuscany. The English Romantic novelist, like the Italian Communist, sought to alter the political order through humanistic reform and an engagement with popular culture.

9. Observing that daughters care for their blinded fathers in each of Shelley's first three novels, I argued, in an earlier article, that both female education and female self-sacrifice, expressed through the role of nurse, were predicated upon the symbolic castration of the father (James P. Carson, "Bringing the Author Forward: *Frankenstein* Through Mary Shelley's Letters," *Criticism* 30.4 [Fall 1988]: 442).

10. While Euthanasia dei Adimari is Shelley's fictional creation, the historical figure Castruccio Castracani was born in 1281 and ruled Lucca from 1316 until his death in 1328. The Guinigi were a prominent Lucchese merchant family who were not exiled from Lucca in 1301, when the White Guelph faction (Shelley's *bianci*) was. The White Guelphs, who included Castruccio's Interminelli (Antelminelli) family, were subsequently aligned with the Ghibellines. See Louis Green, *Castruccio Castracani: A Study on the Origins and Character of a Fourteenth-Century Despotism* (Oxford: Clarendon Press, 1986), 20, 41, and 86.

11. William Godwin, *Enquiry Concerning Political Justice*, ed. Isaac Kramnick (Harmondsworth, England: Penguin, 1976), 730.

12. That is to say, Godwin adumbrates Gramsci's notion of the "organic" intellectual. Unlike the "professional" intellectual, whose independence from manual labor permits a delusory autonomy from class background, the organic intellectual integrates science and work, theory and practice, and serves a directive function for his or her class from within (Gramsci, *Selections from the Prison Notebooks*, 3–23).

13. For Mary Shelley's views on the peasants of Tuscany, see "The English in Italy," in *The Mary Shelley Reader*, 349–50.

14. Shelley, *Frankenstein*, 8.

15. For Barbara Jane O'Sullivan, Beatrice is an avatar of the Cassandra figure that frequently appears in nineteenth-century women's texts. This figure serves as an image of the female artist, and the discourses in which she appears expose, according to O'Sullivan, a patriarchal conspiracy for the suppression "of female spiritual and imaginative power" ("Beatrice in *Valperga*: A New Cassandra," in *The Other Mary Shelley: Beyond Frankenstein*, 141). O'Sullivan regards Mary Shelley as complicit with patriarchal "social strictures" when she discredits "the creative woman" in the figure of Beatrice, as well as "female spiritual power" and "female self-assertion" in the figure of the witch Fior di Mandragola (150–51). Such a narrowly "feminist" perspective unfairly denigrates the rationalist feminism of Shelley and, indeed, of Wollstonecraft. In contrast to O'Sullivan, I argue that the rational and dutiful Euthanasia is Mary Shelley's central figure for the female author.

16. Contemporary reviewers accused Shelley of an anachronistic, if not sentimental, conception of Castruccio's character in her tracing of the development of a medieval tyrant "out of an innocent, open-hearted and deeply-feeling youth. We suspect, that in the whole of this portraiture, far too much reliance has been laid on thoughts and feelings, not only modern, but modern and feminine at once" (*Blackwood's Edinburgh Magazine* 13 [March 1823]: 284). While little is known about the private life of the historical Castruccio, he (unlike Shelley's character) was married. He had nine children by his wife, Pina Streghi, and at least two illegitimate children, whom he acknowledged in his will (Green, *Castruccio Castracini*, 190–92).

17. In *The Origins of the English Novel 1600–1740* (Baltimore, Md.: Johns Hopkins University Press, 1987), Michael McKeon refers to these epistemological concerns as "questions of truth."

18. David McCracken, "Godwin's Literary Theory: The Alliance Between Fiction and Political Philosophy," *Philological Quarterly* 49 (1970): 122.

19. Allan Gilbert, trans., *Machiavelli: The Chief Works and Others* (Durham: Duke University Press, 1965), 2:533.

20. Niccolò Machiavelli, *The Life of Castruccio Castracani of Lucca*, in ibid., 2:553.

21. "To Jane Williams," 19–20 February 1823, in *The Letters of Mary Wollstonecraft Shelley*, 3 vols., ed. Betty T. Bennett (Baltimore, Md.: Johns Hopkins University Press, 1980–88), 1:312.

22. Mary Wollstonecraft, *A Vindication of the Rights of Woman*, 2nd ed., ed. Carol H. Poston (New York: W. W. Norton, 1988), 183.

23. I am drawing here upon Foucault's notion of disciplinary power, which has an exemplary locus in the military sphere. See Michel Foucault, *Discipline and Punish: The Birth of the Prison*, trans. Alan Sheridan (New York: Pantheon/Random House, 1977), 168, 171. The "disciplines" operate through the accumulation and recording of data about individuals obtained through policing, surveillance, and other forms of detailed observation. The disciplines answer to a new demand linked to industrialization: "to construct a machine whose effect will be maximized by the concerted articulation of the elementary parts of which it is composed" (164). I would dissent, however, from Foucault's antihumanist perspective. For him, it is from the knowledge and data about individuals produced by disciplinary techniques that "the man of modern humanism was born" (141).

24. In her valuable analysis of Percy Shelley's revisions to the manuscript of *Franken-stein*, Anne Mellor disagrees with critics who have argued for Mary Shelley's anxiety of authorship by noting that Percy "introduced all the references to Victor Frankenstein as the 'author' of the creature" (Mellor, *Mary Shelley: Her Life*, 65). If the word *author* in the 1818 text of *Frankenstein* is in Percy Shelley's hand, then the word *mechanist* from the phrase "the author and mechanist of these crimes" in *Valperga* likewise has a relevant source in Percy Shelley's works. In *A Defence of Poetry* (written in 1821), Percy Shelley establishes an opposition between poets, who employ the faculty of imagination, and "reasoners and mechanists," who exemplify "the calculating faculty" (*Shelley's Prose; or, The Trumpet of a Prophecy*, ed. David Lee Clark [Albuquerque: University of New Mexico Press, 1954], 291, 292). Percy Shelley's targets are utilitarian educators, who assume that reform will arise automatically from an accumulation of information rather than from the creative power to use the wisdom we already possess, and classical political economists, who believe that increasing the wealth of nations is more important than its equitable distribution:

> While the mechanist abridges and the political economist combines labor, let them beware that their speculations, for want of correspondence with those first principles which belong to the imagination, do not tend as they have in modern England to exasperate at once the extremes of luxury and want. (292)

I am arguing that Mary Shelley in *Valperga* shares her husband's critique of utilitari-anism and classical political economy.

25. William Shakespeare, *Hamlet*, in *The Riverside Shakespeare*, ed. G. Blakemore Evans (Boston: Houghton Mifflin, 1974), 3.2.364–67. Anne Mellor believes that by the time Shelley had revised *Frankenstein* in 1831, she had come to view human beings as machines: "Mary Shelley adopts a behavioristic model of human nature. Human beings are, like nature itself, only machines manipulated by external forces" (Mellor, *Mary Shel-ley: Her Life*, 173). Given Shelley's explicit critique of the reduction of human beings to machines in 1823, I would hesitate to equate the determinism of the 1831 *Frankenstein* with behaviorism.

26. Today, criticism of this base/superstructure model is everywhere apparent: for example, in Homi Bhabha's quotation of Stuart Hall's acknowledgment "that, though influential, 'material interests on their own have no necessary class belongingness'" (Homi K. Bhabha, *The Location of Culture* [New York: Routledge, 1994], 28).

27. Pamela Clemit observes that Mary Shelley's contemporaries situated her within the Godwinian "school" and that both Godwin and Percy Shelley admired *Valperga*, especially the highly original character of Beatrice, the prophetess of Ferrara. According to Clemit, Mary Shelley follows Godwin in focusing on the imaginative realization of "theoretical concerns," while departing from Godwin's preferred mode of first-person narration, in order to experiment "with multiple points of view"—in the case of *Valperga*, especially the alternative viewpoints of women (Pamela Clemit, *The Godwinian Novel: The Rational Fictions of Godwin, Brockden Brown, Mary Shelley* [New York: Oxford University Press, 1993], 7, 179).

28. Shakespeare, *Hamlet*, 3.2.396.

29. William Godwin, *Caleb Williams*, ed. David McCracken (Oxford, 1970; rprt., New York: W. W. Norton, 1977), 314.

30. I am thinking here of "the reversal of the political axis of individuation" that Fou-cault situates at the moment when the "disciplines" arise. In older regimes, such as feu-dalism, "individualization is greatest where sovereignty is exercised. . . . In a disciplinary

regime, on the other hand, individualization is 'descending'" (Foucault, *Discipline and Punish*, 192–93).

31. François-Auguste-Marie-Alexis Mignet, "Historical Notice of the Life and Works of M. de Sismondi," in *Political Economy, and the Philosophy of Government*, by M. de Sismondi (London: John Chapman, 1847), 6–7.

32. Ibid., 30–31.

33. J. C. L. de Sismondi, *A History of the Italian Republics, Being a View of the Origin, Progress, & Fall of Italian Freedoms* (London: J. M. Dent, [1907]), 122–23. I quote from this convenient Everyman edition, which is a republication of the one-volume abridgment of his comprehensive work that Sismondi contributed to Dionysius Lardner's *The Cabinet Cyclopaedia*, vol. 14 (1832).

34. Simon Schama has supplied this list of exemplary sites of liberty for the *philosophes*, except that he does not include the medieval communes of Tuscany ("The Enlightenment in the Netherlands," in *The Enlightenment in National Context*, ed. Roy Porter and Mikulás Teich [Cambridge: Cambridge University Press, 1981], 56).

35. See Green, *Castruccio Castracani*, 45.

36. In fact, the republican government of the commune of Florence did permit substantial "popular" and artisanal participation by the end of the thirteenth century. Laws were passed to control the violence of Florentine aristocrats, who were "compelled to pay a surety as an earnest of good behaviour, liable to mutilation for wounding a *popolano*, and to immediate execution and the demolition of their houses for killing one" (Green, *Castruccio Castracani*, 22).

37. Godwin, *Political Justice*, 644.

38. At the end of the first volume, when Euthanasia holds a May festival at Valperga in order to celebrate peace in Tuscany, Shelley defines the inclusiveness of the term *Uomini di Corte*: "Then arrived a multitude of *Uomini di Corte*; story-tellers, *improvisatori*, musicians, singers, actors, rope-dancers, jugglers and buffoons" (*Valperga*, 1:256).

39. Niccolò Machiavelli, *The Prince*, in Allan Gilbert, trans., *Machiavelli: The Chief Works and Others*, 1: 84.

40. *Blackwood's Edinburgh Magazine*, 13 (March 1823): 284. I have remarked that Shelley, like Godwin, prefers individual history to national history; but we should note that, at the same time, she follows her mother's insistence that the individual life be placed within the broader context of the progress of civilization: "The reading of history will scarcely be more useful than the perusal of romances, if read as mere biography; if the character of the times, the political improvements, arts, &c. be not observed" (Wollstonecraft, *Rights of Woman*, 148).

41. Like piazzas and squares, bridges were centers for popular culture (Peter Burke, *Popular Culture in Early Modern Europe* [New York: Harper & Row, 1978], 111). My knowledge of the late-eighteenth- and early-nineteenth-century "discovery of the people" derives in large part from Burke. I am likewise indebted to his discussion of the complex interrelationship of elite and popular traditions, which can be reduced neither to a trickle-down model nor to one in which high culture is energized from below (see, especially, Burke, *Popular Culture*, 28–29, 58–63).

42. It may be instructive once again to compare Shelley with Gramsci. On the one hand, Gramsci approved of a fundamentally conservative educational system because it "combated folklore" (Gramsci, *Selections from the Prison Notebooks*, 34). On the other, Gramsci believed that "a molecular diffusion of a new humanism, an intellectual and

moral reformation" of the proletariat and peasantry was essential for revolutionary change in fascist Italy (David Forgacs, "National-Popular: Genealogy of a Concept," in *The Cultural Studies Reader*, ed. Simon During [London: Routledge, 1993], 186). Such a cultural reformation must start by drawing upon "popular culture *as it is*." The new literature that Gramsci would create must "sink its roots in the humus of popular culture as it is, with its tastes and tendencies and with its moral and intellectual world, even if it is backward and conventional" (Antonio Gramsci, *Selections from Cultural Writings*, trans. William Boelhouer, ed. David Forgacs and Geoffrey Nowell-Smith [Cambridge: Harvard University Press, 1985], 102).

The Apocalypse of Empire:
Mary Shelley's *The Last Man*

Paul A. Cantor

1

Mary Shelley's husband, Percy, was a great visionary, but sometimes his visions took peculiar forms. Thomas Love Peacock, in his *Memoirs of Shelley* (1858–62), records one of Percy's weirder moments:

> About the end of 1813, Shelley was troubled by one of his most extraordinary delusions. He fancied that a fat old woman who sat opposite to him in a mail coach was afflicted with elephantiasis, that the disease was infectious and incurable, and that he had caught it from her. He was continually on the watch for its symptoms; his legs were to swell to the size of an elephant's, and his skin was to be crumpled over like goose-skin. He would draw the skin of his own hands, arms, and neck very tight, and if he discovered any deviation from smoothness, he would seize the person next to him, and endeavour by a corresponding pressure to see if any corresponding deviation existed. . . . His friends took various methods of dispelling the delusion. I quoted to him the words of Lucretius:
>
> > Est elephas morbus, qui propter flumina Nili
> > Gignitur Aegypto in media, *neque praeterea usquam*.
>
> He said these verses were the greatest comfort he had. When he found that, as the days rolled on, his legs retained their proportion, and his skin its smoothness, the delusion died away.[1]

It is strangely appropriate that the idealist Shelley, with all his contempt for the material limitations of humanity, should fear nothing so much as a disease that would compound his fleshliness. It also rings true that in his phobia, Shelley could be reassured only by the words of one of his favorite poets: "There is elephantiasis, for instance, which is bred in the heart of Egypt on the banks of the Nile and nowhere else."[2] But why should Shelley be comforted by Lucretius's assurance that elephantiasis has its source only on the banks of the Nile? After all, his fellow traveler might have been an Egyptian, or at least have been returning from a trip up the Nile. In Peacock's account, Shelley acts as if England were a self-contained nation and not a great imperial power with commercial and political interests in both the Near and the Far East. Peacock's words of comfort work only if they can be taken to prove that the dread disease is safely quarantined in the distant world of the Orient.

Whether Mary Shelley ever learned of this peculiar episode in her husband's life I do not know, but she always had an uncanny feel for the nightmare side of his imagination, and eventually she wrote a novel in which Percy's fears in the mail coach are writ large. More aware of material reality than her husband, Mary Shelley recognized that in the emerging imperialist world of the early nineteenth century, the population of England was no longer necessarily safe from diseases that might have their origin in distant lands. In *The Last Man*, first published in 1826, she tells the story of a plague arising in the East that spreads across the globe, eventually engulfing England and gradually obliterating the entire human race. Related to several poems dealing with the "last man" theme,[3] the novel is apocalyptic in mode and mood. Shelley, however, shapes a negative apocalypse, a systematic unwriting of all the revolutionary hopes for the paradisiacal transformation of the human condition that fueled Romantic poetry, perhaps best represented by Percy Shelley's *Prometheus Unbound* (1819).[4] Whereas in Percy's poem the liberation of the imagination frees humanity from material limits and leads to the universal triumph of love, in Mary's novel the material pressures of disease work to bring out the worst in humanity, especially a competitiveness for dwindling resources that eventually results in armed conflict.

In her greatest and most famous work, *Frankenstein*, Shelley portrays an idealistic young scientist who hopes to better the human condition but who ends up companioned by the monstrous product of his experiments, a terrifying doppelgänger who acts out the aggressive impulses that the seemingly benevolent Victor tries to deny in himself.[5] *The Last Man* is more diffuse and hence less powerful as a narrative than *Frankenstein*, but it goes further in bringing out the dark side of Romanticism. In

Prometheus Unbound, a male hero out of Greek mythology is shown reuniting with a female figure named Asia; the result is a dizzying vision of paradise regained.[6] In the sobering vision of *The Last Man*, East and West come together again, but this time their embrace proves fatal to both and indeed to all humanity.[7] It is as if the germ of fear contained in Percy's elephantiasis phobia had grown into a nightmare of worldwide proportions.

The Last Man is indeed one of the first works of imaginative literature to take the entire earth as its stage. Though the directly narrated action is centered in Europe, reported events take place as far away as America and Australia. Shelley is strikingly modern in *The Last Man* in the way she imagines a world in which events that happen in remote corners of the planet have almost immediate and wholly disastrous consequences halfway around the globe. Like many Romantics, Percy Shelley envisioned a world united by the release of the creative impulses of humanity, but Mary sees a world brought together by the forces of destruction. At first glance, these forces may seem to be nonhuman; it is, after all, a plague that Shelley shows destroying humanity, and although she lived before the germ theory was developed and thus could not understand the biological basis of the disease she portrays, she does present it as a force of nature. Yet, at every stage, the spread of the plague is hastened, and its destructive effects are exacerbated by human actions. Thus, although the plague seems to confront humanity as an external blow of fate, for which no person can be blamed, in fact it brings out certain destructive tendencies in human nature that are in the end as much responsible for the extermination of the race as the disease itself. As the futuristic setting of the novel suggests—it takes place in the twenty-first century—Shelley presents the plague as a *modern* phenomenon; only in the conditions of the modern world could the plague take the universally destructive course it does. Indeed, we will see that in a certain sense the fundamental plague for Shelley is modernity itself.

Of all the forces in the modern world Shelley links to the plague, none is more important than imperialism. In *Frankenstein,* Shelley proved to be remarkably prophetic in anticipating the moral dilemmas to which modern science would give rise. Perhaps because *The Last Man* has not been as popular, Shelley has not been given corresponding credit for the way her later novel anticipates the problems European imperialism was to create in the modern world. When most of her contemporaries were still untroubled by the issue of imperialism, Shelley created a narrative that raises profound doubts about England's attempt to reach out and embrace the whole of the globe. The plague in *The Last Man* begins to spread as a result of a British-led expedition to free Greece from Turkish rule, an enterprise presented as a triumph of the West over the East. The further spread of the plague follows the great imperial trade routes. What new dangers, Shelley seems to be asking, is England exposing itself to by creating a worldwide empire? Wouldn't the British be better off staying at home, tending to their domestic concerns, instead of sailing off to remote corners of the earth and bringing back deadly diseases along with their imperial spoils? Like *Frankenstein*, *The Last Man* participates in Shelley's defense of the domestic sphere, only this time the force propelling her heroes away from the safety of hearth and home is the lure not of scientific discovery but of foreign conquests.[8]

2

A reading of *The Last Man* as a critique of imperialism is most powerfully suggested by a scene that occurs after the ravages of the plague have forced masses of people to migrate:

> A number of people from North America, the relics of that populous continent, had set sail for the East with mad desire of change, leaving their native plains for lands not less afflicted than their own. Several hundreds landed in Ireland. . . . At length they began to interfere with the inhabitants, and . . . ejected the natives from their dwellings. . . . A few events of this kind roused the fiery nature of the Irish; and they attacked the invaders. . . . The Americans were eager to escape from the spirit they had roused, and . . . embarked for England. Their incursion would hardly have been felt had they come alone; but the Irish . . . began to feel the inroads of famine, and they followed in the wake of the Americans for England also. . . . Many went up as high as Belfast to ensure a shorter passage, and then journeying south through Scotland, they were joined by the poorer natives of that country, and all poured with one consent into England. (213–14)

It is hard to believe that as early as the 1820s Shelley created this vision of the refuse of the British empire pouring back into the home country. In contemporary criticism of postcolonial fiction, this kind of movement has come to be known as "the Empire Strikes Back." The geographic symbolism of the passage is unmistakable; the path the marauders follow into England simply reverses the path English colonialism took outward into Scotland, Ireland, and America. Shelley makes explicit the idea that the Scottish, the Irish, and the Americans are paying the English back for the wrongs they suffered under colonial rule: "They talked of taking

London, conquering England—calling to mind the long detail of injuries which had for many years been forgotten" (215).

In *The Last Man,* the sins of Britain's imperialist past come back to haunt it.[9] To be sure, written as it was in the 1820s, Shelley's nightmare vision of England invaded reflects fears lingering from the era of the Napoleonic Wars, when the English worried about French expeditions to their shores.[10] However, Shelley gives a specifically ironic twist to her scene of England invaded: it is not a rival imperial power that sets out to conquer England but a force composed of its present and former colonial subjects. I do not know if *The Last Man* is the first example of this motif of "reverse colonization," but it is surely one of the earliest. Once again, Shelley proved to be ahead of her time; by the end of the nineteenth century, stories of England falling victim to forces from its colonies began to form a minor genre.[11] A good example is Bram Stoker's *The Jewel of Seven Stars* (1903), in which an Egyptian mummy brought to London exerts a demonic power over the unsuspecting inhabitants of the imperial metropolis.

Once one is alerted to the connection Shelley establishes between imperialism and the plague, one can find anxieties over empire throughout *The Last Man.* From its inception, the plague is associated with the great fields of European imperialism: America and Asia.

> In the still uncultivated wilds of America, what wonder that among its other giant destroyers, Plague should be numbered! It is of old a native of the East, sister of the tornado, the earthquake, and the simoom. Child of the sun, and nursling of the tropics, it would expire in these climes. It drinks the dark blood of the inhabitant of the south, but it never feasts on the pale-faced Celt. If perchance some stricken Asiatic come among us, plague dies with him, uncommunicated and innoxious. (169)[12]

Here Shelley shows the initial impulse to establish a sharp opposition between the colonizer and the colonized, the same distancing of disease to foreigners that had reassured her husband in his elephantiasis panic. The English hope that, although their imperial subjects suffer from the rampaging disease, they themselves will prove immune to its spread. In the talk of "dark blood" and the "pale-faced Celt," Shelley even suggests a racial dimension to this thinking.[13]

At first, the English suffer only economic disruptions as a result of the plague, once again linked to the issue of imperialism: "Even the source of colonies was dried up, for in New Holland, Van Diemen's Land, and the Cape of Good Hope, plague raged" (170). By the time Shelley has finished, *The Last Man* reads like an atlas of European colonialism, and of course the English hope of being spared the plague proves vain. It is in the nature of plague, both as a reality and as a literary symbol, to cut across boundaries and thus to break down all sorts of binary oppositions, to infect the good as well as the bad, the rich as well as the poor, the native as well as the foreigner, the colonizer as well as the colonized.[14] The fact that a plague is what destroys Britain reflects a very real fear of the imperialist enterprise, the fear of contracting strange diseases while conquering and occupying distant lands.[15] In perhaps the most famous narrative of English colonizers being colonized themselves, H. G. Wells's *The War of the Worlds*, the plot turns on the insidious connection between imperialism and disease. Wells's Martians are defeated not by any human weapons but by the earth's microbes, to which the aliens lack all immunity.

The infection of the plague is a deadly reality in *The Last Man*, but it also has a symbolic dimension. Shelley establishes a metaphorical link between the plague and the spirit of modern commerce; indeed in many ways for Shelley the most pervasive plague becomes the market economy itself. As we have seen, England first feels the effects of the plague in economic terms: "Foreign distresses came to be felt by us through the channels of commerce" (168). The plague interrupts the worldwide flow of imperial trade:

> Trade was stopped by the failure of the interchange of cargoes usual between us, and America, India, Egypt and Greece. . . . These disasters came home to so many bosoms, and, through the various channels of commerce, were carried so entirely into every class and division of the community, that of necessity they became the first question in the state. (169)

For Shelley, the "channels of commerce" become virtually indistinguishable from the channels of the plague. Economic troubles spread just like the plague, moving unimpeded throughout international and domestic markets.[16] What strikes Shelley so forcibly is the interconnectedness of a modern market economy, what she calls "the fictitious reciprocity of commerce" (169). In *The Last Man,* troubles at any one point in the market economy cause problems at all the others, leaping like a contagious disease over boundaries of class. The "channels of commerce" are ultimately responsible for the speed and extent of the spread of the plague. In Shelley's dark vision, only because the whole world has become entangled in the web of international trade is the plague able to claim the whole of humanity. Ultimately, she seems to view the plague as a kind of retribution for the economic sins of the modern world:

Of old navies used to stem the giant ocean-waves betwixt Indus and the Pole
for slight articles of luxury. Men made perilous journies to possess themselves of earth's splendid trifles, gems and gold. Human labour was wasted—
human life set at nought. (230)

Here we see how Shelley's critique of imperialism in *The Last Man*
links up with her critique of science in *Frankenstein*. She objects to any
form of human endeavor that leads people away from domestic happiness
in pursuit of supposedly greater goals. As she writes in *Frankenstein*:

If the study to which you apply yourself has a tendency to weaken your
affections and to destroy your taste for those simple pleasures in which no
alloy can possibly mix, then that study is certainly unlawful, that is to say, not
befitting the human mind. If no man allowed any pursuit whatsoever to
interfere with the tranquillity of his domestic affections, Greece had not been
enslaved, Caesar would have spared his country, America would have been
discovered more gradually, and the empires of Mexico and Peru had not been
destroyed.[17]

In *Frankenstein,* Shelley was already criticizing the imperialist impulse
for destroying domestic tranquillity.[18] For Shelley, the ultimate human
good is to be found in the family, or at least in a small circle of human
beings who genuinely care for each other.[19]

Appearing to speak for Shelley, Lionel Verney of *The Last Man*
champions the home as a refuge from the evils of the social world:

How unwise had the wanderers been, who had deserted its shelter, entangled
themselves in the web of society, and entered . . . that labyrinth of evil, that
scheme of mutual torture. . . . I have joined in ambitious hopes . . . : now,—
shut the door on the world, and build high the wall that is to separate me from
the troubled scene. . . . Let us live for each other and for happiness; let us
seek peace in our dear home. (158)

The Last Man moves between the two poles of Shelley's imagination: the
nuclear family and humanity as a whole. In a sense, the course of the
narrative involves a massive process of contraction. Beginning with the
whole earth as her field of action, Shelley progressively narrows her
narrative horizons from the worldwide network of imperialism and trade
to England as a nation-state refuge from the plague, to isolated villages in
the English countryside, to groups of human beings banding together to
flee the plague, to the pseudo-family grouping of Lionel, Adrian, and
Clara toward the end of the story, and finally to the Last Man of the title
himself.

Though this narrowing of focus in the story reflects the disastrous depopulation of the earth, in an emotional countermovement, Shelley shows human beings frequently treating each other better as they unite against the plague: "The loving heart, obliged to contract its view, bestowed its overflow of affection in triple portion on the few that remained" (197). Shelley clearly prefers human existence on a smaller scale. She consistently associates the plague with the large scale of modern civilization: "The vast cities of America, the fertile plains of Hindostan, the crowded abodes of the Chinese, are menaced with utter ruin" (169). True to the facts about epidemics, Shelley presents the plague as largely an urban phenomenon in its inception. One might say that, for her, urbanization *is* the plague; the great enemy in *The Last Man* is the "overgrown metropolis" (188; see also 292). Though ultimately the plague encompasses every corner of the earth, Shelley shows its development and diffusion to be largely the product of a complex of phenomena specifically associated with modernity: urbanization, imperialism, international trade, and the market economy. This is the sense in which one might say that for Shelley modernity is the true plague. To be sure, the plague remains a force of nature, but when one looks at its results, one sees that it simply accelerates and brings to a catastrophic conclusion the destructive tendencies that Shelley associates with the process of modernization. Beginning in the massive cities that characterize the modern world, the plague eventually spreads out to destroy the countryside, rural life, and finally the family itself, in short, the traditional way of life Shelley appears to prize.

Thus, *The Last Man* is in many respects conservative in its political implications, as its quotations from Edmund Burke would tend to suggest. [20] Hearing that the novel associates modern capitalism with the plague, one might assume that Shelley's sympathies were radical, but one must remember that capitalism can be criticized from the right as well as from the left. Against the plague of the modern market economy, with its worldwide interconnections, Shelley sets up the old ideal of the English country estate, with the local landed gentry caring for their tenants. Her political sympathies in the novel seem at times patriarchal and even feudal. She seems to have contempt for modern democratic politics, in part because of "the commercial spirit of republicanism" (43). The parliamentary forces in the novel prove utterly incapable of dealing with the problems created by the plague; in the person of their chief representative, Ryland, they simply abandon the English to their fate. [21] Thus, *The Last Man* becomes a kind of aristocratic fantasy in which a few great men have to come to the rescue of England. Though the novel is premised on the idea that England has finally become a republic rather than a monarchy, Shelley suggests that all political virtue remains with the old aristocrats and that the country must be led by a series of Protectors, first Lord Raymond and then Adrian, the Earl of Windsor. The fact that Shelley modeled these characters on Lord Byron and Percy Shelley, respectively, shows that she has in mind not so much an aristocracy of birth as an aristocracy of merit. Specifically, by fantasizing a situation in which first her Byron figure and then her Percy figure rules England, Shelley seems to champion an aristocracy of *artistic* merit, going her husband one better in imagining a state in which poets might become the *acknowledged* legislators of the world.[22]

As radical as this notion may be in one sense, in another it is reactionary. In true Romantic fashion, Shelley has no faith in institutional political arrangements and can only imagine individual great men, preferably artists, doing any good for their country.[23] She proves to be curiously sympathetic to the English landed gentry, who use their privileges and their wealth to help their fellow human beings in distress:

> [Adrian] made proposals in parliament little adapted to please the rich; but his earnest pleadings and benevolent eloquence were irresistible. To give up their pleasure-grounds to the agriculturist, to diminish sensibly the number of horses kept for the purposes of luxury throughout the country, were means obvious, but unpleasing. Yet, to the honour of the English be it recorded, that, although natural disinclination made them delay awhile, yet when the misery of their fellow-creatures became glaring, an enthusiastic generosity inspired their decrees. . . .The high-born ladies of the country would have deemed themselves disgraced if they had now enjoyed, what they before called a necessary, the ease of a carriage. (171–72)

One shudders to think what Percy Shelley would have made of this passage had he lived to see this image of himself making common cause with the English landed gentry. This sympathy for the English aristocracy is also difficult for twentieth-century readers to swallow, but there can be no doubt that it suffuses Mary Shelley's political vision. Her narrator reports: "Those writers who have imagined a reign of peace and happiness on earth, have generally described a rural country, where each small township was directed by the elders and wise men" (195). The political rhetoric of the novel is pervasively Burkean, as Shelley celebrates the virtues of the traditional British constitution and, above all, the grace of its aristocratic way of life.[24] At one point, she even writes glowingly of "the patriarchal modes in which the variety of kindred and friendship fulfilled their duteous and kindly offices" (223).

3

Thus, the politics of *The Last Man* is deeply conflicted, in complicated ways that seem characteristic of Romanticism. From one perspective, Shelley appears to criticize aristocratic ideology, but from another she appears to participate in it. As a critique of imperialism and of the way it threatens to destroy all that is truly valuable in human life, *The Last Man* seems to be antiaristocratic, an attack on the kind of heroic ethos that leads men to abandon their homes and families to seek glory on foreign shores. Shelley even seems to be aware of how the Romantic poets were implicated in the imperial dreams of their day. She gives her Byron figure, Lord Raymond, a Napoleon complex:

> My first act when I become King of England, will be to unite with the Greeks, take Constantinople, and subdue all Asia. I intend to be a warrior, a conqueror; Napoleon's name shall vail to mine; and enthusiasts, instead of visiting his rocky grave, and exalting the merits of the fallen, shall adore my majesty, and magnify my illustrious achievements. (40)

As Shelley was painfully aware, Byron had in fact died in the course of fighting for the cause of Greek independence (in 1824, just when Shelley was beginning to write *The Last Man*).[25] However, she makes a point of presenting the noble project of liberating Greece in the more dubious imperial context of subduing the Ottoman Turks and all of Asia.[26] Lord Raymond seems to be taking not just Napoleon but Alexander the Great as his model, hoping to become the champion of the West against the East.[27] Once again, Shelley demonstrates her acute sensitivity to the way in which the highest impulses of Romanticism were often inextricably bound up with lower motives. As in *Frankenstein*, she shows in *The Last Man* that what appears in the Romantic to be the idealistic motive of helping humanity may conceal a will to power. The would-be liberator or benefactor of his fellow human beings expects to be worshipped by them as a god. In the way Raymond seeks "to govern the whole earth in his grasping imagination" (40), Shelley seems to suggest something imperialist about the chief Romantic faculty itself.

For all her suspicions about the heroic ethos, and her sharpsightedness in uncovering the sophisms by which men seek to cast their quest for self-aggrandizement in a benevolent light, in the end Shelley seems herself a captive of a form of aristocratic ideology. Although she questions the restless, adventurous spirit of aristocracy, she seems to have a Burkean faith in a settled aristocracy as the only way of providing the stability she thinks necessary for the good life. Shelley's hope seems to be to tame the aristocratic spirit, to purge it of its dangerous aggressiveness and to domesticate its energies.[28] She holds up the English country estate as an ideal precisely because of its patriarchal character; she praises an aristocracy that would care for its dependents as if they were members of one big family, thus contrasting the personal bonds of a feudal world with the impersonal interdependence of a worldwide, capitalist economy. To the extent that an aristocracy can be conceived on the model of a family, Shelley seems to endorse its leadership and way of life.

Moreover, Shelley seems taken with the sheer glamour of aristocracy. Although she raises doubts about the aristocratic figure of Lord Raymond, she clearly is fascinated with his lordly aura (no doubt reflecting her ambivalence about Byron himself). While on one level a critique of aristocracy, *The Last Man* thus becomes at the same time an aristocratic fantasy. The plot allows Shelley, in the person of the narrator, Lionel Verney, to project herself into an aristocratic position in an almost stereotypical rags-to-riches story. This point becomes clearest when one views *The Last Man* as an example of travelogue, one of the genres Shelley had in mind in shaping the novel. In the last section of the book, the remaining characters band together, leave England for the Continent, and head south in the hopes of bettering their condition. The way the action sweeps across Europe bears comparison with many of the famous travel books of the Romantic era. In particular, *The Last Man* seems to retrace the itinerary of *Childe Harold's Pilgrimage*; one might even argue that Shelley was rewriting the book that made Byron famous, as she unfolds a similar pageant of Europe in ruins, exhausted from war, and experiencing a cultural despair. In having her characters travel through France and Italy, Shelley was more specifically retracing ground she had covered in tours with her husband.

With one difference, however: this time the Shelleys travel first-class. That is, the characters in *The Last Man* stay not in cheap hotels but in palaces along their route.[29] When in Paris, for example, they check in at Versailles. This may seem like a facetious observation, but it reveals something important about Shelley's novel. Because the plague has already exterminated most of humanity, when her tourists come to a city, they find its grandest dwellings unoccupied and available. Thus, Shelley's characters experience what a travel brochure would call "the vacation of their dreams":

> In about a fortnight the remainder of the emigrants arrived from England, and they all repaired to Versailles; apartments were prepared for the family of the

Protector in the Grand Trianon, and there, after the excitement of these events, we reposed amidst the luxuries of the departed Bourbons. (278)

Here Shelley imagines the party of her Percy figure, Adrian, almost literally stepping into the shoes of the French aristocracy. The scene embodies a form of wish fulfillment:[30] with the old regime destroyed by the French Revolution and the aftermath of the Napoleonic Wars, Shelley dreams of appropriating the ancient privileges for a new aristocracy, an aristocracy of talent, the aristocracy of artistic talent most perfectly embodied in her husband. Throughout *The Last Man,* Shelley fantasizes situations in which her Percy figure finally receives the forms of recognition she felt her dead husband had been denied during his lifetime.[31] Adrian achieves political recognition as Lord Protector of England and eventually experiences the ultimate in aristocratic splendor at Versailles. As much as Shelley questions the cult of the Great Man in politics, especially insofar as it leads to imperial ambitions, she herself indulges in the cult, at least when the Great Man is an image of her husband, in whose glory she is happy to share.

It is indeed striking how much of *The Last Man* ends up being devoted to a version of the traditional aristocratic Grand Tour of Europe, as Shelley's characters, fleeing the plague, make their way through the ruins of France and Italy. Shelley portrays a Europe in which the grand forces of modernity have played themselves out in a universal apocalypse of empire. For Shelley, a Europe ravaged by plague becomes an image for a Europe exhausted by the ideological and military struggles of the French Revolution and the Napoleonic Wars. With the exhaustion of political forces, Shelley finds only the realm of the aesthetic left; indeed, Europe turns into an aesthetic spectacle in *The Last Man*. In effect, what Shelley shows in *The Last Man* is a posthistorical Europe turned into one vast museum, with all its cultural achievements on view.[32] Throughout the novel, Shelley creates a sense of artistic belatedness among her characters. Perdita's avenue of artistic activity, for example, is not to create her own visions but to paint "copies of the finest pictures of Raphael, Correggio, and Claude" (35).[33] The idea of the last man is in fact the ultimate image of cultural belatedness: to stand at the final moment of human history and thus to be able to survey the whole of human cultural achievement. In this sense, the popularity of the "last man" theme in nineteenth-century literature can be related to the developing historicist sense of the age: the pervasive nineteenth-century feeling of "lastness," of coming at the end of a long cultural development, which finally makes a retrospectively synoptic view of human history possible. The vision of Shelley's last man is strangely akin to that of Hegel, who believed that he came at the end of history and hence was the first to be able to comprehend fully its movement (is it too much to point out that Hegel died of cholera?).

Living at the end of history, Shelley's characters stroll through the empty streets of Paris and Rome, taking in the sights, gawking at the monuments:

> In the towns, in the voiceless towns, we visited the churches, adorned by pictures, master-pieces of art, or galleries of statues. . . . In the morning we rode in the adjoining country, or wandered through the palaces, in search of pictures or antiquities. (313)

It is the realization of any English tourist's dream—to be able to tour France without having to put up with the French, and Italy without the Italians. Indeed, there is something sinister about the tourist spirit embodied in Shelley's characters. Their behavior may reflect the democratizing spirit behind the growth of museums in the nineteenth century, the effort to make great art, once the exclusive property of the aristocracy, finally available to the general populace, a movement encapsulated in the transformation of the Louvre from a royal palace to a public building open to all. However, this movement at the same time involved a comodification of art, an attempt to market it to a middle-class public, which is reflected in the way Shelley's characters appropriate cultural artifacts for their own consumption.[34]

Verney, the character with whom Shelley most closely identifies, lives out the perfect dream of the tourist as aesthete:

> Having determined to make Rome my abode, at least for some months, I made arrangements for my accommodation—I selected my home. The Colonna Palace was well adapted for my purpose. Its grandeur—its treasure of paintings, its magnificent halls were objects soothing and even exhilarating. . . . I passed long hours in the various galleries—I gazed at each statue, and lost myself in a reverie before many a fair Madonna or beauteous nymph. I haunted the Vatican, and stood surrounded by marble forms of divine beauty. (338)

It is striking how the emerging language of European tourism and museum going saturates the final pages of *The Last Man*; at times, one seems already to be in a novel by Henry James. Moreover, the implications of this image of Verney appropriating an Italian palace and its works of art for himself are disturbing; he himself sees his actions as those of a "robber" (338). For a novel that seems so profoundly anti-imperialist, it is curious to see the hero finally acting out a kind of imperialist fantasy, betraying the same impulse that led Lord Elgin to bring the famous marbles back with him to London. In a strange way, the final movement of Shelley's travelers through Europe recapitulates the imperialist sins that originally unleashed the plague's destructive power. Verney talks of his group colonizing France (279) and even at one point proclaims triumphantly, in rather loaded words written so soon after the Napoleonic Wars: "The English took uncontested possession of Paris" (273).

For all her critique of imperialism, then, Shelley in the end seems to accept a form of aesthetic imperialism. When all else drops out of the lives of her characters, they are left with the pursuit of beauty. For the Last Man, life becomes a kind of perpetual Grand Tour. More generally, for all her doubts about aristocracy, Shelley seems willing to justify it as an aesthetic phenomenon. Her hope, of course, is that by aestheticizing aristocracy, she will defang it, as it were, but as Verney's behavior as a robber suggests, even an aestheticized aristocracy seems to have its grasping claws. As always happens in Shelley's writings, *The Last Man* illuminates the phenomenon of Romanticism in unexpected ways. The Romantics criticized the old regime and welcomed its overthrow, but as tendencies like Romantic medievalism suggest, in many ways the Romantics had a reactionary side to their vision and were eager to appropriate the privileges of the old regime for themselves. One way of characterizing Romanticism is to say that it sought to replace the old aristocracy of birth with a new aristocracy of artistic talent. This paradoxical democratization of the aristocratic idea is in its own way admirable, but *The Last Man* reminds us that even an aestheticized aristocracy is still an aristocracy and hence subject to the same imperial impulses as the rest of nineteenth-century culture. Toward the end of *The Last Man*, Shelley's characters are appropriating cultural artifacts just the way colonial officers did throughout the British Empire.

4

As the novel ends, the Last Man, Verney, strikes a quintessentially Byronic pose, saying "Farewell, Italy!—farewell" (341) and sets off to sea in a manner that recalls another literary model, the *Odyssey*, as he confesses himself willing to "dare the twin perils of Scylla and Charybdis" (341). However, even as Shelley looks back to Homer's Ulysses, she uncannily looks forward to Tennyson's as well:

I should reach the pillars of Hercules. And then—no matter where—the oozy caves, and soundless depths of ocean may be my dwelling, before I accomplish this long-drawn voyage, or the arrow of disease find my heart as I float singly on the weltering Mediterranean; or, in some place I touch at, I may find what I seek—a companion; or if this may not be—to endless time, decrepid and grey headed—youth already in the grave with those I love—the lone wanderer will still unfurl his sail, and clasp the tiller—and, still obeying the breezes of heaven, for ever round another and another promontory, anchoring in another and another bay, still ploughing seedless ocean, leaving behind the verdant land of native Europe, adown the tawny shore of Africa, having weathered the fierce seas of the Cape, I may moor my worn skiff in a creek, shaded by spicy groves of the odorous islands of the far Indian ocean. (341–42)

Verney could say, along with Tennyson's Ulysses: "I cannot rest from travel: I will drink / Life to the lees;" he, too, is a "gray spirit yearning in desire," setting out "to follow knowledge like a sinking star." In the remarkable conclusion to *The Last Man*, Romanticism modulates into Victorianism as Mary Shelley comes to terms with the failure of her husband's apocalyptic expectations. Indeed, the valedictory tone of the passage sounds like an answer to Percy Shelley's youthful hope in *Hellas* that "the world's great age begins anew." Romanticism was a poetry of youth, looking forward to a glorious future. In this passage, however, Mary Shelley captures perfectly the tone of a latecomer, looking back on a past irrevocably lost. That is why the parallels with Tennyson's "Ulysses" are so striking: both characters are desperately searching for one final opportunity for heroism in a world of diminished and perhaps extinguished expectations.

Yet, as Verney plots out the route of his last voyage, he does have a goal in mind and plans on following precisely the path of European colonization, indeed the route Vasco de Gama pursued to India. Just as in Tennyson's "Ulysses," at the end of *The Last Man* the rhetoric of Romanticism becomes curiously indistinguishable from the rhetoric of British imperialism. When Verney states his credo, the Romantic's craving for experience blends into the conquistador's craving for danger:

I form no expectation of alteration for the better; but the monotonous present is intolerable to me. Neither hope nor joy are my pilots—restless despair and fierce desire of change lead me on. I long to grapple with danger, to be excited by fear, to have some task, however slight or voluntary, for each day's fulfillment. I shall witness all the variety of appearance, that the elements can assume—I shall read fair augury in the rainbow—menace in the cloud—some lesson or record dear to my heart in everything. (342)

One can almost hear the voice of Keats in a line like "I shall read fair augury in the rainbow." However, "I long to grapple with danger" sounds more like an imperialist adventurer such as Cortez. Yet this opposition may not be as sharp as it at first sounds; in "On First Looking Into Chapman's Homer," Keats compares himself to Cortez, reminding us that in the will to conquer experience, the Romantic aesthetic shades imperceptibly into the imperial ethos. In *The Last Man*, Mary Shelley gives one more portrait of how Romantic idealism and the heroic impulse can lure men away from the family life she cherished, but, as her identification with Verney suggests, she herself was not immune to the siren song of the Romantic/imperial imagination.

Notes

All quotations from *The Last Man* are taken from the edition of Hugh J. Luke Jr. (Lincoln: University of Nebraska Press, 1965), which is based on the 1826 London first edition. Page numbers are given in parentheses in the body of the essay.

1. Thomas Love Peacock, *Memoirs of Shelley and Other Essays and Reviews*, ed. Howard Mills (New York: New York University Press, 1970), 40–41. For a fuller and somewhat different account of this episode, see Thomas Jefferson Hogg, *The Life of Percy Bysshe Shelley* (London: George Routledge, 1906), 457–59. For a discussion of the significance of Shelley's fear of elephantiasis, see Nigel Leask, *British Romantic Writers and the East: Anxieties of Empire* (Cambridge: Cambridge University Press, 1992), 6–7.

2. Lucretius, *On the Nature of the Universe*, trans. R. E. Latham (Harmondsworth, England: Penguin Books, 1951), 251. The passage comes at the end of book 6, in Lucretius's discussion of epidemics.

3. Thomas Campbell and Thomas Hood both wrote "Last Man" poems, and fragments survive of a play by Thomas Lovell Beddoes with that title, but perhaps the most important influence on Mary Shelley was Byron's poem "Darkness" (written in 1816, around the time she was writing *Frankenstein*). For a survey of this subject, see A. J. Sambrook, "A Romantic Theme: The Last Man," *Forum for Modern Language Studies* 2 (1966): 25–33; Steven Goldsmith, *Unbuilding Jerusalem: Apocalypse and Romantic Representation* (Ithaca: Cornell University Press, 1993), 265–71; and Fiona J. Stafford, *The Last of the Race: The Growth of a Myth from Milton to Darwin* (Oxford: Clarendon Press, 1994), 197–231.

4. For a discussion of Shelley's work as a negative apocalypse, in particular in relation to *Prometheus Unbound*, see Morton D. Paley, "*The Last Man*: Apocalypse Without Millenium," in *The Other Mary Shelley: Beyond "Frankenstein,"* ed. Audrey A. Fisch, Anne K. Mellor, and Esther H. Schor (New York: Oxford University Press, 1993), 107–23. See also Lee Sterrenburg, "*The Last Man*: Anatomy of a Failed Revolution," *Nineteenth-Century Fiction* 33 (1978): 324–47.

5. For a discussion of *Frankenstein* as "The Nightmare of Romantic Idealism," especially in relation to *Prometheus Unbound*, see my *Creature and Creator: Myth-making and English Romanticism* (Cambridge: Cambridge University Press, 1984), 103–32.

6. On the importance of Asia in *Prometheus Unbound*, see Leask, *British Romantic Writers*, 146–54.

7. On the complicated relation of East and West in *The Last Man*, see Barbara Johnson, "The Last Man," in *The Other Mary Shelley*, 264.

8. Though several discussions of *The Last Man* touch on the issue of imperialism in the work, I have found none centrally devoted to that subject. The one that comes closest is Audrey A. Fisch, "Plaguing Politics: AIDS, Deconstruction, and *The Last Man*" in *The Other Mary Shelley*, 267–86. See also Goldsmith, *Unbuilding Jerusalem*, 291–92.

9. Though *The Last Man* conveys an anti-imperialist message, it must be granted that Shelley seems to remain captive of English stereotypes of the Irish in her portrait of their encounter: "Our soldiers [the English] . . . advanced to quickest time, but in perfect order: their uniform dresses, the gleam of their polished arms, their silence, and looks of sullen hate, were more appalling than the savage clamour of our innumerous foe. Thus coming nearer and nearer each other, the howls and shouts of the Irish increased; the English proceeded in obedience to their officers" (217). This contrast between civilized and barbaric soldiers goes all the way back to Homer's portrayal of the difference between the Greeks and the Trojans at the beginning of book 3 of the *Iliad*.

10. See Jane Blumberg, *Mary Shelley's Early Novels* (Iowa City: University of Iowa Press, 1993), 136.

11. Patrick Brantlinger discusses this development in the chapter called "Imperial Gothic: Atavism and the Occult in the British Adventure Novel, 1880–1914," in his *Rule of Darkness: British Literature and Imperialism, 1830–1914* (Ithaca: Cornell University Press, 1988); see especially pp. 230–38 for his treatment of the theme of the "invasion of civilization by the forces of barbarism or demonism." Brantlinger does not discuss Mary Shelley or *The Last Man*; she was in effect too far ahead of her time to be included in his analysis. The best discussion of "reverse colonization" I have seen (and my source for the term) is Stephen D. Arata, "The Occidental Tourist: *Dracula* and the Anxiety of Reverse Colonization," *Victorian Studies* 33 (1990): 621–45. I do not know if Bram Stoker was influenced by Shelley, but there is a remarkable parallel between the scene in *The Last Man* in which a plague-infected ship from America arrives in England (157–58) and the scene in *Dracula* (chap. 7) when the *Demeter* brings the vampire to Britain.

12. For other associations of the plague with Asia, see *The Last Man,* 134, 139, 140, and 162–63. Reminiscent of Percy Shelley's elephantiasis phobia, here is the first mention of plague in the book: "This enemy to the human race had begun early in June to raise its serpent-head on the shores of the Nile" (127).

13. The racial aspect of the plague is reinforced later in the story when, in a nightmarish scene, the narrator, Lionel Verney, contracts the disease from "a negro half clad" (245) who seems to come out of nowhere.

14. See Kate Ferguson Ellis, "Subversive Surfaces: The Limits of Domestic Affection in Mary Shelley's Later Fiction," in *The Other Mary Shelley*, 225.

15. In many ways *The Last Man* reflects fears generated by the spread of Asiatic cholera in the early nineteenth century. See the excellent article on "Cholera" in the 11th edition of the *Encyclopaedia Brittanica* and also Stafford, *Last of the Race*, 218–19. A major outbreak of Asiatic cholera occurred in 1823; it was the first time the disease spread into Asia Minor and Russia, thus creating great anxiety in Europe. On this point, see Paley, "Apocalypse Without Millenium," 120. Asiatic cholera finally reached England in 1831; a year later, in yet another case of Shelley's fiction eerily anticipating disas-

ters in her own family, the disease claimed the life of her half brother, William Godwin Jr. (William St. Clair, *The Godwins and the Shelleys: A Biography of a Family* [New York: W. W. Norton, 1989], 483).

16. Goldsmith is the only critic I have found who discusses the economic aspects of *The Last Man*; see *Unbuilding Jerusalem*, 294.

17. *Frankenstein* (New York: New American Library, 1965), 54.

18. The issue of imperialism comes up at several points in *Frankenstein:* for example, in Walton's polar exploration (linked to England's imperialist obsession with finding the Northwest Passage) or in the creature's plan in effect to invade "the vast wilds of South America" (139).

19. For Shelley's "idealizing of the bourgeois family," see Anne K. Mellor, *Mary Shelley: Her Life, Her Fiction, Her Monsters* (New York: Methuen, 1988), especially the chapter on *The Last Man*, 141–76. For a contrary view, see Blumberg, *Mary Shelley's Early Novels*, especially 115–16.

20. For the quotations from Burke, see *The Last Man,* 116, 165, and 300.

21. On Shelley's critique of Ryland and democratic ideology, see Mellor, *Mary Shelley*, 161.

22. Consider the famous conclusion of Percy Shelley's *A Defence of Poetry*: "Poets are the unacknowledged legislators of the World" (Donald H. Reiman and Sharon B. Powers, eds., *Shelley's Poetry and Prose* [New York: Norton, 1977], 508).

23. On this point, see Stafford, *Last of the Race*, 226.

24. Mellor recognizes Shelley's "sympathy for Edmund Burke's vision of an organic society" but argues that ultimately she is critical of Burke (*Mary Shelley*, 162–63). On Shelley's view of Burke, see also Sterrenburg, "Anatomy," 331–33, and Blumberg, *Mary Shelley's Early Novels*, 141.

25. See Luke's "Introduction" to *The Last Man*, x.

26. Later, Raymond's dual motives in fighting for Greece are run together; he aims "to secure liberty, probably extended empire, to the Greeks" (117).

27. At the gates of Constantinople, Raymond explicitly adopts Alexander as his model (see *The Last Man,* 141). For the way in which Shelley "indicts the Romantic cult of the heroic leader," see Sterrenburg, "Anatomy," 345–46.

28. On this subject, see my essay "Mary Shelley and the Taming of the Byronic Hero: 'Transformation' and *The Deformed Transformed*," in *The Other Mary Shelley*, 89–106.

29. For an account of the shabbiness of the conditions during the Shelleys' first trip to France and Italy, see St. Clair, *Godwins and Shelleys*, 364–65. Toward the end of *The Last Man* (314), Shelley's travelers stay at the Villa Pliniana, near Lake Como. We know from a letter Percy Shelley wrote to Thomas Love Peacock on 30 April 1818 that he and Mary once actually tried to rent this villa. On this point, see Safaa El-Shater, *The Novels of Mary Shelley* (Salzburg: Institut für Englische Sprache und Literatur, 1977), 83.

30. It may seem odd to speak of "wish fulfillment" in the context of such a dark and depressing novel, but Fredric Jameson offers a way of doing so when discussing a science fiction film similar to *The Last Man* in its vision of the end of the world:

> The last people on earth . . . emerged into a forbidding landscape in which they could fill their car without charge from the gas pumps and take cans of food off the shelves in empty grocery stores; California, for them, was returned to the stage of a paradisal landscape free of overpopulation. . . . The show thus offered existential terror and

melodramatic grief, backed with the very real advantages of a reduction in competition." (Fredric Jameson, *Postmodernism, or The Cultural Logic of Late Capitalism* [Durham, N.C.: Duke University Press, 1991], 384)

Jameson's capsule description of the film—"a Utopian wish fulfillment wrapped in dystopian wolf's clothing" (384)—serves as an equally apt characterization of *The Last Man.*

31. In a specific inflection of this theme, Shelley is concerned in *The Last Man* with compensating for the fact that Lord Byron was so much more famous than Percy Shelley during their lifetimes; see Verney's comments on page 27: "Relations of what [Raymond] had done, conjectures concerning his future actions, were the neverfailing topics of the hour. I was not angry on my own account, but I felt as if the praises which this idol received were leaves torn from laurels destined for Adrian." In effect, the plot of *The Last Man* works so that Adrian's fame can eclipse Raymond's. For further speculations on the way in which the relationship of Byron and Percy Shelley is figured in *The Last Man*, see William D. Brewer, *The Shelley-Byron Conversation* (Gainesville: University Press of Florida, 1994), 151–55.

32. In this context, it is interesting that one of Raymond's most cherished projects as Lord Protector is the creation of a "national gallery for statues and pictures" (76). For the idea that the "world has become a veritable museum of human limitations" for Verney, see Robert Lance Snyder, "Apocalypse and Indeterminacy in Mary Shelley's *The Last Man*," *Studies in Romanticism* 17 (1978): 450.

33. On this point, see Paley, "Apocalypse Without Millenium," 114. Although Shelley sets her novel in the late twenty-first century, she fails to imagine any art created later than the early nineteenth century; her characters are, for example, still listening to Mozart and Weber as the ultimate in music (99, 173, 280). This lapse in imagination in *The Last Man* serves to increase the sense of artistic belatedness in the work; it is as if Shelley is writing after the death of European art.

34. In my thinking about museums in the nineteenth century, I have been guided by the work of my student Barbara Black in her 1991 University of Virginia dissertation, "Fragments Shored Against Their Ruin: Victorian Museum Culture" (*DAI*-A 53/02 [August 1992]: 501).

The Triumph of Death:
Reading and Narrative
in Mary Shelley's *The Last Man*

Lynn Wells

The Tender Offspring of the Reborn World

"Friend, come! I wait for thee!" (*LM,* 332) writes Lionel Verney in the towns emptied by the plague, but "friends" were slow to materialize for the narrative bearing his (final) name. As has been noted, Mary Shelley's *The Last Man* suffered from extreme critical neglect, to the point of near extinction, until its rescue from obsolescence.[1] A novel so fixated on the identity of its future readership should leave us, as critics, wondering whether we are the anticipated readers for whom the text longs. If we are, our seeming task would be to decipher this cryptic inscription of English Romantic culture that openly solicits our sympathy and understanding yet remains puzzlingly unclear about the exact message of its "instruction" (*LM*, 291).

Critics who have studied this monumental document since its revival in the 1950s and 1960s have treated it as though it is scrutable from specific vantage points: they read it primarily as a *roman à clef*, or as a text whose biographical elements are subordinate to its various critiques of Romanticism.[2] Their discussions of *The Last Man* often define themselves directly against the biographical context, frequently relegating it to an antiquated and reductive critical methodology. For instance, in his analysis of Shelley's revision of apocalyptic thought, Morton D. Paley quickly dismisses such considerations: "As the autobiographical aspect of *The Last Man* is widely recognized, it requires only brief mention

212

here."[3] Others keep biographical connections only to the extent that they confirm a particular reading; for these readers, real-life figures become markers of certain identifiable positions or dogmas. Lee Sterrenburg, for example, detects the besieged presences of William Godwin and Percy Shelley behind the novel's attack on utopian political optimism.[4] Nonetheless, either approach—biographical or postbiographical—usually assumes two kinds of textual stability: first, that Romanticism itself is a unified text with definite properties that can be unproblematically brought to and/or discerned in the novel; and second, that *The Last Man* records early-nineteenth-century events mimetically, despite its futuristic setting. Starting with these assumptions, commentators have tended to engage the novel as if its meaning, though perhaps partially concealed by the veil of fiction, is intact and need only be discovered.

What these critics fail to do is to disclose some unitary and preformed truth hidden within the novel; they do not, as Lionel claims his own purpose in writing to be, "solve the riddle" and "reveal the meaning of the enigma" (*LM*, 311). On the contrary, any interpretation actively replicates the text's own compositional practice. As Shoshana Felman explains, critics unwittingly "perform" and "reproduce," through repetition, what texts themselves do.[5] *The Last Man* weaves together selected narratable components of Romantic culture—personal referents, aesthetic theories, historical events, and so on—into a cohesive narrative. This work of cultural compilation is plainly figured in the "Author's Introduction" when the *I* "model[s]" certain of the sibylline leaves "into a consistent form" (*LM*, 4). In their interpretations, critics not only repeat and redo this procedure, but they also undo it, separating the interwoven narratable strands and reconstructing them as new stories (i.e., different sorts of readings) that parallel the text. Barbara Johnson, for instance, isolates those elements that support her reading of the novel as a eulogy for the defunct humanist subject; Anne K. Mellor locates those features that reinforce her study of the nuclear family in Shelley's work.[6] In all cases, critics foreground specific aspects; like Lionel, they bring "forward the leading incidents" (*LM*, 193) and place others in the background. As the "Author's Introduction" makes clear, the combinations possible in this mosaic are endless, and they vary according to the predilections of the "artist" who (re)arranges the cultural "shards" (4). There is no final interpretation, no single static vision of English Romantic culture to be espied in pristine form behind the text's fabric.

I will treat *The Last Man* not as a finished artifact to be de-composed but as a work whose meaning fluctuates with, and is inseparable from, the movement of the narrative itself. The novel can be seen as an imaginary process as described by Julia Kristeva in "The Adolescent

Novel": it is an ongoing open structure that enables Shelley, through writing, to fashion and refashion the cultural text subjectively and provisionally.[7] Rather than mimetically transcribing a preexistent reality, *The Last Man* acts like a "duplex mirror of a former revelation" (*LM*, 264): it presents historical actuality refracted through Shelley's complex perceptions of the culture in which she lived. As a result, the novel's characters and events are overdetermined in the same sense as dream-images: they are multivalent, representing several things at once. While characters may correspond with biographical personalities such as Percy Bysshe Shelley or George Gordon Lord Byron, they also act as a series of Romantic figures who concurrently embody contemporary literary stereotypes and entire sets of ideas. These condensed identities or masks are temporarily tried on, displaced, and moved around as Shelley tries to come to terms with the moribund society of which she feels herself to be the sole survivor. She projects onto the text, and it reflects back to her, images of a dying world that she attempts to delimit and within which she strives to create a position for herself, even as it recedes from her sight.

If we think of *The Last Man* as a transferential medium on which Shelley works through her responses to the passing of Romantic culture (on every level), we can see the text as exhibiting the traits of what Sigmund Freud terms "ambivalent mourning"; it manifests cycles of attachment and detachment from a lost object that is both lovingly recalled and utterly repudiated.[8] The narrative structure itself also enacts the mourning process: it functions both as a site of recovery, through the buildup of potential narrative action, and of loss, through the elimination of that same action. *The Last Man* becomes a "triumph of death" (*LM*, 291), as Lionel calls his story, in several ways at once, including the sense of triumphing over death, similar to how Jacques Derrida rereads the title of Percy Shelley's *The Triumph of Life* to encompass the notion of "surviving beyond."[9] The plague can be thought of as an agent of narrative annihilation, allowing the text to lay to rest various elements and to revive others, obsessively repeating key scenes and ideas, in its drive to achieve a satisfying cultural image. Lastly, we can diagnose Shelley's failure to resolve successfully her conflicting attitudes toward Romanticism in the novel's anxious projection of a future ideal reader, both in the narrative proper and in the introduction, where we will begin our discussion.

Transfiguration

The "Author's Introduction" to *The Last Man* is misleadingly named, since its authority over the main narrative is only provisional and its relationship with that narrative is far more than introductory. The *I* who has ostensibly put together Lionel's story implies that another artist might arrive at a superior arrangement of the sybilline leaves according to "his own peculiar mind and talent" (*LM, 4*). Because of the acknowledgment that this particular collation of the prophecies is not authoritative, we do not read the future universal plague as unavoidable but merely as one possible outcome.[10] Despite its narrative coherence, the text that follows seems always on the verge of breaking up into its constituent parts and being re-formed, the conditionality of the introduction imbuing the whole. What Felman says about Henry James's *The Turn of the Screw* can apply equally to *The Last Man*:

> The frame is therefore not an outside contour whose role is to display an inside content: it is a kind of exteriority which permeates the very heart of the story's interiority, an internal cleft separating the story's content from itself, distancing it from its own referential certainty.[11]

The introduction to Shelley's novel likewise suffuses the main narrative, disrupting its illusion of representational stability. Although placed before the text, the introduction penetrates the story to its end, where the apparent ultimatum of Lionel's fate opens back onto limitless other possibilities.

However, the introduction is a "pre/text," as Giovanni Franci suggests,[12] not only by virtue of its position in the novel but also because it supplies a reason for the narrative's being written in the first place. The *I* tells us that the activity of "giving form and substance" to the gathered leaves has transported her or him from an "imperious" and "once benignant" world to another "glowing with imagination and power" (*LM, 3, 4*). While the speaker does not specify what caused the alteration from benignity to grief, it is clear that the circumstances were worsened by the disappearance of the "matchless companion" (3) without whom she or he continues sorrowfully and alone. Nonetheless, composition is said to "have cheered long hours of solitude"; thus, by preparing a tale of "woeful change" (4), the writer finds a means of coping, through art, with a similar change in his or her life. The narrative shaped from the sybilline materials therefore fulfills two purposes: it furnishes a comforting reflection of the speaker's bereavement as well as a textual surrogate for what is gone. In "On the melancholic imaginary," Kristeva explains the double connection between death and artistic creation: "If loss, mourning, absence set the imaginary act in motion and fuel it as much as they menace and undermine it, it is also undeniable that the fetish of the work of art is erected in disavowal of this mobilizing affliction."[13] At the same time as it temporarily replaces a lost object, a text can operate as a surface on which mourning can be expressed in imaginary terms. The "Author's Introduction," with its symbolic descent into a cave, announces how the main narrative will function as a projection of Shelley's unconscious responses to what she perceives to be vanishing around her. Within this economy, the original companion represents the whole nexus of personal and cultural losses that Shelley confronts through writing.

Just as the companion stands for more than any one biographical personage, the *I* does more than designate authorial presence: she or he signifies the first stage in the process whereby Shelley creates for herself a series of provisional identities through which she can safely explore her situation with regard to her culture. That this narratorial figure is not meant to be identical with Shelley herself is obvious in the careful elision of any defining sexual features, either for the *I* or for the friend, whose gender, if mentioned, would perhaps influence our assumptions about the speaker's gender. However, neither is the *I* supposed to be completely distinct from Shelley, given the introduction's pretense of explaining the genesis of the text at hand and its insistence on using accurate biographical detail (e.g., the date of the Shelleys' trip to Naples). The introduction's narrator therefore is akin to a mirror image of the author, like her and yet dissimilar, existing in a necessarily simultaneous relation with her. The *I* and Shelley maintain a dialogic equipoise, separated by what Kristeva, in "Word, Dialogue, Novel," calls "a blank space" across which the author's individuality is "negated" and "transformed." After passing through this tranformational "space," the author is "born" anew as a "character" who is not simply the real person camouflaged but an independent entity. In Kristeva's terminology, the *I* of the "Author's Introduction" is not a direct translation of Shelley as a subject (i.e., S -> S); she or he is the end product or addressee of a conversion of life into text (S -> A).[14] This transposition results in a textual hybrid to which Tilottama Rajan refers as "auto-narration":[15] *The Last Man* is neither pure autobiography nor pure fiction but some amalgam of the two. This generic crossover is signaled by the initial self-modifying "per-mutation"[16] from Shelley to the first-person speaker.

Kristeva believes that the character that arises from the author's dissolution in anonymity is at first only pronominal ("he/she"), but it eventually assumes a "proper name"[17] with recognizable characteristics;

Shelley's text marks this elaboration in two discrete steps. With the movement from the introduction to the main narrative, and to Lionel as narrator, the second stage takes place in the author's formation of an alternate, desirable identity. Brought into being by the *I* as she or he models the sybilline leaves, Lionel both transcends that figure and stands in the same dialogic relation to her or him as does the *I* to Shelley herself. That is, Lionel becomes the addressee at the end of the transformational processes of *both* the *I* and Shelley, a doubly projected self-image that has been refined, step by step, to a state of absolute authority.

Many critics regard Lionel as a thinly concealed alias through which they look and see Shelley directly, as though the *I* does not intervene; Muriel Spark confidently declares: "It is clear that the character of Lionel Verney is Mary herself."[18] However, the transition from *I* to Lionel should not be ignored, since there is a significant shift in definition. Whereas the introduction's speaker is delineated quite vaguely— ungendered, nameless—Lionel is drawn in detail, so that the authorial image is brought into sharper focus. Not only does Lionel have a full background, while the introduction's narrator has almost none, but he also surpasses the *I* in terms of artistic ability. Rather than compiling previously written prophecies, Lionel is an author in his own right, studying the world around him and endowing it with narrative shape: "All events, at the same time that they deeply interested me, arranged themselves in pictures before me. I gave the right place to every personage in the groupe, the just balance to every sentiment" (*LM*, 126). Specifically, Lionel is a chronicler, recording the history of his age in a manner that gives him unqualified control, since his viewpoint is the only one available to us. We can only evaluate whatever Lionel admires or condemns based on his descriptions; unlike the *I* of the introduction, his perspective as storyteller is justified and invulnerable. While Perdita occasionally takes over as Shelley's voice in the novel, usually in order to deflect feminine weakness away from her brother, her role is secondary and without creative autonomy. Lionel is more than just another layer of disguise for Shelley: he is the perfect authorial identity. As such, within the main narrative he is both Shelley's mask, an assumed identity that makes it possible for her to express personal criticisms of her culture without fear of reprisal, and an object of desire, an imaginary, idealized version of her self free from any perceptible shortcomings.

As the consummation of successive authorial re-creations, Lionel approximates what Freud theorized as the "ego ideal"—a fabricated, per-fect self-image that coexists with the ego in the psyche. Freud proposes that, when faced with adverse criticism, we retreat into the "ego ideal," which is incapable of error since it replaces the unconditional love enjoyed in childhood; we are thereby able to avoid self-recrimination.[19] This concept is pivotal to Freud's understanding of ambivalent mourning, which differs from normal mourning with its gradual reorientation and abatement of the libidinal energy previously directed to the dead person. If a mourner has negative feelings (usually sublimated) toward someone who has died, she or he undergoes drastic emotional vicissitudes, motivated by guilt, between two opposing attitudes. In the melancholic phase, the mourner accuses him- or herself of wishing (and perhaps causing) the death to happen and consequently reaffirms his or her fidelity to the lost person's memory through passionate idolization. Contrarily, the mourner can yield to the negative emotions and want to be rid of the dead person forever; she or he then indulges in mentally "disparaging," "denigrating," "even as it were slaying"[20] the lost one. The libidinal energy becomes intensively and narcissistically reinvested in the self. In this manic phase, Freud contends, "the ego and the ego ideal have fused together, so that the person in a mood of triumph and self-satisfaction, disturbed by no self-criticism, can enjoy the abolition of his inhibitions, his feelings of consideration for others, and his self-reproaches."[21] For Freud, the cycle between "triumph"[22] and melancholy "can be repeated several times"[23] as the mourner tries to deal with the loss.

A similar cyclical movement between guilt-ridden veneration and smug reproval is discernible in the main narrative of *The Last Man*, which comprises the journal written by Lionel in his attempt to come to terms with his lost society. Owing to his unassailable moral superiority as narrator, Lionel records his impressions without fear of contradiction, frequently alternating between censure and praise of the same character or event. For example, Adrian, whose political naiveté causes him to proclaim that peaceful democracy can rid the world of "evil," "poverty," and "sickness" (*LM*, 159), is undoubtedly at times an object of Lionel's deprecation. Yet elsewhere, especially following the plague's invasion of England, when he commands the desperate population, Adrian is held up as a sincerely admirable leader.[24] Such vacillations in Lionel's account demonstrate an internal irresolution symptomatic of Shelley's views of her own society. With Lionel as a textualized ego ideal, she uses his history as an imaginary backdrop against which she can work out her ambivalent mourning of her culture, indulging in critical attitudes to which she could never openly admit, all the while expiating her guilt through idealization, all from a triumphant position of personal security. This indirectly expressed cultural ambiguity, epitomized by Lionel's merging of relentless critical hindsight with wistful sentimentality, unfolds over the course of his narrative.

Narrative Process-ion

Structurally, the main narrative duplicates the mourning process's mutually contradictory impulses to perpetuate and destroy the memory of someone who has been lost. From its title onward, *The Last Man* foreordains its own ending (as the novel's omens portend its civilization's decline), demarcating a narrative space across which events can only move inexorably toward Lionel's lone survival. Within this circumscribed structure, the text opens the potential for stories to develop, starting with Lionel as a prototypical bildungsroman hero/narrator, similar to Johann Wolfgang von Goethe's Wilhelm Meister. We expect to follow Lionel's career from his origins as an uncultivated youth through his maturation as a social subject; the early stages of this education are present in his introduction to the civilized world after his rustic beginnings, in his growing literary aptitude, and in the intrigues and travels on which he embarks with his new associates. The novel marshals in this context an array of identifiable Romantic stereotypes and motifs: Raymond as the Byronic adventurer (sexual and otherwise), Adrian as both Percy Shelley and an Alastor-like figure, idyllic country settings, political reformation, and so on. This collection of materials immortalizes the cultural gestalt much the way the mourner preserves the image of the dead person through remembrance. However, just as the text temporarily saves the culture from oblivion through amassed representation, it also obliterates what it accumulates. The plague commandeers the bildungsroman plotline near its midpoint, rendering any further development superfluous and setting into motion the systematic killing-off of Lionel's remaining relationships, eventually leading to his complete isolation. After the plague's appearance, the remainder of the novel literally degenerates into a funereal triumph or procession with an ever-increasing number of disparate corpses, so that this text curiously reverses *Frankenstein*'s initiatory creative act of sewing together and reanimating dead bodies. In a sense, the narrative itself is put to death, since the plague precludes any advancement; regardless of the promise that a tale involving Romantic figures will ensue, any real progression is doomed from the outset.

While the narrative of *The Last Man* goes out of its way to foreclose its own plot, it resists closure as well. Lionel frequently comments that he wants to proceed swiftly to finish his tale: "But the same sentiment that first led me to pourtray scenes replete with tender recollections, now bids me hurry on. The same yearning . . . makes me now recoil from further delay. I must complete my work" (*LM*, 173). Despite these hints of acceleration, he continues to prolong his account, prolixly lingering over details. As a result, the reader's reaction to the text may be somewhat like the Countess of Windsor's impression of her carriage ride: "Though I was assured that we travelled speedily, it seemed to me that our progress was snail-like, and that delays were created solely for my annoyance" (267). The narrative's paradoxical tendency both to hurry and postpone its forward propulsion relates to its primary impetus: the text does not rush haphazardly from creation to total destruction but rather sets about, by means of a painstaking process of rearrangement and elimination, to reach the best final configuration. As Peter Brooks argues in *Reading for the Plot*, narrative seeks "the right death, the correct end," with the "complicated detour" of the plot leading to the achievement of that end.[25] Through the deviations of Lionel's story, Shelley methodically reworks certain ideas in an effort to form a picture of a culture to which she can reconcile herself.

Within this revisionist operation, Shelley uses the plague as a kind of antisignifier, making it possible to remove peripheral actors from the plot once they have served their purposes and are no longer needed to support the cultural tableau built up around the principal characters. Ryland, for instance, after playing his part as the self-serving "democrat," has a gruesome demise, his body found "half-devoured by insects" (*LM*, 232). However, such Gothic removals are reserved for background figures. In a novel about a pandemic, surprisingly only one of the central characters (and a minor one at that)—Alfred, the son of Lionel and Idris—actually seems to die of the plague, and he does so in extraordinary circumstances. All of the others, with the exception of Lionel, die from other causes. Although the plague is not directly responsible for doing away with the central figures, it nonetheless contributes to an atmosphere in which their deaths seem natural and inevitable. The distinctive manners in which these deaths occur reveal Shelley's attitudes toward those aspects of her culture that are represented by those characters and retired from the text with their departures.

The sorting out of cultural paradigms occurs continuously, as Shelley attaches to the central characters traits associated with figures from her personal life and social milieu. These traits do not stay affixed permanently; they circulate throughout the narrative as Shelley splits off and reassigns them, searching for the best combination. The characters are not separate individuals so much as figures in a cultural dream-text, repeating and displacing one another. Owing to this fluidity, Shelley is able to shift between characters, using them alternately as positions from which to act out, observe, vilify, and/or cherish different Romantic stances. In this overdetermined system of signification, sexual relationships warrant particular attention, since they provide Shelley with a means of examining various characteristics by bringing them into contact with one another. The interplay early in the novel between the two couples comprising the nucleus—Raymond and Perdita, and Lionel and Idris—forms a sequence over which certain properties are tested, then either adapted or expunged from the text.

Shelley portrays in Raymond the supreme Romantic individualist so that she can glorify that cultural figure while showing up its deficiencies. As a virile egotist, Raymond shares many traits with his closest biographical equivalent, Byron, and with Byronic heroes such as Childe Harold. Raymond's eloquent defense of British aristocracy and monarchy, and his ambition to reclaim that eminence for himself by defeating the democratic forces, are presented appealingly but also nostalgically; as a societal alternative, his program is no longer viable. Disdaining domestic tranquillity, he is easily lured away from the Romantic idyll of Windsor castle, thereby becoming the vehicle through which Shelley can vicariously experience the recklessly active lives (as she imagines them) available to her male contemporaries but denied to her. Although Lionel glowingly evokes his heroism, there is also implicit rejection: upon returning from Greece, Adrian wonders at Raymond's impassiveness to the inhumanity of battle: "He is able to contemplate the ideal of war, while I am sensible only to its realities" (*LM*, 116). Together with political and military aggressiveness, Raymond represents an overweening masculine sexuality that is repugnant yet captivating— Lionel is noticeably more sympathetic than outraged by Raymond's betrayal of his sister with Evadne. Like the shadowy female figures in Byron's *The Giaour* and Percy Shelley's *Alastor*, Evadne emanates a dangerous sexuality carefully abstracted from the other women characters. This double sexual menace is largely neutralized by Evadne's martyred death and Raymond's remorseful reconciliation with Perdita. Although Raymond is a seductive figure, in the end Shelley cannot recuperate him into any acceptable cultural grouping, except through the apotheosis of death. By having Raymond die in a mysterious explosion following Evadne's curse, Shelley metes out a conspicuously violent end to a life that placed self ahead of others, effectively purging the male Romanticism that offends her[26] while simultaneously trying to exorcise her own involuntary attraction to Byron. Raymond's unsavory features are expelled from the text with his departure, and Perdita's and Lionel's enshrined memory of him is cleansed of all negative associations.

Perdita personifies womanly self-sacrifice and acquiescence to male domination, a cultural stereotype with which Shelley tries to come to terms through the creation of an exaggerated version of women's predicament. Beginning as a Wordsworthian "solitary," trailing pensively through the woods and living in a cottage, Perdita is reluctantly convinced to leave her protected environment in support of her husband's ambitions. Through Perdita's worship of Raymond, Shelley permits herself to desire Byron (in every sense) as well as to cast herself provisionally as the long-suffering wife of an unfaithful husband, a plight with which she had considerable familiarity. Further, Perdita's presence allows Shelley to have an enunciative position from which she can dispassionately give expression to otherwise distressing feminine emotions. This ventriloquism is evident in the fact that, though he makes it clear that he was not there, Lionel intimately describes Perdita's thoughts and actions during her scenes with Raymond; in addition, the narrative voice occasionally slips into the first person: "He, she thought, can be great and happy without me. Would that I also had a career!" (*LM*, 117). Despite her characteristic helplessness, Perdita still has the strength to rescue with Lionel the captured Raymond in Greece, though mostly as a tearful onlooker. As soon as Raymond dies, Perdita quickly loses her vitality; she later mails her corpse to the address of her husband's grave site by drowning herself clutching a piece of paper saying "To Athens" (156). Shelley's disposal of Perdita indicates that female deference to this degree is unreasonably painful and self-destructive. In spite of the beauty of prostrate sorrow, Perdita is only limitedly useful or attractive as a figure and is consigned to the same idealized remembrance as Raymond.

Perdita and Raymond in tandem occupy extremes of weakness and forcefulness, of passivity and activity, with which Shelley experiments but finally rejects as excessive. That their constitutions had been essentially flawed and prone to disaster is emphasized by Lionel's regretful condemnation of them when he regains the security of Windsor Castle: "How unwise had the wanderers been, who had deserted its shelter, entangled themselves in the web of society, and entered on what men of the world call 'life'" (158). Nevertheless, the qualities embodied by Raymond and Perdita are not entirely absent following their deaths early in the text; they reappear in tempered forms among the other central characters.

After remaining in the background during the focus on Perdita and Raymond's defective relationship, Idris and Lionel reemerge as the ideal couple, combining exemplary femininity with a less flamboyant, more sensible masculinity. Like Perdita, Idris is compliant to her husband's wishes; however, since her marriage is free from infidelity, she can be passive without exposing herself to harm. Whereas Perdita's monomania causes her to neglect her daughter Clara, Idris divides her attention between husband and children. Though prepared to leave the refuge of

Windsor in order to protect her family, she never makes it across the English channel, succumbing first to an indefinite malady seemingly brought on by exhaustion and worry. Idris meets a fittingly selfless end in familiar surroundings, avoiding the trials of life and lonely death that Perdita must endure as punishment for venturing outside the domestic enclave. In spite of her fragility, Idris is valiant in her weakness rather than pathetic; Lionel does not attribute to her the debilitating emotional frailties that he assigns to his sister. While Perdita is the voice of stereotypically female anxieties, Idris objectifies "the admired type of feminine perfection" (262) that Shelley, via Lionel, can revere and desire.

At the same time, through Lionel's interaction with Idris, Shelley is able to modify and soften the representation of male behavior in the novel. In contrast to Raymond, Lionel engages in political and military affairs only for the benefit of others, and only for as long as he is needed, always returning promptly to care for his family. In spite of his feint at the nomination for the protectorship, he is not a leader, preferring to follow Raymond and Adrian's plans rather than initiate any of his own. Courageous but not arrogant, active but not heroic, Lionel (as does Adrian) absorbs and sustains the positive traits left by the removal of the figure of male egomania. Together, Lionel and Idris act as a resurrected and improved version of the ideal marriage being developed over the course of the text.

In his role as loving husband, Lionel also enables Shelley to work out the implications of bereavement in a narrative context. Through two parallel scenes, both involving Lionel's trying to deliver Idris from imminent harm, Shelley exerts imaginative control over death by summoning, then deferring, it. Early in the novel, when Idris is endangered by the Countess's plot to marry her to another man, she escapes through a snowstorm to Lionel, who restores her to safety. This situation is replayed after the appearance of the plague but with some changes and fatal results. They are stranded in another blizzard, but by the time Lionel finds shelter, Idris, owing to her failed health, has already died. In strikingly similar conditions, the deprivation held at bay by the first occurrence is deliberately invoked by the second.

These scenes, inverted through the inner mirror of the plague, are part of a circuit in the novel of abductions, abandonments, and rescues (successful and otherwise). Raymond is held captive by the Turks, then released; Lionel abducts his sister in an ill-fated attempt to coerce her away from Greece; an abandoned charity-girl is aided by Adrian and Lionel. While such incidents apparently occur independently of each other, together they form an underlying pattern, a paradigmatic text that preoccupies the actual plotline. Through these recurrent nightmares and fantasies, Shelley acts out various cultural experiences (such as the fantasy of being an active male) by recasting them in imaginary terms. The narrative obsession with moments of separation and reunion exposes the latent dynamic in *The Last Man* whereby Shelley selectively saves some aspects of her culture and discards others.

By going back to scenes of recovery and loss, the text is either, as Shlomith Rimmon-Kenan explains, moving forward to some resolution or caught in a loop from which it cannot break free: "Narration-as-repetition . . . may lead to a working through and an overcoming, but it may also imprison the narrative in a kind of textual neurosis, an issueless re-enactment of the traumatic events it narrates and conceals."[27] With Lionel's second and failed rescue attempt, the narrative may be laying to rest flawless femininity, having reached a point of satisfaction or satiety with that figure; this reading would be borne out by the way Lionel dwells on Idris's burial, suggesting a meticulously wrought finality. Conversely, the repetition of these scenes may signal not a wholesale eradication of this figure but rather its metamorphosis. In its relentless drive to settle on a lasting cultural image, the text narrows down the number of characters, retaining the good qualities of those it excises and reallocating them to increasingly idealized characters.

Throughout this culling process, Adrian is pivotal, since only he manages to outlive his unfavorable traits. As the fictional equivalent of Percy Shelley, Adrian has highly charged biographical significance. Early on, Shelley goes out of her way to distract sexual attention away from Adrian by making him permanently single, peripheral to the two couples. However, the manner in which Adrian's celibacy is established reveals that desire for him is merely shunted temporarily onto Idris. In yet another rescue scene, Lionel races to the side of Adrian, who has been declared "irrecoverably mad" (*LM*, 40) after having been disappointed in his love for Evadne. When Adrian gets well, any sexualized characteristics have disappeared; it is as if his sexuality is part of the "madness" from which he has to recover, an unwanted element that has to be repressed in order for the text to proceed. Lionel, meanwhile, wins Idris's heart in gratitude for his aid, so that the desire circulating for Adrian in the novel is safely redirected to his sister, who stands in as a female double. Shelley distances herself from Adrian so that she can impartially approach certain ideas associated with her husband. While Adrian is dreamy and introspective, he is not literally a poet in the same sense that Lionel is an author. By divorcing Adrian from the act of writing, Shelley can still cherish his character while deriding the rarified esotericism of Romantic poetics; Lionel alludes to enjoying, as a quaint diversion after the plague, "poets of times so far gone by, that to read of them was to read of Atlantis and Utopia; or such as referred to nature only, and the workings of one particular mind" (314). Nonetheless, even indirect incriminations of Adrian diminish as the narrative advances, and he gradually becomes the repository for virtually every admirable quality.

The evolution of Adrian as paragon is accomplished through the redistribution of his shortcomings to other characters and the replaying of previous episodes. His political foibles are divided between Merrival, the absent-minded astronomer, a caricature of the utopian thinker, and Ryland, the pragmatist, a flat-footed and self-absorbed leader who fails to inspire the populace in an emergency. Once dissociated from these two extremes, Adrian arises as the master politician, reconciling democratic principles with royal blood and aristocratic nobility. A similar conciliatory spirit informs Lionel's notion of setting up community governments, with local elders ascending to power through "spontaneous regal elections" (196); however, the fact that this plan is given only scant reference implies that any momentous venture is Adrian's prerogative. Like Lionel, Adrian is ambitious only in the service of others, but his altruism goes beyond his friend's compromise between domestic and public life, as he assumes a paternal role for the survivors. In a scene echoing Raymond's vainglorious entry into Constantinople, Adrian arrives in plague-ridden Paris, a martial ruler intent on negotiating peace and resolving disputes. Such obvious repetitions accentuate how Adrian is progressively enhanced, shedding his own weaker characteristics and taking on the better ones left behind by others, until he develops into the epitome of male virtue.

Because the text concentrates its organization of traits on Adrian, he becomes a more fully defined version of the introduction's companion, a polyvalent figure who acts as a site for the working through of cultural loss. That Adrian is the focal point of the mourning process enacted in *The Last Man* is suggested by his intermittent and extensive absences. When he is away from Adrian, Lionel is more actively independent— going into battle with Raymond, leading a company of men in France. When he is with Adrian, however, Lionel tends to retire into the background, assisting his friend in his exploits and rhapsodizing on his goodness. Lionel's separations from and returns to Adrian simulate the cycles in which an ambivalent mourner engages and disengages the memory of the lost one. Shelley's perplexity about this crucial character is clear in that she keeps him "for ever on the verge of annihilation" (158); she prefigures Adrian's death well before the spread of the plague and leaves the possibility open that he could die at any time, giving herself leeway to get rid of him whenever he becomes unmanageable. However, he makes it to the end, and Lionel's final reunion with him is a fantasy of emotional fulfillment: "Half in exhaustion, half voluntarily, I threw myself at my length on the ground—dare I disclose the truth to the gentle offspring of solitude? I did so, that I might kiss the dear and sacred earth he trod" (295). Along with Clara, Adrian near the close of the novel is the condensation of all that is desirable; Lionel says of them: "I was conscious that every other sentiment, regret, or passion had by degrees merged into a yearning, clinging affection for them" (328). Following Idris's death, her attributes are split and subsumed by these two: Clara replaces her as the paragon of womanly goodness but apparently devoid of sexual energy, while Adrian moves unequivocally into his role as the object of Lionel's desire. Since these idealized figures are the last to predecease Lionel, the narrative should conclude on a note of satisfied regret.

Yet there are signs that the elimination process is inadequate. Before the survivors dwindle to three, new characters are brought forward as if in a last-ditch effort to put to rest some unfinished problems. The impostor-prophet challenges the sanctity of Adrian's benevolent governance, raising the suspicion that democracy is inherently fallible, since people may voluntarily submit to tyranny when given freedom of choice. One of the impostor's victims, Juliet, though introduced earlier, gains prominence near the end. With the failure of Lionel's attempt to rescue Juliet, owing to her hostaged child,[28] the text relapses to the question of feminine self-sacrifice that ostensibly had been settled with Perdita's suicide. In addition to Juliet's story, there are the embedded accounts of Lucy and the young organist, both concerned with women in distress over invalid parents. By multiplying tales of female helplessness, the novel seems to be worrying certain ideas that it has not resolved satisfactorily, impeding its own forward motion. Nonetheless, following these hints of chronic uneasiness, the narrative intuits its unstoppable progress toward its ending, sensed within the textual world as a kind of cosmic "Necessity" (290).[29] Lionel records his and Adrian's inexplicable realization that the plague had "vanished from the earth" (310); this suspension gives Shelley the latitude to shape the concluding scene, preparing appropriately meaningful deaths for the two characters who should represent the culmination of her cultural imaginings.

After the epidemic ceases, the final set of three (plus Lionel's remaining child, Evelyn) is initially harmonious, withdrawn from the travails of life, as had been the family at Windsor. All wants can be instantly fulfilled with little labor, so that the earth, despite its ghastly reminders of destruction, becomes to the survivors an Eden, their abode at Lake Como a "paradisiacal retreat" (315). Within this perfect community, democracy unites with a kind of symbolic monarchy. Lionel and Adrian playfully dub Clara the "little queen of the world" (313), whom they attend equally; she completes a series of "queens" in the text, replacing those that are negative—the countess and the plague (252)—and surpassing Idris as the positive model. As sovereign, Clara is matriarchal, adopting toward Evelyn the role of "a young mother" (315). So long as Clara is occupied with the child, the threesome lives in unanimity. However, once Evelyn dies, the fellowship declines, indicating the persistence of disturbing aspects even among these most idealized figures.

The novel's increasingly tenuous attitude toward Adrian and Clara before their deaths signals that they are somehow unsatisfactory. When Clara is relieved of her maternal duties, the sense of balance in the group falters; Lionel becomes extraneous as his niece grows closer to Adrian: "She crept near him, drinking in his speech with silent pleasure" (319). Fisch sees in Adrian's nascent power over Clara a sexual threat (275), the same desire repressed with his madness and "buried" with Raymond and Evadne. The resexualizing of Adrian at this point revokes the distance put in place by Shelley so that she could safely admire him as a figure, and it raises the spectre of homosexual desire in Lionel's undisguised affection for him. Further, Adrian regresses to a behavioral habit from before his madness, a tendency to recklessness that Lionel had criticized earlier: "Are you weary of life, O Adrian, that you thus play with danger?" (57). Adrian's impulsiveness, together with Clara's excessive fatalism, leads to the disastrous sailing trip to her parents' graves. Unlike her mother, Clara is unsuccessful in delivering herself to Greece, a short circuit that suggests an inability to return to origins, to finish meaningfully. Adrian's and Clara's deaths therefore accentuate their shortcomings rather than their perfection. Although Lionel lyricizes them in memory, their inglorious ends denote that Shelley ultimately finds them lacking as cultural representatives.

While only Lionel demonstrates the pragmatism and "instinctive love of life" (323) needed to avoid the fate of Adrian and Clara, after their demises he does not immediately fulfill the final role of the typical bildungsroman hero, as the novel's opening had seemed to promise that he would. Rather than reflecting sagely on his experiences from a position of weary but enlightened maturity, he regresses gradually to the primitive condition from which he first arose. He wanders like a "wild-looking, unkempt, half-naked savage" (331), with only a dog for a companion, effectively undoing all of his previous development and reverting to his beginnings as a shepherd. Despite his narratorial infallibility, Lionel does not emerge at the text's conclusion as an ideal character to succeed the imperfect standards of Adrian and Clara.

The failure to reach a resolution of cultural ambivalence through the working out of idealized figures is underscored by the fact that the narrative does not end with their deaths (as it does in *Matilda*) but literally drifts, with Lionel, for some time thereafter. The narrative continues past its natural life span, acquiring new vitality when it should be drawing to a close. In this respect, the chronicler and his tale are cognate, since Lionel lives on in three separate ways. When his son Alfred, the only main character to die of the plague, falls ill, Lionel too becomes infected from the breath of a mysterious "negro" (245). Yet Lionel revives, like Frankenstein's monster, from certain death, as if Alfred's sacrifice purchases his recovery.[30] This resurrection is repeated in Lionel's escape from drowning; he awakes on the beach having "lain long deprived of life" (324). Lastly, Lionel survives his own narrative, leaving his completed manuscript behind to venture out into the deserted world.

Shadows, Arise, and Read Your Fall!

Lionel proffers a number of reasons for deciding to commit his story to paper at a time when writing had become "vanity" (223). Foremost is edification: he chronicles humanity's last years so that any descendants may learn about their ancestors and avoid the same fate. Beyond this social value, though, Lionel's composition performs a therapeutic duty: "I had used this history as an opiate; while it described my beloved friends, fresh with life and glowing with hope; active assistants on the scene, I was soothed; there will be a more melancholy pleasure in painting the end of all" (192). The manuscript not only ends some time after the "beloved friends" have died but begins with their deaths as well. Lionel commences writing only once he is convinced that he is truly alone; the project therefore serves the double purposes of filling the emptiness caused by his friends' absence and of prolonging their lives in his text. As Gregory O'Dea puts it, "The physical text of Verney's history assumes the place of the lives and episodes it describes."[31] Lionel also perpetuates his own past existence by posing as the narrator of his tale and as a character within it. As long as Lionel is engaged creatively, he maintains his identity by projecting it onto a medium outside of himself that returns to him a comforting image, unlike the endlessly alienating self-reflection that he sees in the mirror shortly after the shipwreck. However, when he reaches the end of his manuscript, he faces the same void of nonsignification into which the plague victims have disappeared; because there is no one left to listen to him, he risks sliding from virtual anonymity ("The Last Man") back into the utter silence temporarily put in abeyance by his narrative. This loss of selfhood reverses the process at the novel's opening when Adrian civilizes Lionel by restoring his lost name, the honor of his family, thereby making him into a social being and ending his separation from the rest of humanity. Like the monster in *Frankenstein*, Lionel, once again finding himself isolated, is unable to procreate; and, like the monster, he despairs of ending his days in solitude, unable to ease his suffering by sharing his experiences with another of his own kind: "To none could I ever relate the story of my adversity; no hope had I" (*LM*, 326). His need to narrate drives him first to produce his text and then to pursue further solace by looking for a new companion.

For Lionel, the act of writing finds its impetus in an accident of reading occasioned by his search for survivors. In a Roman house, he happens upon a manuscript, parts of which "lay scattered about" (339), much like the sybilline leaves in the Neapolitan cave. Significantly, this partial document is a "learned disquisition on the Italian language" (339), a tongue with which Lionel is evidently conversant. He thus becomes the projected reader, the posterity to whom the manuscript's author dedicates his work. By coming across the text and being able to understand it, Lionel answers its wish as an object to be found and appreciated, since it too would remain silent without an other to intercept its message. Lionel also addresses his own manuscript to some unknown recipient in the hope that it will be likewise fortunate in being delivered, that is, discovered by its readership, which it frequently apostrophises. These future readers are consistently described as the offspring of "some surviving pair" (291), the children of some ideal couple more durable than Adrian and Clara, a new Adam and Eve. According to his direct appeals to them, Lionel fantasizes that these readers will be characterized by a "gentle disposition," a facility to be "compassionate" and patient (291). When Lionel recounts situations where his judgment has been questionable, such as his imprudent decision to abduct Perdita, he asks outright for reader approval: "I believe that most people in my situation would have acted in the same manner" (154). In addition, Lionel expects readers to be able to comprehend the point of his rather oblique instruction. Yet the dubious prospect that his manuscript will someday be interpreted correctly is insufficient for Lionel with his intense desire to be heard. The alternative readers whom he craves in the form of a living audience for his tale would necessarily have to possess these same qualities of sympathy and understanding; they must want to hear his story as much as he wants to tell it. The circumstances surrounding the genesis of Lionel's narrative establish that writing and reading are not only inextricably related activities but also two mutually sustaining desires that seek one another out.

In its competing version of how Lionel's narrative is conceived, the introduction cites another act of reading precipitated by exploration—the perusal and compilation of the prophetic leaves, whose original author is the sybil.[32] At first, the *I* and her or his companion are joint readers of this disparate manuscript, together choosing which fragments to carry away and which to leave behind. The basis of this selection process is linguistic cogency: the explorers select those leaves "whose writing one at least of [them] could understand" (3) from among the various ancient and modern languages represented. When the companion is lost, so too is this cooperation, and the *I* must proceed solely according to his or her own knowledge. The *I* makes the transition from reader to writer only after the companion has gone, using the task of arranging the leaves in order to ward off loss and solitude. However, at the moment of composing the introduction, the *I* has supposedly already concluded this work and is adding an explanation of its origins after the fact, to render the narrative more intelligible. Like Lionel, the *I* continues past the end of the story as such, projecting into the future in anticipation of a readership. That the reaction sought by the *I* is a sympathetic one is clear in the effusive apologies made in the introduction for the ensuing manuscript. By asking to be "excuse[d]" (4) for the subjectiveness of the textual production, the *I* implicitly offers to share his or her authority, inviting the reader to rearrange the mosaic at will, to rewrite what has been written. Of necessity, the reader of the text in this form must comprehend the language in which it is presented, the language spoken by the *I*; the reader consequently assumes the collaborative position vacated by the companion. In effect, the reader desired by the *I* would replace the companion, providing the kind of mutual understanding that initiated the act of writing. The introduction, then, repeats the same duplex pattern as the narrative it circumscribes: writing begins as a response to loss, with the absent companion reconstituted textually, and in turn transfigured, resurrected as a new object of desire, the projected reader.

Finally, this pattern within a pattern is enclosed and repeated by the novel itself, which performs the same double actions of reading and writing, recovery and projection. As a cultural document, *The Last Man* is process and product, an ongoing effort by Shelley to read that which is disappearing around her and to render her perceptions of it in a form legible to others. We come to the text in the belief that it conceals, in its runic condition, an authentic legend of the English Romantic world; we therefore invest Shelley with the authority of what Jacques Lacan calls "le sujet supposé savoir" [the subject presumed to know], the holder of meaning that we lack and seek.[33] At the same time, the novel casts its desire forward to us as readers, looking ahead to an ideal audience that will not only listen sympathetically but interpret authoritatively, resolve its ambivalences, tell it what it means.

Notes

I would like to thank Tilottama Rajan for her helpful advice with regard to this article.
All references in this essay to Mary Shelley's *The Last Man* are to Hugh J. Luke Jr.'s edition (Lincoln: University of Nebraska Press, 1965) and are cited parenthetically in the text as *LM*.

1. Morton D. Paley, *"The Last Man*: Apocalypse Without Millenium," 107–23, in *The Other Mary Shelley: Beyond "Frankenstein"*, ed. Audrey A. Fisch, Anne K. Mellor, and Esther H. Schor (New York: Oxford University Press, 1993); Muriel Spark, *Child of Light: A Reassessment of Mary Wollstonecraft Shelley* (Hadleigh, Essex: Tower Bridge, 1951); and Robert Lance Snyder, "Apocalypse and Indeterminacy in Mary Shelley's *The Last Man*," *Studies in Romanticism* 17 (fall 1978): 435–52 all begin their analyses of the novel with speculations as to why it had been ignored for so long. Spark believes that the reason is self-evident: *The Last Man*, she says, evaded nineteenth-century classification (as either a "domestic tale," a Gothic, or a "sociological" novel) and therefore was unable to find a readership (150). Snyder explains the work's neglect in Shelley's lifetime as a consequence of its critical reception, which "denounced" (435) it as morbid and its author as depraved; he attributes later neglect to the novel's "stylistic vagrancies and occasionally forced prose" (436). Paley also refers to contemporary critics' harsh appraisal of the novel but within the context of the controversy over originality raised by the numerous "last man" narratives being written at the time by Thomas Campbell and others. Shelley's novel, arriving late on an already crowded scene, seemed "not apocalyptic but ridiculous" (107); nonetheless, Paley argues, the critical vehemence may have concealed "a certain eschatological anxiety" (108).

2. The two critical poles to which I refer align themselves for the most part according to general methodological trends in literary theory. Thus, Walter Edwin Peck's "The Biographical Element in the Novels of Mary Wollstonecraft Shelley," *PMLA* 38 (1923): 196–219, discusses *The Last Man* in completely biographical terms consistent with the critical attitudes of his day, the vestiges of which persist in Spark's book, *Child of Light*. Both Snyder, "Apocalypse and Indeterminacy," and Lee Sterrenburg, *"The Last Man*: Anatomy of Failed Revolutions," *Nineteenth Century Fiction* 33 (1978): 324–47, writing in the late 1970s, go out of their way to distance their arguments from the biographical, though largely without the vocabulary of new theory to assist them; they focus on how the novel critiques and undermines prevalent Romantic cultural notions. Giovanni Franci, "A Mirror of the Future: Vision and Apocalypse in Mary Shelley's *The Last Man*," 181–91, in *Mary Shelley: Modern Critical Views*, ed. Harold Bloom (New York: Chelsea House, 1985); Paley, "Apocalypse Without Millenium"; and Barbara Johnson, "The Last

Man," 258–66, and Audrey Fisch, "Plaguing Politics: AIDS, Deconstruction, and *The Last Man*," 267–86, both in *The Other Mary Shelley*, have brought poststructuralist theory to the text, variously identifying it as Shelley's project to deconstruct her culture at large rather than to represent it in any strictly personal sense. With Anne K. Mellor's *Mary Shelley: Her Life, Her Fiction, Her Monsters* (New York: Methuen, 1988), many of the earlier biographical considerations seem to have reasserted themselves, albeit within a more sophisticated theoretical framework; in her preface, Mellor clarifies that she is working from the assumption that "authors" speak, not "language" per se: "But I am thinking of the author in Bakhtinian terms, as the nexus of a 'dialogue' of conflicting ideological discourses or allegiances produced by sex, class, nationality, and specific economic, political, and familial conditions" (xii–xiii). Gregory O'Dea's article "Prophetic History and Textuality in Mary Shelley's *The Last Man*," *Papers on Language and Literature* 28 (1992): 283–304, brings new light to *The Last Man* by using current historiographic theories, focusing on how the text's self-consciousness about its own narrative construction reveals "the relationships between time, history, and eternity, and the difficulties of representing those relationships" (293). With his emphasis on the boundary between futuristic fiction and prophetic history, O'Dea counters those arguments, which see the novel as unproblematically mimetic. My own approach borrows from psychoanalytic narrative theory in order to diagnose both the text and our readings of it.

3. Paley, "Apocalypse Without Millenium," 109.

4. Sterrenburg, "Anatomy."

5. Shoshana Felman, "Turning the Screw of Interpretation," *Yale French Studies: Literature and Psychoanalysis: The Question of Reading: Otherwise* 55.6 (1977): 101.

6. Johnson, "The Last Man"; Mellor, *Mary Shelley*.

7. Julia Kristeva, "The Adolescent Novel," in *Abjection, Melancholia and Love*, ed. John Fletcher and Andrew Benjamin (New York: Routledge, 1989), 8–23.

8. Sigmund Freud, "Mourning and Melancholia," trans. James Strachey, in *The Standard Edition of the Complete Psychological Works*, ed. James Strachey (London: Hogarth, 1957), 14:237–60.

9. Jacques Derrida, "Living On/Border Lines," trans. James Hulbert, in *Deconstruction and Criticism* (New York: Continuum, 1979), 76.

10. O'Dea likens the speculative future envisioned by the introduction to the provisionality of historians' various accounts of the past compiled from the same "raw materials" ("Prophetic History," 292).

11. Felman, "Turning the Screw," 123.

12. Franci, "A Mirror of the Future," 183.

13. Kristeva, "On the Melancholic Imaginary," trans. Louise Burchill, in *Discourse in Psychoanalysis and Literature*, ed. Shlomith Rimmon-Kenan (New York: Methuen, 1987), 105.

14. Kristeva, "Word, Dialogue, Novel," trans. Alice Jardine et al., in *The Kristeva Reader*, ed. Toril Moi (New York: Columbia University Press, 1986), 34–61.

15. See Tilottama Rajan's "Autonarration and Genotext in Mary Hays' *Memoirs of Emma Courtney*," *Studies in Romanticism* 32.2 (1993): 149–76, and "Mary Shelley's *Mathilda*: Melancholy and the Political Economy of Romanticism," *Studies in the Novel* 26.2 (1994): 43–68.

16. Kristeva, "Word," 45.

17. Ibid.

18. Spark, *Child of Light*, 152.

19. Freud, "Group Psychology and the Analysis of the Ego," trans. James Strachey, in *Standard Edition*, 18:67–143.

20. Freud, "Mourning and Melancholia," 257.

21. Freud, "Group Psychology," 132.

22. Derrida, "Living On/Border Lines" (see especially p. 108 and following), suggests the Freudian understanding of "triumph" in the mourning process as a means of approaching Percy Shelley's *The Triumph of Life* as well as Maurice Blanchot's *L'arrêt de mort*—both texts intimately concerned with death, narrative, and beyond.

23. Freud, "Group," 133.

24. Fisch, "Plaguing Politics," concludes that all of the characters (including Adrian) representing political systems in *The Last Man* are equally targets of Shelley's deconstructive project, in which she sets out to expose the hegemony of male-centered, imperialistic forms of government.

25. Peter Brooks, *Reading for the Plot: Design and Intention in Narrative* (Cambridge, Mass.: Harvard University Press, 1984), 103–4.

26. For a discussion of Shelley's views toward the male aspect of her culture, see Mellor's "Why Women Didn't Like Romanticism: The Views of Jane Austen and Mary Shelley," in *The Romantics and Us: Essays on Literature and Culture*, ed. Gene W. Ruoff (New Brunswick, N.J.: Rutgers University Press, 1990), 174–287; and Meena Alexander, "Femininity and Betrayal: *The Last Man*," in *Women in Romanticism: Mary Wollstonecraft, Dorothy Wordsworth and Mary Shelley* (Savage, Md.: Barnes and Noble, 1989), 155–60, 185–91.

27. Shlomith Rimmon-Kenan, "Narration as Repetition: The Case of Günter Grass's *Cat and Mouse*," in *Discourse in Psychoanalysis and Literature*, 178.

28. Juliet's child changes mysteriously from a boy (*LM*, 283) into a girl (286), an inconsistency easily put down to hasty writing on Shelley's part. However, given the shift in this sequence from male heroism to female desperation, the error may be a significant one.

29. While I discuss the emphasis on "Necessity" toward the end of the novel as the narrative's self-conscious premonition of its own imminent expiry, O'Dea sees it as a force of historical determinism along the lines of that hypothesized by William Godwin and Percy Shelley ("Prophetic History," 297).

30. In relating his revival, Lionel notes that he was the only person ever known to have survived infection (*LM*, 250). Yet, earlier in his account, he mentions "old Martha," who equally claims to have "recovered" following exposure (196). Lionel's insistence on his uniqueness in this regard serves to increase his sense of isolation, his "monstrousness" in comparison with the rest of his race, and therefore makes him more deserving of reader sympathy. From our standpoint, this (seemingly inadvertent) contradiction is more confusing and perhaps relates to Shelley's ongoing engagement with her text—i.e., the possibility of additional plague survivors, at least temporarily, may have been an option that she wished to keep open. In addition, Martha, associated by name with the biblical Lazarus and hence with the ability to escape death, could signify an interpenetration between textual levels; she may be a shadow of the sibyl in the main narrative, just as the "shout of shepherd-boy" (3) in the introduction echoes Lionel as a youth.

31. O'Dea, "Prophetic History," 299.

32. A further twist to the dynamic interplay of writing and reading is O'Dea's inclusion of the sibyl, the introduction's "I," and their subsequent readers as part of Lionel's narrative's "audience" ("Prophetic History," 301).

33. Jacques Lacan, "Du sujet supposé savoir, de la dyade première, et du bien" (1964), in *Le Séminaire—Livre 11: Les Quatres Concepts fondamentaux de la psychanalyse*, ed. Jacques-Alain Miller (Paris: Seuil, 1973), 209–20.

Women in the Active Voice:
Recovering Female History in Mary Shelley's
Valperga and *Perkin Warbeck*

Ann M. Frank Wake

At the level of history, it was not clothes that made the woman, but virtues—
or vices.

—Diane Owen Hughes, "Invisible Madonnas"

However replete with event, the past is but a point to us; however empty, the
present pervades all things.

—Mary Shelley, *The Letters of Mary Wollstonecraft Shelley*, vol. 2

Shortly following the publication of *Perkin Warbeck* in 1830, Mary Shelley wrote a letter to her publisher, John Murray, pronouncing an interest in women's history two decades before such study even existed as a distinct discipline in the Academy. She suggested several topics for future books, writing "I have thought also of the Lives of Celebrated Women, or a history of Woman—her position in society and her influence upon it—historically considered, and a History of Chivalry" (*Letters*, 2:115). She wrote neither of these books, nor a proposed biography of Mme de Staël, but her intention to do so begs us to explore her fiction with similar purpose. In many ways, Shelley's novels *Valperga* (1823), set in fourteenth-century Italy, and *Perkin Warbeck* (1830), in Tudor England, prepared her to write a formal historical treatment of women.[1] They gave her a forum to investigate her research interests and to devise her attitudes about how women had fared in the past. My point here is to suggest that Shelley not only used the fiction to voice her concerns about women's traditional roles and positions but that in the process she came to challenge and ultimately reject two of the more tantalizing views of history in her day, namely, the doctrine of meliorism and the notion that the Middle Ages were somehow a "golden age." I attempt to characterize a plausible psychological framework by which to consider Shelley's views of historical and contemporary events, using Ellyn Kaschak's recent work in feminist psychotherapy as my model. Shelley's attitudes about women are then considered from a new historicist, poststructuralist, feminist perspective of history, to suggest that Shelley was "deconstructing" ideas of text, history, and gender roles long before we had an appropriate framework for acknowledging her efforts.

The notebook in which Shelley recorded her research on Italian medieval customs (for the writing of *Valperga*) shows a keen interest in women's legal and social status. This document notes that husband and wife "sometimes lived by different laws—generally the wife lived by her husbands and if a widow returned to her own." She noted that

> in Modena the law exists of a husband being able to kill his wife & her lover taken in the fact. The usual law was that he might sell his wife or punish her (but not corporally) & if the lover could not pay the fine he might sell him too. a free woman marrying a slave she was killed or sold by her relations— or became property of the king—he was killed—a free man gave liberty to a slave before he married her.

Of interest is how Shelley capitalizes on this information in her fiction, often depicting married or engaged men with lovers, and women who feel punished, betrayed, or bound by unreciprocated fidelity, and who sometimes view marriage as bondage. She also recorded in the notebook women's fashions in some detail (including clothes and hair), social customs surrounding marriage, the epithalamium, dowries, funerals ("women were forbidden to attend"), "insults to widows and widowers remarrying" ("the same now practiced at Genoa"), inheritance, jousts and tournaments, gypsies, knighthood ("apparently less honorable more universal and far less romantic in Italy than elsewhere"), a list of nunneries of Pavia, and finally, dangers that threatened lady pilgrims.[2] Her commentaries on these laws and customs, indicated above in parentheses, reveal a critical stance toward both past and contemporary practices as they restricted or inhibited women. We see her draw comparisons, formulate positions, and note historical facts about women, such as the list of Pavia nunneries.

Had Shelley followed through on her proposed "history of Woman" or "Lives of Celebrated Women" (*Letters*, 2:115) she would have led an early charge for women's studies that caught hold later in the century. Women with important political connections have appeared in history writing through the centuries, but the topic of "women in history" only began receiving serious academic attention from the middle of the nineteenth century (and that obviously minimal and intermittent, based on Virginia Woolf's narrative about trying to find a history of women for *A Room of One's Own*). As it was, Shelley turned to fiction rather than politics to devise her own "history of Woman," which shows us that history, in particular the Middle Ages, was debilitating, regardless of a woman's class or privilege. Barbara O'Sullivan claims that "in many ways Shelley was a forerunner of the Victorian women authors who adapted and strengthened the portrayal of the gifted woman."[3] Yet always in the background for any woman was the reality that custom was, in Shelley's words, a "silken net" (*Perkin Warbeck*, 3:177).

Women as Icons: A Psychological Context

Not merely a record of laws, fashions, religion, and domestic and social rewards and punishments, history became for Shelley a record of female virtues, or vices, as medieval women's historian Diane Owen Hughes has noted (see the epigraph to this essay). Hughes points to the tradition of female representations that she claims ultimately, in fiction, led to iconic portrayals of women. The pscyhological effects that iconic expectations in the media have on today's women are addressed frequently, but less often do we look at this problem for women in the past. Hughes suggests that women's exclusion from public life became a function of the narrative constructions of histories themselves, finding that historical writing from fourteenth-century Italy, the setting for *Valperga*, reveals "the consistent impulse to see women in iconic rather than in narrative terms" that "inevitably reduced their historical presence, perhaps almost as much as those legal barriers that had kept them from a public life." Women were "denied an active public persona and hence excluded from history's narrative as they had never been excluded from the poetry of myth and epic. In the historic age of men, these static women, frozen out of the flow of history, were best described and understood not by narrative devices but rather by iconic means."[4] Perhaps Shelley was on to something in using iconographic language to depict women in *Valperga* and *Perkin Warbeck*, as male historians (noticeably in the fourteenth century) had done before her. She was able to describe not only how men perceived and ultimately defined women but to suggest how women responded to gender conditioning. Not only did she play with the problems and implications of iconography in her texts but she also imagined a significant historical presence for women, one that highlighted both public and private roles, thus preserving a voice and narrative that represented forgotten, unacknowledged, or misunderstood women such as Lady Katharine Gordon (wife of the "Pretender" to the English throne, Perkin Warbeck). She imagined a wider sphere for women than nineteenth-century custom would allow, in which she could explore the likely outcomes for women with intelligence and political sensibilities from a protective historical distance that freed her own creativity and ability to comment on women's roles and great men's failures in any age.

Kaschak's model of feminist psychotherapy proves compelling when trying to understand Mary Shelley's perceptions of women and uses of language, together with history. The assumptions that Kaschak makes about women's psychology provide a possible link between the impact of historical, cultural, social, and personal forces that exert themselves on women writers and how they become translated into fiction, particularly into iconic symbols. Kaschak assumes that feminist psychotherapy "includes the work of mourning the various losses for every woman, central among which is the loss of the possible as a function of gender restrictions." She continues, "disappointment is well embedded in female psychology and must be acknowledged before the work of regaining the possible can begin." If a woman is to move beyond disappointment in order to "regain the possible," she must be able and allowed to feel anger. Anger, says Kaschak, is "directly related to power and the ability to change."[5]

A familiar example from *Frankenstein* can illustrate this psychoanalytic conceptual framework. When Justine is condemned to death for killing Frankenstein's brother, William, Elizabeth's reaction to the justice system merits scrutiny. In the first printing (1818), Elizabeth boldly articulates her frustration and anger toward patriarchal constructs, proclaiming:

> Oh! how I hate its [the world's] shews and mockeries! . . . The executioners, their hands yet reeking with the blood of innocence, believe that they have done a great deed. They call this retribution. Hateful name! . . . Yet this is not consolation for you . . . unless indeed that you may glory in escaping from so miserable a den. Alas! I would I were in peace with my aunt and my lovely William, escaped from a world which is hateful to me, and the visages of men which I abhor.[6]

Elizabeth's heart-wrenching reaction, combined with a death wish, portrays at once her anger and its futility. Nothing will change either the circumstances by which the innocent are punished or the system that created "so miserable a den." In the 1831 revised edition the passage is completely cut, replaced by Justine's hope that Elizabeth "learn from me, dear lady, to submit in patience to the will of Heaven!" (246). From a willingness to speak out, to reflect anger, Shelley's revision points to resignation as the only feasible reaction a woman could have to Justine's plight. Justine's martyrdom hints of the telling use of iconic images to come in *Valperga* and *Perkin Warbeck*.

These passages from *Frankenstein* also prove telling in suggesting how Shelley understood the psychological implications of anger and disappointment, the key emotions highlighted in Kaschak's model. Elizabeth's rage in the 1818 text might suggest a relationship to "power and the ability to change" that Shelley herself may have envisioned before her twentieth year, inspired by her father (William Godwin), her memory of her mother (Mary Wollstonecraft), the idealism of her husband (Percy Shelley), and the general tenor of the spirit of the age. Yet even the young Elizabeth sees neither hope nor possibility for change. By 1831, when the third edition of *Frankenstein* was published and Shelley was thirty-four, anger seemed so futile, change so impossible, the status quo so entrenched in her daily life, that putting up a fight of any kind may have seemed ludicrous.[7] A younger Shelley's Elizabeth could voice her frustration and pain, perhaps even imply a belief in anger. Once life with Percy Shelley became more frustrating, followed by his sudden death in 1825, hope for personal and social change seemed doomed to a limbo of loneliness and disappointment, noted repeatedly by scholars as characteristically imprinted in her fiction. Rarely elsewhere in Shelley's fiction following Elizabeth's impassioned speech in the 1818 edition of *Frankenstein* does a female character express outright anger. Shelley's female characters show resignation and frequent hope, but the necessary anger that could be channeled to produce power and change is rare and virtually always defeated by certain disappointment or betrayal.

A New Historical, Feminist Deconstruction of Meliorism

A major feminist literary project has been to demonstrate ways in which women writers' texts deconstruct the very institutions, cultures, and notions of self and identity that others have taken for granted, embraced, or simply refused to recognize as damaging or debilitating to women. Such revisions of history have questioned some of the most fundamental tenets of history writing's purpose, which has been typically to reflect broad-based ideologies, undercurrents of thought and movement within cultures, and actions of great men. History, too, has a personal lens that reveals individual psychologies and personal agendas of its writers. Deconstructionist, Marxist, new historicist, and feminist critics have often taught us not merely to question the very possibility of "objectivity," "fact," and "meaning" but ultimately to identify the personal as political and all writing, including the writing of history, as contextual and idiosyncratic. Much of our most interesting history reflects the creative insight and revisions of what we now perceive as culturally biased minds in ingratiating or revolutionary response to their worlds.

The tenets of new historicism, as summarized by H. Aram Veeser, have provided "new" "fundamental themes and concerns" in their problematizing of ideas of history, foremost among them:

> the idea that autonomous self and text are mere holograms, effects that intersecting institutions produce; that selves and texts are defined by their relation to hostile others (despised and feared Indians, Jews, Blacks) and disciplinary power (the King, Religion, Masculinity); that critics hoping to unlock the worship of culture should be less concerned to construct a holistic master story of large-scale structural elements directing a whole society than to perform a differential analysis of the local conflicts engendered in individual authors and local discourses.[8]

These claims for the "local" and the "individual" in history writing also describe the underpinnings of much historical fiction written by women (and, of course, Mary Shelley) before we had the terms "deconstruction," "poststructuralism," "new historicism," and "jouissance" to describe ways of critiquing, illuminating, or transcending cultural power and assumptions. Shelley understood texts as cultural products of individual negotiation and "intersection" with "hostile others" and "disciplinary power." The readings of women that follow point to Shelley's constant scrutiny of large cultural forces: the concept of male and female spheres, for example, and the problematic tendency to focus on the universal "large-scale structural elements" rather than on the lives of individuals making choices within often misunderstood historical contexts.

Shelley wrote in many of the genres most closely associated with "women's writing" (with the notable exception of conduct books), among them the romance, the sentimental novel, the Gothic, journals, diaries, and letters. When considered among other women writers in these genres, Shelley has been recognized as a significant, unconventional voice for women by feminist critics, including Anne Mellor, who makes the case that Shelley rejected the masculine ideology implicit within the Romantic "I" as subject. Others, including Laurie Langbauer, Kate Ferguson Ellis, and Jane Blumberg, have pointed out ways in which Shelley's fiction subverts domestic and social institutions, gender roles, and Romantic idealism and narcissism. Earlier work by Elaine Showalter and Sandra Gilbert and Susan Gubar helped to uncover ways that women writers questioned and exposed accepted notions of "meaning," "fact," "objectivity," "masculine," "feminine," and "universal" that collectively prescribe Western notions of "tradition" by looking at the "subtexts" in every woman's story.[9] Shelley used fiction to define power in order to deconstruct it—to challenge or expose limited access to power. She recognized the debilitating consequences for women inherent in Western dualism, which placed man and God, nature and nurture, reason and imagination, masculine and feminine, in fundamental opposition, generally to the disadvantage of woman. In this context, meliorism proves equally problematic, since it ignores signs of decay or inequality within a culture.

By the second half of the eighteenth century, meliorism had become the accepted view of history, as a belief in "man's indefinite progress towards perfection on earth" was purported by important scholars.[10] Godwin, David Hartley, and Joseph Priestly, according to A. J. Sambrook, became the "prominent gospellers of perfectibility," while even the "less starry-eyed" Edward Gibbon could "acquiesce in the pleasing conclusion that every age of the world has increased, and still increases, the real wealth, the happiness, the knowledge and perhaps the virtue of the human race." Sambrook notes that Sir Isaac Newton's discoveries had led his admirers to believe that inevitable progress would be found in previously undiscovered scientific "truth," and to them he offered "dramatic evidence of the godlike powers of human reason." In Shelley's adulthood, proponents of meliorism predicted happy endings in spite of the increasing evidence of physical and social decay. The effort to perpetuate the myth of progress seemed to shift in some eyes from faith in human reason to faith in capitalism.[11] Yet Thomas Macaulay, perhaps the staunchest defender of the meliorist position at that time, attacked Robert Southey in his *Colloquies* (1830) for being too Romantic (my term) in his judgments about England's future, even though many of the now canonized Romantic writers inherently tended, as did Macaulay himself, to look forward with optimism.

Macaulay glibly summarized Southey's position with regard to the effects of rising industrial growth: "And what is this [Southey's] way? To stand on a hill, to look at a cottage and a factory, and to see which is the prettier." Macaulay provided the classic position for those who believed, much evidence to the contrary, that nineteenth-century England was destined for "natural progress":

> History is full of the signs of this natural progress of society.... We see the wealth of nations increasing, and the arts of life approaching nearer and nearer to perfection, in spite of the grossest corruption and the wildest profusion on the part of rulers.... We firmly believe that, in spite of all the misgovernment of her rulers, she [England] has been almost constantly becoming richer and richer. Now and then there has been a stoppage, now and then a short retrogression; but as to the general tendency there can be no doubt. A single breaker may recede; but the tide is evidently coming in.[12]

Macaulay misses Southey's point, that aesthetics can tell us about the state of a culture, but he does so for good reason. Macaulay's view, based on increasing material wealth associated with capitalism (England was getting richer), was not the only evidence that the tide was coming in. For very different reasons, radicals such as William Blake and Percy Shelley felt compelled to believe in humankind's intrinsic goodness, which if unfettered, could materialize into the good future. The Romantic aesthetic shifted as poets could no longer ignore the signs of increasing decay and materialism engendered by the shift to urban industry and commerce. Poetry staved off the uncertain future, becoming Percy Shelley's "unacknowledged legislator"—the force that might continue to inspire imaginative purity and social change. But this future remained unimaginable to Mary Shelley, who saw from the often painful vantage point of the "other."[13]

There were plenty of meliorist naysayers who rejected the theory on socialist and feminist grounds. William Thompson, a revolutionary democrat and feminist in Wollstonecraft's vein, represented the more pessimistic view of England's condition. In a disagreement with James Mill's social arguments against female enfranchisement in his 1824 *Essay on Government*, in 1825 Thompson published *Appeal of One-Half the Human Race*, which, according to historian Barbara Taylor, "first spelled out the rudiments of a Socialist feminist position." Thompson wrote: "The present arrangements of society, founded on individual competition . . . are absolutely irreconcilable with equality . . . of women with men." "Even were all the unequal legal and unequal moral restraints removed," he continued, "in point of independence arising from wealth they [women] must under the present system of social arrangements, remain inferior."[14] Taylor interprets this statement thusly: "How could women achieve equality with men as long as childbearing and family responsibilities prevented them from acquiring equal wealth?" Even Percy Shelley became increasingly aware of the impossibility of realizing "universal emancipation." Taylor notes that in "Queen Mab" he sounds more pessimistic in lines such as "the harmony and happiness of man/Yields to the wealth of nations" and "gold is a living god."[15]

Kenneth Neill Cameron argues that for Percy Shelley history is "essentially a struggle between two sets of forces, the forces of liberty and the forces of despotism."[16] Betty Bennett has agreed, adding that Mary Shelley's histories work out her husband's thesis, depicting "a cycle of historical struggle" that illustrates her own theme of "the inadequacy of personal love when linked to personal ambition."[17] Yet Shelley also seemed interested and inclined to identify intellectually with the Tudor historians' function to "furnish political or moral instruction,"[18] and to take seriously the view that history owes a moral lesson to its readership. Although this dimension of history writing was compatible with Percy Shelley's view in the *Defence of Poetry* that poetry was the moral legislator of humankind, the Shelleys fundamentally differed on the locus of moral vision. Mellor has determined that Mary Shelley's writings "support a feminist position that argues that female culture is morally superior to male culture, that men should become more like women, more 'feminine' in their behavior."[19] Shelley links morality directly to gender, repeatedly depicting women in morally superior positions to men. In a letter written in 1825, Shelley observed, "Most women I believe wish that this [for they] had been men—so do not I—change my sex & I do not think my talents would be greater—& I should be like one of these—selfish, unkind—either pursuing for their own ends or deserting—because those ends cannot be satisfied" (*Letters*, 1:491). Yet the imperative to translate "political or moral instruction" based on an assumption of the superiority of feminine qualities is more complicated in her fiction. Some of the women characters encourage male cultural values outright through their actions and desires, in effect to reflect the self-abnegating virtues of the "proper lady" of Shelley's day.[20] Others, in particular the heroines Euthanasia and Katharine, present a superior moral compass and view that defies the stereotype of the proper lady.

Meliorism and the "Golden Age" of Medievalism

Sir Walter Scott's historical fiction is largely credited with making medievalism popular with the broad public of the early nineteenth century. According to medieval historian Barbara Hanawalt, the Romantic movement "did stimulate interest in the Middle Ages, if not specifically in the women living then." "Memorable women appeared in Scott's novels of the Middle Ages and in the ballads and snatches of poetry that antiquarians sought out," she continues, "but they were not the centerpieces of either the novels or collections."[21] Shelley, however, made women the centerpieces: in *Valperga,* only twelve of the thirty-seven chapters focus on Castruccio, the presumed male hero, while twenty-five chapters focus on the two women who most influence him and provide moral instruction. Similarly, in *Perkin Warbeck* we are also drawn into the women's lives and see things most often from their points of view.

A new breed—the woman historian—is credited with giving serious consideration to the problems with meliorism in the nineteenth century, although Shelley clearly had the same concerns earlier. Hanawalt found that "by the end of the nineteenth-century British historians had for the most part adopted a theory of progress in history." Yet women historians of the same period, with the exception of Annie Abram, overwhelmingly attacked the doctrine of meliorism by showing that "the position of women deteriorated rather than improved" over the centuries. By this time, women were researching and writing history and making independent judgments that differed from the traditional judgments of mainstream historians. Having "surveyed the social and economic status of women," women historians showed ways that women's positions within British society had "deteriorated rather than improved over the centuries."[22] They suggested that women had more control over their own destinies before industrialism forced commerce outside of the home and into the public sphere. Ultimately, they concluded that on some level the Middle Ages must have somehow been better for women—a kind of golden age.

This myth may have actually held true for a small portion of women, the mystics. Medieval historian Elizabeth Alvilda Petroff has studied the writings of medieval women mystics and concluded that "we see what is missing in the literature of the rest of the medieval world" in their writings, namely "a female subject, living autonomously in a world she defines, speaking a language she invents and controls." Only mystic women identified as prophets were taken seriously and allowed a public voice, and for many of these women "self-identification as prophet was the key to having a public voice, for as a woman lacking a systematic education . . . [she] had no individual voice."[23] In writing about Hildegard of Bingen (1098–1179), for instance, historian Sabina Flanagan points out that "a woman could be a prophet without upsetting the perceived natural order, since no particular attributes of her own were required, except, possibly, humility. Indeed, there was some suggestion that God might specifically choose the weak and despised to confound the strong. Thus to be a female prophet was to confirm women's authority, rather than to deny it."[24]

Yet Shelley's writing shows that for neither the mystic nor the nonmystic woman was there a true outlet for public or individual voice. According to Petroff, it is women's mysticism that is "connected to freedom."[25] Yet, as will emerge from the discussion to follow of the character Beatrice in *Valperga*, Shelley could not envision a life of freedom even for the mystic woman. She did not accept the myth of a lost golden age for women: if anything, her fiction suggests that cultural perceptions of women's roles had changed little by the nineteenth century and that the negative impact of iconic treatment of women remained a constant problem, controlling how they were defined within culture and history. It is in this respect that she attacks meliorism: by "localizing" and "individualizing" history (to use Veeser's terms), Shelley presents some key flaws in the popular myth that impacted on women and girls. She thereby obliterates the distinctiveness assigned to given historical periods by male historians and implicates the historian for leaving women out of history altogether or assigning to them a static, mundane role.

Wives and Historical Perception:
Elizabeth and Katharine in *Perkin Warbeck*

Shelley's stories themselves speak of her interest in female survivors: the psychology that shows how they coped and the history that begs to be told. As Diane Owen Hughes points out, women have any visibility at all in history primarily through the public institution of marriage, "a fundamental political act, one that allowed women a collective way back into history."[26] According to Shelley's research notes on the medieval period, men "placed their chief glory in arms & horses" and no doubt judged each other by this criterion.[27] In *Perkin Warbeck*, Shelley added her own commentary on what mattered in the telling of history: "Whoever writes concerning the actions of the men of olden times must sadden the reader by details of war, descriptions of fields of battle, narrations of torture, imprisonment, and death. But here also we find records of high virtues and exalted deeds" (1:140). Here, Shelley carefully and deliberately moves from what Veeser calls the "large-scale structural elements directing a whole society" to "a differential analysis of the local conflicts engendered in individual authors and local discourses."[28] Remarkably, the "exalted" records of moral behavior Shelley describes belong not to the heroes but to their wives, who also serve as our interpreters of male failure and masculinity itself. Elizabeth and Katharine measure men by the criteria to which they are held accountable as women, namely, fidelity and adherence to duty. "Duty," in this context, refers to both the private and public realms, where the men repeatedly fare poorly on the judgement scales. If history and male historians judge public virtue, wives and lovers judge both the private and the public behaviors.

   In *Perkin Warbeck*, both Elizabeth, queen of Henry VII, and Katharine, the pretender's wife, are measured by and measure others based on their fidelity and fulfillment of duty. Shelley imagines what has otherwise been ignored in the histories of these women—their feelings, domestic roles, perceived obligations, and the conflicts and consequences of political marriages for both. Of Katharine, Shelley writes, "As a woman her glory and all her honour must consist in never deviating from the strait line of duty, which forbade her absence from his [Warbeck's/Richard's] side" (3:2–3). Katharine is repeatedly described using iconic language that is undercut at other times. For instance, at one time we are told that she "looked a Queen, as she yielded herself a slave" (3:180) and later that "her form; something like it dwells in Raphael's Madonnas and Guido's Angel of Annunciation" (3:256). She marries for love rather than political power or position, questioning: "What is there in the name or state of king, that should so take captive our thoughts that we can imagine no life but on a throne?" (3:2–3). Yet her life becomes controlled by that very "state of king," for Warbeck's/Richard's entire adult life is consumed in pursuit of the crown. Certain of endless bloodshed and his inevitable death, Katharine pleads with her husband to assume a quiet life with her, remote from his ambitious goals. "Katharine simply suggests total abandonment of Richard's public role," writes Betty Bennett, "thereby offering him a love ideal which is personal and restricted rather than general; an ideal which is as insufficient for him as it would have been for [Percy] Shelley."[29] O'Sullivan describes Katharine as "pathetic in her hand-wringing ineffectuality."[30]

   Both descriptions miss the point, however, that Katharine provides the moral that we are to learn from this story. Shelley, in fact, identified Katharine as one of her favorite characters. Accepting that "feminine excellence" will be judged by quality of love, Shelley's Katharine delights in "exhausting her treasures of devoted love on the fallen, because they need it most" (3:257). Katharine becomes the great moral arbiter who harbors the lesson that Warbeck/Richard must come to learn and does learn before he is put to death. Thus, Shelley's history provides powerful "political or moral instruction"[31] true to the medieval setting and to the ways in which medieval historians depicted the age, but she does so via the central female character. Katharine's life was admittedly compromised because she chose fidelity to her husband even though she thought he was wrong to pursue the throne at all costs. The institution of marriage combined with iconic expectations for women could hardly prevent manipulations and survival techniques from being necessary. O'Sullivan notes that surviving women in Shelley's fiction "have to change tactics; they have to learn accommodating strategies which their companions would never have dreamed of."[32] Yet in refusing to remain silent, Katharine wins a victory over her husband after he comes to realize that he gave up too much to wed ambition. Katharine never abandons her values, and shortly before he dies, Richard understands her point.

Katharine was a prime target for historically harsh treatment because she remained in Henry VII's court after Richard's death and until hers. She was thereby perceived both as a traitor to her husband and to Henry as her supposed lover. Shelley quite naturally comes to the defense of the widow with no means to support herself. She adds a telling footnote that both defends and justifies Katharine's actions, and probably reimagines them to suit her own position as a misunderstood widow in a rigidly judgmental society. The note reveals Shelley's own tenuous questioning of how she fits into society and how the public must perceive her:

> I do not know how far these concluding pages may be deemed superfluous: the character of the Lady Katharine Gordon is a favourite of mine, and yet many will be inclined to censure her abode in Henry the Seventh's court, and other acts of her after life. I desire therefore that she should speak for herself, and show how her conduct subsequent to her husband's death, was in accordance with the devotion and fidelity with which she attended his fortunes during his life. (3:339)

Allowing Katharine to "speak for herself" gives her a moral authority and a human face unconsidered in "objective" public accounts. She transcends the historical bounds of other narrators to publicly voice her own private story.

Before we even learn Katharine's story, Shelley addresses Henry VII's marriage to Elizabeth, daughter of Edward IV and Elizabeth Woodville, the dowager queen. This marriage historically became for both families a crucial political act that united Lancaster and York after the bloody Wars of the Roses that placed Henry VII on a precarious throne. The nineteen-

year-old Elizabeth eagerly anticipates her wedding, believing her
position will give her the power to assist her Yorkist party: "Her
imagination fed on the good she would do for others, when raised to
royal dignity: the hope of liberating Warwick [her childhood friend and
Henry's enemy], and of fulfilling her mother's wishes in conferring
benefits on various partisans of the White Rose [York], filled her bosom
with purest joy" (1:59). Interestingly, Elizabeth marries not for love but
for her imagined public role, which of course is denied her. Henry "hated
to owe his title to the crown to any part of the House of York; he
resolved, if possible, to delay and break the marriage; but his own friends
were urgent to comply and prudence dictated it—thus effectually to
silence the murmurs of the party of the White Rose" (1:53). The dowager
queen, Elizabeth's savvy, experienced mother, knows well that Henry
hates the White Rose and "his chief pride lay in establishing himself on
the throne, independent of the claim he might acquire by his marriage
with the Lady Elizabeth" (1:60).

Ironically, while their union is historically depicted as fairly
compatible, in *Perkin Warbeck* Shelley depicts the marriage as a
potential fairy tale turned nightmare. As a queen with no influence on her
husband, still in love with her childhood friend Warwick, Elizabeth
becomes a victim of her ancestral inheritance and her political party's
necessity. While this certainly is not an original plot, Shelley's emphasis
on Elizabeth's feelings of betrayal, longing for her lover, and hatred for
her husband stretch our notions of history's objectivity. The nuptials,

> which before elated, now visited her coldly: for without the hope of
> influencing her husband, the fate of a Queen *appeared mere bondage.* In her
> heart she wished to reject her uncourteous bridegroom; and once she had
> ventured to express this desire to her mother, who, filled with affright, laid
> aside her intrigues, devoting herself to *cultivate a more rational disposition* in
> her daughter. Henry paid the doomed girl one visit, and saw little in her
> except a bashful child; while his keener observation was directed towards the
> dowager queen. (emphasis added) (1:62)

The dowager queen's complicity in her daughter's enslavement shows us
a telling by-product of politics for women in women's history. The
agonizing conflict when motherhood and public duty collide, when
domestic responsibility is co-opted for the sake of a public role, results in
a physical and emotional bondage for these women. What, in a woman's
education, could have prepared Elizabeth to "cultivate a more rational
disposition" simply when it proved most convenient for an indifferent
fiancé or unfeeling public?

Many bitter years later, Elizabeth, then queen, tells her now intimate friend Katharine: "It is a bad world . . . and if I become bad in it, perchance I shall prosper, and have power to save: I have been too mild, too self-communing and self-condemning . . . faded, outworn, a degraded slave—*I am not Elizabeth*" (emphasis added) (3:316–17). The combined effect of missing out on love and accepting her political fate as her only option causes Elizabeth to lose herself completely over the years. She also tells Katharine, "I am not pure, not innocent, much you mistake me. . . . Wicked impious thoughts harbour in my heart, and pollute my soul, even beyond the hope of meditation. Sometimes I hate my beautiful children because they are his" (3:317). This anger with no outlet shows the extent of cruelty, suffering, hatred and bondage in this privileged woman's history.

Shelley then uses the intimacy she created between Elizabeth and the widowed Katharine as the vehicle by which Katharine can save face, remain in Henry's court without shame, and, importantly, protect her dead husband's reputation. Queen Elizabeth pleads with Richard to allow her dear friend Katharine to live with her: "On my knees I do implore you to bide her not to leave me a dead—alive, a miserable, bereft creature, such as I was ere I knew her love" (3:335). Katharine agrees to submit to the humiliation of living in the court because she loves Elizabeth and Richard has sanctioned it. She again fulfills a duty to others while sacrificing her own desire, and we must acknowledge that she remains completely misunderstood by the court (and presumably the history books). Edmund, a member of the court who remains ignorant of her personal situation, taunts her: "Yours is another existence, Lady; you need the adulation of the crowd—the luxury of palaces; you purchase these, even by communing with the murderer of him who deserved a dear recompense at your hands" (3:348). How, other than out of a duty-bound fidelity to a friend, or a bitter economic reality, does someone live with such accusations—accusations not unlike those Shelley herself received following Percy Shelley's death? Katharine, having been judged by an assumption of privilege, is stripped of the reality of her existence. She is not allowed to feel her pain. Yet Katharine has the last word, perhaps Shelley's own plea to her public: "Permit this to be, unblamed—permit a heart whose sufferings have been, are, so many and so bitter, to reap what joy it can from the strong necessity it feels to be sympathized with—to love" (3:354). She could again be misunderstood, for she refers to her friendship with Elizabeth rather than to any possible attentions from the king. Female community sustains these women in an alien, impersonal environment in which their only perceived role is political. They are the privileged pawns of history.

Lovers and Codependency: Euthanasia and Beatrice in *Valperga*; Monina in *Perkin Warbeck*

Unlike Katharine in *Perkin Warbeck*, in *Valperga*, Euthanasia rejects marriage altogether when it means that she must sacrifice fidelity to her own political and social values to those of her future husband, Castruccio. She is a special case in that she rejects the domestic realm when it does not coincide with her politics, unlike Katharine and Elizabeth in the later novel. Not surprisingly, things do not go well for Euthanasia. She inherited her father's revolutionary spirit and learned Latin by reading to her ailing father (in a remake of Milton's daughters?). She saw herself in a hero's quest that incorporated moral good into Italy's future: "her soul, adapted for the reception of all good"; "her young thoughts darted into futurity, to the hope of freedom for Italy, of reviving learning and the reign of peace for all the world: wild dreams, that still awake the minds *of men* to high song and glorious action" (emphasis added) (*Perkin Warbeck*, 1:30). The irony is clear: Euthanasia is naive and idealistic enough to believe that her high thoughts, not her gender, will dictate her role in her land's future.

Castruccio's education was quite different in that he learned by fighting beside feudalists on the battlefield. As the Ghibelline leader, his political position remains irreconcilable with Euthanasia's democratic ideal, leading Betty Bennett to claim that "their love relationship fails in political terms; a personal love would not suffice."[33] I would suggest that Euthanasia's choice is less "politics or love" and more clearly the need to reconcile the two. Ultimately, both Castruccio and Euthanasia reject love altogether when it implies political compromise, for Euthanasia refuses to abandon her own party. Like Katharine, Euthanasia also provides another moral lesson to the male protagonist. However, Castruccio, unlike Richard in *Perkin Warbeck*, never accepts Euthanasia's moral position, and the two become physically and emotionally estranged until her death. Castruccio ultimately exiles Euthanasia from her home (Valperga) and country, presumably because his vulnerability to her libertarian streak provides a continual threat to his ability to lead with conviction. By stripping her of those things that have defined her and given her identity, Castruccio multiplies the debilitating consequences of having abandoned Euthanasia for the battlefield, leaving her alone. Shelley has little choice but to kill her off and thus secure Euthanasia's own moral high ground, which highlights personal sacrifice unnoticed by a misunderstanding public. She drowns at sea in an exile Castruccio imposed to remove her political and personal threat to his leadership.

The eulogy for Euthanasia proves telling in that it enlarges her tragedy to a kind of maternal lamentation for all forgotten women in history. Euthanasia, Shelley writes, "was never heard of more; even her name perished." Earth, we are told, "felt no change when she died; and men forgot her. Yet a lovelier spirit never ceased to breathe, nor was a lovelier form ever destroyed amidst the many it brings forth" (3:262). We are told of the "endless tears" that "might well have been shed of her loss" as she "quitted a life replete with change and sorrow" (3:262). She ends up dead, in effect, because she refused the codependent's role—unlike Katharine, who supported her husband even when she knew he was destined to destroy himself and risk many other lives. Joseph Lew finds that Euthanasia "spends her life trying to preserve the anonymous domesticity, concern for others, rationality, and attention to duty Mellor sees as central to the female Romantic tradition."[34] "Shelley's female characters explain to us 'why women didn't like romanticism,'" writes Lew, quoting Mellor, "why Austen and Shelley seem to be anachronistic, preferring Enlightenment traditions to the newly dominant Romantic ideology."[35] Euthanasia may also be viewed as a character who maintains her political integrity and thus must be punished in the end for, in the first place, having it, and in the second place, having it "wrong" (from Castruccio's perspective). It also seems appropriate to ask, in this context, "why women didn't like history as written."

Euthanasia's story abandons much historical accuracy in search of a moral, for historical facts are not Shelley's concern in the work. Shelley's primary source on Castruccio Castracani, Morieri, describes him as "one of the most celebrated captains of his time": "Nothing seemed to oppose his courage and good fortune, when he was taken off by a premature death in 1330, in the forty-seventh year of his age" (*Perkin Warbeck,* 1:iii–iv). Although reputed to be a tyrant ruler in the annals of history, Morieri's assertion of Castruccio's "courage and good fortune" did not go unchallenged by Shelley. Euthanasia is a purely fictitious invention who casts the hero in a very critical light. (The historical Castruccio Castracani had married at a very young age through an arrangement that united two families whose combined strength made it possible for him to place the Ghibellines in power. In the novel, he remains unmarried and childless; in life he had many children.)[36] Euthanasia's story provides romance and punishes Castruccio for his bad choices, but Euthanasia suffers equally in speaking of the personal aspects of the "great man's" life that challenge historical perceptions of him. Because we can never hear from Castruccio's actual wife, Shelley invents a woman who freely contradicts the historical celebration of Castruccio's conquests. Shelley set out to challenge that untested claim for greatness by exploring his life from the point of view of the "other" who had political and personal ambitions of her own that, in the fiction, Castruccio deliberately and cruelly thwarts.

On the other hand, Beatrice, Castruccio's mystic lover, and Monina, Warbeck's/Richard's protegé, depict women in collusion with the male Romantic tradition.[37] They serve the role that we might now call "codependent," in that they encourage and support the desires of some-one else at their own expense but without finding happiness or fulfill-ment in the process. Castruccio discovers the very young, beautiful, and mysterious Beatrice in a convent as he passes through a village in be-tween battles. Captivated by her, he inquires of her parentage and cir-cumstances (though he is still engaged to Euthanasia), asking if she is really "an angel descended upon earth for the benefit and salvation of man" (*Perkin Warbeck,* 2:25). From this question, which depicts iconic language, Shelley steps into the seat of the mystic and, more explicitly, into issues of female power, motherhood, and origins. Beatrice's mother, of whom Beatrice is deliberately kept ignorant, was burned at the stake as a heretic for threatening the traditional church hierarchy, having, ac-cording to a bishop, "secretly formed a sect, founded on the absurd and damnable belief, that she was the Holy Ghost incarnate upon earth for the salvation of the female sex" (2:26). Indeed, the identified mother, Wil-helmina of Bohemia, actually lived, and Shelley's creation of a daughter for her points to her concern for voicing the loss of empowered women but also the futility of challenging the status quo. Wilhelmina's powers threatened the very religious, social, sexual, and ethical codes of the cul-ture, as well as of the church itself, for her "tenets were intended entirely to supersede those of our beloved Lord Jesus, and her friend Magfreda was to be papess, and to succeed to all the power and privileges of the Roman pontiff" (2:27). With a mission to provide "female salvation," and thus to implicate the church for inscribing women as inheritors of Eve's disobedience, Wilhelmina so cleverly hid her powers that she was initially buried as a saint. After her death, the church officials uncovered the existence of her sect and called her a "lurking pestilence," "so impi-ous, so absurd, so terrifically wicked" (2:22).

Despite being kept in ignorance over the truth of her mother, Beatrice grows up to display similar mystic traits and to draw followers. Castruccio cannot resist her beauty and eventually saves her from a martyred death as a religious heretic. Her powers confuse and unsettle him, and he "fled as the daemon might have fled from the bitter sorrows of despoiled Paradise; he left her aghast, overthrown, annihilated" (2:97). Beatrice transfers her spiritual power and emotional desire into an obsessive love for Castruccio, knowing that he was already pledged to

Euthanasia. She goes through a series of catastrophes, eventually joins the Paterin sect, but finally meets Euthanasia, who shelters and protects her. Euthanasia describes for Beatrice the woman's mind, an "inner cave," "difficult of access, rude, strange, and dangerous." She tellingly adds, "Let those beware who would explore this cave" (3:300–301). She thinks to herself, "Ah! I wonder not that [Castruccio] cast away my affections, since he can spare no deeper sympathy for Beatrice" (3:103).[38] Even a witch who enters into Beatrice's tribulations "knew how powerless she [the witch herself] was" but "desired to fill in every part the character attributed to her" (2:117). This woman "looked evil as her daily bread, and . . . had sold her soul to the devil to do ill alone" (ibid.). Role definition, Shelley shows us, is a self-fulfilling prophecy. We are meant to see, through these fantastic characters, the damage women were dealt through established institutions (religion, militia, proper lady) and careless men. The injustices Beatrice experiences multiply in relation to the degree that she represses or denies her own desires. Yet even the conspiracy to prevent Beatrice from knowing about her mother does not prevent her from intuiting Wilhelmina's power, experiencing "the inexplicable emotions which seemed to link her to other existences" (3:127), a description uncanny in its resemblance to Shelley's own mystic link with her dead mother, Mary Wollstonecraft. Beatrice is denied the authority due to a mystic woman of the period because others know of her feminist origins and fear them. She also sacrifices her career as a mystic prophet in order to obtain Castruccio's love, but he leaves her psychologically traumatized. This fantastic depiction of female power destroyed by male institutions, customs, culture, and personal cruelty shows Shelley's commitment to exposing the tendencies of history to leave out, misrepresent, and misjudge.

In a less fantastic but equally unlikely scenario, the female warrior Monina in *Perkin Warbeck* vies for Warbeck's/Richard's love by encouraging him to pursue his ambition at all costs. As his "guardian angel" on the battlefield (1:238–39), Monina plays a very different role than does Katharine, but similar to Beatrice she sacrifices herself for the great hero. Monina too has "some strange sorcery about [her]" but no authority because of it (2:5–6). Shelley compares the influences of Monina and Katharine on Richard, writing that

it was strange that a girl of royal birth, bred in a palace, accustomed to a queen-like sovereignty . . . should aim at restricting the ambitious York to mere privacy; while Monina, the humble daughter of a Moorish mariner, would have felt honour, reputation, all that is dear to man, at stake, if her friend had dreamed of renouncing his claims to the English crown. His cause was her life; his royalty the mainspring of all her actions and thoughts. (3:59)

This moment gives pause to reflect on the impact of class positioning on behavior and desires. Monina shows unwavering faith in Richard's destiny, yet her love and ambition blind her to the consequences of his pursuits, while Katharine suffers deeply from her recognition of them. We are told that for Monina, Richard's "cause was her life; his royalty the main spring of all her actions and thoughts" (ibid.). Katharine saw, however, "a vain mask in all the common-place pomp of palaces. . . . It was but being an actor in different scenes, to be a potentate or a peasant; the outward garb is not the livery of the mind" (3:60). We might conclude that Katharine can afford to be noble as a woman of privilege and that Monina is the true heroine here, except that Monina has lived through and for someone else without finding herself in the process. She feeds off of Richard and consequently proves to be equally shortsighted. Katharine sees the larger picture but, although in the midst of privilege, has no real power to be heard. She speaks truth for her author, but no one hears it. She has no more hope of being taken seriously than does Monina. Richard admires Monina merely for her loyalty and presumed weakness: "What a wondrous creation woman was—weak, frail, complaining when she suffers for herself; heroic fortitude and untired self-devotion are hers, when she sacrifices for him she loves" (2:132). Monina proves "wondrous" to Richard because of the depth of her self-sacrifice, never for her political involvements in his quest per se. Yet Richard views Katharine as Truth itself (2:211), even though he never listens to her. Her perfection, we are told, "led him to every thought associated with the charms and virtues of woman" (2:213). Both women are primarily viewed in iconic terms. Monina is put to death for her public role in Richard's attempt to overthrow Henry VII, while Katharine, as described in the prior section, must live in public disgrace. Only Elizabeth and the reader know of her noble spirit.

Transcending the Gaze of Power

These narratives raise significant questions regarding how women were or might have been treated in history and fiction, in both their private and public lives. They reveal Shelley's determination to undercut the iconic portrayals of women and to refuse the historical perspectives that perpetuate women's psychological pain and exclusion from full lives. Shelley's historical moment called for her to reconsider some of the very myths that secured power and voice for the public realm, which perpetuated the exclusion of women. Above all, Shelley was a keen psychologist whose capacity for perceiving and portraying the problems in her culture continue to astound us. Ellyn Kaschak describes an important task of feminism and of feminist therapy "to maintain the tension between women as a category and each individual woman, between micro details and broad strokes, similarities and differences."[39] This tension resonates not only with the aims of new historicism itself as Veeser describes it, but with a feminist deconstruction of Shelley's dilemmas in writing historical fiction. While men perceived women through iconographic visions and symbols, there were individual women trying to be heard (Katharine, Elizabeth, Euthanasia, Shelley herself), or women who accepted unquestioningly how men perceived them (Beatrice, Monina).

Using Marilyn Frye's notion of the "loving eye,"[40] Kaschak identifies Shelley's message in her writing of history: "Change involves replacing the arrogant oedipal gaze with ... the loving eye, which 'does not prohibit a woman's experiencing the world directly, does not force her to experience it by way of the interested interpretations of the seer in whose visual field she moves.'" To achieve independence from the male gaze, Shelley reconsidered some of the key assumptions about history in her time. If "seeing is believing and knowing for oneself," writes Kaschak, the future must contain its very possibility for women to achieve real progress. Shelley changed the terms: progress was not Macaulay's materialism or Percy Shelley's idealism or comfortable retreat into "golden pasts" or history accepted uncritically, it was seeing for oneself even when the gaze of power limited the space for hope and future. Shelley attempts in her fiction to find space for anger, the means that has helped women through the ages to "regain the possible."[41] As O'Sullivan has said, one of the "most remarkable aspects" of Shelley's writing is that it "highlights the dilemma of the survivor."[42] The women in Shelley's historical fictions indeed show this strength and resistance.

Notes

This essay is an expanded version of a chapter from my dissertation, *Factitious States: Mary Shelley and the Politics of Early Nineteenth-Century Women's Identity and Fiction*, submitted at the University of Michigan, Ann Arbor, ca. 1989.

The Letters of Mary Wollstonecraft Shelley, 3 vols., ed. Betty T. Bennett (Baltimore, Md.: Johns Hopkins University Press, 1983), is cited parenthetically in the text as *Letters*.

The Fortunes of Perkin Warbeck; A Romance, by Mary Wollstonecraft Shelley, 3 vols. (London: Henry Colburn and Richard Bentley, 1830), is cited parenthetically in the text as *Perkin Warbeck*.

1. Mary Wollstonecraft Shelley, *Valperga; or Castruccio, Prince of Lucca*, 3 vols. (London: G. and W. B. Whittaker, 1823), and *The Fortunes of Perkin Warbeck; A Romance*, 3 vols. (London: Henry Colburn and Richard Bentley, 1830). Brief plots of each novel follow. For a much more detailed plot summary of *Valperga* that includes attention to "new theoretical, historic, and philosophical contexts" for the work, see Joseph Lew, "God's Sister: History and Ideology in Valperga," in *The Other Mary Shelley: Beyond Frankenstein*, eds. Audrey Fisch, Anne K. Mellor, and Esther H. Schor (New York: Oxford University Press, 1993). For a more detailed summary of events and political connections in *Perkin Warbeck*, see Jane Blumberg, *Mary Shelley's Early Novels: "This Child of Imagination and Misery"* (Iowa City: University of Iowa Press, 1993), 216–19.

Summary of *Valperga*: The novel chronicles a highly fictionalized version of fourteenth-century Castruccio Castracani's life from childhood to his eventual role as celebrated warrior and tyrant ruler of Lucca. Castracani eventually overtakes the castle Valperga, seat of the opposition Guelphs and home of his former childhood friend and fiancée, Euthanasia. Educated by supporters of the Ghibelline Party (feudalist followers of the German emperor) following his parents' early death, Castruccio grows up to value, in Joseph Lew's words, "the dominant ideology of Renaissance Italy, of fame achieved through military deeds" (165) and soon distinguishes himself in battle. Euthanasia grows up to be an instrumental leader of the opposition Guelph Party (republicans, rebellious against feudalism, "supporters of the pope" [175]). However, although the two pledge to marry, their politics keeps them apart, based on a conscious decision by Euthanasia that she will not give up her politics and honor. While they are still engaged, Castruccio meets Beatrice, a beautiful but haunted Paterin ("a heretical sect which believed that the evil spirit is ascendant in this world" [175]), and we trace her self-demise, along with Euthanasia's, as both try to overcome loss and powerlessness. In the end, the story is more about these two women than it is about Castruccio. They both die, and Castruccio, while moved to question his priorities and choices, continues to lead the Ghibellines, implement their feudalist politics, and secure a spot in Italian and world history.

Summary of *Perkin Warbeck*: The novel (subtitled "a romance") fictionalizes a familiar and controversial moment in British history in which Warbeck claimed to be the surviving second little prince, the duke of York, the uncrowned Richard IV. From childhood, Warbeck pledges his life to overthrow Henry VII and regain his throne and inheritance. The papers that could prove his identity are destroyed, and Warbeck must enlist arms to achieve his aim. He is set up by Scotland's James IV to meet his cousin, Katharine Gordon, to fall in love with her, and ultimately to strengthen James's and his political ties. Katharine opposes Warbeck's obsession to obtain the throne at any cost, much as before her Euthanasia had protested against Castruccio's feudalism and activities as a warrior, but Katharine stays with Richard and supports him, never doubting the legitimacy of his claim. In contrast, a woman from his humble upbringing, Monina, encourages him and even assists him in his fight for the throne. We are meant to see that, like both Castruccio and Frankenstein, Warbeck/Richard's ambition ultimately blinds him to the consequences of fulfilling his desire, including the lives that will be lost and the relationships that will suffer or be destroyed. Similarly, women with ambition not directly attached to a moral system are suspect to Shelley.

2. "Notes for *Valperga*" in the Abinger Collection, Bodleian Library, Oxford University (Dep. e. 274); quoted with the permission of Lord Abinger. Blumberg also refers to this document in a note in *Mary Shelley's Early Novels*, 233–34.

3. See Barbara Jane O'Sullivan, "Beatrice in *Valperga*: A New Cassandra," in *The Other Mary Shelley*, 141.

4. Diane Owen Hughes, "Invisible Madonnas? The Italian Historiographical Tradition and the Women of Medieval Italy," in *Women in Medieval History and Historiography*, ed. Susan Mosher Stuard (Philadelphia: University of Pennsylvania Press, 1987), 29, 27.

5. Ellyn Kaschak, *Engendered Lives: A New Psychology of Women's Experience* (New York: Basic Books, 1992), 222.

6. Mary Wollstonecraft Shelley, *Frankenstein; or, the Modern Prometheus The 1818 Text,* with a new preface, ed. James Rieger (Chicago: University of Chicago Press, 1982), 83.

7. In particular, her dependence on Sir Timothy Shelley (Percy Shelley's father) for money to raise their son following her husband's death made her especially embittered. Sir Timothy refused to ever receive her, and the two never met. He nevertheless reliably sent maintenance allowances for his grandson, who inherited his title upon the death of Percy Shelley's first son by his first wife, Harriet.

8. H. Aram Veeser, ed., "Introduction" to *The New Historicism* (New York: Routledge, 1989), xiii.

9. For more information on the topics identified here, see Anne K. Mellor, "On Romanticism and Feminism," in *Romanticism and Feminism* (Bloomington: Indiana University Press, 1988); and Laurie Langbauer, "Swayed by Contraries: Mary Shelley and the Everyday," and Kate Ferguson Ellis, "Subversive Surfaces: The Limits of Domestic Affection in Mary Shelley's Later Fiction," both in *The Other Mary Shelley*; Jane Blumberg, *Mary Shelley's Early Novels*; Elaine Showalter, "Feminist Criticism in the Wilderness," in *Writing and Sexual Difference*, ed. Elizabeth Abel (Chicago: University of Chicago Press, 1982); and Sandra Gilbert and Susan Gubar, *The Madwoman in the Attic: The Woman Writer and the Nineteenth-Century Literary Imagination* (New Haven: Yale University Press, 1979).

10. A. J. Sambrook, "A Romantic Theme: The Last Man," *Forum for Modern Language Studies* 2 (1966): 25.

11. Stephen Greenblatt, "Towards a Poetics of Culture" in *The New Historicism*, ed. H. Aram Veeser (New York: Routledge, 1989), 5.

12. Thomas Babington Macaulay, "A Review of Southey's Colloquies," *Edinburgh Review* (1830): 1623.

13. For a more blatant example of Shelley's rejection of meliorism, see her novel *The Last Man* (London: Hogarth Press, 1985), in which she imagines the end of the world as a plague that destroys all of humanity as punishment for its misguided deeds and poor treatment of nature.

14. Barbara Taylor, *Eve and the New Jerusalem* (New York: Pantheon, 1983), 17, quoting William Thompson, *Appeal of One-Half the Human Race, Women, against the Pretensions of the other Half, Men, to retain them in political, and then in civil and domestic Slavery: in Reply to a Paragraph of Mr. Mill's celebrated "Article on Government"* (1825).

15. Taylor, *Eve*, 17.

16. Kenneth Neill Cameron, "The Social Philosophy of Shelley," *Sewanee Review* 50 (1942): 458.

17. Betty T. Bennett, "The Political Philosophy of Mary Shelley's Historical Novels: *Valperga* and *Perkin Warbeck*," in *The Evidence of the Imagination: Studies of Interactions Between Life and Art in English Romantic Literature*, eds. Donald H. Reiman, Michael C. Jaye, Betty T. Bennett, et al. (New York: New York University Press, 1978), 363.

18. Leonard Fellows Dean, *Tudor Theories of History Writing* (Ann Arbor: University of Michigan Press, 1947), 3.

19. Anne K. Mellor, *Mary Shelley; Her Life Her Fictions Her Monsters* (New York: Methuen, 1988), 216.

20. Mary Poovey's *The Proper Lady and the Woman Writer* (Chicago: University of Chicago Press, 1984) identifies the "Proper Lady" as a construct whose primary concern was appearances. Poovey ultimately concludes that Shelley became so preoccupied in her fiction with the appearances of her proper ladies that she herself became one so that she "would seem to be only what a lady should be" (144). Rather, I would argue that Shelley read the culture through this figure, which does not mean that she unequivocally accepted for herself the iconic images that she portrayed. On the contrary, her language, often hyperbolic in its descriptions of proper ladies, suggests an ironic distancing from this construct.

21. Barbara Hanawalt, "Golden Ages for the History of Medieval English Women," in *Women in Medieval History and Historiography*, ed. Susan Mosher Stuard (Philadelphia: University of Pennsylvania Press, 1987), 3.

22. Ibid., 7.

23. Elizabeth Alvilda Petroff, *Body and Soul: Essays on Medieval Women and Mysticism* (New York: Oxford University Press, 1994), 21, 11.

24. Ibid., 11, quoting Sabina Flanagan, *Hildegard of Bingen, 1098–1179: A Visionary Life* (London: Routledge, 1989), 14–15.

25. Ibid., 20.

26. Hughes, "Invisible Madonnas?" 42.

27. Shelley, "Notes for *Valperga*."

28. Veeser, xiii.

29. Bennett, "Political Philosophy," 367.

30. O'Sullivan, "Beatrice in *Valperga*," 153.

31. Dean, *Tudor Theories*, 3.

32. O'Sullivan, "Beatrice in *Valperga*," 153.

33. Bennett, "Political Philosophy," 363.

34. Lew, "God's Sister," 163.

35. Lew, "God's Sister," 162–63, quoting Anne K. Mellor, "Why Women Didn't Like Romanticism: The Views of Jane Austen and Mary Shelley," in *The Romantics and Us*, ed. Gene W. Ruoff (New Brunswick, N.J.: Rutgers University Press, 1990).

36. Louis Green, *Castruccio Castracani; a study on the origins and character of a fourteenth-century Italian despotism* (Oxford: Clarendon Press; New York: Oxford University Press, 1986), 1:iii–iv.

37. For an extensive treatment of Beatrice in *Valperga*, who represents for O'Sullivan "the predicament of the creative female" and "an alternative to the Promethean optimism of Romanticism," see "Beatrice in Valperga," 140–58.

38. See David Marshall, *The Surprising Effects of Sympathy; Marivaux, Diderot, Rousseau and Mary Shelley* (Chicago: University of Chicago Press, 1988), for a detailed treatment of sympathy as a significant major theme in Shelley's work.

39. Kaschak, *Engendered Lives*, 224.

40. Ibid., 225, quoting Marilyn Frye, *The Politics of Reality: Essays in Feminist Theory* (Trumansburg, N.Y.: Crossing Press, 1983), 82.

41. Ibid., 225, 222.

42. O'Sullivan, "Beatrice in *Valperga*," 153.

The Self and the Monstrous:
The Fortunes of Perkin Warbeck

Lisa Hopkins

When Lionel Verney, hero of Mary Shelley's novel *The Last Man*, finds himself deprived of his last two companions, he sits down to write the story of his life. At the outset of the book, he writes:

DEDICATION
TO THE ILLUSTRIOUS DEAD.
SHADOWS, ARISE, AND READ YOUR FALL!
BEHOLD THE HISTORY OF THE
LAST MAN.[1]

Although Verney goes on to speculate that his lost world may be "re-peopled" by "the children of a saved pair of lovers, in some to me unkown and unattainable seclusion" (339), it is still hard to think of a more fruitless enterprise than dedicating to the dead, or a more inherently contradictory one than an invitation to "behold the history of the last man." This readerless narrator implicitly propounds a theory of narrativity, and of history in particular, that seems to find echoes elsewhere in Mary Shelley's work. Sharing something of the impulse to tell for its own sake, which perhaps finds its most powerful expression in *The Rime of the Ancient Mariner*—the poem to which the young Mary listened so intently[2]—it also shares much of the aesthetic that led Sir Philip Sidney to condemn history as inferior to poetry, since it offers merely the particular and factual, as opposed to the ideal and inspiratory realm of poetry, from which example and instruction may be drawn.[3] *The Last Man*, for all its ostensible status as spelled from Sibyl's leaves, offers a similar view of history as a discipline that is, in essence, useless,

260

since the very specificity of the narratives that it offers us prevents us from drawing any universally applicable lessons from it. Even the fact that *The Last Man* is, formally, prophecy rather than history does not preserve it from this indictment. The figure of the prophet is one that recurs frequently in Mary Shelley's works—but it does so in the shape of Cassandra, whose accuracy was precisely equalled by the incredulity she inspired in all around her that rendered her warnings worthless.[4] And it may be worth noting that what Frankenstein's monster learns from the history of Plutarch's *Lives* can prepare him very little for the world he lives in, but that in the literature of *Paradise Lost* he finds some very telling correspondences to his own situation.

It is worth this detour for some thoughts on Mary Shelley's views of history to approach her fascinating and much neglected historical novel *The Fortunes of Perkin Warbeck*. In it, Shelley does not follow the procedure of the great model of the historical novel, Scott's *Waverley*, by taking an orthodox account of events and attempting to render them more intelligible to a contemporary reader by clothing them in authorial sympathy and believable characters who are, nevertheless, avowedly fictional; instead, she steers the historical novel toward historiography proper as she uses her text to challenge rather than reinforce the version of events that we think we know. Her Perkin Warbeck is not a Flemish adventurer masquerading as the duke of York but the rightful prince himself; her Richard III is not the cold-blooded child murderer of Shakespeare and Sir Thomas More but a usurper with a conscience who does not scruple to seize the throne but stops short of murder. Instead, he allows his high-minded nephew, the earl of Lincoln, to secrete the Princes in the Tower in a location where their lives will be saved but where the political threat they could pose to their uncle will be neutralized. Moreover, Shelley's Richard even has right on his side, since she subscribes to the story that Edward IV was precontracted before he married the boys' mother, which would indeed bastardize them; however, Shelley also opines that Elizabeth Woodville had, however erroneously, been thought to be the rightful queen for so long that her children should have been considered the heirs to the throne.[5] This is also the view of the Yorkist nobility of the novel, who mean eventually to reinstate the young Edward V; their plan is frustrated, however, when he dies of natural causes and his younger brother Richard is too young to be offered as a realistic alternative to Henry Tudor. After a touching farewell to his mother, Elizabeth Woodville, the boy is smuggled to the Continent, where he lives safely under the alias of Perkin Warbeck before embarking on the series of adventures that lead him, eventually, to his death at Tyburn. For this latter part of his career, Shelley's account is largely the same as the conventional narrative, although she does insert much circumstantial detail and a spectacularly improbable account of how Richard made a foray into the Tower of London itself and escaped scot-free. The major difference, of course, is that at every turn she recounts his adventures from the perspective not of an impostor but from that of a true prince.

The suggestion that the man known as Perkin Warbeck, the Anna Anderson of his day, might in fact have been the real Richard, Duke of York, did not originate with Shelley. In the early seventeenth century, Sir George Buc, one-time Master of the Revels, argued in *The History of the Life and Reigne of Richard III* that Richard III had been unfairly traduced by More and that the younger of the two princes had survived. The play by the seventeenth-century dramatist John Ford (who had shared family connections with Percy Shelley's ancestors in the Gages of Firle in Sussex), *The Chronicle History of Perkin Warbeck* (1634), while stopping short of formally endorsing Perkin's claims, does pointedly omit his confession of imposture, which Ford would undoubtedly have read in his sources, and presents the pretender in a romantic and, on the whole, a highly positive light;[6] and the claim of Perkin's authenticity was unhesitatingly advanced by Horace Walpole in his *Historic Doubts on the Life and Reign of King Richard the Third* (1768).[7] Shelley even claims (*Perkin Warbeck*, Preface, 2), that Sir Francis Bacon hints as much in his *History of the Reign of King Henry VII* (1622) but for political reasons felt unable to speak out clearly.

I have argued elsewhere that for the seventeenth-century revisionists, Perkin Warbeck actually represented an important and surprisingly relevant figure, since any suggestion of his legitimacy could in effect be used as leverage against the increasingly unsettled Stuart crown.[8] For Walpole, the issue seems to have been a rather different one: he appears to have wanted to put right what he saw as a serious miscarriage of justice by granting Richard III the historical equivalent of a posthumous pardon. The first word of his title is "Historic"; the book is offered as a serious piece of investigation, a counter to Sir Thomas More. What, though, was Mary Shelley's motive, and what kind of purpose did she think her book would serve?

If Walpole is to be thought of as an eighteenth-century antagonist to More, perhaps Shelley can in some ways at least stand as a nineteenth-century alternative to Shakespeare. Her engagement with Duke Richard of York and his story is primarily on the level of the imaginative, not of the historical, in the sense in which Sidney might have divided them. Shakespeare's relationship with the historical minutiae of his text is notoriously an uneasy one: however much interpretative ink may be

spilled over Richard III's decision to send the bishop of Ely for strawber-
ries, or Buckingham's entrance in rotten armor, the simplest explanation
seems to be that Shakespeare found these details in Holinshed and simply
transferred them wholesale without any attempt to rationalize them. He
is, too, certainly confused about titles, thinking that "Earl Rivers" and
"Lord Scales" are two different people, rather than separate titles of the
same man. Adopting a radically different point of view from the other
work on Warbeck that came out in the same year as her own, Alexander
Campbell's *Perkin Warbeck; or the Court of James the Fourth of
Scotland*, which sees Perkin straightforwardly as an impostor, Mary
Shelley is similarly cavalier, not so much with historical fact (the scarcity
of this in Perkin's case means that it could place very few restrictions on
her) but with probability: besides the totally fictitious and indeed totally
fantastic episode of Duke Richard's escape *into* the Tower, there is the
highly unlikely circumstance of Jane Shore, the mistress of his late
father, appearing not once but twice, on each occasion by total chance, to
save the young duke's life. In this demonstration of the workings of
poetic rather than actual justice, Mary Shelley clearly aligns herself with
Sidney's poet rather than his historian, and she does so too when she
allots herself a liberally free hand in the creation of character and
incident. Her James IV of Scotland, for instance—arguably the most
subtly drawn and most interesting character in the book—allows himself
to be led into scruples about the morality of taking mistresses that are
obviously far more the product of the nineteenth than of the fifteenth
century, to which they would be totally alien; Elizabeth Woodville, for
whom few contemporaries had a good word, becomes a respectable,
agonized, sentimental matron. Additionally, Mary Shelley deliberately
draws on popular legend rather than serious historiography when she
gives credence to the tale of the bastard son of Richard III, who is called
to his tent on the eve of the Battle of Bosworth, escapes the slaughter,
and ends as a carpenter and committed recluse. Other extrahistorical
sources are similarly apparent: the angelic goodness of Monina, of
Katherine, and (in many respects) of Duke Richard himself, is obviously
contrasted with the quasi-demonic, obsessive evil of Meiler Trangmar
and Clifford and with the scheming self-interest of Frion and King
Henry. Such characterological chiaroscuro clearly belongs more to the
absolutes and the polarities of the Gothic (a genre with which Mary
Shelley had of course already shown herself aligned in *Frankenstein,* not
to mention her father's *Caleb Williams*) than to the more muted, balanced
palette with which characters are more generally painted in historiography. We are, for instance, a long way here from the dispassionate irony
of a Gibbon or the sobriety of a Hume.

Mary Shelley, however, seems ultimately uninterested in such models as these. She is not aiming at the cool dissection of causes and events that characterizes Gibbon; she shows no desire to write magisterially or to treat material comprehensively. She might indeed be better compared with another female author reacting against the historiography of great men to produce a far more impassioned and personal account—the young Jane Austen with her furiously partisan *History of England*—and she is also clearly related to the tradition of apology for Richard III that culminated in the scathing warmth of Horace Walpole. As the most recent chronicler of the Perkin Warbeck affair has written, "despite drawing information from the Tudor chronicles she stands in the line of the seventeenth-century reaction against the damning criticism of Richard III."[9] Her repeated insistence on the fact that Duke Richard's personal badge was the White Rose—later to be adopted as the Jacobite emblem of the 1715 and 1745 rebellions—and that he was indeed called by that name, also serves to align her visibly with Tory rather than with Whig versions of history. This brings with it its inevitable concomitant, that since Whig rather than Tory was ultimately perceived as in the ascendant trajectory, the Tory view of events was essentially colored with the elegiac sense of a world now lost. This is certainly well expressed in the tale of a doomed prince whose very identity was ultimately traduced, and it also serves to link Mary Shelley very closely to her literary predecessor, John Ford. Writing, as I have argued elsewhere, for a disaffected aristocracy in a country drifting toward civil war, Ford similarly concentrates on the inherent and inimitable nobility of what is doomed to worldly failure. In this, he and his circle can be seen as subscribing to the Tacitean view of history that the historian Mervyn James views as the keynote of the honor cult surrounding the earl of Essex and those, like Ford's aristocratic patrons, who survived and lamented his death:

> That Fate, irrational, incomprehensible and uncontrollable, rules over human history. Events were inevitable and their causes obscure: no explanation was possible why this rather than that should have come to pass. . . . [f]or the man of honour events were therefore hag-ridden by Fate. For this reason, although the quality of the assertive will was displayed in the encounter with Fate, honour was not authenticated at the bar of success, or diminished by failure.[10]

In this view, too, as in Sidney's of the ultimate futility of history because of its inability to provide edifying examples, the true function of historiography can only be that of lamentation.

Mary Shelley's own extensive dependence on Ford's play is clearly signaled by her repeated inauguration of chapters with quotations from it. These are, appropriately enough, clustered particularly thickly in the Scottish and English sections of Perkin's life, which is what Ford drama- tizes (he is silent on the subject of Perkin's upbringing and says little about his trips to Ireland and virtually nothing about his time in Spain and France). Chapter 29, "Welcome to Scotland," has a chapter heading taken from the equivalent section of Ford; so do chapters 32, 36, and 42; and when Richard tells King James, "Your majesty imparts no strange truth to me,"[11] Shelley alludes directly to the subtitle of Ford's play, which is called *The Chronicle History of Perkin Warbeck: A Strange Truth*. The characterization of King James as impetuous, honorable, at first genuinely devoted to Duke Richard and then increasingly alienated by his baffled inability to comprehend the finer feelings of the duke's character, also owes something to Ford, as does the drawing of Katherine as a paragon of beauty, virtue, and, above all, loyalty (although Mary Shelley interestingly omits totally the high-minded Dalyell, who is Katherine's unsuccessful suitor in the Ford play: this may be because she was aware that Ford, for reasons of his own, had invented the character). Above all, her Duke Richard is, at times, virtually a carbon copy of Ford's Perkin in his unfailing nobility, his utter conviction of his own right, and, most of all, his hopeless revulsion at the suffering that the short-lived invasion of Northumberland imposes on the inhabitants there. Although Mary Shelley fleshes this out by adding the episode of the death of Edmund Plantagenet's foster father, the hero's sentiments are precisely the same in both texts, as is the rapidity with which his lack of martial eagerness disgusts and alienates King James.

In relying on Ford, however, Mary Shelley does more than merely find models for certain of her characters and incidents. Ford's version of events, as part of the early-seventeenth-century reappraisal of Richard III, is clearly concerned to stand in conspicuous opposition to the version of events offered by More and, above all, by Shakespeare. Mary Shelley, too, despite the comparison I have drawn between her own artistic impulse and that of Shakespeare, must surely have been acutely aware that in retelling this particular story she was choosing to go directly counter to the work of England's national writer. She does not, of course, ignore Shakespeare altogether: James of Scotland tells Duke Richard that his cousin Katherine is "no frail floweret, to be scared when the rough wind visits her cheek" (234), and the narrator herself tells us that "Katherine could assume nothing, not even a virtue, if she had it not" (237) (it is an interesting coincidence—or trick of memory or psychology—that both quotations should occur at the point where the text is also most heavily dependent on Ford). Both these allusions, however, refer to *Hamlet*: Hamlet remembering his father as so solicitous to his mother that he would not let the wind visit her cheek too roughly, Hamlet adjuring his mother to assume a virtue, if she has it not. There is no reference to *Richard III*.

And yet *Richard III* might well be thought to have been a text that would have been of particular interest to Mary Shelley. As well as its obvious applicability to the events that she is covering in *The Fortunes of Perkin Warbeck*, it also centers on a concern that, as she had clearly demonstrated, was vital to her: monstrosity. The deformity of Richard renders him monstrous in precisely the same ways as the deformity of Frankenstein's monster does, or as the deformity of the dwarf in *Transformation*. The analogies become even closer when we remember that Richard III's preferred solutions to his problems are always sought through associating himself with women—first the Lady Anne, for reasons to which even he himself cannot put a name, then Queen Elizabeth, in a bizarre scene of proxy wooing—just as Frankenstein's monster deflects his own quest for vengeance away from his master directly, choosing instead to focus first on Justine and then on Elizabeth. So much does Mary Shelley choose *not* to pursue this potential connection, however, that the only reference in her text to Richard III's deformity is an ambiguous one, when Duke Richard says of his uncle, "This Welsh earl, whom you call king, grinds the poor people he has vanquished to the dust, making them lament him they named Crookback, who, though an usurper, was a munificent sovereign" (61). "Him they named Crookback," while definitely implying some kind of deformity in the king, does not unequivocally confirm it, imposing the crucial qualifier of "him they named" rather than offering the straightforward testimony of Duke Richard himself, who had seen and known his uncle.

Despite the absence of a limping, hunchbacked Richard III, Mary Shelley's novel is, nevertheless, centrally structured by an ongoing tension between the self and its monstrous other, an unceasing, polymorphous conflict that proves as central here as it does in *Frankenstein*. One obvious manifestation of it is the varying comparisons between Duke Richard and his other possible selves. On the one hand, there is the grasping, unfeeling Henry VII, who sits on the throne that Richard himself should possess; on the other, there is James IV of Scotland, his brother in arms and, briefly, his brother in spirit too, from whom he becomes divided through the superiority of the ducal over the kingly notions of honor in love and war. There is also the earl of Warwick, the prisoner in the Tower with whose fate Duke Richard's own is so intimately bound up and for whom he was initially mistaken in Ireland: first cousins, they will eventually plot escape together and die together, but not until, we are told, they "had changed characters" (388), with the formerly timid Warwick becoming the more eager of the two for escape. It is a suggestive phrase and conveys much of the fluidity of the boundary between self and other in this text, where even a husband and wife can be seen as ultimately interchangeable when Katherine becomes known by the name of the White Rose, which had previously been her husband's sobriquet.

Most telling, perhaps, is that most troubling of all *alter egos*, Sir Robert Clifford, the childhood playfellow whose envy of Richard eventually drives him to turn traitor before he and the duke (like Frankenstein and his monster) come to a deadly conflict in the sea. Clifford is always, from the beginning, seen as verging on the physically deformed—we hear of "the slight, stunted figure of Clifford" (68)—and it is not long before he becomes so mentally too. "He hated the prince, because he was his opposite" (151). There is an obvious link here with the sense of unbordered selfhood that will later link Richard to Katherine, where mirror imagery, so important in the formation of identity in *Frankenstein*,[12] is found again: "Richard had found in the Lady Katherine a magic mirror, which gave him back himself, arrayed with a thousand alien virtues" (230). Later, Richard, placed in the stocks, will become a mirror in which all kings are reflected, following the prophecy "This last vile act of his enemy must awaken each sovereign on his throne to indignation; each would see in him a mirror of what might befall themselves, if fallen" (375). Clifford uses the mirror that the duke represents to him to very different purpose: "Among the partizans of York sometimes he felt remorse; beside the bright contrast of his own dark self, never" (162). Ultimately, his own body will take on the outward deformity of his inner mind, as he becomes virtually unrecognizable to his former associates: "Now his gait was shuffling, his appearance mean, his speech hesitating and confused" (168).

Clifford, however, does not provide the only example of the "own dark self" in the novel. There is also Meiler Trangmar, obsessed by the deaths of his three sons to the point that his only waking thought is vengeance on the House of York; and Trangmar can serve as a pointer to a persistent strain of metaphors that are connected with monstrosity in one very particular and perhaps rather unexpected form—motherhood. To some extent, the connection was already present in the story as she found it in Ford, where Oxford says of Margaret of Burgundy, protectress of Perkin and of Lambert Simnel:

> In her age
> Great sir, observe the wonder—she grows fruitful,

Who in her strength of youth was always barren.
Nor are her births as other mothers' are,
At nine or ten months' end; she has been with child
Eight or seven years at least; whose twins being born—
A prodigy in nature!—even the youngest
Is fifteen years of age at his first entrance,
As soon as known i'th'world; tall striplings, strong
And able to give battle unto kings,
Idols of Yorkish malice.[13]

Moreover, it was also a connection strongly suggested by the circumstances of Mary Shelley's own life. It has often been suggested that the
image of the monster in *Frankenstein* derives ultimately from Mary
Shelley's own image of herself, as a mother whose children died; it is a
commonplace to link the young Frankenstein's experiments with creating
life from corpses with the young Mary Shelley's dream about reviving
her dead daughter by placing her near the fire. It is certainly the case that
motherhood was to prove to be an issue deeply fraught with anxieties and
problems not only for Mary but for the majority of her friends and
family. Her mother, Mary Wollstonecraft (who had already endured the
stigma of giving birth to an illegitimate daughter), died of puerperal fever
after Mary was born; several of her own children—the first, an unnamed
daughter, and later William and Clara—died, leaving her with only Percy
Florence. She suffered a miscarriage that would have killed her had it not
been for the prompt thinking of her husband; her stepsister Claire Clairmont suffered the loss of her only child, Byron's daughter Allegra; and
her husband's first wife, Harriet Westbrook, is often said to have been
pregnant when she drowned herself (although this rumor may perhaps be
due merely to the bloated appearance of drowned corpses).

As one might perhaps expect with so profound and fundamental an
anxiety, the trauma surrounding motherhood appears not directly in Mary
Shelley's text but manifested in marginality and displacement. The actual
mothers in *The Fortunes of Perkin Warbeck* are, like Victor's mother in
Frankenstein, ostensibly beyond reproach. The devoted Madeline does
everything possible for both her own daughter Monina and her adopted
son Duke Richard; Richard's natural mother, Elizabeth Woodville, shows
a most tender (though ultimately unavailing) solicitude for all her children. Interestingly, Mary Shelley chose to ignore the unequivocal statement in Buc (which is sometimes repeated by later historians) that Duke
Richard and Katherine had children, and Jane Shore too is, like her historical counterpart, childless. So much for the actual female characters,
but another element of the text tells a very different tale. When Meiler

Trangmar is first mentioned, his introduction is accompanied by a power-ful narratorial simile:

> Meiler Trangmar felt every success of [the Yorkists] as a poisoned arrow in his flesh—he hated them, as the mother may hate the tiger whose tusks are red with the life-blood of her firstborn—he hated them, not with the measured aversion of a warlike foe, but the dark frantic vehemence of a wild beast deprived of its young. (99)

Trangmar's actual status as a triply bereaved father is forcibly transferred here into a terrifying image of the monstrous *mother*. Initially figured as human, this mother is quickly dissolved by the complex syntax into a suggestion of equivalence with the red-tusked tiger itself, a suggestion that is immediately confirmed by her actual metamorphosis into "a wild beast deprived of its young."

This startling association of motherhood with predation proves to be only the first of several in the text. Sometimes motherhood is more positively imaged:

> A mother draws not more instinctively her first-born to her bosom, than does the true and passionate lover feel impelled to hazard even life for the sake of her he loves, to shield her from every danger, or to share them gladly with her. (171)

Even here, however, the apparently reassuring image of the mother embracing her child soon gives way to a more troubling one of hazard and danger. Both of these, too, recur in the description of Katherine awaiting the news of Richard's fate in the West Country:

> To one thus aware of the misfortune that awaits her, the voice of consolation is a mockery. Yet, even while she knows that the die is cast, she will not acknowledge her intimate persuasion of ill; but sits smiling on any hope brought to her, as a mother on the physician who talks of recovery while her child dies. (338)

Here the mother is presented as virtually imbecilic: passively acquiescing in the most futile of voluntary self-deceptions, she "sits smiling" like an idiot in these grossly inappropriate circumstances and neglects even to offer her dying child comfort because she has renounced her role as pri-mary caregiver in favor of the useless, and indeed positively deceptive, physician (there may perhaps be echoes here of Mary Shelley's own guilt at having failed to notice that her first daughter was dead when, waking in the night to give her suck, she thought the child was merely sleeping soundly).

Perhaps most chilling of all is the novel's only instance of actual bad mothering, which is withheld until very late in the unfolding of the narrative, when we meet again the beautiful but ineffectual Elizabeth of York. When first introduced, she was a nurturing figure, protective of her adoring cousin Warwick; when the story moves to her again, however, she has been forced into a loveless marriage with Henry VII and is presented as a very different person. Deeply embittered, she confesses to Katherine, "Sometimes I hate my beautiful children because they are his" (397). This profound insight into the perception of children as both the products of the self and the monstrous products of the other provides the climax of the recurrent image of the bad mother. This sits startlingly in a text that steadfastly refuses to incriminate bad fathering, as when Richard declares at his trial, "My very good lord, I ask nothing, save that a little mercy be extended to the memory of my gracious uncle, my lord of Gloucester, who was no child-murderer" (400–401). But perhaps the text's strongest, most self-lacerating indictment of mothering as ineffectual is a silent one, contained in a purely structural irony. Challenged after the death of her husband about her reasons for continuing to live at court, Katherine cites as her prime motivation the necessity to nurture the heir to the throne, the promising young Prince Arthur. In this way, she hints, she can at least feel that the succession, which has been wrongly diverted to Henry Tudor, will fall into safe hands again. Yet in another part of the same conversation, her interlocutor, her husband's bastard cousin Edmund Plantagenet, refers to the tombstone of Monina as showing "half the date, the 14–, which showed that she died before the century began, in which we now live." We are, then, in the early years of the sixteenth century, and Arthur died at the age of sixteen, of the sweating-sickness, in 1502, so that the succession fell instead to his less fine-grained brother Henry VIII, who was to extirpate all that remained of the House of York. If Mary Shelley here is showing even the slightest respect for historical accuracy, we must be forced to suppose that the conversation between Katherine and Edmund is taking place in 1500, 1501, or early 1502 (Mary Shelley merely calls it "years" after Richard's death), and that this remark of Katherine's is, therefore, shadowed by the bitterest of ironies, that nurturing here will prove useless, since the treasured Arthur is shortly to die. Any endorsement of Katherine's position that Mary Shelley seems to be holding out must surely be at least partially undercut by our knowledge that her efforts in this respect are doomed.

Yet it seems beyond doubt that Mary Shelley *is* endorsing Katherine, in however circumscribed a manner. Indeed, she tells us so herself in a rare note to the text (the paucity of footnotes is in general accord with the practice deemed, at the time, particularly appropriate to history that was meant to be read by women):

> The character of Lady Katherine Gordon is a favourite of mine, and yet many will be inclined to censure her abode in Henry the Seventh's court, and other acts of her after-life. I desired therefore that she should speak for herself, and show how her conduct, subsequent to her husband's death, was in accordance with the devotion and fidelity with which she attended his fortunes during his life. (406)

Critics have not been slow to point out that, in speaking "for herself," Katherine is surely speaking for Mary Shelley also. As Barbara Jane O'Sullivan argues, "there is little doubt that Katherine was a vehicle for Shelley's own message to those who criticized her lifestyle after Percy Shelley's death."[14] Like *The Last Man*, which Barbara Johnson has called "the story of the one who remains,"[15] the end of *The Fortunes of Perkin Warbeck* is primarily concerned with the guilt of the survivor. The intense applicability of this to Mary's own situation is neatly pointed up for us by a brief reflection toward the end of the book: "Nor do we hate nor blame the wild winds and murderous waves, though they have drunk up a life more precious and more beloved than words have power to speak" (399). Here, it is clearly Percy Shelley's death by drowning, rather than Richard's by hanging, that is remembered. Interestingly, however, Mary Shelley is silent about the fact that the historical Katherine Gordon remarried after the death of Perkin Warbeck not just once but a striking three times. Again, personal feelings seem the most likely explanation. Conceivably, Mary Shelley could have been reluctant to deal with this section of the story because one of the three remarriages took Katherine to Swansea (a tomb for her survived there until the Second World War, although she was in fact buried elsewhere), where Mary Shelley's half sister Fanny Imlay had committed suicide. More probably, she may well have felt that it touched too closely on the story of her own thought of remarriage after the death of Percy Shelley; this seems to be made more likely by the fact that a footnote to *The Fortunes of Perkin Warbeck* commends one of the novels of Washington Irving, who five years before had seemed to be a possible suitor for her. In this novel structured so closely round the seeming polarities and disturbing similarities of the self and the monstrous other, there can be little doubt that, to Mary Shelley, Katherine *is* the self.

What then does that make Duke Richard, the enigmatic prince whose elusive identity is so well captured by the fact that he never even has a name? Known at various times as the duke, the prince, or simply the

White Rose, his own eponymous text mistitles him as Perkin Warbeck, the "nick-name" that causes him so much agony of soul in the novel. He also steadfastly refuses to assume the title of king, although, if his pretensions are correct, that in fact is what he is. If his wife seems so clearly to be Mary Shelley, surely the husband should be a portrait of Percy Shelley? In many ways, that is exactly what Richard resembles: the high-souled idealism and the hatred of violence are very close to Percy Shelley, and it is easy to see in the natural, honorable king whose society rejects him a type not only of Adrian in *The Last Man*, an acknowledged portrait of Percy Shelley, but also of the latter's concept of the poet as the "unacknowledged legislator" of society.

In other respects, however, the picture in the mirror is a less flattering one. Many critics have found in *Frankenstein* an indictment of the irresponsibility of the artist, directed particularly at Percy Shelley; *The Fortunes of Perkin Warbeck* offers an equally telling analysis of the chaos that one well-intentioned but exceptional being can wreak on the lives of those around him. It is notable that, despite her enthusiastic conviction of the truth of Richard's claims to be the rightful heir of York, Mary Shelley is decidedly more lukewarm about his decision to pursue those claims by force. As I have already pointed out, she paints the desolation inflicted upon the Northumbrian peasants in far more vivid colors than Ford does, and she also goes out of her way to offer a pointedly authorial reflection on the subject:

> Our motives—we believed them disinterested or justifiable; we have advanced a wondrous step in life before we can concede even to ourselves that alloy may be mingled with that we deemed pure gold: ignorant of the soil and culture of our own hearts, we feel sure that no base mixture can form a part of what we fancy to be a mine of virgin ore. Richard would have stood erect and challenged the world to accuse him—God and his right, was his defence. His right! Oh, narrow and selfish was that sentiment that could see, in any right appertaining to one man the excuse for the misery of thousands. (235)

Admirable in many ways though the hero may be, therefore, he is not free from fault.[16] A very different picture is offered by the following description of his bastard cousin, Edmund Plantagenet:

> During his hazardous journey to Flanders, Edmund was supported by that glowing sensation which borrows the hues and sometimes the name of happiness; it was an ecstatic mood that soared above the meaner cares of life, and exalted him by the grandeur of his own ideas. Self-devotion is, while it can keep true to itself, the best source of human enjoyment; there is small

alloy when we wholly banish our own wretched clinging individuality, in our entire sacrifice at the worshipped shrine. (57)

Even here the endorsement is not complete: there is marked scepticism expressed about the possibility of keeping self-devotion entire, and even when it is, the best that can be promised of it is that it will produce "human enjoyment"—there is no mention of usefulness or of any grander purpose. Nevertheless, the two quotations together offer an apt summary of one of the many dualities that structure the novel: that between self-interest and altruism, or, as Mary Shelley terms it, self-devotion. The former is exemplified by Henry VII and by Robert Clifford; the latter not so much by the hero as by Edmund Plantagenet and Katherine, who are also (and one presumes not coincidentally but in a kind of poetic justice) the only two characters who survive the general wreck of the Yorkist cause.

Even within the hero, then, "alloy" is found, and indeed we may well be invited to see his very exceptionalness as a form of monstrosity, a deformity from the normal that society cannot readily tolerate, any more than it could accommodate the restless talents of Victor Frankenstein or of Raymond in *The Last Man*. The sensitive exploration of the self in society provided by the novel can be seen as offering us a number of insights. For one thing, the individual imposture of which the hero is accused is soon revealed to stand merely as a metaphor for the problematics of all identity as the self adjusts to the pressures exerted on it by the multiplicity of other selves and selfish others of whom it finds its society to be constructed. In a related point, the boundary between the self and the monstrous—apparently so firmly fixed in the cases of the polarities between Duke Richard and Robert Clifford—is revealed as irrevocably collapsed not only in the potent image of the monstrous mother (which in turn plays on the fears of Mary Shelley's own self about elisions between the categories of self and other) but also in the "right" that can drive Duke Richard to so disastrous a war and to bring death on so many of those he values. In the end, indeed, the story of Duke Richard can never be told; the pressures of Mary Shelley's own society on a woman writer who seeks to purvey history instead of fiction led her to market it instead as *The Fortunes of Perkin Warbeck*.

Notes

1. Mary Shelley, *The Last Man*, ed. Brian Aldiss (London: Hogarth Press, 1985), 339.

2. Muriel Spark, *Mary Shelley* (London: Constable, 1988), 13.

3. Compare Laurie Langbauer, "Swayed by Contraries: Mary Shelley and the Everyday," in *The Other Mary Shelley: Beyond Frankenstein*, ed. Audrey A. Fisch, Anne K. Mellor, and Esther H. Schor (Oxford: Oxford University Press, 1993), 185–203.

4. See Barbara Jane O'Sullivan, "Beatrice in *Valperga*: A New Cassandra," in *The Other Mary Shelley*, 140–58, for the importance of the Cassandra figure in Shelley's work.

5. Mary Shelley, *The Fortunes of Perkin Warbeck* (1830; rprt., London: G. Routledge and Co., 1857).

6. Ford's *The Chronicle of Perkin Warbeck* is found in *John Ford: Three Plays*, ed. Keith Sturgess (Harmondsworth, England: Penguin, 1970). Muriel Spark feels that "Ford . . . implies his own leaning towards Warbeck's claim" (*Mary Shelley,* 204).

7. Horace Walpole, *Historic Doubts on the Life and Reign of Richard the Third*, ed. P. W. Hammond (Gloucester, England: Alan Sutton, 1987), 69, 75, 79.

8. See Lisa Hopkins, "*Perkin Warbeck*: A Stuart Succession Play?" in *John Ford's Political Theatre* (Manchester, England: Manchester University Press, 1994), chap. 2.

9. Ian Arthurson, *The Perkin Warbeck Conspiracy* (Gloucester, England: Alan Sutton, 1994), 26.

10. Mervyn James, *Society, Politics and Culture* (Cambridge, England: Cambridge University Press, 1986), 315.

11. Shelley, *The Fortunes of Perkin Warbeck*, 268.

12. See Lisa Hopkins, *A Hall of Mirrors: Mary Shelley's "Frankenstein"* (Sheffield, England: Sheffield Hallam University Publications, 1992).

13. Ford, *Chronicle*, 1.1.52–62.

14. O'Sullivan, "Beatrice in *Valperga*," 153.

15. Barbara Johnson, "The Last Man," 258–66, 262.

16. Betty T. Bennett comments that "Richard's failure is made amply clear to the reader" ("The Political Philosophy of Mary Shelley's Historical Novels: *Valperga* and *Perkin Warbeck*," in *The Evidence of the Imagination*, ed. Donald H. Reiman, Michael C. Jaye, and Betty T. Bennett [New York: New York University Press, 1978], 354–71, 364). Bennett offers an acute analysis of the novel.

The Illusion of "Great Expectations": Manners and Morals in Mary Shelley's *Lodore* and *Falkner*

Charlene E. Bunnell

Having astounded the literary world with *Frankenstein*'s originality, shocked it with *The Last Man*'s bleak determinism, and earned its grudging respect with *Valperga*'s and *Perkin Warbeck*'s historical representations, Mary Shelley took a different approach with her last two novels, *Lodore* (1835) and *Falkner* (1837).[1] Indebted both to novels of manners and to sentimental domestic fiction, these works depict contemporary settings, commonplace characters, and detailed examinations of the manners and morals of society, all of which represent a marked departure from the metaphysical, futuristic, or historical features dominating Shelley's earlier fiction.[2]

In the tradition of the novel of manners established by such writers as Eliza Haywood, Frances Burney, and Jane Austen, *Lodore* demonstrates how fully social customs and mores dictate a character's behavior as she makes her entrance upon the world's stage. However, rather than emphasizing how her heroine, Cornelia Lodore, must accommodate her expectations to those of conventional society, Shelley suggests that she is too subservient to manners and image. Cornelia discovers that she cannot rely on "society's glass" as the barometer by which to conduct her life, for in so doing she loses self-esteem and forgoes familial duty. In contrast to Haywood's Betsy Thoughtless and Austen's Emma Woodhouse, who need to moderate their self-will to assimilate into the public sphere, Cornelia needs to exert her will to break free of social hypocrisy. In *Falkner,* Shelley continues to examine the tension between social codes and individual desires. Voicing a warning similar to Charlotte Lennox's in her novel *The Female Quixote* (1752), Shelley explores the devastating consequences of a character's mores, grounded in romantic ideals and illusions, colliding with society's expectations and stark reality. While Lennox's misguided Arabella provides comic delight with her interpretation of French romances as conduct books and historical accounts, Shelley's Falkner suggests only dark despair. Acting the part of a rescuing sentimental hero, he inadvertently causes the death of the woman he loves and subsequently experiences a public spectacle resulting from such illusory romantic role-playing.

Although in both novels Shelley indicts a society that represses independence and self-esteem and that exalts public over private virtue, she also criticizes the protagonists. Cornelia Lodore and John Rupert Falkner are responsible for much of their unhappiness as a result of envisioning "great expectations" for themselves upon the world's stage. Employing theatrical metaphors to spotlight her social commentary, Shelley depicts the dangerous and often disastrous results when such expectations are grounded in illusions fostered both by the characters' perceptions of life as theater and of themselves as actors and by a society more concerned with superficial manners than moral integrity.

Both *Lodore* and *Falkner* proved successful novels for Mary Shelley, no small feat given her family's notoriety amid the growing conservatism of the emerging Victorian reading public.[3] Despite many prepublication problems, when it was finally published on 7 April 1835 by Richard Bentley and Henry Colburn, *Lodore* was an unqualified success, second only to *Frankenstein*.[4] Critics praised its treatment of believable, ordinary characters, and Leigh Hunt reviewed it favorably, noting that its major weakness was simply that it lacked the power of *Frankenstein*, a novel, he admitted, which is a "thing to happen only once in many years."[5] The success of *Lodore* prompted Charles Ollier to ask Shelley for another novel, which she began in late 1835.[6] She sold her finished work to Saunders and Otley, who, according to Shelley biographer Emily Sunstein, offered more generous advances and payment than did Bentley.[7] Published in February 1837, *Falkner* did not receive the critical acclaim accorded to its predecessor. Nevertheless, it sold well and generated salutary notices, including one by the *Monthly Review*, which called it the "finest, and most powerful, in regard to sentiment, of Mrs. Shelley's novels."[8] Despite their initial successes, today both novels are Shelley's least known and studied.[9]

Focusing on two generations, *Lodore* presents the stories of three characters—Lord Lodore, Cornelia Santerre Lodore, and Ethel Lodore Villiers. Volume 1 of the novel opens with Lodore, a melancholy

Byronic figure, who has recently returned to England after an unsuccessful love affair on the Continent. He meets and marries the young Cornelia Santerre, and they have a daughter, Ethel. The unhappy marriage is strained further when Countess Lyzinski (Lodore's earlier love) visits with her son Casimir, who is unaware that he is Lodore's biological son. Complications ensue with the threat of a duel between father and son, and Lodore elects to leave England for America. At her mother's urging, Cornelia refuses to accompany her husband, and he takes three-year-old Ethel to live in Illinois for twelve years until he decides to rectify the past and return. However, he is killed in a duel, and Ethel goes back to England to live with Lodore's sister, Elizabeth Fitzhenry, on the family estate in Longfield, Essex. The second and third volumes focus on Cornelia and Ethel. Although aware of each other's existence, mother and daughter avoid establishing a relationship: Ethel assumes that her mother does not wish to see her, and Cornelia believes herself bound by her late husband's outdated will, which stipulates her losing a generous settlement should she acknowledge her daughter. Ethel marries the worthy Edward Villiers, and the couple experiences debtor's prison as a result of the senior Villiers's gambling. Learning of her daughter's situation from a mutual friend, Fanny Derham, Cornelia ignores social conventions and legal restrictions to help Ethel and Edward. Through a series of fortuitous events, they all reconcile and discover that benevolent virtue is indeed ultimately rewarded.

Although the novel's title might lead one to infer that Lord Lodore is the featured character, Mary Shelley specified that Cornelia and Ethel are the protagonists: "A Mother & Daughter are the heroines—The Mother who after safrifising *all* to the world at first—afterwards makes sacrifises not less entire, for her child—finding all to be Vanity, except the genuine affections of the heart" (*Letters*, 2:185). Arguably, the central figure is Cornelia, whose story interconnects with the lives of all the others and most explicitly demonstrates the "Vanity" and hypocrisy of social expectations and manners. From both her education and her own youthful self-centeredness, Cornelia Lodore perceives society as a stage on which to enact the role of a fashionable lady, and she is conditioned to adopt its accepted manners and to create an image that will earn its approbation. Dominated by her mother and married at sixteen, Cornelia has had little chance to have a variety of life experiences or to establish any sense of self-identity or esteem. As authority figures, neither Lady Santerre nor Lodore respect Cornelia as an individual; rather, they see her as a means to an end: the furthering of their own social or personal ambition. By delineating the characters of Lady Santerre and Lord Lodore, Mary Shelley provides the background for understanding her protagonist's weakness and for recognizing that, although Cornelia is to blame for her problems, society is at fault as well.

The parasitic Lady Santerre realizes that, through her daughter's marriage to Lodore, she herself can achieve social prominence that will befit her title. The narrator tells us that "she was a clever though uneducated woman: perfectly selfish, soured with the world, yet clinging to it. To make good her second entrance on its stage, she believed it necessary to preserve unlimited sway over the plastic mind of her daughter" (*Lodore*, 31). "Unlimited sway" she does hold. She sets herself up as a barrier to an intimate relationship between Cornelia and Lodore and does not educate her daughter to be self-reliant or independent; rather, Lady Santerre ensures that she herself will "direct the machinery of the drama" (30).

This and other theatrical metaphors reinforce Shelley's criticism of Lady Santerre's privileging of image and affectation over substance and genuine emotion; they also reveal this character's superficial view of life, as evidenced in her equating life with a dramatic spectacle and people with actors on a stage. When Cornelia asks her mother for advice, following Lodore's request that she accompany him to America, Lady Santerre instructs her daughter to ignore his plea, assuring her that he will abandon his plans: "You are as lost as he, if you yield. A little patience, and all will be right again. He will soon grow tired of playing the tragic hero on a stage, surrounded by no spectators" (49). Lady Santerre, so accustomed to adopting roles to obtain public acceptance, assumes that everyone else does the same. Attempting to reassure Cornelia, who is genuinely concerned about losing her daughter, she insists that Lodore will tire of being a father and will be "too glad to find that you will still be willing to act the mother towards his child" (49). Her choice of words—"act the mother"—indicates that she applies role-playing to the domestic sphere as well as the public one and that lives are merely projected images and roles to be played. The narrator's description of Lady Santerre in her last years is hardly flattering: "Withering away in unhonoured age, still she appeared in the halls of the great, and played the part of Cerberus in her daughter's drawing-room" (54). The allusion to the three-headed dog guarding the entrance to Hades is apt. Lady Santerre is diligent in orchestrating and protecting the daughter's image that she has so carefully constructed for her own gain. As a woman who has taught her daughter "to view society's glass by which to set her feelings, and to which to adapt her conduct" (31), she remains to her dying day more concerned with appearance than with substance, with acting rather than living.

Lord Lodore must also share in the guilt for Cornelia's social education. His young and impetuous character has several literary antecedents: Charlotte Smith's Frederic Delamere, the rakish pursuer in *Emmeline* (1788); Eliza Fenwick's Arthur Murden, the compulsive abductor in *Secresy* (1795); and William Godwin's Ferdinando Falkland, the brooding antagonist in *Caleb Williams* (1794). All these figures are perpetually haunted and ultimately destroyed by their youthful passions and ambitions. Having experienced unrequited love for the strong-willed Countess Theodora Lyzinski, Lodore views the young Cornelia as a plastic figure that he can mold according to his perception of the perfect wife. Aware of Lady Santerre's financial problems, he is entranced with playing the role of benefactor to his young wife and thinks "how proud a part was his, to gift her with rank, fortune, and all earthly blessings, and to receive in return, gratitude, tenderness, and unquestioning submission" (29). Cornelia's inexperienced and impressionable nature does not, however, satisfy Lodore's purpose. She is inextricably bound to her mother, a tie that is even stronger than the one with her husband. Well-schooled by her mother, Cornelia indeed regards her relationship as Lodore's wife merely as a role to play on the stage of English society, and her husband soon realizes the emptiness of such posturing. Lodore's intention is also thwarted by Lady Santerre, who "inspired him . . . to play a god-like part" while she simultaneously denied him the authority to do so (30). Resenting his supporting role, Lodore is unsympathetic to the needs and foibles of his young wife, whose reliance upon her mother displaces him as the center of her life.

As if Mary Shelley felt that readers might overlook Lodore's manipulative nature, she emphasizes it further by detailing the father's philosophy of educating his daughter. Although Lodore had failed in his Pygmalion plan for Cornelia, and although he had criticized Lady Santerre's strong hold on her daughter, he repeats his earlier mistake and imitates his mother-in-law's very example in his instruction of Ethel. Borrowing from stock images and archetypes, such as Milton's Eve, Shakespeare's Miranda, Byron's Haidèe, and Thomas Campbell's Gertrude, he molds the plastic Ethel so that "she [grows] into the image on which his eye doted" (10).[10] The parallels to *Frankenstein* are evident: Lodore is as intent on creating a perfect specimen for selfish motives as was Victor. His aim is to shape a daughter who will not only bless him as a father but will also represent his ideal image of woman, an image that, for different reasons, neither Theodora Lyzinski nor Cornelia can achieve. None of these heroines presents a model of independence or selfhood for Ethel; rather, they represent the type of woman that Lodore has imagined is the ideal: submissive, pliable, and dependent.

Given her education by Lady Santerre and Lodore, Cornelia is understandably susceptible to the allures of high society and quickly learns to enjoy the benefits of Lodore's wealth and rank, which facilitate her entrance onto the public stage. Like Frances Burney's Evelina and Eliza Haywood's Betsy Thoughtless, she discovers the painful ramifications of misjudging social situations. Her playful flirting with Casimir, harmless in intent, is instrumental in causing Lodore's and her downfall. As her husband reminds her following the fateful party where he struck Casimir, she is partly to blame, and he scolds her for "the part you have had in bringing on this catastrophe" (40). Cornelia continues the dramatic allusion to identify their situation, seeing, perhaps, an analogy between their lives and those of characters in a sentimental play by Kotzebue.[11] She remarks to Lodore, "This sounds very like a German tragedy, being at once disagreeable and inexplicable" (41). As it did for Lady Santerre, the dramatic metaphor appropriately describes their predicament, at the same time highlighting Cornelia's realization that image and public virtue are the means to acquiring social status and approbation. Shelley neither condones Cornelia's thoughtless behavior with Casimir nor validates her protagonist's reason for the remorse that results from concern with appearance rather than from genuine care about her husband's plight and her role in it.

After the death of her mother, Cornelia no longer has anyone to direct her life. Yet by this time, having learned how to play effectively to the conventions of society, she has difficulty in abandoning the role so painstakingly cultivated over the years. After hearing of Lodore's death, Cornelia is free to pursue a relationship with Horatio Saville, who has come to love her very much. A second son with scholarly rather than political or social ambitions, Horatio seems an unlikely match for the more worldly Cornelia. Nevertheless, she is attracted to his sincerity and his affection for her as a person rather than as a commodity. However, Cornelia cannot easily remove the mask she has worn so long. Playing the part of the coquette, she allows the "artificial courtesies of society" to dictate her actions (89). As a result of her behavior, Horatio concludes that Cornelia cannot be serious about a titleless second son. Learning that he has gone abroad, she is sure that he will return to her, just as she was convinced that Lodore would abandon his plan to go to America; however, Sophia Saville later tells her that her brother has married a Neapolitan woman, Clorinda.[12] Once again, Lady Lodore learns that the social manners she adopts do not accomplish her desire, and she wonders" "at the part she had acted" (93).

Cornelia reveals her obsession with maintaining her social status by nonmaternal actions generated from fear that public spectacle could harm her image. In an exchange with Edward Villiers, whom she has come to know by way of Horatio, Edward's cousin, she learns that Ethel has returned to England. Not aware that, directly prior to his death, Lodore was revising his will to reunite mother and daughter, Cornelia believes that she must forfeit her jointure should she assume the role of mother and guardian of her daughter. To avoid a public confrontation with Ethel should they chance to meet at a social function, Cornelia plans to spend the summer season in Paris; she would not, she tells Edward, "present a domestic tragedy or farce to the Opera House—we must not meet in public" (95). "A domestic tragedy" played out in public is repugnant to Cornelia, who, since the Lyzinski episode, has so diligently acted with propriety and decorum. Having very carefully polished her image over the years, Cornelia is unwilling to risk tarnishing it. At this point, the lonely young woman recognizes the emptiness of her life and begins to regret her adherence to society's expectations. However, she cannot yet bring herself to give up the social amenities to which she is accustomed, nor does she have any motivation to do so, for she fears that the daughter whom she truly loves has been taught to despise her.

Although despondent over losing Horatio and resigned to keeping a distance from Ethel, Cornelia forces herself to "adopt as a mask, the smiling appearance which had been natural to her for many years" (176). The mask remains intact until she hears of Ethel's and Edward's financial troubles. Cornelia then decides that, despite social pretenses and legal dictates, she will intervene to help them and to convince her daughter, whom she imagines to be weak-willed, to come stay with her.[13] Consciously acting rather than instinctively reacting, Cornelia performs the role of mother, projecting a detached concern that does not compromise her social status. She determines to visit her daughter, "making up her mind to perform her part with grace, and every show of kindness" (179). Meeting Ethel privately for the first time in nearly fifteen years, Cornelia realizes how wrong she has been to cast her daughter into the role of a weak, insipid character. Impressed by Ethel's fortitude and self-assurance, Cornelia promises to help her. Unable to bear her own loneliness any longer and inspired by her daughter's genial disregard for pretense, she finally decides that playing the part of the wronged wife for social appearances cannot supply the happiness or fulfillment that disinterested love and familial support can. As Katherine Hill-Miller notes, motherhood frees Cornelia: "Cornelia's new life of devotion to her daughter, for all its conventionality, allows her to escape some of the configurations of traditional marriage—in particular the patterns of dominance and dependence involved in her relationship to Lodore."[14] One might also add that she has at last cast off social posturings as well as the dominance and dependence associated with

Lady Santerre. Cornelia secretly arranges to help Ethel by selling her jointure and by turning her London house over to her daughter. In prior days, Cornelia either would have continued to enjoy her status among the well-connected without concern for Ethel or would have ensured a public fanfare that celebrated her generosity and benevolence. Now, ridden with guilt and sadness, she places her daughter's happiness above her own and, abandoning her role as a fashionable society matron, exits the public stage.

In the tradition of sentimental fiction, reward does come for Cornelia: she and her daughter reunite, and Horatio Saville returns, free to marry her. The homey, rural setting of their sentimental reunion is a pastoral contrast to the artifices of London society. For the epigraph of the second chapter, Mary Shelley quotes a passage from Seneca that aptly sums up Cornelia's newfound happiness: "Settle in some secret nest, / In calm leisure let me rest; / And far off the public stage, / Pass away my silent age" (*Lodore*, 6). This epigraph provides an effective contrast to the characters and fates of Lodore and Cornelia. Both of them seek "calm leisure" in rural homes: he in the wilds of Illinois, she in the outskirts of Longfield, Essex. However, Lodore escapes to evade his past and merely casts off one mask to assume another: in Illinois, he drops his title and uses his family name, Fitzhenry. Cornelia, on the other hand, chooses the quiet, natural setting, once she has discarded her mask and has attained self-esteem and independence from society's expectations. The setting is an escape not from herself but from social theatrics. Indeed, she has finally found herself and genuine happiness.

Mary Shelley intended Ethel to be the other heroine of *Lodore*, and through this character, she presents a successful alternative to Cornelia's life. Despite the parallels in education and upbringing, Ethel sharply contrasts with her mother in many ways. Although observing social standards of propriety and decorum, she regards self-esteem and domestic happiness as truer measures of one's worth. When she and Edward experience the degradation of a debtor's prison, she remains with him, refusing to live comfortably with her aunt. The narrator remarks, "Love in a cottage is the dream of many a high-born girl, who is not allowed to dance with a younger brother at Almack's; but a secluded, an obscure, an almost cottage life, was all that Ethel had ever known, and all that she coveted" (111). This passage reveals Mary Shelley's strong indictment of society's manners that often deny young women or men the chance for love with a partner who is compatible, though not perhaps the most desirable for social advancement. Although Edward at times worries about appearance, Ethel does not: "A splendid dwelling, costly living, and many attendants, were with her the adjuncts, not the material, of life. If the stage on which she played her part was to be so decorated, it was well; if otherwise, the change did not merit her attention" (165). Lady Santerre reveres society's glass and the public stage; Ethel's actions mirror her authentic character and demonstrate her disdain for actions motivated solely by consideration for appearance and custom.

Although brought up to be dependent, like the heroines of Radcliffe and Smith, Ethel quietly but deliberately challenges the boundaries imposed by marriage and social manners. She disobeys her husband's requests when she believes they will adversely affect either her or their relationship. She also understands that to achieve happiness one must at times abandon romantic ideals or social propriety. Reading Shakespeare's *Troilus and Cressida* with Edward while they nervously wait for a close friend, Fanny Derham, to bring them money, Ethel remarks, "Would Troilus and Cressida have repined at having been left darkling a few minutes? How much happier we are than all the heroes and heroines that ever lived or were imagined! They grasped at the mere shadow of the thing, whose substance we absolutely possess" (168). Ethel refuses to compromise her principles to accommodate a social image, and she is quite aware of the distinction between reality and illusion. For her, domestic happiness is more important than self-interest and public masks, a lesson that Cornelia fortunately learns in time to enjoy the remainder of her life with her daughter. "To thine own self be true," Polonius tells Laertes, for "Thou canst not then be false to any man." [15] In a world that privileges appearance above sincere principles and morals and prefers public masks to genuine character, Polonius's advice is difficult to live by. Nevertheless, the "personages who formed the drama of this tale" (*Lodore*, 228), especially Cornelia Lodore, discover that roles played for the sole purpose of social acceptance, gain, or approbation result in unfilled and unhappy lives.

Mary Shelley's indictment of social hypocrisy in *Lodore* extends into her final novel, *Falkner*, again a generational tale. Framed within the story of the protagonist's life with Elizabeth Raby, his adopted daughter, is the autobiographical history of John Falkner's youth and crime. This epistolary narrative reveals the egocentric and self-pitying perspective of a character whose romantic idealism and desire for social respect become a nightmare of domestic tragedy and public spectacle. The novel opens with the sad story of the six-year-old orphan Elizabeth Raby, who first encounters Falkner as he is about to commit suicide at the gravesite of Elizabeth's mother. Thinking he means to harm her mother's spirit, the child prevents his death. Falkner then accompanies her to the Baker home, where she resides, and he learns from Mrs. Baker that Elizabeth's mother may have been a friend to Alithea Rivers Neville, the woman he has accused himself of murdering. Out of sympathy and guilt, he adopts Elizabeth, who lovingly calls him her father. The entire first volume of this two-volume novel deals with Falkner's and Elizabeth's lives over approximately a ten-year period as they travel the Continent so that Falkner can avoid the authorities who he believes must be searching for him. Eventually they return to England, and Elizabeth enjoys the friendship of Lady Cecil and her stepbrother, Gerard Neville, Alithea's son. Elizabeth's and Gerard's growing affection for each other prompts Falkner to reveal his past crime in a letter, which begins the second volume. [16]

Falkner opens his letter stating that his intent is to exonerate Alithea, whose husband, Sir Boyville, wrongly believes that she had voluntarily left him. Boyville has portrayed Alithea as an unfaithful wife and uncaring mother. That even the local public accepts this image, despite its awareness of her integrity and devotion to her family, reinforces Shelley's scorn of society's collective obsession with appearance and public virtue. In his narrative, Falkner professes, "I am not writing my life; and, but for the wish to appear less criminal in my dear child's eyes, I had not written a word of the foregone pages, but leaped at once to the mere facts that justify poor Alithea, and tell the tragic story of her death" (*Falkner*, 2:39). However, Alithea's story, as Katherine Hill-Miller has observed, is "buried at the work's emotional center." [17] Although proving her innocence by refuting the false rumors about her character, the letter does not leap "at once to the mere facts that justify poor Alithea," as Falkner claims; rather, it focuses on Falkner and his life. Like the confessional histories of Godwin's Caleb Williams and James Hogg's Robert Wringham Colwan, [18] the letter reveals Falkner to be both protagonist and antagonist, both victim and villain. Mary Shelley's choice of the frame story enables her to criticize her central character's romantic illusions as well as the unjust and hypocritical society that fuels his actions.

While undeniably to blame for Alithea's death, Falkner is indeed a victim of social inequities and customs. Neglected and abused by his father, who is embittered at being a second son with little future, Falkner experiences an undeservedly miserable childhood. Upon his father's death, he is taken in by his uncle's family and, though not abused, is treated as a second-class citizen. Inherently benevolent, he is expelled from school for fighting with bullies who tried to hurt a family of mice that Falkner was protecting. Frustrated, he decides to become as degenerate as his family and teachers have expected him to be: "I declared war with my whole soul against the world; I became all I had been painted; I was sullen, vindictive, desperate. I resolved to run away; I cared not what would befall me" (*Falkner*, 2:12). Falkner indeed becomes what he "had been painted," thus projecting the self-image that others have determined for him. Like William Godwin, Shelley asserts that society often corrupts the individual.

Fortunately, Falkner rejects that self-image upon meeting Mrs. Rivers, a childhood friend of his mother's. At her home, he experiences the love and warmth he had never known, and there he meets her daughter, Alithea, whom he quickly idolizes. Insecure and desperate for approval, he exchanges one set of great expectations for another, and although the new ones are commendable, Falkner's fanatical adherence to them is not. No longer the rebel, he determines to conform to society's ideal of a worthy, promising gentleman. When Mrs. Rivers arranges for Falkner to attend a military school, he resolves to make good the faith that she and Alithea have in him. The profession of soldier, he decides, is a role that will ensure their and society's approbation:

> My determination was to enlist as a soldier; I believed that I should so distinguish myself by my valour, as speedily to become a great man. I saw myself singled out by the generals, applauded, honoured, and rewarded. I fancied my return, and how proudly I should present myself before Alithea, having carved out my own fortune, and become all that her sweet mother entreated me to be—brave, generous, and true. (2:26)

Falkner envisions a heroic future and easily imagines a dramatic scenario of his life. He will be "singled out" and honored, and his reward will be Alithea's hand and an idyllic life. With "generous ambition and ardent gratitude," Falkner departs for school, striving to assure himself of his motivation, and his theatrical references suggest his view that life is a stage on which to play this desired role:

> The drama of life, methought, was unrolling before me, the scene on which I was to act appeared resplendent in fairy and gorgeous colours; neither vanity, nor pride, swelled me up; but a desire to prove myself worthy of those adored beings who were all the world to me, who had saved me from myself, to restore me to the pure and happy shelter of their hearts. (2:29)

Although Falkner's intent is a worthy one, his motivation is based on an image and idealization of life, not on personal inclination or realism. His desire to achieve fame and glory is prompted by a desperation to demonstrate the worthiness of the only love he has known. Once he has done so, the "drama of life" will conclude with his union to Alithea, and as a sentimental hero, his virtue will surely be rewarded.

Mary Shelley again denounces primogeniture: Mr. Rivers derides

Falkner's station as the son of a second son, despite the young man's having attained a respectable career. Once again, Falkner leaves, this time for India to make his fortune and to achieve the status that will meet with Rivers's approval. Ten years later, learning that he is unexpectedly the heir to the family estate, he returns to England, assuming that, having overcome the barriers of poverty and station, he will marry Alithea. At last his dream will be realized, and he again invents a scenario that depicts not only his romantic ideal but also his reward as a respectable member of society: "My imagination had created home, and bride, and fair beings sprung from her side, who called me father" (2:46). Unfortunately, his vivid imagination creates a world that can never exist for him; it is a vision with no basis in reality. As he ruefully notes later, "Living in a dream, I had not considered the chances and the storms, or even the mere changes, of the seasons of life. . . . I had lived in a fool's paradise" (2:45). Falkner returns to find Alithea married to Sir Boyville, a man unworthy of her. Subsequently, his dream becomes a nightmare: "One word defaced my whole future life and widowed me for ever" (2:46). He has so convinced himself of the domestic drama he has envisioned with Alithea and children that its failure to materialize has widowed him before he is even married.

Desperate, Falkner conceives a plan to reconstruct his life: "Now began that chain of incidents that led to a deed I had not thought of. Incidents or accidents; acts, done I know not why; nothing in themselves; but meeting, and kindled by the fiery spirit that raged in my bosom, they gave such direction to its ruinous powers, as produced the tragedy for ever to be deplored" (2:46). Once again, Falkner finds that his efforts to accommodate social customs and manners and to realize his romantic quest for happiness fail miserably. Up to this point in his narrative, we have readily sympathized with Falkner. He has performed all the proper acts expected by society in order to assume a respected position in it, yet he is still denied his reward. We might have continued to sympathize and to admire him had he quietly abandoned a dream whose fulfillment could only destroy others' happiness. However, he does not. Instead, he substitutes the social construct of a successful, titled suitor with a fictional one of a romance hero saving his love from an unhappy marriage. Like Charlotte Lennox, Shelley suggests that such a plot is well and good for a romance epic, but it is too often disastrous when enacted in real life, especially if motivated more by self-interest than sympathy.

Initially, Falkner does not plan to abduct Alithea against her will; he merely wants to convince her to take her two children, Gerard and an infant daughter, and run away with him. Struggling with his bitterness toward society and with his passion for Alithea, he realizes that "surely there is no greater enemy to virtue and good intentions, than the want of self-command" (2:71). He decides not to coerce her, recognizing that true heroism requires neither theatrics or egocentric playacting: "For a moment I had become virtuous and heroic" (ibid.). But passions overtake him, and he forces Alithea into the carriage, as his overly excited accomplice, Osborne, drives off before the child Gerard can get in with his mother. Alithea falls into a faint, both from astonishment at Falkner's actions and from horror at having been separated from Gerard, who runs down the road after the carriage crying for his mother. Falkner cannot fathom the extent of Alithea's love for her children despite her earlier informing him that the name "mother" is more dear to her than that of "wife" (2:64). Despondent already that his long-held dream to marry her cannot become reality, he is again shocked that primal maternal instinct is greater than romantic love. Falkner once again bitterly experiences the illusion of romance with Alithea's accidental drowning: he was to have been her savior, not her executioner. After her death, Falkner imagines the scene of Alithea awakening in the cottage and her futile effort to escape: "I saw it all; and how often, and for ever, do I go over in my thoughts what had passed during the interval of my absence" (2:81). Reliving the scene time and time again reinforces his guilt, but it never prompts him to absolve Alithea, even when he hears the slanderous version Sir Boyville has concocted. He aptly acts the part of the Byronic figure but is unable to achieve real heroism. Instead, he slips into an increasingly debilitating despondency that intensifies his self-victimization.

Although Mary Shelley claimed that fidelity was her last novel's theme, the text also warns that a passion ungoverned by reason ultimately destroys one's hopes and dreams. For Falkner, the passion is love for a married woman. Early in the novel, the narrator remarks on Falkner's inability to control his emotions: "All his life he had cherished a secret and ardent passion, beyond whose bounds every thing was sterile—this had changed from the hopes of love to the gnawing pangs of remorse—but still his heart fed on itself—and unless that was interested, and by the force of affection he were called out of himself, he must be miserable" (1:59). That passion, of course, is for Alithea. Falkner's love is not the self-sacrificing or disinterested one that Alithea and Elizabeth Raby possess but an obsessive one fed first by his desperate attempts to enact socially prescribed roles and then by a self-produced image of a romance hero whose daring deeds will earn him the reward of his heart's desire. Even Elizabeth's redemptive love cannot lift Falkner out of his despair. After the failed suicide attempt in the Cornwall cemetery, Falkner immerses himself in caring for Elizabeth, but he cannot forget the past or forgive himself. Watching Falkner, the narrator tells us, one notes "his piercing eyes fixed in vacancy, as if it beheld there a heart-moving tragedy" (1:158).

As in *Lodore*, Shelley reinforces her condemnation of hypocritical role-playing in her depiction of supporting characters. Sir Boyville, who earlier had so willingly denounced his wife in order to protect his own image, decides to have Falkner tried as the murderer of an innocent woman. The publicity, he believes, will not only destroy Falkner but also elevate his own character and elicit sympathy for him as a wronged husband cheated of a wife. Unfortunately for Boyville, the trial, a theatrical production in itself, strips away everyone's mask and reveals the true character. Boyville realizes his own culpability and dies a broken but penitent man. It is also during the trial that Falkner fully comprehends how such incidents or accidents, well-intentioned though they may have been, lead to unwanted spectacle:

> He was, indeed, thinking of things more painful than even the present scene; the screams and struggles of the agonized Alithea—her last sad sleep in the hut upon the shore—the strangling, turbid waves—her wet, lifeless form— her low, unnamed grave dug by him: had these been atoned for by long years of remorse and misery, or was the present ignominy, and worse that might ensue, fitting punishment? (2:278)

Mary Shelley leaves the question to the reader. Although Falkner is exonerated of the murder charge, he will carry his sentence until death. After the trial, he reflects, "The purity of his honour was tarnished" (2:290). In response to a similar situation in Eliza Fenwick's *Secresy*, Caroline Ashburn writes, "Fatal end of an ungoverned passion—virtuous in its object, but vicious in its excess."[19] Both Boyville and Falkner tragically realize the import of this observation too late to change the course of events that led to their misery.

Another character who is drawn to playing roles is Gerard Neville, whose determination to discover the truth contributes significantly to Falkner's confession. Elizabeth Raby draws a parallel between Gerard and Shakespeare's Hamlet: just as Hamlet exalts and exonerates his father, so Gerard tries to clear and elevate his mother's name. He is indeed very much like Hamlet; he is moody and introspective and, though wanting to take action, inclined to wait and watch; "I am tied," he confesses when Sir Boyville implements his plan to publicize Falkner's crime, "forced to inaction—the privilege of free action taken from me" (*Falkner* 2:143). When his mother's body is exhumed, Gerard nearly throws himself into the grave, paralleling Hamlet's reaction to Ophelia's death. Elizabeth's apt comparison of Gerard to Hamlet is one that Gerard himself is quite conscious of:

> "I have read that play," said Neville, "till each word seems instinct with a message direct to my heart—as if my own emotions gave a conscious soul to every line. Hamlet was called upon to avenge a father—in execution of his task he did not spare a dearer, a far more sacred name—if he used no daggers with his mother, he spoke them; nor winced though she writhed beneath his hand. Mine is a lighter—yet holier duty. I would vindicate a mother—without judging my father—without any accusation against him, I would establish her innocence. Is this blameable?" (1:181)

Shelley would agree that such a reaction is not "blameable"; however, likening events to a dramatic work is dangerous if one tries to construct, or reconstruct, reality according to a literary representation of life. Despite his determination for revenge, as revealed in the above passage, Gerard cannot avenge his mother's death in any bloody fashion once he contemplates Falkner's narrative. Initially, he plans to challenge Falkner to a duel: "He ended the tale, and he thought—"Yes, there is but one termination to this tragedy; I must avenge my sweet mother, and by the death of Falkner, proclaim her innocence'" (2:121). However, he stops short of extending the dramatic analogy to its completion. Gerard is moved by Falkner's story and is convinced of its truth. Furthermore, his love for Elizabeth prevents him from taking the life of the only man she has known as a father. Although he experiences some of Hamlet's indecisiveness, Gerard eventually asserts himself in opposition to his father's plan to create a public spectacle by making Falkner stand trial.

If Falkner, Sir Boyville, and, to some extent, Gerard depict the dangers of privileged social manners and literary heroes, Elizabeth Raby represents the alternative. Herself a victim of unfortunate circumstance, she never attempts in turn to victimize others. She is open to meeting her father's family, the wealthy, Catholic Rabys, despite their having disowned him for marrying his poor, Protestant mother. She remains faithful to Falkner throughout the worst of his dark moods and during the ordeal of the trial. However, she never adopts roles herself and, while always adhering to propriety, does not let any manners of society dictate her actions. The analogy Gerard draws between himself and Hamlet prompts Elizabeth to reread Shakespeare's tragedy:

> She was soon buried, not only in the interest of the drama itself, but in the various emotions it excited by the association it now bore to one she loved more even than she knew. It was nothing strange that Neville, essentially a

dreamer and a poet, should have identified himself with the Prince of Denmark; while the very idea that he took to himself, and acted on sentiments thus high-souled and pure, adorned him yet more in her eyes, endowing him in ample measure with that ideality which the young and noble love to bestow on the objects of their attachment. (1:186)

Although she is caught up as a spectator of a drama unfolding rapidly before her bewildered eyes, Elizabeth refrains from playing roles in it. She may draw parallels between real life and fictional/dramatic people; however, she does not equate them or expect events to play out as a Shakespearean tragedy. She has a firm grasp on the realities of life and a pragmatic rather than idealistic outlook. Elizabeth, like Ethel Lodore, is more concerned with real life than with theatricality. She possesses neither an obsessive, dramatic sensibility nor a debilitating subjectivity. When Falkner reads about historic heroes, his reaction to literature is to reconstruct the events according to his perspective; in contrast, Elizabeth's is to contemplate them and learn from them: "When they read of the heroes of old, or the creations of the poets, she dwelt on the moral to be deduced, the theories of life and earth, religion and virtue, therein displayed; while he compared them to his own experience, criticized their truth, and gave pictures of real human nature, either contrasting with, or resembling, those presented on the written page" (1:161–62). Like the dark, Romantic figures in Gothic novels such as Charles Maturin's *Melmoth the Wanderer* or William Godwin's *Caleb Williams*, Falkner can see only the weak or malevolent side of humanity; guiltless, Elizabeth recognizes the duality of human nature and accepts it. He confuses the boundaries between life and art; she may use dramatic analogies, but she always distinguishes metaphor from life.

In both *Lodore* and *Falkner*, Mary Shelley drew on the conventions of the novel of manners and sentiment to expose the artificiality of social roles that often adversely affect one's ability to modify "great expectations" to the exigencies of reality. Although Shelley offers typically happy endings to the trials endured by the characters of *Lodore* and *Falkner*, the warning message is not diffused by the end result: donning masks and playing roles on a public stage can compromise the private self and the ability to see beyond social facades. As the narrator of *Falkner* remarks, "there are moments when the future, with all its contingencies and possibilities, becomes glaringly distinct to our foreseeing eye; and we act as if that was, which we believe must be" (1:288). A "foreseeing eye" can easily misrepresent reality when it lacks objectivity and a sympathetic sensibility; too readily we "act" or enact a role to promote self-interest and to ensure a socially validated image. Not an explicit moralist, Mary Shelley nonetheless depicts in her last two novels the debilitating and often tragic results of social theatrics as she indicts the society and the individuals who privilege manners over morals.

Notes

The Letters of Mary Wollstonecraft Shelley, 3 vols., ed. Betty T. Bennett (Baltimore, Md.: Johns Hopkins University Press, 1980–83), are cited parenthetically in the text as Letters.

References to Mary Shelley's Lodore (New York: Wallis & Wallis, 1835) are cited parenthetically in the text as Lodore.

Parenthetical citations in the text to Falker refer to the original two-volume American edition, published in New York in 1837 by Saunders and Otley.

1. Frankenstein was published in 1818; The Last Man, in 1826; Valperga; or the Life and Adventures of Castruccio, Prince of Lucca, in 1823; and The Fortunes of Perkin Warbeck, in 1830. Shelley's second major work, Mathilda, was written in 1819 but remained unpublished until 1959.

2. Several of Shelley's tales and short stories, however, do incorporate conventions of domestic, sentimental fiction. See, for example, "The Mourner" (1823), "The Trial of Love" (1834), and "The Parvenue" (1836), in Mary Shelley: Collected Tales and Stories, ed. Charles E. Robinson (Baltimore, Md.: Johns Hopkins University Press, 1976).

3. The "radical" philosophies and concerns of her parents, Mary Wollstonecraft and William Godwin, had long lost their initial appeal among even the literati. Although her husband, Percy Bysshe Shelley, was still admired as a poet, his character remained blemished by his political writings and by the often exaggerated stories of his life.

4. Shelley experienced difficulties in getting Lodore published. Bentley's and Colburn's literary agent, Charles Ollier (who had been Percy Shelley's publisher), questioned if the novel were long enough for the three-volume format. Then the printers lost two packets of manuscripts that Shelley had sent them. In letters to Ollier on 4 and 30 April 1833, Shelley revealed her frustration with having to rewrite the missing pages from memory, as she had no copies (Letters, 2:200–202). Although printed as early as August 1834, Lodore was not published until nine months later; see the 19 August 1834 letter to Maria Gisborne in which Shelley writes that Lodore was finally printed (2:213).

5. Leigh Hunt, review of Lodore, London Journal 58 (6 May 1835): 138–39.

6. Initially, Shelley was hesitant to begin another novel. She was busy researching and writing biographies for Dr. Dionysius Lardner's Cyclopaedia, whose volume 3, Lives of the Most Eminent Literary and Scientific Men of Italy, Spain and Portugal, was published in November 1837 by Longman, Orme, Brown, Green, and John Taylor of London. Furthermore, she nursed her father prior to his death in 1836. However, she changed her mind about writing the novel and, in a letter to Ollier a few months later, wrote, "I began to reflect on the subject—and a story presented itself so vividly to my mind that I began to write almost directly—and have finished one volume—the whole will be ready in the Autumn. It is in the style of Lodore, but the story more interesting & even, I should think,

more popular" (*Letters*, 2:263). She later admitted to Leigh Hunt that *Falkner* was "a favourite of mine" (*Letters*, 2:285).

7. Emily Sunstein, *Mary Shelley: Romance and Reality* (Boston: Little, Brown, 1989), 334.

8. *Monthly Review* 1:3 (March 1837): 376–80. Critics for *The Athenæum, Literary Gazette*, and *Monthly Repository* were others who recommended the novel. See W. H. Lyles, *Mary Shelley: An Annotated Bibliography* (New York: Garland, 1975), 181–83.

9. One study that offers a noncondescending reading of these works is Katherine Hill-Miller's *"My Hideous Progeny": Mary Shelley, William Godwin, and the Father-Daughter Relationship* (Newark: University of Delaware Press, 1995). There are no modern editions of the two novels other than *The Novels and Selected Works of Mary Shelley*, an eight-volume Pickering Masters Series edited by Nora Crook (Brookfield, Vt.: Pickering and Chatto, 1996). *Lodore* is volume 6; *Falkner*, volume 7.

10. Most readers will be familiar with *Paradise Lost*'s Eve, *The Tempest*'s Miranda, and *Don Juan*'s Haidèe. Gertrude is the title character of Campbell's narrative poem *Gertrude of Wyoming* (1809) and is the most immediate source for Shelley's reference.

11. Lodore's and Cornelia's circumstances are similar to those of the husband and wife in Kotzebue's *Menschenhass und Reue*, which Richard Brinsley Sheridan brought to the English stage in 1798 as *The Stranger*. Shelley records Kotzebue's autobiographical work *Das merkwüdigste Jahr meines Lebens* (1801) in her 1815 reading list (*Journals of Mary Shelley*, 2 vols., ed. Paula Feldman and Diana Scott-Kilvert [Oxford: Clarendon Press, 1987], 1:90). However, it is not known if she had been familiar with this particular play. German tragedies notwithstanding, the bizarre and unforeseen situation of Cornelia and Lodore also resembles those in English Gothic plays of the period; for example, see Joanna Baillie's *De Montfort* (1798).

12. Clorinda is quite likely modeled after Emilia Viviani, who was also in a convent (awaiting an unhappy marriage) and whose beauty and plight captured Percy Shelley's interest and sympathy in 1820. She is a variation of the title character in Mary Shelley's 1824 short story "The Bride of Modern Italy," also named Clorinda.

13. Edward, whose dissolute father has squandered the family fortune, is serving a prison sentence, and he and Ethel share a shabby apartment in the prison section of London.

14. Hill-Miller, *"My Hideous Progeny,"* 159.

15. *Hamlet*, 1.3.82–84.

16. Falkner recorded this narrative several years prior to Elizabeth's reading it. Like Lord Raymond of *The Last Man*, he left England to fight for Greece, hoping to die a hero and thus expiate his guilt and redeem his reputation.

17. Hill-Miller, *"My Hideous Progeny,"* 191.

18. James Hogg, *The Private Memoirs and Confessions of a Justified Sinner* (1824; rprt., London: Penguin, 1983).

19. Fenwick, *Secresy*, 298.

Part 4
A Bibliographical Update

Mary Shelley's Other Fiction:
A Bibliographical Census

Frederick S. Frank

Mary Shelley's "other" fiction, the approximately forty tales, six novels, and four plays written after *Frankenstein* (1818), has long been regarded as either a mere biographical appendix to her equivocal relationship with Shelley, Byron, and Godwin or an index to her deviation from Romantic ideals. When read at all, the post-*Frankenstein* novels and tales were dismissed as artistically inferior and worthy of study solely for the ways in which they could illuminate her single work of genuine genius, her mythic novel of miscreation. In his *History of the English Novel*, Ernest Baker expressed the conventional view of the ineptitude of *Perkin Warbeck*, *Lodore*, *Falkner*, and *Valperga* and extended his negative assessment to *The Last Man*, the only post-*Frankenstein* novel to maintain an audience in the twentieth century. Wrote Baker: "The few living people who have read these novels agree that they are painstaking, not incorrect but devoid of historical imagination, too often grandiloquent, and generally dull."[1] Similar strictures were leveled against the short stories, even by critical proponents of *Frankenstein*. In 1972, William Walling opened his chapter on Mary Shelley's "other" fiction in the Twayne English Authors Series by warning the reader that "aside from her first three novels, little of Mary's fiction repays attention"[2] and by relegating the entire post-*Frankenstein* canon to a subsidiary position. Such dismissive attitudes persisted until the early 1980s, when three trends in criticism and literary taste gave a new impetus to an interest in a substantial body of writing done after *Frankenstein*.

The first trend was the consequence of shifting theoretical perspectives. The new historicist, feminist, and postmodernist critical methods and Lacanian and Derridian models rendered Mary Shelley's entire corpus readable again not only for its ideological content but as autonomous literary achievements that were not necessarily eclipsed by *Frankenstein*. A second trend, the expansion and proliferation of Gothic studies, made other works by the creator of the protomonster novel attractive objects of study in the context of the terror tradition. Third, Mary Shelley's legitimate place and contribution to the science fiction genre could certainly be argued by cultural historians on the basis of much of her short fiction as well as *Frankenstein*. In his bibliographical essay on Mary Shelley criticism in *The English Gothic: A Bibliographic Guide to Writers from Horace Walpole to Mary Shelley* (1983), Robert D. Spector recognized these trends.

> Increased interest in Gothic novels and science fiction and greater emphasis on feminist studies have made Mary Shelley an important literary figure, but there are still critical and scholarly works that reflect the earlier attitude expressed by Richard Garnett's account in the *Dictionary of National Biography* which describes her life and writing in terms of her parentage and marriage.[3]

With the publication in 1993 of Jane Blumberg's *Mary Shelley's Early Novels*[4] and the critical anthology edited by Audrey A. Fisch, Anne K. Mellor, and Esther Schor, *The Other Mary Shelley: Beyond Frankenstein*, the period of neglect had clearly ended. Mary Shelley was now seen as "an independent artist of complexity and depth"[5] whose philosophic achievement could only be comprehended by going "beyond *Frankenstein*."

The present bibliography graphs these shifts in opinion toward the total Shelley canon and directs the user to modern primary and secondary sources relevant to further study of the entire post-*Frankenstein* canon of tales and novels. The bibliography also documents the gaps and lacunae in the field, although these gaps are rapidly being closed. Two tales, "Hate" and "Maurice," remain lost, and the possibility exists that other signed, unsigned, or pseudonymous pieces remain interred in the keepsakes and annuals.[6] Eleven stories originally appearing in various periodicals have never been reprinted. Among the longer works, the mythological dramas *Midas* and *Proserpine* and the novels *Perkin Warbeck* and *The Last Man* now have reliable scholarly texts. Additionally, 1996 saw the publication of *The Novels and Selected Works of Mary Shelley* in eight volumes of the Pickering Masters Series under the general editorship of Nora Crook and Pamela Clemit.[7]

To achieve maximum usefulness, the bibliography should be scrutinized in its entirety and consulted in tandem with the critical essays in this volume. The three segments of the bibliography are self-explanatory, with some overlapping and intersection. The middle section, "The Prose Canon," arranges all the titles of the novels and tales in alphabetical order to facilitate identification. The user who wishes to conduct further investigation should also be aware that the Lord Abinger Collection of Shelleyana in the Bodleian Library contains extensive unpublished material, such as page fragments from the unpublished story "Cecil."

The scholarly reprintings of many of the short stories in anthologies edited by Charles E. Robinson and Betty T. Bennett[8] have now awakened readers to the fact that Mary Shelley was a highly active participant in the world of letters up until her death in 1851. Her many unique fictional contributions to the annuals and her intelligent activity as a novelist reveal not a reclusive Victorian scribbler but a working author who thought of herself as a career writer rather than a the creator of a single sensational book. This is the full and true portrait of the artist that the present collection of essays and this bibliography endeavor to rediscover and restore.

Key to Abbreviations

Abensour, *L'Endeuillée et autres récits,* refers to Liliane Abensour, trans., *L'Endeuillée et autres récits* [The mourner and other tales] (Paris: José Corti, 1993).

Aldiss, "Origin," refers to Brian Aldiss, "Mary Shelley: The Origin of the Species," in *Billion Year Spree: The True History of Science Fiction* (Garden City, N.Y.: Doubleday, 1973); rprt., *Extrapolation* 14 (1973): 186–89; rprt., "Part One: Out of the Gothic; On the Origin of the Species: Mary Shelley," in *Trillion Year Spree: The History of Science Fiction* (New York: Athenæum, 1986), 46–50.

Alexander, *Women in Romanticism,* refers to Meena Alexander, *Women in Romanticism: Mary Wollstonecraft, Dorothy Wordsworth, and Mary Shelley* (Savage, Md.: Barnes & Noble, 1989).

Clemit, *The Godwinian Novel,* refers to Pamela Clemit, *The Godwinian Novel: The Rational Fictions of Godwin, Brockden Brown, Mary Shelley* (Oxford, U.K.: Clarendon Press, 1993).

CT refers to *Mary Shelley: Collected Tales and Stories,* edited by Charles E. Robinson (Baltimore, Md.: Johns Hopkins University Press, 1976).

El-Shater, *The Novels of Mary Shelley,* refers to Safaa El-Shater, *The Novels of Mary Shelley,* Salzburg Studies in English Literature 59

(Salzburg, Austria: Institut für Englische Sprache und Literatur, Universität Salzburg, 1977).

Gilbert & Gubar, *Norton Anthology*, refers to Sandra W. Gilbert and Susan Gubar, eds., *Norton Anthology of Literature by Women* (New York: W. W. Norton, 1989).

Grylls, *Mary Shelley*, refers to R[osalie] Glynn Grylls, *Mary Shelley* (London, New York, Toronto: Oxford University Press, 1938).

Haining, *Gothic Tales of Terror*, refers to Peter Haining, ed., *Gothic Tales of Terror: Classic Horror Stories from Great Britain, Europe and the United States, 1765–1840* (New York: Taplinger, 1972).

Hill-Miller, *My Hideous Progeny*, refers to Katherine Hill-Miller, *My Hideous Progeny: Mary Shelley, William Godwin, and the Father-Daughter Relationship* (Newark, Del.: Delaware University Press; London and Cranbury, N.J.: Associated University Presses, 1994).

Mary Shelley's Early Novels refers to Jane Blumberg, *Mary Shelley's Early Novels: "This Child of Imagination and Misery"* (Iowa City: University of Iowa Press, 1993).

MSR refers to *The Mary Shelley Reader*, edited by Betty T. Bennett and Charles E. Robinson (New York: Oxford University Press, 1990).

Nitchie, *Mary Shelley*, refers to Elizabeth Nitchie, *Mary Shelley–Author of "Frankenstein"* (New Brunswick, N.J.; Rutgers University Press, 1953); rprt., Westport, Conn.: Greenwood Press, 1970.

Nochimson, "Mary Wollstonecraft Shelley," refers to Martha Nochimson, "Mary Wollstonecraft Shelley," in *Critical Survey of Long Fiction*, ed. Frank Magill (Englewood Cliffs, N.J.: Salem Press, 1983), 2385–95.

Norton, *Masters of Horror*, refers to Alden H. Norton, ed., *Masters of Horror* (New York: A Berkley Medallion Book, 1968).

The Other Mary Shelley: Beyond Frankenstein refers to the work by that name edited by Audrey A. Fisch, Anne K. Mellor, and Esther H. Schor (New York: Oxford University Press, 1993).

Palacio, *Mary Shelley dans son oeuvre*, refers to Jean de Palacio, *Mary Shelley dans son oeuvre: contribution aux études Shelleyennes* (Paris: Klincksieck, 1969).

The Parent's Offering refers to *The Parent's Offering: Or, Interesting Tales for Youths of Both Sexes* (London: Baldwin and Cradock, 1829).

Richardson, "*Proserpine* and *Midas*," refers to Alan Richardson, "*Proserpine* and *Midas*: Gender, Genre, and Mythic Revisionism in Mary Shelley's Dramas," in *The Other Mary Shelley: Beyond Frankenstein*.

Roberts, "Mary Shelley," refers to Marie Roberts, "Mary Shelley and the Mortal Immortal: 'Transformation' and 'The Evil Eye,'" in *Gothic*

Immortals: The Fiction of the Brotherhood of the Rosy Cross (New York: Routledge, 1990).

Robinson & Bennett, *The Bodleian Shelley Manuscripts*, refers to Charles E. Robinson and Betty T. Bennett, eds., *The Bodleian Shelley Manuscripts. Volume X. Mary Wollstonecraft Shelley. Mythological Dramas: Proserpine and Midas. Relation of the Death of the Family of Cenci* (New York: Garland, 1992; Brookfield, Vt.: Pickering & Chatto, 1996, ed. Nora Crook).

Sayers, *Great Stories,* refers to Dorothy L. Sayers, ed., *Great Stories of Detection, Mystery, and Horror* (London: Victor Gollancz, 1931).

Skarda & Jaffe, *The Evil Image,* refers to Patricia L. Skarda and Nora Crow Jaffe, eds., *The Evil Image: Two Centuries of Gothic Fiction and Poetry* (New York: New American Library, 1981).

Spark, *Mary Shelley*, refers to Muriel Spark, *Mary Shelley—A Biography* (New York: E. P. Dutton, 1987; London: Cardinal, 1989).

Spector, *Seven Masterpieces*, refers to Robert D. Spector, *Seven Masterpieces of Gothic Horror* (New York: Bantam Books, 1963).

Sunstein, *Mary Shelley,* refers to Emily Sunstein, *Mary Shelley: Romance and Reality* (Boston: Little, Brown, 1989).

Thompson, *Romantic Gothic Tales*, refers to G. R. Thompson, ed., *Romantic Gothic Tales, 1790–1840* (New York: Harper & Row, 1979).

Veeder, *Mary Shelley and Frankenstein*, refers to William Veeder, "Appendix B: Plot Summaries of Mary Shelley's Novels After 1818," in *Mary Shelley and Frankenstein: The Fate of Androgyny* (Chicago: University of Chicago Press, 1986), 223–24.

Walling, *Mary Shelley*, refers to William A. Walling, *Mary Shelley*, TEAS number 128 (New York: Twayne; 1972).

Williams, *The Lifted Veil*, refers to A. Susan Williams, ed., *The Lifted Veil: The Book of Fantastic Literature by Women, 1800–World War II* (New York: Carroll & Graf, 1992).

Collections, Editions, and Anthologies
Containing Mary Shelley's Short Fiction

Abensour, *L'Endeuillée et autres récits.* A French translation of selected tales, including "The Mourner," "The Mortal Immortal," and "The Parvenue."

MSR. Contains the tales "Recollections of Italy," "The Bride of Modern Italy," "Roger Dodsworth: The Reanimated Englishman," "The False

Rhyme," "Transformation," "The Dream," and "The Mortal Immortal: A Tale"; *Frankenstein;* and selected essays, reviews, and letters. The stated purpose of the collection is to "advance a contextual reading of Mary Shelley so that we may better understand her masterpiece, the author her-self, and the multifaceted Romanticism that extends from her time to ours" (Introduction, 10).

Garnett, Richard, ed. *Tales and Stories by Mary Wollstonecraft Shelley—Now First Collected.* Introduction by Richard Garnett. London: William Paterson, 1891. Collects and prints seventeen Mary Shelley tales for the first time since their periodical publication. Garnett's anthology is a bibliophile's labor of love specifically intended to apprise readers of her literary genius in the art of the short story and to reveal "a lonely, thwarted, misunderstood woman ... whose precise place in the contemporary constellation of genius remains to be determined" (Introduction, xi).

Gilbert & Gubar, *Norton Anthology.* Contains one Mary Shelley story, "The Mortal Immortal."

Haining, Peter, ed. *The Gentlewomen of Evil: An Anthology of Rare Supernatural Stories from the Pens of Victorian Ladies.* London: Robert Hale, 1967. Reprint, New York: Taplinger, 1967. Among the thirteen tales is Mary Shelley's "Transformation."

———, *Gothic Tales of Terror.* Prints Mary Shelley's story "The Dream," "a fine example of the Gothic romance story dating from the hey-day of the genre." Believes that Mary Shelley was most at home in the short-story form.

Norton, *Masters of Horror.* Contains one Mary Shelley story, "Transformation."

CT. The authoritative edition of Mary Shelley's post-*Frankenstein* prose fiction. Contains twenty-five stories and nineteen plates. Printed for the first time since their periodical publication are "The Bride of Modern Italy," "The Trial of Love," and "An Eighteenth-Century Tale: A Fragment." Also prints two newly discovered stories, "Roger Dodsworth: The Reanimated Englishman" and "The Smuggler and his Family." Of the general characteristics of the tales, Robinson notes that they offer the reader "graphic incident, realistic dialogue, and an ironic point of view. ... It is also possible to read Mary Shelley's fictions as idealiza-tions of her own life" (Introduction, xiv). Robinson's notes on each story provide sources, publication history, and critical observations.

Russ, Joanna, ed. *Tales and Stories.* Boston: Gregg; Boston: G. K. Hall, 1975. A modern edition of the 1891 Garnett edition of Mary Shel-ley's short fiction with introduction. Russ believes that modern Gothics such as Daphne Du Maurier's *Rebecca* descend from Mary Shelley's vision of woman.

Sayers, *Great Stories*. Contains one Mary Shelley story, "The Mortal Immortal."

Skarda & Jaffe, *The Evil Image*. Prints Mary Shelley's short story "Transformation."

Spector, *Seven Masterpieces*. The first modern printing of "The Heir of Mondolfo," a story in which "the castle itself has ceased to be the location of the action; the supernatural has been reduced to the terrors of the weather, and both sentimental and didactic interests are egalitarian rather than aristocratic" (332).

Thompson, *Romantic Gothic Tales*. Contains Mary Shelley's short story "Transformation."

Williams, *The Lifted Veil*. Contains Mary Shelley's story "The Mortal Immortal."

The Prose Canon:
Mary Shelley's Tales, Novels, and Dramas

"The Bride of Modern Italy"
Type: short story (unsigned)
First Printing: *London Magazine* 9 (April 1824): 357–63.
Modern Editions: *CT*, 32–42; *MSR*, 263–73.
Criticism:
Donner, H. W., ed. *The Works of Thomas Lovell Beddoes*, 586. London: Oxford University Press, 1935. A Beddoes letter to Thomas Forbes Kelsall attributes this unsigned story to Mary Shelley, the sole basis for Mary's authorship.
Nitchie, *Mary Shelley*, 64–66, 132–34. The character of Clorinda Saviani is a mixture of Harriet Westbrook and Emilia Viviani, while Marcott Alleyn, the young English go-between, is "a more earthy Shelley."
CT, 376–77. The character of Clorinda is modeled on Emilia Viviani. Together with skillful transposition of autobiographical detail, the story has "precise description and unity of plot."
Sunstein, *Mary Shelley*, 254–55. This realistic story is "Mary's version of Shelley's romance with Emilia Viviani."

"The Brother and Sister, An Italian Story"
  Type: short story
  First Printing: *The Keepsake for MDCCCXXXIII* [1833], 105–41.
    London: Longman, Rees, Orme, Brown, Green, 1832.
  Modern Editions: *CT*, 166–89.
  Criticism:
    CT, 385–88. Describes the story as "a sophisticated study of a
      young girl's idealization of her brother."
    Sunstein, *Mary Shelley*, 174. Comments on the father-daughter
      conflict in several stories.

"Cecil"
  Type: novella (unfinished in manuscript)
  First Printing: none. Manuscript (c. 1834, thirty-three pages) in the
    Abinger Collection, Bodleian Library.
  Criticism:
    Sunstein, *Mary Shelley*, 327, 449. "Cecil" is an unfinished chil-
      dren's story. Mary Shelley's critique of the English public school
      system may be seen in the attitudes of Cecil's mother.

"The Choice. A Poem on Shelley's Death"
  Type: poetic narrative or short story in verse written in July 1823.
  Modern Editions: H. Buxton Foreman, ed. London: Printed for the
    Editor for Private Distribution, 1876.
  Criticism:
    Sunstein, *Mary Shelley*, 239. Refers to the long autobiographical
      poem as reflective of Mary Shelley's resolve "never again to fail
      to express her affections." She reproached herself for her cold-
      ness in the lines, "My heart was all thine own,—but yet a shell
      closed in its core."
    Veeder, *Mary Shelley and Frankenstein*, 164. Mary Shelley charac-
      terizes herself as "impenetrable" and is honest about her own
      will to power.

"The Clouds; A Dream"
  Type: short story (unsigned)
  First Printing: *London Magazine* 8 (November 1823): 482–84.
  Modern Editions: Grylls, *Mary Shelley*.
  Criticism:
    Sunstein, *Mary Shelley*, 247–48. Describes the story as "an amusing
      tale, a spoof of London's climate and pollution, padded with
      quotations from famous authors."

"The Dream"
  Type: short story (signed by "the Author of 'Frankenstein'")
  First Printing: *The Keepsake for MDCCCXXXII* [1832], 22–38. London: Longman, Rees, Orme Brown, and Green, 1831.
  Modern Editions: Haining, *Gothic Tales of Terror*, 287–300; *CT*, 153–65; *MSR*, 301–13.
  Criticism:
    CT, 383–85. Maintains that the story derives directly from Keats's *The Eve of St. Agnes*. "Constance awakes from her night on St. Catherine's couch to choose human over divine love."
    Sunstein, *Mary Shelley*, 174. The story contains the frequent theme of conflict with the father.

"An Eighteenth-Century Tale: A Fragment"
  Type: short story (in manuscript)
  First Printing: none. Manuscript (c. 1824) in the Abinger Collection, Bodleian Library.
  Modern Editions: *CT*, 345–46.
  Criticism:
    CT, 398–99. Comments on the story's structure as "characteristic of Mary Shelley's use of a scenic frame by which to enclose a retrospective narrative."
    Sunstein, *Mary Shelley*, 164. Describes the story's style as "in a mode inspired by Boccaccio."

"The Elder Son"
  Type: short story
  First Printing: *Heath's Book of Beauty* (1835), 83–123. London: Longman, Rees, Orme, Green, 1834.
  Modern Editions: *CT*, 244–65.
  Criticism:
    Sunstein, *Mary Shelley*, 33. Assigns autobiographical identities to the characters. "The unremarried widower and his daughter in her story "The Elder Son" (1834) may well depict Mary and Godwin's relations."
    CT, 392. Mary Shelley adjusted the tone of the story for the fashionable readership of *Heath's Book of Beauty* by ruling out supernatural events and using a contemporary heroine, Ellen, who naively idealizes her father and is victimized by a false lover.

"Euphrasia: A Tale of Greece"
  Type: short story
  First Printing: *The Keepsake for MDCCCXXXIX* [1839], 135–52.
    London: Longman, Brown, Orme, Green, 1838.
  Modern Editions: *CT*, 295–307.
  Criticism:
    Nitchie, *Mary Shelley*, 126. Believes that the tale was influenced by
      Trelawny's recitation of strange tales to the group in Pisa.
    CT, 394–95. Comments on the outer frame story and the inner
      frame story with nested narrators. She chose not "to return the
      reader to the circumstances of the outer frame leaving the plight
      of the original narrator, Henry Valency, unresolved."

"The Evil Eye"
  Type: short story (signed by "the Author of 'Frankenstein'")
  First Printing: *The Keepsake for MDCCCXXX* [1830], 150–75. Lon-
    don: Hurst, Chance, 1829.
  Modern Editions: *CT*, 100–16.
  Criticism:
    Nitchie, *Mary Shelley*, 126. Notes the possible influence of
      Trelawny's strange storytelling at Pisa.
    Raitt, A. W. *Prosper Mérimée*, 375–82. New York: Charles Scrib-
      ner's Sons, 1970. Reprints Mary Shelley's review from the
      Westminster Review for January 1829 of Mérimée's tale of the
      evil eye, *La Guzla*. Notes the probable influence of the tale on
      Mary's story "The Evil Eye."
    Roberts, "Mary Shelley," 94–95. Relates the power of the evil eye
      of the Albanian wanderer, Dmitri, to Shelley's Ginotti in *St.
      Irvyne* and other Rosicrucian characters. "The supernatural
      device of the evil eye heightens the drama of a story which is
      bound up with passion and intrigue."
    CT, 379–80. Identifies the sources of the story to be Byron's *Childe
      Harold*, Thomas Hope's *Anastasius*, and Mérimée's *La Guzla*.
      "That 'The Evil Eye' was influenced by Mérimée's work is fur-
      ther suggested by Mary's translation of three of the poems in *La
      Guzla*."

Falkner. A novel
  Type: novel
  First Printing: London: Saunders and Otley, 1837.
  Modern Editions: Folcroft Library Editions, 1975; Pamela Clemit, ed.
    Brookfield, Vt.: Pickering & Chatto, 1996.

Criticism:

Blumberg, Jane. "Appendix D: The Late Novels: *Perkin Warbeck, Lodore, Falkner.*" In *Mary Shelley's Early Novels*, 216–23. Compares the character of Falkner to Falkland in Godwin's *Caleb Williams* and maintains that Mary Shelley presents a new heroine who is feminine, submissive, angelic, and conventionally virtuous. "These new women are raised onto a Victorian pedestal of dizzying height." The study is based on Blumberg's Oxford University dissertation "Mary Shelley's Early Novels," *IT* 41 (1992): 244–45.

El-Shater, "Epilogue, *Falkner.*" In *The Novels of Mary Shelley*, 156–64. The novel registers "a final decline in Mary Shelley's powers as a novelist" and her exhaustion of autobiographical sources. Falkner's character is based on Edward John Trelawny.

Hill-Miller, "*Falkner.*" In *My Hideous Progeny,* 165–201. *Falkner* was written specifically "to depict and endorse the limits of conventional womanhood and to celebrate the renunciations of motherhood." The theme of the failed father is also depicted in a daughter "who unselfishly submits herself to her father's desires and, by doing so, paradoxically gains control over him."

Nitchie, *Mary Shelley*, 122–31. Summarizes the novel and compares its hero with Byron's Manfred. Also suggests that Falkner's physique and character might be based on Trelawny, "six feet tall, with his Moorish face, his dark gray expressive eyes, telling 'strange stories of himself, horrific ones.'"

Nochimson, "Mary Wollstonecraft Shelley." Reads the work as a Gothic novel that ends happily in "the restoration of an estranged father." "The plot is a characteristic tangle of Gothic convolutions invoking old secrets and sins, obdurate Catholic families, and the pure love of a young girl."

Poovey, Mary. "Fathers and Daughters: The Trauma of Growing Up Female." *Women & Literature* 2 (1982): 39–58. A psycho-analytic reading that compares the father-daughter relationship of *Falkner* with Fanny Burney's *Evelina*.

Sunstein, *Mary Shelley*, 36–37, 333–34. Cites Mary Shelley's journal for the novel's autobiographical content. The book has "'a strong conjuring up of fictitious woes' and is uniquely revealing in painful biographical specificity."

Veeder, *Mary Shelley and Frankenstein*, 71–72, 82–83, 134–35. In the later fiction, "Suitors replace sires. Neville can replace Falkner so smoothly because he is the same character."

Walling, "Other Fictional Prose and the Verse, The Three Remaining Novels." In *Mary Shelley*, 101–9. Sees *Falkner* as Mary Shelley's commentary on Byronic egoism. "Unhappily, the complete irrelevance of Mary's concern with Byronism is revealed in the changed taste evident in the reading public of 1837."

"The False Rhyme"

Type: short story (signed by "The Author of 'Frankenstein'")

First Printing: *The Keepsake for MDCCCXXX* [1830], 265–68. London: Hurst, Chance, 1829.

Modern Editions: *CT*, 117–20; *MSR*, 283–85.

Criticism:

CT, 380–81. Considered by Robinson to be one of Mary Shelley's finest tales "successfully coordinating action and theme."

"Ferdinando Eboli: A Tale"

Type: short story (signed by "the Author of 'Frankenstein'")

First Printing: *The Keepsake for MDCCCXXIX* [1829], 195–218. London: Hurst, Chance, 1828.

Modern Editions: *CT*, 65–80.

Criticism:

CT, 378–79. Connects the tale with the Gothic tradition since "the ostensibly unique frustrations of Count Eboli have antecedents in Gothic romances where heroes are assailed by villainous twins or diabolical doppelgängers."

Sunstein, *Mary Shelley*, 289. Comments on her work for *The Keepsake*.

"The Fisher-Boy of Weymouth"

Type: attributed children's short story (signed by "C. Barnard")

First Printing: London: M. W. Juvenile Library, 1819.

Criticism:

Sunstein, *Mary Shelley*, 433. The story is reminiscent of Godwin's *Caleb Williams*.

The Fortunes of Perkin Warbeck, a Romance

Type: novel

First Printing: London: Henry Colburn and Richard Bentley, 1830.

Modern Editions: Betty T. Bennett, ed. Norwood, Pa.: Norwood Editions, 1976; Doucet Devin Fischer, ed. Brookfield, Vt.: Pickering & Chatto, 1996.

Criticism:

Bennett, Betty T. "The Political Philosophy of Mary Shelley's Historical Novels: *Valperga* and *Perkin Warbeck*." In *The Evidence of the Imagination: Studies of Interactions Between Life and Art in English Romantic Literature*, edited by Michael C. Jaye, Betty T. Bennett, Doucet Devin Fischer, and Ricki B. Herzfeld, 354–71. New York: New York University Press, 1978. Examines the political egotism and desire for power inherent in the characters of *Perkin Warbeck* (Richard IV Plantagenet) and Castruccio and compares their Napoleonic personalities to similar self-centeredness in Raymond in *The Last Man* and Victor Frankenstein. There can be no ideal social structure until human beings improve themselves.

Blumberg, Jane. "Appendix D: The Late Novels: *Perkin Warbeck, Lodore, Falkner*." In *Mary Shelley's Early Novels*, 216–23. Describes the novel as "an historical romance in the popular and lucrative style of Walter Scott." Mary Shelley believed Perkin Warbeck to be the legitimate Duke of York and legal claimant to the English throne.

Dunleavy, Gareth W. "Two New Mary Shelley Letters and the 'Irish' Chapters of *Perkin Warbeck*." *Keats-Shelley Journal* 13 (1964): 6–11. Prints two Mary Shelley letters to Thomas Crofton Croker that "divulge the source of the descriptive details used in certain chapters of the historical romance." She also sought Croker's help with Irish geography and place names.

El-Shater, "*The Fortunes of Perkin Warbeck*." In *The Novels of Mary Shelley*, 111–26. Views the historical romance as stylistically inept, "a novel that requires the reader's maximum patience to plod his or her way in the quagmire of its rambling and disconnected episodes. The truth is that historical romance was not Mary Shelley's forte."

Nitchie, *Mary Shelley*, 168–69, 206. Notes the historical accuracy of the novel based on Mary Shelley's meticulous research as she drew on Godwin and John Murray. "She had put into it more careful study than into *The Last Man* and less personal feeling than into *Valperga*."

Nochimson, "Mary Wollstonecraft Shelley." The novel is flawed by its "grandiose superfluity of expression and incident," but it "attempts to explore once more man's fruitless quest for power and glory."

Santagostino, Federica. "Storia e fiction in *Perkin Warbeck* di Mary Shelley," *Confronto Letterario: Quarderni del Dipartimento di*

Lingue e Letterature Straniere Moderne dell'Università di Pavia 11:21 (1994): 111–18. Discusses Mary Shelley's adherence to and departure from historical fact in *Perkin Warbeck*. The novel is more factual than fictive.

Spark, "*Perkin Warbeck.*" In *Mary Shelley*, 199–212. Suggests that the novel was inspired by her reading of the Waverley novels. Scrupulously researched, the novel rejects the notion of Warbeck, the pretender. "Mary Shelley's story offers the theory that Warbeck was, in fact, the younger of the princes in the Tower," Edward IV's legitimate son, and legal claimant to the English crown.

Sunstein, *Mary Shelley*, 299–300, 301, 309. Mary Shelley's belief in the legitimacy of Perkin Warbeck reflects her Romantic politics. She also defends the adultress Jane Shore, "condemns capital punishment, and obliquely declares her sympathy with current working-class protests."

Veeder, *Mary Shelley and Frankenstein*, 39–40, 161–62. Mary Shelley conformed to her androgynous ideal by balancing traditionally male and female traits in various characters.

Walling, "Other Fictional Prose and the Verse, The Three Remaining Novels." In *Mary Shelley*, 101–9. Refers to *Perkin Warbeck* as "essentially a lifeless novel although it deserves our respect for the quality of intelligence which is intermittently displayed."

"Hate"

Type: short story (lost) (c. 1814)
Criticism:

Sunstein, *Mary Shelley*, 87. Mentions that Mary Shelley began writing this lost story at Marsluys, France, in September 1814.

Veeder, *Mary Shelley and Frankenstein*, 243. Refers to this lost story in connection with Mary's generic role in Moore's *Life of Byron*.

"The Heap of Stones"

Type: attributed children's short story (signed by "Mrs. Caroline Barnard")
First Printing: *The Parent's Offering*.

"The Heir of Mondolfo"

Type: short story
First Printing: *Appleton's Journal: A Monthly Miscellany of Popular Literature* n.s. 2 (January 1877): 12–23.
Modern Editions: *CT*, 308–31; Spector, *Seven Masterpieces*, 331–61.

Criticism:

Nitchie, *Mary Shelley*, 131. Notes the possible use of Sir Timothy Shelley in Ludovico's father.

CT, 395–97. Notes that this posthumously published story was found among the papers of Leigh Hunt.

Spector, *Seven Masterpieces*, 332. The story demonstrates "one of the directions that the later Gothic took. The supernatural has been reduced to the terrors of the weather, and both sentimental and didactic interests are egalitarian rather than aristocratic."

Sunstein, *Mary Shelley*, 450. Suggests that Mary Shelley gave this story to Leigh Hunt. It turned up many years later among Hunt's papers.

"The Invisible Girl"

Type: short story (signed by "The Author of 'Frankenstein'")

First Printing: *The Keepsake for MDCCCXXXIII* [1833], 210–27. London: Longman, Rees, Orme, Brown, Green, 1832.

Modern Editions: *CT*, 190–202.

Criticism:

Nitchie, *Mary Shelley*, 131. Mary Shelley drew on the character of Sir Timothy Shelley for father figures.

CT, 389. Regards the first-person narrator as "relatively functionless" and the story itself as one of Mary Shelley's weakest pieces.

Sunstein, *Mary Shelley*, 174. Like several other tales, the story contains father-daughter conflict.

"Lacy de Vere"

Type: short story (unsigned)

First Printing: *Forget-Me-Not* for 1827, 275–94. London: Rudolf Ackermann, 1826.

The Last Man

Type: novel

First Printing: London: Henry Colburn, 1826.

Modern Editions: Muriel Spark, ed. *Child of Light: A Reassessment of Mary Wolstonecraft Shelley,* abr. ed. Hadleigh, Essex, U.K.: Tower Bridge Publications, 1951; Hugh J. Luke Jr., ed. Lincoln: Nebraska University Press, 1965. Reprint, with an introduction by Anne K. Mellor, 1993; Brian Aldiss, ed. London: Hogarth Press, 1985; Monaco: Éditions du Rocher, 1988; Morton D. Paley, ed. New York: Oxford University Press, 1994; J. Blum and Nora Crook, eds. Brookfield, Vt.: Pickering & Chatto, 1996.

Criticism:
Aaron, Jane. "The Return of the Repressed: Reading Mary Shelley's *The Last Man*." In *Feminist Criticism; Theory and Practice*, edited by Susan Sellers, Linda Hutcheon, and Paul Perron, 9–21. Toronto: Toronto University Press, 1991. Applies feminist critical theory to explore the theme of repressive patriarchy in the novel.
Aldiss, " Origin," 31–34. Views *The Last Man* as "a transitional novel," "a scientific romance," "a transposition of reality rather than a fantasy."
Aldiss, Brian. "Mary Wollstonecraft Shelley, 1797–1851." In *Science Fiction Writers: Critical Studies of the Major Authors from the Early Nineteenth Century to the Present Day*, edited by E. F. Bleiler, 3–9. New York: Charles Scribner's, 1982. A brief biocritical portrait of Mary Shelley emphasizing the importance of *Frankenstein* and *The Last Man* in the formation of the science fiction genre.
Aldiss, Brian. "Introduction." In *The Last Man*, edited by Hugh J. Luke Jr., vi–xi. Lincoln: University of Nebraska Press, 1965. Mary Shelley's novel belongs to several genres, including science fiction, futuristic and eschatological prophecy, Gothic romance, travelogue, and autobiography.
Alexander, "Femininity and Betrayal: *The Last Man*" and "Confronting Chaos: (Mary Shelley's *The Last Man*)." In *Women in Romanticism*, 155–60 and 185–91. Discusses the character contrast of Perdita and Evadne as alternative feminine role models and the thematic importance of the Drury Lane Theatre episode in *The Last Man*. "With art turned into a veritable opium for the people, true reality of poverty, wretchedness and death by the plague is masked over."
Blumberg, Jane. "'The Earth is not, nor Ever Can be Heaven': *The Last Man*." In *Mary Shelley's Early Novels*, 114–55. Sees *The Last Man* as reflective of Mary Shelley's loneliness and intellectual independence from the memories and subservience to Shelley and Byron. "*The Last Man* is in some sense a tribute to Shelley but it is an ironic one, an unmistakable swipe at Shelley's most cherished ideal."
Clemit. "*The Last Man*, Mary Shelley's Novels of the 1820s: History and Prophecy." In *The Godwinian Novel*, 183–210. Mary Shelley made "an innovative contribution to the Godwinian tradition in *The Last Man*. The narrator is faced with the impossibility of controlling history, society, or nature, and this

dwarfing of the individual is central to the plot's oppressive imaginative power."

Dingley, R. J. "An Allusion in Hazlitt." *Notes & Queries* n.s. 30 (1983): 229–30. Suggests *The Last Man* as a source for Hazlitt's "On a Sun-Dial."

El-Shater, *"The Last Man."* In *The Novels of Mary Shelley*, 67–110. Mary Shelley conceived of the writing of *The Last Man* "as a means of writing her husband's biography under cover." In Adrian, "Mary pictured the essential traits of her husband and tried to realise his ideas."

Fisch, Audrey. "Plaguing Politics: AIDS, Deconstruction, and *The Last Man.*" In *The Other Mary Shelley: Beyond Frankenstein*, 267–86. Analyzes the politics of the novel in several modern contexts, including a contemporary version of the plague in the form of AIDS. The narrator (Lionel Verney) "represents Mary's answer to the faulty politics" of the other characters and becomes a working model for our own politics of survival amidst moral pestilence and egomania.

Franci, Giovanni. "Lo Specchio del Futuro: Visione e Apocalisse in *The Last Man* di Mary Shelley" [The voice of the future: vision and apocalypse in Mary Shelley's *The Last Man*]. *Quaderni di Filologia Germanica della Facolté di Lettere e Filosofia dell'Université di Bologna* 1 (1980): 75–84. Reads the novel as the science fiction prototype for the common theme of global extinction of civilization.

Friedlander, Saul, Gerald Holton, Leo Marx, and Eugene Skolnikoff. *Visions of Apocalypse: End or Rebirth?* 68. New York: Holmes and Meier, 1988. Alludes to the pessimistic finality of *The Last Man.*

Goldsmith, Steven. "Of Gender, Plague, and Apocalypse: Mary Shelley's *Last Man.*" *Yale Journal of Criticism* 4 (1990): 129–73. A deconstructive analysis of the novel's themes demonstrating Mary Shelley's implicit and explicit rejection of the millennial idealism of both her parents and her husband. "Shelley alters an exclusively masculine theme even as she imitates it."

Goldsmith, Steven. "Apocalypse and Gender: Mary Shelley's Last Man." In *Unbuilding Jerusalem: Apocalypse and Romantic Representation,* 261–313. Ithaca, N.Y.: Cornell University Press, 1993. Views the novel as "dystopian and counterapocalyptic, a utopian inclination which Mary Shelley imagined but could not know and a text that distantly anticipates the current work of various French feminist writers." Relates counterapocalyptic themes to gender in the following subsections: "'Last Man' Poetry; or, The Last Man Who Would Not Leave," "The 'Last Man' and Subjectivity," "The 'Last Man' and Gender," "'My Sibylline Leaves,'" "The Sibyl's Story," "The Sibyl's Story Revised," "The Sibyl's Story Expanded: The Structure of the Novel," "Beyond Man and Humanism; or, The Last Man, at Last," "Novelistic Subversion," and "Apocalypse, Plague, and Narrative Contagion."

Grylls, R[osalie] Glynn. "Mary Shelley's Novels." *Times Literary Supplement*, 11 April 1935, p. 244. A twenty-four-line letter to the editor stating that the only other novel besides *Frankenstein* that "repays reading is *The Last Man* where she succeeds in rendering a terror beyond that of 'Frankenstein.'"

Johnson, Barbara. "'The Last Man.'" In *The Other Mary Shelley: Beyond Frankenstein*, 258–66. A philosophical discussion that links the novel with Derrida's article "The Ends of Man." Mary Shelley "takes over a typically Romantic style in order to say what she sees as the end of Romanticism; she mourns for a certain type of universal vision."

Kadish, Doris Y. "Allegorizing Women: *Corinne* and *The Last Man*." In *Politicizing Gender: Narrative Strategies in the Aftermath of the French Revolution,* 15–36. New Brunswick, N.J.: Rutgers University Press, 1991. Compares *The Last Man* with Madame De Staël's *Corinne*. Both novels allegorize "women characters as symbolic participants in the collective story of the French Revolution." The writing of both novels "helped to assert women's political role."

Ketterer, David. "Mary Shelley and Science Fiction: A Select Bibliography Selectively Annotated." *Science Fiction Studies* 5 (1978): 172–78. Intermittent references to criticism of *The Last Man*.

Klein, Mary Ann. "Conceptual and Artistic Limits of Eight Nineteenth Century British Literary Utopias." *Dissertation Abstracts* 35 (1974): 1048A–1049A (Marquette University). Mary Shelley's *Last Man* is a Romantic pessimist's version of the alternate world that is more ominous than attractive. She pioneered in the development of the dystopic fantasy.

Kuczynski, Ingrid. "Katastrophe und Hoffnung: Eine Gesellschaftsvision der Romantik: Mary Shelleys Roman *The Last Man*" [Catastrophe and hope: a social vision of the romantic: Mary Shelley's novel *The Last Man*]. In *Literarische Diskurse und Historischer Prozess: Beiträge zur Englischen und*

Amerikanischen Literatur und Geschichte, edited by Brunhild de la Motte, 139–50. Potsdam, GDR: Pädagogische Hochschule "Karl Liebknecht": Potsdamer Forschungen, 1988. Interprets the novel to be not entirely a pessimistic prophecy. Global annihilation is balanced by hope and Romantic faith in the human spirit.

Leighton, Angela. Review of *The Last Man*. *Keats-Shelley Review* 2 (1987): 144–48. Review of the Hogarth Press edition of the novel edited by Brian Aldiss. *The Last Man* is "infused with passionate regret for a dead generation of poets and idealists and has a disturbing timelessness."

Lomax, William. "Epic Reversal in Mary Shelley's *The Last Man*: Romantic Irony and the Roots of Science Fiction." In *Contours of the Fantastic: Selected Essays from the Eighth International Conference in the Fantastic in the Arts*, edited by Michele K. Langford, 7–17. Westport, Conn.: Greenwood Press, 1990. Treats the novel as a seminal contribution to the modern science fiction genre and demonstrates how Mary Shelley intentionally subverts and inverts traditional patterns of epic heroism in Lionel Verney's wanderings.

Nellist, Brian. "Imagining the Future: Predictive Fiction in the Nineteenth Century." In *Anticipations: Essays in Early Science Fiction and Its Precursors*, edited by David Seed, 111–36. Syracuse, N.Y.: Syracuse University Press, 1995. Compares the dark vision of the future in *The Last Man* with other nineteenth-century utopias by Samuel Butler and William Morris.

Luke, Hugh J., Jr. "Introduction." In *The Last Man,* vii–xviii. Lincoln: University of Nebraska Press, 1965. The novel shares the themes of isolation and life-threatening science with *Frankenstein*. "Whereas *Frankenstein* immediately gripped the imagination, *The Last Man* had little popular success and was damned by the critics."

Luke, Hugh J., Jr. "*The Last Man*: Mary Shelley's Myth of the Solitary." *Prairie Schooner* 39 (1966): 316–27. Serious modern criticism of Mary Shelley's prophetic fantasy begins with Luke's essay that establishes the book's relationship to the Gothic and Romantic traditions and relates its themes to the figure of the solitary in a lonely and empty universe.

Middleton, Victoria Sharon. "The Exiled Self: Women Writers and Political Fiction." *Dissertation Abstracts International* 41 (1980): 263A (University of California-Berkeley). Argues that Mary Shelley's "estrangement from her family and from society impeded her self-definition." The resultant isolation is seen in the "anti-political vision of *The Last Man*, which upholds society's status quo at the expense of reform."

Middleton, Victoria Sharon. *Elektra in Exile: Women Writers and Political Fiction,* 45–49. New York: Garland Publishing, 1988. Restates the argument that *The Last Man* is politically and morally pessimistic in defending the social order against reform.

Miller, Arthur McA. "*The Last Man*: A Study of the Eschatological Theme in English Poetry and Fiction from 1806 Through 1839." *Dissertation Abstracts* 28 (1966): 687A (Duke University). Traces the rise of cataclysmic literature in the early 1800s and refers to some of Mary Shelley's sources, including the anonymous *The Last Man; or, Omegarus and Syderia* (1806), Lord Byron's "The Darkness," and Thomas Dale's *Irad and Adah* (1822). Mary Shelley's *The Last Man* "resumed the format of *Omegarus*. The central episode of her novel recasts Byron's 'Darkness' into prose. The novel also injects unorthodox religious and political speculation into the eschatological genre."

Mishra, Vijay. "Mary Shelley's Personal Trauma; The Literary Intertexts; Apocalyptic Narratives: Tales of Ends." In *The Gothic Sublime,* 158–60, 162–71. Albany, N.Y.: SUNY at Albany University Press, 1994. Refers to *The Last Man* as "an exceptional text, one of the more successful apocalyptic narratives. It unites a narrative millenarianism with the return of the repressed, which, as the sublime, threatens to consume our erstwhile and secure constructions of meaning."

Nitchie, *Mary Shelley*, 30–38, 141–42, 150–53, 184–85, 193–94. Discusses the inception, publication, and reception of the novel and her reaction to such contemporary events as balloon flight. Her progressive and republican England is no millenium because "the whole system was as weak as the individual men who directed it, men who had not been educated so as to form 'the character of social man.'"

Nochimson, "Mary Wollstonecraft Shelley." The novel's subjects are "the degenerating spiral of history" and "the plague of man's will to power." But Lionel Verney's survival "carries with it a suggestion of responsibility in the tragedy of mankind."

O'Dea, Gregory Sean. "The Temporal Sublime: Time and History in the British Gothic Novel." *Dissertation Abstracts International* 52 (1992): 2563A (University of North Carolina). Discusses *The Last Man* as one of several literary examples of time as a generator of the sublime in Gothic fiction. "Time and history are important to three main features of Gothic fiction: temporally distant settings, suspenseful plots, and supernatural intrusions upon human action."

O'Dea, Gregory. "Prophetic History and Textuality in Mary Shelley's *The Last Man*." *Papers on Language and Literature* 28 (1992): 283–304. Analyzes *The Last Man* as futuristic and historical fantasy and sees it as both a type of Gothic novel and an example of apocalyptic history.

Palacio, Jean de. "Mary Shelley and *The Last Man*, a Minor Romantic Theme." *Revue de Littérature Comparée* 42 (1968): 37–49. Investigates the success of the "Last Man" motif and studies Mary Shelley's sources in poems by Thomas Hood, Thomas Campbell, and Cousin de Grainville's prose epic *Le Dernier Homme* (1805). "The Last Man motif fell in her way at a time when she was most in need of an allegorical or symbolic pattern."

Palacio, *Mary Shelley dans son oeuvre*, 286. Suggests that the novel is a vehicle for Mary Shelley's worst pessimistic fears concerning an evil universe sanctioned by an evil deity and doomed by human ineffectuality.

Paley, Morton D. "Mary Shelley's *The Last Man*: Apocalypse Without Millenium." *Keats-Shelley Review* 4 (1989): 1–25. Reprint, *The Other Mary Shelley: Beyond Frankenstein*, 107–23. Details the negative reviews of the novel and discusses its dystopic vision through its themes of the failure of imagination, the failure of art, and its "ambivalence toward millenarianism, denying the linkage of apocalypse and millenium that had previously been celebrated in some of the great works of the Romantic epoch."

Paley, Morton D. "Introduction." In *The Last Man*, edited by Hugh J. Luke Jr., i–xxxviii. Lincoln: University of Nebraska Press, 1965. Views the novel as a refutation of visionary social change and a work that runs counter to the millenial optimism of other Romantic thinkers, including Shelley himself.

Parrinder, Patrick. "H. G. Wells and the Fiction of Catastrophe." *Renaissance and Modern Studies* 28 (1984): 40–58. Mentions *The Last Man* as an atmospheric and thematic analogue to Wells's *The War of the Worlds* (1898).

Paschetto, Anna. "Un Primo e Ultimo Uomo: Il Problemo Mary Shelley da *Frankenstein* a *The Last Man*" [A first and last man: Mary Shelley's problem from *Frankenstein* to *The Last Man*]. In *Sheherazade in Inghilterra: Formule Narrative nell'Evoluzione Inglese*, 143–81. Milan, Italy: Cisalpino-Goliardica, 1983. Compares and contrasts *Frankenstein* with *The Last Man*. While *Frankenstein* "debates a fundamental problem of life," *The Last Man* deals almost exclusively with death and permanent isolation of spirit.

Porte, Joel. "In the Hands of An Angry God: Religious Terror in Gothic Fiction." In *The Gothic Imagination: Essays in Dark Romanticism*, edited by G. R. Thompson, 55–57. Pullman: Washington State University Press, 1974. Briefly discusses "Mary Shelley's eschatological fantasy." Sees the plague as the book's controlling metaphor that symbolizes the incorrigibly corrupt human spirit that renders the world "that labyrinth of evil, that scheme of mutual torture."

Russell, Elizabeth. "'All Is Show—and I but Shadow': Mary Shelley; Self and Text." In *Representations of the Self in Women's Autobiography*, edited by Vita Fortunati, 17–28. Bologna, Italy: University of Bologna, 1993. Examines the theme of tragic self-consciousness in *Mathilda*.

Sambrook, A. J. "A Romantic Theme: *The Last Man*." *Forum for Modern Language Studies* 2 (January 1966): 25–33. A historical survey of apocalyptic literature in France and England emphasizing the prototypical role of Mary Shelley's novel in stating and developing the motif of the final survivor of destroyed worlds. Like other users of the theme, Mary Shelley questioned and rejected millennial idealism.

Snyder, Robert Lance. "Apocalypse and Indeterminacy in Mary Shelley's *The Last Man*." *Studies in Romanticism* 17 (1978): 435–52. Discusses the novel's "conceptual uniqueness" by examining the plague as a conveyer of the theme of catastrophic indeterminacy. "The plague figures as a grotesque enigma mocking all assumptions of order, meaning, purpose, and causality."

Spark, Muriel. "Mary Shelley: A Prophetic Novelist." *The Listener* 45 (1951): 305–6. On the ominous contemporaneity of the doomsday themes of *The Last Man*. Utopia building leads to social and political hells. Draws parallels between *The Last Man* and *Frankenstein*. Both stories "culminate in the Romantic motif of man in search of himself and in conflict with himself and combine rational and natural themes with the imaginative elements of Gothic fiction."

Spark, "The Last Man." In *Mary Shelley*, 179–98. Suggests that the "ruthlessly pessimistic" tone of the novel was caused in part by the deaths of Byron and Shelley. Also reads the novel as an autobiographical allegory, since "it is clear that the character of

Lionel Verney is Mary herself; Adrian is an idealised version of Shelley; and Raymond, a more realistic portrait of Byron."

Spatt, Hartley. "Mary Shelley's Last Men: The Truth of Dreams." *Studies in the Novel* 7 (1975): 526–37. Views *The Last Man* as having "all the elements which make for a powerful work of Gothic fiction," including the Promethean impulse, situations of primal loneliness, and "a group of characters whose powers work at cross-purposes to their desires."

Spector, Robert D. "'Mary Shelley;' The Inheritors: Charles Robert Maturin and Mary Shelley." In *The English Gothic: A Bibliographic Guide to Writers from Horace Walpole to Mary Shelley*, 227–48. Westport, Conn.: Greenwood Press, 1983. Reviews the reviews of the novel and summarizes the modern scholarship. Notes the negative opinions of Ernest Baker and Sir Edmund Gosse, both of whom found *The Last Man* absurd or of interest only for its portraits of the Byron-Shelley circle.

Sterrenberg, Lee. "*The Last Man*: Anatomy of Failed Revolutions." *Nineteenth Century Fiction* 33 (1978): 324–47. Relates Mary Shelley's "disaster novel" to other post-Napoleonic works of literature and painting in an attempt to place the book as an "anatomy of the revolutionary age, an encyclopedic survey of political positions including utopianism, Bonapartism, and revolutionary enthusiasms of various kinds."

Sunstein, *Mary Shelley*, 269–72. Rates the novel as "impressive fiction in which she tried to forecast what the twenty-first century might be, not what she wished it to be." The novel is also "an extended metaphor of her life experience, as well as a mine of her vocabulary of images, history, myth, literature and the arts, and of her prophetic gift."

Veeder, *Mary Shelley and Frankenstein*, 72–76, 160–63. *The Last Man* presents various negative arguments against "the efficacy of the will. Beneath our conscious intentions are drives which do from within what events do from without—shape us to their whim."

Wagar, W. Warren. *Terminal Vision: The Literature of Last Things*. Bloomington: Indiana University Press, 1982. Brief mention of Mary Shelley's contribution to apocalypse. Has an extensive primary bibliography of doomsday novels.

Walling, "*The Last Man*." In *Mary Shelley*, 72–100. Regards the novel as "a book of genuine power, less readable than *Valperga*, less intense and richly symbolic than *Frankenstein*." She infused the work with "all her actual and profound social and political uncertainty about the future."

Zimmerman, Phyllis. "Some Lines of Italian Poetry in the Introduction to *The Last Man*." *Notes & Queries* 37 (1990): 31–32. Identifies Petrarch's verse as the source for the lines.

Lodore

Type: novel

First Printing: London: Richard Bentley, 1835; New York: Wallis & Newell, 1835.

Modern Editions: Fiona Stafford, ed. Brookfield, Vt.: Pickering & Chatto, 1996.

Criticism:

Blumberg, Jane. "Appendix D: The Late Novels: *Perkin Warbeck, Lodore, Falkner*." In *Mary Shelley's Early Novels*, 216–23. Calls the novel "a more developed and certainly more socially acceptable version of *Mathilda*" that is related to her other fiction in its portrayal of "a perilously close relationship between father and daughter."

El-Shater, "*Lodore*." In *The Novels of Mary Shelley*, 127–55. Describes this novel of family corruption and disintegration as "disproportionate with a clumsy sequence of events. She refrained, perhaps on purpose, from inculcating any serious political or radical ideas."

Hill-Miller, "*Lodore*." In *My Hideous Progeny,* 128–64. Focusing on three daughters in the novel—Ethel Fitzhenry, Fanny Derham, and Cornelia Santerre—shows how "*Lodore*, more overtly than Shelley's other novels, analyzes the many varieties of the daughter's education at the father's hands and portrays the impact of this education on the daughter's behavior and life."

Nitchie, *Mary Shelley*, 76–87, 117–21, 134–36. Comments on the biographical content as seen in the characters, especially her attitudes toward Shelley and Byron and the social and domestic tensions created by their personalities. "There are echoes of Shelley's education and of his first marriage and its disaster in the events of Lodore's life, but none of Shelley's personality in Lodore himself."

Nochimson, "Mary Wollstonecraft Shelley." Comments on the "forests of Illinois" section of the novel and maintains that "in *Lodore*, an extremely long parade of misunderstandings" creates "the central image [of] the recovery of a lost mother."

Sunstein, *Mary Shelley*, 320–24. The style projects Mary Shelley in "an unforced, contemplative mood. She reappraises aspects of the past with significant insight. In three heroines, Mary Shelley distributes reflections of herself."

Veeder, *Mary Shelley and Frankenstein*, 67–68, 101–2, 159–60. Mary Shelley's relationship to androgyny is to be seen in "her feminine and masculine aspects as they appear in the two heroines of Lodore."

Walling, "Other Fictional Prose and the Verse, The Three Remaining Novels." In *Mary Shelley*, 101–9. *Lodore* is marred by a pervasive sentimentality, "an absence of serious ideas, and its almost total lack of creative vitality; it is the weakest of all her fiction."

"The Magician of Vicenza"
Type: attributed short story
First Printing: *Forget-Me-Not* for 1829, 273–83. London: Rudolf Ackermann, 1828.

"Manfred"
Type: drama (unfinished and lost)
Criticism:
Nitchie, *Mary Shelley*, 158–59. In 1824, Mary Shelley had written several scenes and tried to interest a publisher but abandoned the project after being discouraged and perhaps dissuaded by Godwin. This verse tragedy was "not Byron's Manfred but the Ghibelline King of Naples who she had used in 'A Tale of the Passions.'"

Mathilda
Type: novel (unpublished)
First Printing: *Studies in Philology,* extra series no. 3, ed. Elizabeth Nitchie. Chapel Hill: North Carolina University Press, 1959.
Modern Editions: Elizabeth Nitchie, ed., North Carolina University Press, extra series no. 3, *Studies in Philology*, 1959; Janet Todd, ed. London: Penguin Books, 1991; *MSR*, 173–246; Gabriella Agrati and Letizia Magini, trans. Milan, Italy: Edizione delle Donne, 1980; Nora Crook, ed. Brookfield, Vt.: Pickering & Chatto, 1996.
Criticism:
Abe, Miharu. "Monstrous Images in Mary Shelley's *Mathilda*, a 'Double-Voiced' Narrative." In *Centre and Circumference: Essays in English Romanticism*, 609–22. Tokyo, Japan: Kirihara, for the Association of English Romanticism in Japan, 1995.

Abensour, Liliane and Françoise Charras, eds. *Romantisme Noir* [Dark romanticism]. Paris: Herne, 1978. Contains excerpts and brief commentary on the novella.

Alexander, "Mary Shelley's *Mathilda*." In *Women in Romanticism*, 160–66. Suggests that *Mathilda* is "a feminine myth of origin" based on the incestuous fable of Oedipus and the infernal imprisonment of Persephone. "The myth rewritten has brought no comfort. Fusion with the dead mother cannot rebeget the self."

Bowen, Arlene. "'Colui da cu'io tolsi/lo bello stilo': Dante's Presence in Mary Shelley's *Mathilda*." *Italian Culture* 12 (1994): 59–84. An influence study that identifies Mary Shelley's use of Dante's versions of love and lust in the *Divine Comedy* with the writing of *Mathilda*.

Champagne, Rosaria Margaretha. "Crimes of Reading: Incest and Censorship in Mary Shelley's Early Novels." *Dissertation Abstracts International* 53 (1992): 1524A (Ohio State University). Applies poststructural, Foucaultian, and psychoanalytic theory to *Mathilda* to show how the novella presents "fragmented representations of her 1819 nervous breakdown and the aftereffects of childhood sexual abuse." In Mary Shelley's case, "canonical literary history demands that she fail in a great way."

Dalles, Mary Patricia. "Crystallization and the Self: Revising Passionate Love in Stendhal's 'De l'amour,' John Keats' Fanny Brawne Poems, William Hazlitt's 'Liber Amoris,' Ann Batten Cristall's 'Poetical Sketches,' and Mary Shelley's *Mathilda*." *Dissertation Abstracts International* 55 (1994): 971A (University of Colorado). All of these Romantic writers "represent passionate love as neither regressive nor compensatory but rather liberatory." In *Mathilda*, Mary Shelley "represents passionate love in the language of nature to strengthen that link and to veil the intensity of feminine passion."

Harpold, Terrence. "'Did You Get *Mathilda* from Papa?': Seduction Fantasy and the Circulation of Mary Shelley's *Mathilda*." *Studies in Romanticism* 28 (1989): 49–67. A psychobiographical reading applying the criteria of Marie Bonaparte. In *Mathilda*, Mary Shelley "rehearses the problematic scene of her origin, foregrounds the oedipalization of the primal scene, a scene of seduction between father and daughter recasting her emergence from her parents' embrace as a substitution of the daughter in the place of the mother, the object of the father's desire."

Hill-Miller, *"Mathilda."* In *My Hideous Progeny*, 101–27. The unpublished novel uses the theme of incest "to tell the story of a daughter's induction into womanhood and "filthy materiality." Also connects *Mathilda* with *Frankenstein.* "Like *Frankenstein, Mathilda* paints a portrait of a father and child locked in bitter conflict."

Koyanagi, Yasuko. "Mary Shelley's *Mathilda*: 'My Daughter, I Love You!'" In *Centre and Circumference: Essays in English Romanticism*, 593–608. Tokyo, Japan: Kirihara, for the Association of English Romanticism in Japan, 1995. Studies the incest theme in the novella.

Lanswer, Susan S. *Fictions of Authority: Women Writers and Narrative Voice*, 168–72. Ithaca, N.Y.: Cornell University Press, 1992. Maintains that in *Mathilda* Mary Shelley "uses female voice to write in a gendered history. . . . The female voice 'holds the center' of her text in a plot in which the female body becomes the site of conflict."

Mayfield, John Nash. "Romantic Liaisons: Selves and Subjects in Novels of Female Formation." *Dissertation Abstracts International* 52 (1991): 907A (University of Michigan). Groups *Mathilda* with similar female bildungsromans, or novels of formation, and shows how Mary Shelley's novella raises questions about the adequacy of female education.

Mishra, Vijay. "Gothic Fragments and Fragmented Gothics." In *The Gothic Sublime,* 104–16. Albany, N.Y.: SUNY at Albany University Press, 1994. Discusses the Gothic properties of *Mathilda,* including the feverish nature of Mary Shelley's handwriting in the Abinger manuscript of the novella. Maintains that it is "a highly intense work, in some ways much more intense than *Frankenstein. Mathilda* marks a decisive shift toward the beginnings of a strongly articulated female Gothic (sublime) that had been in the making since Clara Reeve, Mrs. Barbauld, and Mrs. Radcliffe."

Nitchie, Elizabeth. "Mary Shelley's *Mathilda*: An Unpublished Story and its Biographical Significance." *Studies in Philology* 40 (1943): 447–62. Reprint, "Appendix III," in *Mary Shelley: Author of "Frankenstein,"* 211–17, New Brunswick, N.J.: Rutgers University Press, 1953. Important early bibliographical description and history of the Abinger manuscript of *Mathilda.* Also discusses Mary Shelley's attraction to the theme of incest and her guilty grief, and dates the novella. "Into this story Mary poured the suffering and loneliness, the bitterness and self-recrimination" that followed William's death. It expresses "a sense of estrangement from, even a physical repulsion toward, one whom she had deeply loved although she felt he did not love her."

Nitchie, Elizabeth. Introduction to *Mathilda*. In *Mary Shelley–Author of "Frankenstein,"* vii–xv. New Brunswick, N.J.; Rutgers University Press, 1953. Nitchie's edition of *Mathilda* also printed *The Fields of Fancy*, a discarded fragment that contains the fanciful framework of the novella. The introduction emphasizes the autobiographical nature of *Mathilda*. "It would be hard to find a more self-revealing work. For an understanding of Mary's character, especially as she saw herself, and her attitude toward Shelley and toward Godwin in 1819, this tale is an important document."

Nitchie, *Mary Shelley*, 11–15, 59–60, 211–17. "Mathilda is certainly Mary herself. Not even her worst enemy could say harsher things about Mary than Mary says about herself in the obviously autobiographical *Mathilda*."

Palacio, *Mary Shelley dans son oeuvre*, 83. Identifies two dramatic sources for the incest theme, Vittorio Alfieri's *Myrrha* and Shelley's *The Cenci*.

Potniceva, T. N. "Svoeobrazie Romanticheskogo Metoda v. Romane M. Shelli 'Matil'da' (1819)" [The individuality of the romantic method in M. Shelley's novel *Mathilda* (1819)]. *Nauchnye Doklady Vysshei Shkoly. Filologiceskie Nauki* (Moscow) 18.5 (1976): 28–35. Praises Mary Shelley for her ability to transform autobiography into art in the novella.

Potniceva, T. N. "Problema Romanticheskogo Metoda v Romanakh M. Shelli 'Frankenstein' (1818), 'Matil'da' (1819)" [The problem of romantic method in Mary Shelley's novels *Frankenstein, Matilda*]. In *Dissertation, Moskovskii Pedagogicheskii Institut im. N. K. Krupskoy*. Moscow, 1978. Mary Shelley approached the problem of the artist's immersion of the self in the works by using irony and male narrators.

Rajan, Tilottama. "Mary Shelley's *Mathilda*: Melancholy and the Political Economy of Romanticism." *Studies in the Novel* 26 (1994): 43–68. A heavily autobiographical reading of the unfinished novella that regards the work as "her most depressing text, a narrative of trauma. . . . The situation encrypts that of Mary Shelley herself."

Todd, Janet. "Introduction." In *Mary Wollstonecraft; Mary and Maria; Mary Shelley, Matilda*, viii–xxviii. London: Penguin Books, 1991. Identifies the novella's subjects to be filial guilt and psychological imprisonment. "Like her creator, the heroine of *Matilda* is the result of her father's first deadly desire, and the book becomes an even more autobiographical birth-myth than *Frankenstein*."

Sunstein, *Mary Shelley*, 60–61, 64–65, 171–73. Interprets the novella as "important Romantic fiction and a crucial biographical document, one of the first case histories of an acute depression, the more rare for being written by the patient."

Veeder, *Mary Shelley and Frankenstein*, 217–18. Judges *Mathilda* to be "poor fiction because going back to Daddy is poor judgment. Incest in *Mathilda* is a simplistic, finally sentimental response to her involved ties."

Walling, "Other Fictional Prose and the Verse; Shorter Fiction." In *Mary Shelley*, 109–15. Suggests that the central subject of the novella is sexual rejection. "Mary was no longer able to look upon sexuality as the ultimate source of happiness or fulfillment. Confronted by Shelley's physical desire, she retreated into frigidity."

"Maurice"

Type: children's short story (lost)

Criticism:

Sunstein, *Mary Shelley*, 199–200. Written for the children of her friends John and Maria Gisborne in 1820.

Midas

Type: unpublished drama

First Printing: *Proserpine and Midas: Two Unpublished Mythological Dramas*. Edited by A. H. Koszul. London: Humphrey Milford, 1922. Reprint, Folcroft, Pa.: Folcroft, 1973.

Modern Editions: Robinson & Bennett, *The Bodleian Shelley Manuscripts*.

Criticism:

Brill, Elissa. "*Midas*: An Opera in Two Acts." *Dissertation Abstracts International* 52 (1992): 2312A (Temple University). A ninety-minute libretto by Brill based on passages in Mary Shelley's *Midas*. The accompanying essay discusses "the libretto, orchestration, form, melodic and harmonic analysis, contrapuntal techniques and compositional process."

Jones, Frederick T. "Mary Shelley and *Midas*." *Times Literary Supplement*, 25 June 1938, pp. 433–34. A letter to the editor rejecting claims of doubtful authorship of both dramas made by Buxton Foreman and Sylva Norman. Cites two unpublished

Mary Shelley letters "to show beyond all question that Mary was the author of both *Proserpine* and *Midas*."

Nitchie, *Mary Shelley*, 158–59. Both plays were inspired by Shelley, who "had suggested that she write on the subjects which he himself used in *The Cenci* and the unfinished *Charles the First*, and that she translate Vittorio Alfieri's *Myrrha*."

Richardson, "*Proserpine* and *Midas*," 124–39. Mary Shelley's two mythological dramas, written in partial collaboration with Shelley, should be studied seriously "as generic experiments, as a woman writer's innovative assault on classical mythology, and as unusual collaborative ventures which raise questions regarding the differences between female and male approaches to poetic invention."

Robinson & Bennett, *The Bodleian Shelley Manuscripts*. The editors offer the textual hypothesis that both dramas were originally written for children. Mary Shelley revised *Proserpine* for an adult audience before its appearance in *The Winter's Wreath for 1832*.

Sunstein, *Mary Shelley*, 193, 275, 398. Comments on the publication history, including A. H. Koszul's 1922 edition of the dramas.

"The Mortal Immortal: A Tale"

Type: short story (signed by "the Author of 'Frankenstein'")

First Printing: *The Keepsake for MDCCCXXXIV* [1834], 71–87. London: Longman, Rees, Orme, Brown, Green, 1833.

Modern Editions: Sayers, *Great Stories,* 1080–92; James Agate, *A Century of Thrillers from Poe to Arlen,* 113–22. London: Daily Express, 1934; Sam Moskowitz, ed. *Masterpieces of Science Fiction,* 44–59. Cleveland: World Publishing, 1966; *CT*, 219–30; *MSR*, 314–26; Gilbert & Gubar, *Norton Anthology,* 241–52; Williams, *The Lifted Veil*, 95–107.

Criticism:

Gilbert & Gubar, *Norton Anthology*, 241–52. Views this "vigorously inventive" tale as autobiographic in that it "expresses her anguished sense of having survived what seemed to be the deaths of everyone around her."

Jennings, Gary. "Ms. Found in an Oxygen Bottle." *The Magazine of Fantasy and Science Fiction* December 1973: 88–100. Mary Shelley's story is a prototype for the theme of posthumous survival. Deals with the theme in Poe, Wells, and other science fiction writers.

O'Donohoe, Nick. "Condemned to Life: 'The Mortal Immortal' and 'The Man Who Never Grew Young.'" In *Death and the Serpent: Immortality in Science Fiction and Fantasy*, edited by Carl B. Yoke and Donald M. Hasler, 83–90. Westport, Conn.: Greenwood Press, 1985. Compares Mary Shelley's story with Fritz Leiber's short story "The Man Who Never Grew Young." Both stories display "a yearning for annihilation and a sense of the worthlessness of immortality." Both deathless characters are "disillusioned and despondent immortals who are alienated by their agelessness."

Roberts, "Mary Shelley," 86–92. The story is "Mary Shelley's most overtly Rosicrucian piece of fiction. In her description of Winzy's torments, she must have drawn upon her own loneliness and despair following her husband's death."

CT, 390–91. Refers to the story of the tragic curse of eternal life as "the most frequently anthologized" of her tales and relates the theme to *Frankenstein,* in which Mary Shelley "uses a supernatural action as a mere device to introduce a study in character."

Venuti, Lawrence. "I. U. Tarchetti's Politics of Translation: or, A Plagiarism of Mary Shelley." In *Rethinking Translation: Discourse, Subjectivity, Ideology,* 196–230. London and New York: Routledge, 1992. On Iginio Ugo Tarchetti (1839–69), "the first practitioner of the Gothic tale in Italy," Venuti says, in his story "Il Mortale Immortale (dall 'inglese), that Tarchetti claimed to have imitated Mary Shelley's "Mortal Immortal" but had actually committed plagiarism. "It adheres so closely to the syntactical and lexical features of Shelley's English as to be less an 'imitation' than an interlingual translation."

Venuti, Lawrence. "The Awful Crime of I. U. Tarchetti: Plagiarism as Propaganda." *New York Review of Books,* 23 August 1992, p. 7. Tarchetti plagiarized Mary Shelley's story "The Mortal Immortal" for political reasons.

"Mounseer Nongtongpaw; Or the Discoveries of John Bull on a Trip to Paris"

Type: attributed children's short story

First Printing: London: Proprietors of the Juvenile Library; M. J. Godwin, 1808.

Criticism:

Sunstein, *Mary Shelley*, 42. A comic story written when Mary Shelley was eleven. It is "an expanded version of the popular comic song, 'Mounseer Nong Tong Paw,' from Charles Dibdin's 1796 musical comedy, *The General Election*."

"The Mourner"
>Type: short story (signed by "the Author of 'Frankenstein'")
>First Printing: *The Keepsake for MDCCCXXX* [1830], 71–97. London: Hurst, Chance, 1829.
>Modern Editions: *CT*, 81–99; Abensour, *L'Endeuillée et autres récits*, 24–45.
>*Criticism*:
>>Hill-Miller, *My Hideous Progeny*, 128–29. Compares Clarice Evesham's passionate love for her father with the similar passion of Mathilda. "The daughter's love, like Mathilda's, kills her father."
>>Nitchie, *Mary Shelley*, 76. The character of Horace Neville "slightly resembles" the young Shelley at Eton.
>>*CT*, 378–79. Identifies the many biographical details in the story such as the orphaned heroine (Ellen Burnet/Clarice Eversham) who "intensely loved her father, became a parricide, and wished to be a suicide."
>>Sunstein, *Mary Shelley*, 34, 298. Mary Shelley was "again under stress" when she wrote this story at age thirty-one. It has patterns found elsewhere in her fiction, since it is "a story of excessive father-daughter love, patricide, and filial suicide."

"The Noise"
>Type: attributed children's short story (signed by "Mrs. Caroline Barnard")
>First Printing: *The Parent's Offering*.

The Parent's Offering; or, Tales for Children
>Type: attributed children's short story collection (signed by "Mrs. Caroline Barnard")
>First Printing: London: M. J. Godwin, Juvenile Library, 1813.
>Modern Editions: *The Parent's Offering: Or, Interesting Tales for Youths of Both Sexes*. London: Baldwin and Cradock, 1829.

"The Parvenue"
>Type: short story
>First Printing: *The Keepsake for MDCCCXXXVII* [1837], 209–21. London: Longman, Rees, Orme, Brown, Green, 1836.
>Modern Editions: Lewis Melville and Reginald Hargreaves, eds. *Great English Short Stories*, 220–28. New York: Viking Press, 1930; *CT*, 266–74.

Criticism:

> Pollin, Burton R. "Mary Shelley as the Parvenue." *Review of English Literature* 8.3 (1967): 9–21. Explores the story's thematic connections with Mary Shelley's artistic and personal life and her melancholy circumstances after the death of Shelley. Her pessimistic views contrast sharply with Shelley's transcendental humanitarianism.
>
> *CT*, 392–93. "'The Parvenue' replaces the Gothic trappings of other supernatural stories with a naturalistic description of contemporary society."
>
> Sunstein, *Mary Shelley*, 333–34. Notes that the story is "uniquely revealing in painful biographical specificity. Mary condemned both father and husband in 'The Parvenue.'"

"The Pet Donkey"

> Type: attributed children's short story (signed by "Mrs. C. Barnard")
> First Printing: *The Fisher-Boy of Weymouth: to which are added, The Pet Donkey and The Sisters*. London: M. J. Godwin, 1819.

"The Pilgrims"

> Type: short story (unsigned)
> First Printing: *The Keepsake for MDCCCXXXVIII* [1838], 128–55. London: Longman, Orme, Brown, Green 1837.
> Modern Editions: *CT*, 275–94.
> *Criticism*:
>
> > *CT*, 393–94. Notes that the story is assigned to Mary Shelley only on Garnett's authority. "The coincidental and elongated plot and the forlorn and orphaned protagonists have antecedents in Mary Shelley's short fiction."
> >
> > Sunstein, *Mary Shelley*, 174. The story is related to other stories that feature heroines "who are orphaned of their fathers before they fall in love, or oppose their fathers and lose their lovers."

"The Pole"

> Type: short story (signed by "the Author of 'Frankenstein'")
> First Printing: *The Court Magazine and Belle Assemblée* 1 (August and September 1832): 64–71, 129–36.
> Modern Editions: *CT*, 347–72.
> *Criticism*:
>
> > Booth, Bradford. "The Pole: A Story by Claire Clairmont?" *Journal of English Literary History* 5 (1938): 67–70. Although the story was signed "by the author of 'Frankenstein'" when it appeared, it is "entirely the work of Claire Clairmont. Internal evidence at

several points lends credence to the conjecture of authorship by Claire."

CT, 399–400. Accepts Bradford Booth's theory that Mary Shelley wrote only the final melodramatic scene of a story that is almost entirely by Claire Clairmont.

Stocking, Marion Kingston, ed. *The Journals of Claire Clairmont*, 438. Cambridge: Harvard University Press, 1968. Cites Claire Clairmont's letter to Mary Shelley dated 24 March 1832 asking Mary to correct the text of "The Pole" and finish the story by writing the final scene.

"The Prize: Or, The Lace Makers of Missenden"

Type: attributed novella for children (signed by "Mrs. Caroline Barnard")

First Printing: M. J. Godwin, Juvenile Library, 1817.

Criticism:

Sunstein, *Mary Shelley*, 428. Describes the story as "a formula novelette with little social criticism, but striking connections with Mary." A possible source is her visit to Thomas Love Peacock at Great Marrow, where she saw the plight of female cottage workers who made lace.

Proserpine, A Mythological Drama in Two Acts

Type: drama

First Printing: *The Winter's Wreath for 1832*, 1–20. London: Whittaker, Treacher, and Arnot, [1831].

Modern Editions: *Proserpine and Midas: Two Unpublished Mythological Dramas*. Edited by A. Koszul. London: Humphrey Milford, 1922; Nora Crook, ed. Brookfield, Vt.: Pickering & Chatto, 1996; Robinson & Bennett, *The Bodleian Shelley Manuscripts*.

Criticism:

Alexander, *Women in Romanticism*, 12–13. Claims that the drama is Mary Shelley's symbolic expression of maternal loss over the death of her son William. "Maternal loss must equal natural devastation, and a mother's rage at the loss of her child can tighten and twist into a vision of universal destruction."

Blumberg, Jane. "Appendix B: Shelley's Reply to Leslie's Short and Easy Method [with the Deists]." In *Mary Shelley's Early Novels,* 203–5. Reveals Mary Shelley's admiration of classical mythology as opposed to the intellectual and emotional restrictions of Christianity. Mary Shelley knew of Charles Leslie's 1820 treatise by way of Byron, who had urged Shelley to compose a refutation.

Jones, Frederick T. "Mary Shelley and *Midas.*" *Times Literary Supplement*, 25 June 1938, pp. 433–34. See Jones under "*Midas.*"

Nitchie, *Mary Shelley*, 158–59. "Her two little classical verse dramas, *Proserpine* and *Midas*, were written under Shelley's guidance and with his help: he supplied the lyrics 'Arethusa,' 'Invocation to Ceres,' and 'The Hymn to Pan.'"

Richardson, "*Proserpine* and *Midas*," 124–39. See Richardson under "*Midas.*"

Robinson & Bennett, *The Bodleian Shelley Manuscripts*. See under "*Midas.*"

Sunstein, *Mary Shelley*, 193, 275, 398. See Sunstein under "*Midas.*"

Veeder, *Mary Shelley and Frankenstein*, 167. Something of Mary Shelley's dark side can be seen in *Proserpine* when she "threatens all living things through the goddess Ceres' vow to strike the earth 'barren.'"

"Recollections of Italy"
Type: short story (unsigned)
First Printing: *London Magazine* 9 (January 1824): 21–26.
Modern Editions: *CT*, 24–31; *MSR*, 255–62.
Criticism:
CT, 375–76. Calls this piece a "narrative essay" that reuses details from her husband's and her own reminiscences of Italian places and scenery.

Sunstein, *Mary Shelley*, 203, 254. One recollection is of the town of Monte Pisano. The story was written when Mary Shelley was short of money.

"The Refusal"
Type: attributed children's short story (signed by "Mrs. Caroline Barnard")
First Printing: *The Parent's Offering.*

"The Ritter von Reichenstein"
Type: attributed short story (signed by "M. S.")
First Printing: *The Bijou for 1828,* 114–38. London: W. Pickering, 1827.
Criticism:
Sunstein, *Mary Shelley*, 168, 282–83, 445. A newly identified Mary Shelley story, it is "set in Austria and combines *Othello* and *Fidelio* themes. One inspiration may have been Schiller's account of the Knight of Taggenburg in *The Sharing of the Earth.*"

"Roger Dodsworth: The Reanimated Englishman"
Type: short story (untitled on first publication)
First Printing: *Yesterday and To-day*, 2:150–65. London: T. Cautley Newby, 1863.
Modern Editions: *CT*, 43–50; *MSR*, 274–81.
Criticism:
> Roberts, "Mary Shelley," 92–94. Sees the story as a satiric extension of the cryogenic hoax. "It may be significant that Dodsworth was born on April Fools' Day. Mary Taunts the hoaxers responsible for the Dodsworth fraud by entreating him to 'no longer bury himself in obscurity.'"
> *CT*, 377. Suggests Mary Shelley's interest in reanimation and her role in a "cryogenic hoax" of 1826.
> Robinson, Charles E. "Mary Shelley and the Roger Dodsworth Hoax." *Keats-Shelley Journal* 24 (1975): 20–28. Discusses Mary Shelley's attraction to the theme of cryogenic transfer and her journalistic participation in the frozen-man hoax. Cyrus Redding published Mary Shelley's playful essay on Dodsworth's reanimation in *Yesterday and To-day* in 1863.

"The Sisters"
Type: attributed children's short story (signed by "Mrs. C. Barnard")
First Printing: *The Fisher-Boy of Weymouth: to which are added, The Pet Donkey, and The Sisters.* London: M. J. Godwin; Juvenile Library, 1819.

"The Sisters of Albano"
Type: short story (signed by "the Author of 'Frankenstein'")
First Printing: *The Keepsake for MDCCCXXIX* [1829], 80–100. London: Hurst, Chance, 1828.
Modern Editions: *CT*, 51–64.
Criticism:
> *CT*, 377–78. Suggests that the story was written simply to accompany the *Keepsake* plate. Its explicit moral lesson is not always related to the "thin plot."
> Sunstein, *Mary Shelley*, 174, 289, 290, 308. Sees the story as autobiographical because it deals with "a girl's love for an outlaw that was forbidden by her father and resulted in the deaths of her sister and her lover." Notes that two stage versions of the story played in London.

"The Smuggler and His Family"
  Type: short story
  First Printing: *Original Compositions in Prose and Verse, Illustrated with Lithographic Drawings; to Which Is Added Some Instrumental Music*, 27–53. London: Edmund Lloyd, 1833.
  Modern Editions: *CT*, 203–18.
  Criticism:
    CT, 389–91. Reads the parable-like story biographically as reflecting "the author's protective love for her own son, Percy Florence."

"The Swiss Peasant"
  Type: short story (signed by "the Author of 'Frankenstein'")
  First Printing: *The Keepsake for MDCCCXXXI* [1831], 121–46. London: Hurst, Chance, 1830.
  Modern Editions: *CT*, 136–52.
  Criticism:
    CT, 382–83. Compares the narrator with the solitary in Wordsworth's poem *The Excursion* and Byron's Bonnivard in "The Prisoner of Chillon." None of these characters can find any meaning in nature.
    Sunstein, *Mary Shelley*, 302. The story reflects Mary Shelley's growing political conservatism, since it "deplored the violence and bigotry of both revolutionaries and aristocrats."

"Story for Leigh Hunt's *The Indicator* for 1821"
  Type: short story (unpublished and lost)
  Criticism:
    Nitchie, *Mary Shelley*, 156. Speculates that the story may be "The Heir of Mondolfo," "a piece of about 6,500 words which was found among the papers of Leigh Hunt."
    Sunstein, *Mary Shelley*, 410. Notes that Hunt's magazine, *The Indicator*, failed in 1820.

"A Tale of the Passions"
  Type: short story (unsigned)
  First Printing: *The Liberal: Verse and Prose from the South* 2 (January 1823): 289–325.
  Modern Editions: *CT*, 1–23.
  Criticism:
    Dilke, Charles W. "The Liberal." *Notes & Queries* 8.4 (1893): 10. On Hunt's favorable opinion of the story and Mary Shelley's other prose contributions.

Gates, Payson G. "A Leigh Hunt-Byron Letter." *Keats-Shelley Journal* 2 (1953): 11–17. In a jointly composed letter from Byron and Hunt to Hunt's nephew, Henry L. Hunt, they write, "I send you in this letter an Italian story of Mrs. Shelley's (a very good one)," but the story "is detained by an accident for the next letter."

Marshall, William H. *Byron, Shelley, Hunt and "The Liberal,"* 149. Philadelphia: Pennsylvania University Press, 1960. Mentions Mary Shelley's contributions to Leigh Hunt's journal, *The Liberal.*

CT, 374–75. Relates the story to her novel *Valperga* and to Shelley's elegy for Keats, *Adonais.*

Sunstein, *Mary Shelley*, 232, 240. In this story, Mary Shelley "established her mature short story style. Her heroine, Despina, does what she herself has not done—conceals her passion for the married Manfred."

A Tragedy
Type: lost, untitled drama

"Transformation"
Type: short story (signed by "the Author of 'Frankenstein'")
First Printing: *The Keepsake for MDCCCXXXI* [1831], 18–39. London: Hurst, Chance, 1830.
Modern Editions: Norton, *Masters of Horror*, 68–87; *CT*, 121–35; Skarda & Jaffe, *The Evil Image*, 116–31; Thompson, *Romantic Gothic Tales*, 238–57; Peter Haining, ed. *The Gentlewomen of Evil: An Anthology of Rare Supernatural Stories from the Pens of Victorian Ladies,* 15–31. London: Robert Hale, 1967; Haining, *Nightmare Reader*, 13–31. Garden City, N.Y.: Doubleday, 1973; *MSR*, 286–300; M. H. Abrams. *The Norton Anthology of English Literature*, 5th ed., 2:885–98. New York: W. W. Norton, 1986.
Criticism:
Aldiss, " Origin," 35–36. Regards Mary Shelley's dwarf story of body exchange as an early example of science fiction and "a remarkable treatment of the doppelgänger theme which lies close to *Frankenstein* in expressing her inner struggle."

Alexander, *Women in Romanticism*, 140–42. A critical summary of the story that concludes that "there is no obvious moral. The monstrous encounter however, clarifies the nature of desire, grants a knowledge that Guido himself is exempt from."

Cantor, Paul A. "Mary Shelley and the Taming of the Byronic Hero: Transformation and *The Deformed Transformed.*" In *The*

Other Mary Shelley: Beyond Frankenstein, 89–106. Mentions Mary Shelley's 1822–23 transcription of Byron's drama and maintains that the story is a "feminist revision and a rewriting of Byron's work" as well as a commentary on Byronism. "Mary Shelley recreates the typical configuration in Byron's poetic tales: a younger man in competition with an older man for a woman's affections."

Langbauer, Laurie. "Swayed by Contraries: Mary Shelley and the Everyday." In *The Other Mary Shelley: Beyond Frankenstein*, 185–203. Considers "the overlooked topic of the everyday in Shelley's writing." Points out that the opening lines of Coleridge's "Rime of the Ancient Mariner" provide the epigraph for "Transformation."

Roberts, "Mary Shelley," 94. Describes the story's doppelgänger as "a demonic guardian angel. Guido's spiritual transformation departs from the model of Faust in that it is the body and not the soul which is forfeit in a diabolical bargain."

Robinson, Charles E. "The Devil as Doppelgänger in *The Deformed Transformed*: The Sources and Meaning of Byron's Unfinished Drama." *Bulletin of the New York Public Library* 74 (1970): 177–202. Although not a straight imitation of Byron's drama, Mary Shelley's tale of satanic bodily exchange was definitely inspired by *The Deformed Transformed*.

CT, 381–82. Suggests that the tale's Gothic theme of the "diabolical doppelgänger" derives from the hunchbacked Arnold in Byron's drama *The Deformed Transformed*; notes its resemblance to Poe's "William Wilson."

Simpkins, Scott. "'They Do the Men in Different Voices': Narrative Crossdressing in Sand and Shelley." *Style* 26 (1992): 400–418. Compares the motif of crossdressing with characters in George Sand's novels.

Skarda & Jaffe, *The Evil Image*, 117. Observes that "the most reverberant echo from *Frankenstein* to 'Transformation' is the doppelgänger or 'double' motif. The misshapen dwarf mirrors the monstrous immorality of Guido."

Sunstein, *Mary Shelley*, 174, 301. The story holds a portrait of Shelley in the "mutinous boy who loved his Maryish foster sister and 'profaned her child's lips with an oath that she would be' his against her father's wishes."

Thompson, *Romantic Gothic Tales*, 1–54. The introduction to the collection "Gothic Fiction of the Romantic Age" relates the story to the orientalized Gothic tale "vaguely in the manner of Beckford's *Vathek* though without its nihilistic irony and surreal sexual fantasy."

"The Trial of Love"
   Type: short story (signed by "The Author of 'Frankenstein'")
   First Printing: *The Keepsake for MDCCCXXXV* [1835], 70–86. London: Longman, Rees, Orme, Brown, Green, 1834.
   Modern Editions: *CT*, 231–43.
   Criticism:
      CT, 391. Credits the story with "unity of action. . . . Instead of a radical alteration or reformation in character, the constant Angeline, the capricious Faustina, and the inconstant Ippolito act in character throughout the narrative."

"Valerius: The Reanimated Roman"
   Type: short story (unpublished)
   First Printing: *CT*.
   Modern Editions: *CT*, 332–44.
   Criticism:
      Roberts, "Mary Shelley," 92–94. Exhibits Mary Shelley's lifelong interest in teleportation. "The reanimated individual and the immortal wanderer are metaphors for the continuity between past and present which is essential for the well-being of any country or society."
      CT, 397–98. The story is a psychological study of Valerius's "reactions to his new existence" rather than the supernatural fact of his reanimation.
      Sunstein, *Mary Shelley*, 164, 434. Comments on the story as an "inter-century conceit between a resurrected first century republican who despises what Rome became thereafter and the contemporary young lady, Isabel Harley, who asserts the inspirational value of imperial Rome and its literature to moderns."

Valperga: or, the Life and Adventures of Castruccio, Prince of Lucca
   Type: novel
   First Printing: London: G. and W. B. Whittaker, 1823.
   Modern Editions: Revolution and Romanticism Series. Plainville, Conn.,Woodstock Books: 1995; Nora Crook, ed. Brookfield, Vt.: Pickering & Chatto, 1996.
   Criticism:
      Blumberg, Jane. "'That Masterpiece of his Malice': *Valperga*." In *Mary Shelley's Early Novels*, 76–113. As a sort of response to Shelley's transcendental optimism and belief in humanity's

amelioration, "*Valperga* remains the darkest and most profoundly pessimistic novel that she ever wrote."

Brewer, William. "Mary Shelley on the Therapeutic Value of Language." *Papers on Language and Literature* 30.4 (1994): 387–407. On the value of language to Mary Shelley in relieving psychological and domestic anguish. Discusses the style of *Valperga* and *Mathilda* in the context of this idea.

Brewer. William D. "Mary Shelley's *Valperga*: The Triumph of Euthanasia's Mind." *European Romantic Review* 5:2 (1995): 133–48. A character analysis of Euthanasia's ethereal nature as opposed to the carnality of Beatrice.

Clemit, "*Valperga*: 'A Book of Promise,' Mary Shelley's Novels of the 1820s: History and Prophecy." In *The Godwinian Novel*, 173–83. The novel is an imitation of Scott's historical romances as well as a character study of tyrannical egotism. "While the historical scope of *Valperga* owes much to Scott's more naturalistic, documentary art, its central imaginative threads reflect the theoretical concerns of earlier Godwinian novels."

El-Shater, "*Valperga*; or, The Life and Adventures of Castruccio, Prince of Lucca." In *The Novels of Mary Shelley*, 34–66. Attributes "real narrative power" to some passages of the novel and refers to it as "a representative Romantic novel. Its theme is Gothic-historical." Also compares *Valperga* to George Eliot's novel of sinister Florentine politics, *Romola*.

Harson, Robert R. "Mary Shelley's 'Tomb of the Capulets.'" *American Notes & Queries* supplement 1 (1978): 197–202. A note on her imaginative use of Romeo and Juliet in *Valperga* and other works with Italian settings.

Lew, Joseph W. "God's Sister: History and Ideology in *Valperga*." In *The Other Mary Shelley: Beyond Frankenstein*, 159–81. Offers an alternative reading for "this unjustly maligned novel" involving Mary Shelley's Romantic ideology. "*Valperga* functions as a Romantic and specifically feminist 'myth of origins' that explains how men and women came to inhabit the worlds we live in."

Nitchie, *Mary Shelley*, 42–43, 61–63, 104–5, 148–49, 192–93. Notes the novel's historical and scenic accuracy as well as Mary Shelley's presentation of Shelley's ideas and ideals in several characters. "Into the person of her heroine, Euthanasia, Mary put her idealization of qualities she loved most in Shelley."

Nochimson, "Mary Wollstonecraft Shelley." Notes that the action of the novel takes place in "a Hobbesian world" in which Castruccio "gains the world at the price of his soul."

O'Sullivan, Barbara Jane. "Beatrice in *Valperga*: A New Cassandra." In *The Other Mary Shelley: Beyond Frankenstein*, 140–58. Argues that Mary Shelley presents her complex heroine, Beatrice, as "a religious prophetess who is hunted, haunted, raped, imprisoned, deceived, and destroyed" and as a symbol of the predicament of the creative female whose fate represents "an alternative to the Promethean optimism of Romanticism."

Rieger, James. "Shelley's Paterin Beatrice." *Studies in Romanticism* 4 (1964–65): 169–84. Studies and compares the two Beatrices of the two Shelleys, Percy's Beatrice in *The Cenci* and Mary's heretical or "paterin" Beatrice, "the most interesting character in *Valperga*." Mary Shelley's paterin Beatrice "does not behold the God above the demiurge. The crude Paterinism of the two Beatrices represents the human understanding in extremis as it wars unaided against the demiurge."

Sunstein, *Mary Shelley*, 33–34, 188–90, 191–92. Assesses the symbolic value of Euthanasia and Castruccio. Euthanasia "affirms Mary Shelley's own love of wisdom, liberty, and a Romantic view of the value of upheaval in personal and political life." Castruccio is seen as "a politicized version of Victor Frankenstein whose gifts and aspiration are perverted by lust for power."

Veeder, *Mary Shelley and Frankenstein*, 71, 162–67. Notes the androgynous characteristics of Castruccio, who has "the attractive vulnerability of Mary's 'delicate' poet-types."

Walling, *"Valperga."* In *Mary Shelley*, 51–71. Discusses the novel's weaknesses, including excessive length and irrelevant episodes. In its handling of the theme of political ambition, however, the novel shows "a genuinely creative sensibility earnestly at work in the hope of destroying the Napoleonic danger at its source."

General Studies:
Biographies, Bibliographies, Critical Studies, and Articles Containing Material on the Novels, Tales, and Dramas

Alexander, Meena. *Women in Romanticism: Mary Wollstonecraft, Dorothy Wordsworth, and Mary Shelley.* Savage, Md.: Barnes & Noble, 1989. Like other women writers, Mary Shelley "had to cut through the bonds of femininity, those structures of patriarchal authority that seemed to stand outside her." Comments specifically on *Mathilda, Proserpine, The Last Man*, and "Transformation."

Beer, Patricia. "Thunderbolts and Daggers." *Times Literary Supplement*, 3 December 1976, p. 1504. A review of Charles E. Robinson's *Mary Shelley: Collected Tales and Stories*, comparing her work to Mrs. Radcliffe's Gothicism. The stories in the collection "develop lurid historical themes, the Gothic horrors, the Romantic sensibilities (freak likenesses, instant repentances) that appealed to her and her readers." "Thunderbolts and Daggers" are the words of Jane Austen's Henry Tilney on the Gothic craze.

Bennett, Betty T. and William T. Little. "Seven Letters from Prosper Mérimée to Mary Shelley." *Comparative Literature* 31 (1979): 134–53. The seven letters, written between July 1828 and February 1829, "are valuable for literary as well as biographical reasons." Mérimée comments on her novels, her short stories, and "her interest in French figures as potential literary subjects."

Bennett, Betty T. *The Letters of Mary Wollstonecraft Shelley*. Baltimore & London: Johns Hopkins University Press, 1980. Many letters are pertinent to the genesis and composition of the stories and novels. Bennett notes that "aside from commentary on *Frankenstein*, critical studies of Mary Shelley have largely deflected inquiry away from her as a creator and a creation of the Romantic period."

Bennett, Betty T. "Finding Mary Shelley in Her Letters." In *Romantic Revisions*, ed. Robert Brinkley and Keith Hanley, 291–306. Cambridge, U.K.: Cambridge University Press, 1992. Comments on autobiographical elements in the prose canon.

Bennett, Betty T. "Feminism and Editing in Mary Wollstonecraft Shelley: The Editor And?/Or? The Text." In *Palimpsest*, edited by George Bornstein and Ralph G. Williams, 67–93. Ann Arbor: Michigan University Press, 1993. Mary Shelley's fiction presents "a revealing example of the need for feminist critics to define the role of feminist editors in the establishment of a feminist canon."

Bigland, Eileen. *Mary Shelley*. New York: Appleton-Century-Crofts, 1959. The biography trivializes and disregards Mary Shelley's short fiction and the novels written after *Frankenstein*.

Bleiler, E. F. *The Guide to Supernatural Fiction*, 453. Kent, Ohio: Kent State University Press, 1983. Has brief summaries of "Roger Dodsworth: The Reanimated Englishman," "Valerius: The Reanimated Roman," "Transformation," "The Mortal Immortal," and "The Dream." Regards her short stories as "for the most part only minor work, in no way as significant as her novels."

Blumberg, Jane. *Mary Shelley's Early Novels: "This Child of Imagina-tion and Misery."* Iowa City: University of Iowa Press, 1993. Ad-dresses the critical neglect of *Valperga* and *The Last Man*. "The real reason for this neglect may lie in the genuine moral horror that her novels instill." Offers four appendixes: "Manuscript Essay: 'A History of the Jews,'" "Shelley's Reply to Leslie's *Short and Easy Method*," "The Byron Manuscripts," and "*Perkin Warbeck, Lodore,* and *Falkner*."

Blunden, Edmund. "Mary Shelley's Romances." In *English Studies in Japan: Essays and Studies Presented to Dr. Yasuo Yamoto.* Tokyo: English Society of the Nihon University, 1958. The monograph ex-presses critical appreciation of *The Last Man,* ranking it as "readable and even reprintable," but rates Mary Shelley's other extra-*Franken-stein* fiction as a mere adjunct to her relationship with Shelley and valuable only in that respect.

Bowen, Arlene. "'The Eternal and Victorious Influence of Evil' in Mary Shelley's First Decade of Fiction (1816–1825)." *Dissertation Abstracts International* 53 (1992): 1921A (SUNY-Stony Brook). Examines the theme of "the loss of transcendental faith" in *Valperga, The Last Man,* and *Mathilda* and argues that these works "demonstrate her skepticism regarding man's potential for regeneration in a world dominated by the spirit of evil."

Carson, James P. "Bringing the Author Forward: *Frankenstein* Through Mary Shelley's Letters." *Criticism* 30 (1988): 432–53. Argues that "Mary Shelley drew whatever literary power she had by submitting to, not struggling with, her husband's influence. She is neither conven-tional nor conservative since she questions the priority and authentic-ity of the authorial and female self in the context of a profound aware-ness of women's position under patriarchy." Comments of *Valperga* that "the situation is characteristic in showing how adoption of the conventional feminine role provides a justification for female educa-tion." Alludes to other non-*Frankenstein* fiction in these contexts.

Church, Richard. *Mary Shelley.* New York: Viking Press; London: Gerald Howe, 1928. The biography contains cursory allusions to *Valperga* ("a tale of love and intrigue in mediaeval Florence when the destinies of lovers were controlled by local politics") and *The Last Man* ("a highly fanciful story of the annihilation of the human race by plague"). Also discusses Mary Shelley's "indefatigable literary labours" for Leigh Hunt's *Examiner.*

Clemit, Pamela. "Mary Shelley's Novels of the 1820s: History and Prophecy." In *The Godwinian Novel: The Rational Fictions of God-win, Brockden Brown, Mary Shelley.* Oxford, U.K.: Clarendon Press,

1993. Offers analyses of *Valperga* and *The Last Man* as Godwinian narratives and examples of Mary Shelley's response to "other models of intellectual fiction in the early 1820s."

Couchman, B. J. *Cassandra (Un)Bound: An Examination of the Fiction of Mary Shelley*. M. Phil. Dissertation, University of York. *IT* 38 (1989): 1458–59. In prophetic novels such as *The Last Man* and in stories such as "The Mortal Immortal," Mary Shelley exercised "a Cassandra voice to predict a bleak and lonely future for human-kind." Surveys her fiction in light of its metaphysical and social pessimism.

Dunn, Jane. *Moon in Eclipse: A Life of Mary Shelley*. New York: St. Martin's Press; London: Weidenfeld and Nicolson, 1978. A competent biography that takes note of Mary Shelley's lifelong devotion to the writing of fiction. "Eclipse" refers to her self-effacement in the sunlight of Shelley's genius and her consequent artistic deference to her husband.

Ellis, Kate Ferguson. "Subversive Surfaces: The Limits of Domestic Affection." In *The Other Mary Shelley: Beyond Frankenstein*, 220–34. Attacks the view of Mary Poovey in *The Proper Lady and the Woman Writer* that Mary Shelley's post-*Frankenstein* novels and stories are conservative, accommodating, and acceptive of woman's domestic subservience. Her radicalism's "passionate protest against the horrors of birth and maternal bonding, the crippling restraints of the domestic sphere, and the overreaching arrogance of men" extend to the later fiction.

El-Shater, Safaa. *The Novels of Mary Shelley*, Salzburg Studies in English Literature 59. Salzburg, Austria: Institut für Englische Sprache und Literatur, Universität Salzburg, 1977. A useful study of Mary Shelley's total output in the field of the novel. Rates her to be "versatile . . . and at her best in her first three novels which have themes of enduring interest." Finds all six novels to be concerned with the exploration of the individual in a variety of repressive social and domestic circumstances.

Favret, Mary. "Mary Shelley's Sympathy and Irony: The Editor and Her Corpus." In *The Other Mary Shelley: Beyond Frankenstein*, 17–38. Notes Mary Shelley's ability to combine the roles of editor, transcriber, critic, and biographer in her own work and the work of Shelley.

Feldman, Paula Renee. "The Journals of Mary Wollstonecraft Shelley: An Annotated Edition." *Dissertation Abstracts* 35 (1975): 6663A (Northwestern University). Annotations refer frequently to Mary Shelley's non-*Frankenstein* fiction.

Feldman, Paula R. and Diana Scott Kilvert, eds. *The Journals of Mary Shelley, 1814–1844*. Oxford, U.K.: Clarendon Press; New York: Oxford University Press, 1987. Offers a valuable section on "The Shelleys' Reading List" (pp. 631–84).

Fisch, Audrey A., Anne K. Mellor, and Esther Schor, eds. *The Other Mary Shelley: Beyond Frankenstein*. New York: Oxford University Press, 1993. Fourteen critical essays grouped under two general headings: "I. Romanticism and Resistance" and "II. Culture and Criticism." The editors' stated purpose is to "bring Mary Shelley to the center of Romantic studies. What these essays discern in the "other" Mary Shelley is a writer whose resistance to Romanticism is in many ways continuous with the insights of contemporary feminist analysis." Reviewed by Fred Botting in *Keats-Shelley Review* 9 (1995): 96–101. Her other fiction raises "issues of writing, identity, democracy and cultural crisis and change" and creates "doubts about progress, purpose, and 'man's' origins." Reviewed by Gary Kelly in *Keats-Shelley Journal* 43 (1994): 201–4. *The Other Mary Shelley* encourages readers to "reject earlier versions of Shelley as a one-book author, literary shadow of her husband, and inferior artist."

Frank, Ann Marie. "Factitious States: Mary Shelley and the Politics of Nineteenth Century Women's Identity Fiction." *Dissertation Abstracts International* 50 (1990): 2495A–2496A (University of Michigan). Explores female characterization and narrative form in Mary Shelley's novels with an emphasis on Mary Wollstonecraft's influence on their content. The female characters "expose the restrictive effects of culturally induced male domination on female self-identity."

Frank, Frederick S. *The First Gothics: A Critical Guide to the English Gothic Novel*. New York: Garland Publishing, 1987. Critical synopses of *Frankenstein*, *Valperga*, *The Last Man*, *Perkin Warbeck*, and *Lodore*. The Gothic impulse in Mary Shelley's post-*Frankenstein* fiction remains an insistent and strong, if not a paramount, means of achieving effects.

Friday, Nancy. *My Mother/Myself: The Daughter's Search for Identity*. New York: Dell, 1977. Popular biography written from a psychoanalytic point of view. Although *Frankenstein* dominates the discussions of her literary works, there are allusions to her identity search for personal and artistic self in the other prose fiction.

Gerson, Noel B. *Daughter of Earth and Water: A Biography of Mary Wollstonecraft Shelley*. New York: William Morrow, 1973. Unscholarly and factually erroneous biography that romanticizes her life and writings. Virtually useless as a critical source for *Frankenstein* or Mary Shelley's other fiction.

Grylls, R[osalie] Glynn. *Mary Shelley*. London, New York, Toronto: Oxford University Press, 1938. Extremely limited critical evaluations of the non-*Frankenstein* fiction. The biographer does not regard Mary Shelley as an author in her own right but sees her writings only in relation to her husband.

Harris, Janet. *The Woman Who Created Frankenstein: A Portrait of Mary Shelley*. New York: Harper, 1979. Semi-scholarly biography with allusions to her other works, but primary position given to *Frankenstein*.

Healy, Dennis. "Mary Shelley and Prosper Mérimée." *Modern Language Review* 36 (1941): 394–96. Mary Shelley met Mérimée in Paris in 1828. In 1829, Mérimée sent a copy of *La Guzla* [*The evil eye*] to his English friend Sutton Sharpe, with instructions that it be delivered personally to Mary Shelley. Prints for the first time two Shelley letters to Victor Jacquemont and Mérimée.

Hofkosh, Sonia. "Disfiguring Economies: Mary Shelley's Short Stories." In *The Other Mary Shelley: Beyond Frankenstein*, 204–19. Examines Mary Shelley's stories appearing in the keepsakes and annuals of the 1820s to 1830s, including the accompanying engravings and their marketing strategies. "Shelley's stories manipulate the visual—face and form—and its relation to meaning to uncover the blemishes not only on the surface but also in the very foundation of beautiful appearances."

Huergo, Elizabeth M. "A Daughter's Exile: Mary Wollstonecraft Shelley and the Politics of Gender and Writing." *Dissertation Abstracts International* 50 (1990): 2497A (Brown University). Analyzes the novels by examining "the conflict between women who write and constricting essentialist definitions of gender which treat femininity and writing as mutually exclusive." Concludes that Mary Shelley resolves such conflict through exile.

Ingpen, Roger. *Shelley in England: New Facts and Letters from the Shelley-Whitton Papers*. Boston: Houghton-Mifflin, 1917. Has random references to Mary Shelley's other novels but asserts that *Frankenstein* is the only one worth reading. Biographically valuable for the conditions under which her other fiction was written.

Jack, Ian. "John Galt and the Minor Writers of Prose Fiction." In *English Literature, 1815–1832, Oxford History of English Literature*, edited by F. P. Wilson and Bonamy Dobrée, 244–45. Oxford, U.K.: Clarendon Press, 1963. A brief discussion of the other novels is appended to remarks on *Frankenstein*. Praises the ending of *The Last Man*. "The dénouement, in which Verney is left alone in the world, is admirably conceived, although the execution does not quite match the conception." All of her novels after *Frankenstein* would be better if they were shorter.

Jones, Frederick L. *Mary Shelley's Journal*. Norman: Oklahoma University Press, 1947. "Appendix IV, Shelley's Reading" (pp. 218–27), is a valuable register of Mary Shelley's wide reading as well as a source indicator for various novels and stories.

Jones, Frederick L. "Unpublished Fragments by Shelley and Mary." *Studies in Philology* 45 (1948): 472–76. Brief commentary on several prose fragments in Mary Shelley's notebook in the Library of Congress, including her translation of Apuleius's "Cupid and Psyche." Although unimportant in themselves, these fragments "help to round out the history of the Shelleys' literary activities."

Klein, Roxanne. "Reading and Writing the Place of Difference: Mary Wollstonecraft, Mary Shelley and Women's Discourse in Late Eighteenth and Early Nineteenth Century Britain." *Dissertation Abstracts International* 49 (1989): 3733A (University of California, San Diego). A Foucaultian analysis of the prose texts of the mother and daughter, focusing on "their strategies for constructing a place for females or any figure of difference." For Mary Shelley, it is "critical that the differences among subjects and objects be recognized and accepted as part of the productive process."

Kopaleishvili, N. G. *Meri Shelli i Problema Filosofsko Fantasticheskogo Romana* [Mary Shelley and the problem of the philosophico-fantastic novel]. Tbilisi, U.S.S.R: Tbilisi University Press, 1980. Studies the relationship between *Frankenstein*, the prototype of the philosophico-fantastic novel, and *The Last Man*, Mary Shelley's extension of the form.

Leighton, Margaret. *Shelley's Mary: A Life of Mary Godwin Shelley*. New York: Farrar, Straus, and Giroux, 1973. A composite portrait of the Shelleys, with commentaries on Shelley's imaginative and pragmatic contributions to Mary's dramas. Has intermittent comments on her short fiction and post-*Frankenstein* novels.

Lovell, Ernest J., Jr. "Byron and the Byronic Hero in the Novels of Mary Shelley." *University of Texas Studies in English* 30 (1951): 158–83. Identifies Byron as Mary Shelley's model and prototype for the characters of Castruccio in *Valperga*, Raymond in *The Last Man*, Lodore in *Lodore*, and Falkner in *Falkner*.

Lovell, Ernest J., Jr. "Byron and Mary Shelley." *Keats-Shelley Journal* 2 (1953): 35–49. Speculates about the central role of Byron in Mary Shelley's career as a novelist and concludes that she was attracted to Byron as a father figure. "And thus beautiful did he appear in her novels, a magnetic and many-sided figure, symbol of one of her most deeply felt needs, that of a father-lover, the desired pillar of masculine power and authority."

Lyles, W. H. *Mary Shelley: An Annotated Bibliography*. New York: Garland, 1975. The authoritative reference source. Covers all aspects of Mary Shelley's fiction and nonfiction as well as secondary materials, including articles, dissertations, book-length studies, reviews, and Mary Shelley criticism in foreign languages. Because of the upsurge in Shelley studies since its publication in the mid-1970s, this bibliography merits a sequel or new separate study.

Marshall, Florence A. [Mrs. Julian]. *The Life and Letters of Mary Wollstonecraft Shelley*. London: Bentley, 1889. A first biography and still a useful source for the circumstances of all of the prose fiction. The biography tended to sentimentalize and deify both Shelleys but also assumed the erroneous position that Mary Shelley subordinated her entire life and art to the genius of her husband.

McGuire, Karen Elizabeth. "Pastoralism in the Novels of Mary Shelley." *Dissertation Abstracts International* 38 (1978): 6145A–6146A (University of Southern California). Investigates the thematic role of pastoralism in the novels and argues that "all of Mary Shelley's novels develop a major Romantic conflict between the desire for power and knowledge as opposed to the desire for contentment and withdrawal from society."

Mellor, Anne K. *Mary Shelley: Her Life, Her Fiction, Her Monsters*. New York: Routledge, 1988. An analytic revaluation of Mary Shelley's life and literary achievements. Six chapters are devoted to *Frankenstein,* with additional chapters on *The Last Man, Mathilda, Lodore, Falkner,* and selected short stories. The basic conflict registered in all she wrote is her ambivalent attitude toward family that she envisioned in opposite terms as an ideal harmony and a destroyer of individuality.

Mellor, Anne K. "A Novel of Their Own: Romantic Women's Fiction, 1790–1830." In *The Columbia History of the British Novel*, edited by John Richetti, 327–51. New York: Columbia University Press, 1994. Mentions but does not discuss in depth "Shelley's later 'society' novels, *Mathilda* (1819), *Lodore* (1835), and *Falkner* (1837)" and the nihilistic *Last Man*. These books "continue to depict the damage done when the mother is absent. Throughout her fiction, Shelley sustains the ideal of an egalitarian family, which she acknowledges to be a fiction in her own experience."

Neumann, Bonnie Rayford. "Mary Shelley." *Dissertation Abstracts* 33 (1973): 5689A (University of New Mexico). Later published as *The Lonely Muse*, the dissertation surveys Mary Shelley's life and writings as these reflect her deviation from Shelleyesque idealism and Byronic Romanticism.

Neumann, Bonnie Rayford. *The Lonely Muse: A Critical Biography of Mary Wollstonecraft Shelley*. Salzburg Studies in English Literature. Salzburg, Austria: Institut für Anglistik und Amerikanistik, Universität Salzburg, 1979. A highly subjective portrait of Mary Shelley offering useful critical insights on the overtly autobiographical content of her short stories, plays, and novels. Her prose is marked by "a personal sense of alienation and transforms this private emotion into a literary theme."

Nitchie, Elizabeth. "Eight Letters by Mary Shelley." *Keats-Shelley Memorial Bulletin* 3 (1950): 23–52. Prints letters to publishers and others concerning the novels that illuminate the autobiographical elements of her fiction. "'I do not know,' she wrote Ollier in sending him the first volume [of *Lodore*] as a sample, 'how briefly to give you an idea of the whole tale. In the daughter I have tried to portray in its simplicity the devotion of a young wife for the husband of her choice.'"

Nitchie, Elizabeth. *Mary Shelley–Author of "Frankenstein."* New Brunswick, N.J.; Rutgers University Press, 1953; rprt., Westport, Conn.: Greenwood Press, 1970. The biography regards most of the post-*Frankenstein* fiction to be survival writing, although "she has a sense of dramatic structure. Except for *Frankenstein*, Mary's fiction reveals little originality and invention in plotting. Their endings are contrived and foreseeable." Does draw attention to her unpublished writing and offers an appendix on *Mathilda*. Appendix 2 (pp. 205–10) is a valuable listing of Mary Shelley's works. Suggests that one of the "lost" stories for Hunt's *Indicator* could be "The Heir of Mondolfo." She fashioned many of her heroes directly on Byron, whose personality is depicted in "the proud and handsome lovers of her short tales— 'The Heir of Mondolfo,' 'Fernando Eboli,' 'The Invisible Girl,' 'The Elder Son,' 'The Pilgrims,' 'The Brother and Sister,' and 'A Tale of the Passions.'"

Nitchie, Elizabeth. "Mary Shelley, Traveler." *Keats-Shelley Journal* 10 (1961): 29–42. On Mary Shelley's travel books, *History of a Six Weeks' Tour Through a Part of France, Switzerland, Germany, and Holland* (1817) and *Rambles in Germany and Italy* (1844). Relates such experiences as the Pantheon by moonlight and the Colosseum to "Valerius; or, the Reanimated Roman," *The Last Man*, and *Valperga*.

Nochimson, Martha. "Mary Wollstonecraft Shelley." In *Critical Survey of Long Fiction*, edited by Frank Magill, 2385–95. Englewood Cliffs, N.J.: Salem Press, 1983. Offers critical synopses of *Falkner* (pp.

2394–95), *Perkin Warbeck* (p. 2393), *The Last Man* (pp. 2390–92), and *Valperga* (pp. 2389–90). Places Mary Shelley's novels in the Gothic tradition. "They deal with extreme emotions, exalted speech, the hideous plight of virgins, the awful abuses of charismatic villains, and picturesque ruins. The sins of the past weigh heavily on their plot structures, and often include previously unsuspected relationships."

Norman, Sylva. "Mary Shelley: Novelist and Dramatist." In *On Shelley.* London: Oxford University Press, 1938. Approves of most of Mary Shelley's other fiction but evaluates it as artistically inferior to *Frankenstein.* Criticizes her uncertain "management of story," sentimental attachment to the Christmas annuals, and mediocrity of imagination. Finds *The Last Man*, for example, to suffer from "an excess of domestic heart throb, too much concern with personal sensibilities" that have no bearing on her intended theme.

Norman, Sylva. "Mary Shelley, 1797–1851." *Fortnightly Review* 175 (February 1951): 112–17. Short, appreciative summary of Mary Shelley's life and art. Implies that she attained an artistic high point with *Frankenstein,* whereas the other fiction is distinctly inferior but still worth studying.

Norman, Sylva. *Flight of the Skylark: The Development of Shelley's Reputation.* Norman: Oklahoma University Press, 1954. Brief and cursory comments on the *Keepsake* stories and the novels. *The Last Man* presents a "strangely fashionable subject, a fantasy of the future, and a vehicle for the Shelley-puppet, Adrian."

Norman, Sylva. "Mary Wollstonecraft Shelley." In *Romantic Rebels: Essays on Shelley and His Circle*, edited by Kenneth Neill Cameron, 59–83. Cambridge, Mass.: Harvard University Press, 1973. A biocritical profile emphasizing the primary position of *Frankenstein* but covering Mary Shelley's other prose fiction. Published previously in *Shelley and His Circle*, ed. Kenneth Neill Cameron (Cambridge, Mass.: Harvard University Press, 1961).

Ozolins, Aija. "The Novels of Mary Shelley: From *Frankenstein* to *Falkner.*" *Dissertation Abstracts International* 33 (1972): 2398A (University of Maryland). An analytic survey of six novels (omits *Mathilda*) designed to show how her other work enhances our comprehension of *Frankenstein.* All of the novels are partially autobiographical and use doubles and dreams, showing that Mary Shelley remained faithful to Gothic and Romantic principles long after Romanticism had subsided.

Palacio, Jean de. *Mary Shelley dans son oeuvre: contribution aux études Shelleyennes.* Paris: Klincksieck, 1969. Critical and evaluative study of Mary Shelley's works and place in literature. Contains valuable comments on her reading and story sources.

Peck, Walter E. "The Biographical Element in the Novels of Mary Wollstonecraft Shelley." *Publications of the Modern Language Association* 38 (1923): 196–219. An important article detailing Mary Shelley's extensive use of herself and members of the Byron-Shelley-Godwin circle in the characterizations of the novels. "On five occasions Mary Shelley drew full-length portraits in prose of her husband and his intimate friends. *Valperga* deals with the life of the Shelleys in Italy; *The Last Man*, with their life in England; *Falkner*, about equally with their life in England and Italy; *The Fortunes of Perkin Warbeck*, with Scotland and their Italian experiences. We meet Shelley under five disguises, Mary and Claire Clairmont each behind three masks, and these: Lord Byron, Emilia Viviani, Harriet Shelley, William Godwin, Edward Trelawny, Fanny Godwin, and the Shelley children, Clara, William, and Percy Florence."

Poovey, Mary. *The Proper Lady and the Woman Writer—Ideology as Style in the Works of Mary Wollstonecraft, Mary Shelley, and Jane Austen*. Chicago: University of Chicago Press, 1984. A feminist reading of defiant styles of authorship that considers Mary Shelley's *Frankenstein*, *Valperga*, and *The Last Man* to be her most radical and ideologically daring texts. Her later prose fiction, however, is markedly conservative, conformist, and submissive to masculine, Romantic criteria. In reconciling the opposing roles, Mary Shelley "capitulates" to convention.

Powers, Katherine R. "The Influence of William Godwin on the Novels of Mary Shelley." *Dissertation Abstracts International* 33 (1973): 4359A (University of Tennessee). An influence study that shows how Godwin's thought, work, and sense of psychological intensity is reflected in the structure of Mary Shelley's novels.

Powers, Katherine R. *The Influence of William Godwin on the Novels of Mary Shelley*. New York: Arno Press, 1980. Published version of the dissertation cited above.

Reddin, Chitra Pershad. *Forms of Evil in the Gothic Novel*. New York: Arno Press, 1980. Categorizes *Valperga* and *The Last Man* along with *Frankenstein* as didactic forms of Gothic fiction and comments on Mary Shelley's vision of social evil in relation to perverted human will. Originally an unpublished doctoral dissertation, Dalhousie University, Halifax, Nova Scotia, 1977.

Rukshina, K. S. *Khudozhestvennoe Tvorchestvo Meri Volskokraft Rannego Perioda (1786–1789)* [The work of Mary Shelley's early period]. Minsk, U.S.S.R.: Sbornik Nauchnykh Rabot, Belorusskii Universitet,

1967, 2:52–70. Covers and evaluates the fiction from *Mathilda* and *Frankenstein* to *Valperga*.

Sencourt, Robert. "Mary Wollstonecraft Shelley." *Contemporary Review* 1102 (October 1957): 215–18. A short appraisal and appreciation of Mary Shelley's artful experimentation with Romantic and Gothic themes in her long and short fiction.

Spark, Muriel. *Child of Light: A Reassessment of Mary Wollstonecraft Shelley*. Hadleigh, Essex, U.K.: Tower Bridge Publications, 1951. Reprinted as *Mary Shelley—A Biography*. New York: E. P. Dutton, 1987; London: Cardinal, 1989. Alludes briefly to the short fiction in *The Keepsake* by noting that "her pen was rarely idle." Has chapters on *The Last Man* and *Perkin Warbeck*. The 1951 volume has an extensively abridged text of *The Last Man*. In 1954, Spark attempted to reissue a complete edition of *The Last Man* with Falcon Press, but the press failed and the edition had to be aborted.

Spears, Marthalee Atkinson. "The Sympathetic Imagination in the Fiction of Mary Wollstonecraft Shelley." *Dissertation Abstracts International* 41 (1980): 2620A (University of Kentucky). Discusses the short stories and each novel in turn and shows how Mary Shelley diverged from the feminist thinking of Mary Wollstonecraft. Develops the thesis that the first five novels "illustrate the failure of sympathetic imagination and fallen societies, but the import of *Lodore* and *Falkner* is positive because spiritually fallen characters are regenerated through sympathetic transcendence of self."

Spector, Robert D. "'Mary Shelley;' The Inheritors: Charles Robert Maturin and Mary Shelley." In *The English Gothic: A Bibliographic Guide to Writers from Horace Walpole to Mary Shelley,* 224–62. Westport, Conn.: Greenwood Press, 1983. Contains secondary bibliographical material on *Perkin Warbeck*, *The Last Man*, *Lodore*, *Mathilda*, and *Valperga* consisting mainly of citations of the reviews. "These reviews of Shelley's fiction comprise by far the largest body of critical material on her writing in the nineteenth century."

Strutkova, T. G. "Romany M. Shelli v Kontekste Literatury Angliiskogo Romantiz-ma" [The novels of Mary Shelley in the context of the literature of English Romanticism]. In *Realizm i Khudozhestvennye Iskaniia v Zarubezhnoy Literature XIX–XX Vekov,* 93–109. Voronezh, U.S.S.R.: Voronezh University, 1980. Measures the artistic success of all the novels, including *Mathilda,* against the criteria of Romantic art and points out significant differences between Mary Shelley's Romanticism and the masculine mainstream of an idealized self and a higher world.

Sunstein, Emily. *Mary Shelley: Romance and Reality.* Boston: Little, Brown, 1989. Valuable both for its biographical substance and its additions to Mary Shelley bibliography. "Appendix B: Mary Shelley's Works" (pp. 409–15) identifies the following new attributions to her short fiction canon: "The Clouds; A Dream," "The Ritter von Reichenstein," "The Magician of Vicenza," and "The Pilgrims." The text has critical commentaries on all of the novels and substantial discussions of several of the short stories.

Tracy, Ann B. *The Gothic Novel, 1790–1830: Plot Summaries and Index to Motifs,* 155–61. Lexington: University Press of Kentucky, 1981. Succinct, accurate synopses of all the novels, including *Mathilda.* Although not every single novel she wrote can be categorized as Gothic, all seven manifest Gothic places, characters, situations, and fatal atmosphere.

Veeder, William. "Appendix B: Plot Summaries of Mary Shelley's Novels After 1818." In *Mary Shelley and Frankenstein: The Fate of Androgyny,* 223–24. Chicago: University of Chicago Press, 1986. Succinct synopses of the six novels written after *Frankenstein.*

Vohl, Maria. *Die Erzählungen der Mary Shelley und ihre Urbilder* [The tales of Mary Shelley and their prototypes]. Heidelberg, Germany: Carl Winter, 1913. Early twentieth-century commentary on the novels and tales that concentrates on Mary Shelley's possible sources in German literature. States that *The Last Man* "steht also auf jeden Fall in engstam Zusammenhang mit Marys Romans" [therefore stands in any case in closest relationship with Mary's novels].

Wade, Philip Tyree. "Influence and Intent in the Prose Fiction of Percy and Mary Shelley." *Dissertation Abstracts* 27 (1967): 3021A (University of North Carolina). Examines the entire body of prose fiction. *Valperga* "escaped her control to degenerate into Gothic melodrama." *Perkin Warbeck* "shows more success at maintaining historical objectivity." *The Last Man* reveals "a pattern of biographical analogies which undergirds its plot." *Lodore* and *Falkner* are "sentimental potboilers with plots and characters that seem almost interchangeable." Has an appendix that provides a bibliographical introduction to Mary Shelley's shorter fiction.

Walling, William A. "Other Fictional Prose and Verse." In *Mary Shelley,* TEAS no. 128, pp. 101–17. New York: Twayne; 1972. Contains detailed discussions of *Valperga* and *The Last Man* and intermittent remarks on *Mathilda,* the mythological dramas, the short stories, and nonfictional prose. Takes the position that "little of Mary's fiction repays attention. The absence of emotional and intellectual significance in Mary's fiction as the years passed after Shelley's death is nowhere seen more nakedly than in her short stories." Brief specific comments on the following short stories: "Transformation," "The Bride of Modern Italy," "Fernando Eboli," and "The Mortal Immortal."

Wolfson, Susan J. "Editorial Privilege: Mary Shelley and Percy Shelley's Audiences." In *The Other Mary Shelley: Beyond Frankenstein*, 39–72. In her editorial capacity, Mary Shelley often "acts as a mediator. Subtly, she was representing herself as the synecdoche of another kind of audience."

Notes

1. Ernest Baker, "The Novel of Sentiment and the Gothic Romance," in *The History of the English Novel* (London: H. F. & G. Witherby, 1929), 5:219.

2. William A. Walling, "Other Fictional Prose and Verse," in *Mary Shelley*, Twayne English Authors Series 128 (New York: Twayne, 1972), 101.

3. Robert D. Spector, "The Inheritors: Charles Robert Maturin and Mary Shelley," in *The English Gothic: A Bibliographic Guide to Writers From Horace Walpole to Mary Shelley* (Westport, Conn.: Greenwood Press, 1983), 224. Additional references to Mary Shelley's fiction are to be found in William H. Lyles's definitive but now dated *Mary Shelley: An Annotated Bibliography* (New York: Garland, 1975) and bibliographies compiled by Clement Dunbar in the annual numbers of the *Keats-Shelley Journal*.

4. Jane Blumberg, *Mary Shelley's Early Novels: 'This Child of Imagination and Misery'* (Iowa City: University of Iowa Press, 1993).

5. Audrey A. Fisch, Anne K. Mellor, and Esther Schor, eds., *The Other Mary Shelley: Beyond Frankenstein* (New York: Oxford University Press, 1993).

6. Emily W. Sunstein, *Mary Shelley: Romance and Reality* (Boston: Little, Brown, 1989). Sunstein locates and lists the following stories not reprinted in Charles E. Robinson's modern edition of the tales: "The Fisher-Boy of Weymouth," "The Heap of Stones," "Lacy de Vere," "The Magician of Vicenza," "Mounseer Nongtongpaw; Or the Discoveries of John Bull on a Trip to Paris," "The Noise," "The Parents' Offering; Or Tales for Children," "The Pet Donkey," "The Sisters," "The Prize; Or the Lace Makers of Missenden," "The Refusal," and "The Ritter Von Reichenstein."

7. Mary Wollstonecraft Shelley, *The Novels and Selected Works of Mary Wollstonecraft Shelley*, ed. Nora Crook and Pamela Clemit (Brookfield, Vt.: Pickering and Chatto, 1996). Vol. 1: *Frankenstein*, ed. Nora Crook; vol. 2: *Matilda*, Dramas, Reviews and Essays, ed. Pamela Clemit; vol. 3: *Valperga*, ed. Nora Crook; vol. 4: *The Last Man*, ed. J. Blum and Nora Crook; vol. 5: *The Fortunes of Perkin Warbeck*, ed. Doucet Devin Fischer; vol. 6: *Lodore*, ed. Fiona Stafford; vol. 7: *Falkner*, ed. Pamela Clemit; vol. 8: Travel Writing, Index, ed. Jeanne Moskal.

8. Charles E. Robinson and Betty T. Bennett, eds., *The Mary Shelley Reader* (New York: Oxford University Press, 1990). Robinson's earlier anthology, *Mary Shelley: Collected Tales and Stories* (Baltimore, Md.: Johns Hopkins University Press, 1976) gave scholars a first full perspective of the "other" Mary Shelley.

Notes on Contributors

Sheila Ahlbrand is an independent scholar who is currently serving as a research and development associate for The Upper Midwest Women's History Center in St. Paul, Minnesota. She is also writing a play about Mary Shelley and Christina Rossetti.

Judith Barbour has recently retired from the Department of English, University of Sydney. She has published articles on Mary Shelley, William Godwin, J. W. Polidori, and Mary Wollstonecraft, and, with Clara Tuite of the Australian National University, is preparing an edition of Mary Shelley's biography of Godwin from the Abinger MSS in the Bodleian Library, Oxford.

Charlene Bunnell recently received her Ph.D. from the University of Delaware, writing a dissertation entitled "'All the world's a stage': Dramatic Sensibility in Mary Shelley's Fiction." She has published articles on Shelley, Romantic fiction, and the Gothic, and has presented papers at national and regional eighteenth-century, popular culture, and women's studies conferences. She is currently an instructor of English at West Chester University.

Paul A. Cantor is professor of English at the University of Virginia and since 1992 has been a member of the National Council on the Humanities. He has also taught at Harvard University and Davidson College. He is the author of several books on Shakespeare as well as *Creature and Creator: Myth-making and English Romanticism*.

James Carson teaches English at Kenyon College. He has published essays on *Frankenstein*, Samuel Richardson, Tobias Smollett and castrati, and celebratory illuminations in relation to Gothic fiction. He is currently completing a book on the Gothic novel.

Ranita Chatterjee is completing a dissertation on the libidinal economy of William Godwin's and Mary Shelley's writings at the University of Western Ontario. She is currently teaching in the Department of English and the Women's Studies Program at the University of Utah.

Syndy McMillen Conger is Director of Graduate Studies in English at Western Illinois University, where she has taught and written about Mary Shelley's *Frankenstein* for many years. She has recently authored *Mary Wollstonecraft and the Language of Sensibility* and edited *Sensibility in Transformation: Creative Resistance to Sentiment from the Augustans to the Romantics* and is currently presenting and/or publishing comparative studies of Mary Wollstonecraft and Mary Shelley.

Audra Dibert Himes is a doctoral student and teaching assistant at the University of Nebraska-Lincoln. Her areas of interest include William Butler Yeats, the Victorian fin de siècle, and Modern poetry, and she has published on Virginia Woolf.

Frederick S. Frank is professor emeritus of English at Allegheny College. In addition to three books published with Scarecrow Press, *Guide to the Gothic: An Annotated Bibliography of Criticism*, *Montague Summers: A Bibliographical Portrait*, and *Guide to the Gothic II: An Annotated Bibliography of Criticism, 1983–1993*, he is the author of other articles, books, and book chapters on Gothic fiction. He is currently writing *The Poe Encyclopedia,* to be published by Greenwood Press.

Ann M. Frank Wake is assistant professor of English at Elmhurst College, Elmhurst, Illinois. Her dissertation, "Factitious States: Mary Shelley and the Politics of Early Nineteenth-Century Women's Identity and Fiction" (University of Michigan, 1989), focused on Shelley as social critic in keeping with Mary Wollstonecraft's legacy. She has presented papers on *Frankenstein*, *Mathilda*, and *Lodore* and is now working on configurations of history and education in early nineteenth-century women's texts.

Diane Long Hoeveler, associate professor of English and coordinator of the Women's Studies Program at Marquette University, is author of *Romantic Androgyny: The Women Within*, coeditor of the MLA volume on *Approaches to Teaching "Jane Eyre,"* and author of the forthcoming book *Gothic Feminism: The Melodrama of Gender and Ideology from Wollstonecraft to the Brontes.* In addition, she also coedited *The Historical Dictionary of Feminism* and has authored numerous articles and reviews on Romanticism and gender, the Gothic, and women's literature.

Lisa Hopkins read English at King's College, Cambridge, and then received an M.A. and a Ph.D. at the University of Warwick. She is now lecturer in English at Sheffield Hallam University. Her publications include *Mary Shelley's "Frankenstein": A Hall of Mirrors, John*

Ford's Political Theatre, and "Engendering Frankenstein's Monster." in *Women's Writing: The Early Modern Period*.

Angela D. Jones is currently at work on a dissertation on bringing life-writing studies and feminist pedagogy to bear on critical production of the Romantic canon and its classroom reproduction. She has a collabo-rative essay on *Ordinary People* forthcoming in a collection on adapting contemporary American's women's fiction to film.

Gregory O'Dea is University of Chattanooga Foundation Assistant Professor of English at the University of Tennessee at Chattanooga, where he teaches courses on eighteenth-century British literature, Romanticism, and the novel. He is the author of several articles on British fiction and aspects of narrative, including studies of Henry Fielding, Mary Shelley, and Charlotte Bronte.

Lynn Wells will receive her doctorate in English from the University of Western Ontario in 1997. Her thesis, "Allegories of Telling: Self-Ref-erential Narrative in Contemporary British Fiction," examines issues of reading, historical representation, and intertextuality in novels by John Fowles, Angela Carter, Graham Swift, and Salman Rushdie. Her publications include "Virtual Textuality" in *Reading Matters: Narra-tive in the New Ecology of the Media* (Cornell University Press, 1997).

Jennifer D. Yocum received her B.A. and M.A. in English from Western Illinois University in Macomb, Illinois. She wrote her master's thesis on P. D. James and the modern mystery novel. She is currently the buyer for Copperfield & Company Booksellers in Macomb.

Index

Entries in Frederick S. Frank's bibliography at the end of this volume are not duplicated in this index.